KEY
WORDS
IN
CHURCH
MUSIC

KEY WORDS IN CHURCH MUSIC

Definition Essays on Concepts, Practices, and Movements of Thought in Church Music

Edited by Carl Schalk

Publishing House
St. Louis

Concordia Publishing House, St. Louis, Missouri
Copyright © 1978 Concordia Publishing House
Manufactured in the United States of America

Library of Congress Cataloging in Publication Data

Main entry under title:

Key words in church music.

    Includes bibliographical references.
    1. Church music—Dictionaries. I. Schalk, Carl.
ML102.C5K5   783′.026′03   77-16277
ISBN 0-570-01317-8

Acknowledgements

In addition to the pictorial material already acknowledged, the following sources deserve special mention. Necessary permission to use material has been granted by the sources indicated: D. Andre Mocquereau & D. Joseph Gajard, *The Rhythmic Tradition in the Manuscripts.* Monographs on Gregorian Chant No. IV. Society of St. John the Evangelist, Desclee, Co. Inc., 1952; facsimile editions of the *Babst Gesangbuch, Das Achtliederbuch,* the *Syntagma Musicum,* the *Neue deutsche geistliche Gesaenge,* the *Musikalische Lexicon,* and the works of Michael Praetorius, Baerenreiter Verlag, Kassel, Germany; *Musikgeschichte in Bildern,* VEB Deutscher Verlag fuer Musik, Leipzig, Germany; K. Penderecki, *Dies irae,* Polskie Wydawnictwo Muzyczne, Krakow, Poland, 1967; Blume, *Protestant Church Music,* and Paul Henry Lang, *Pictorial History of Music,* W. W. Norton Co., New York, 1974 and 1960; Everhard Kraus, *Orgeln and Orgelmusik,* Verlag Friedrich Pustet, Regensburg, Germany, 1972; Peter Williams, *The European Organ 1450—1850,* B. T. Batsford, Ltd., London, England, 1968; Joseph Edward Blanton, *The Organ in Church Design,* Venture Press, Albany, Texas, 1957; Werner Walcker-Mayer, *Die Romische Orgel von Aquincum,* Musikwissenschaftliche Verlagsgesellschaft, Stuttgart, West Germany, 1970; John Rowntree & John F. Brennan, *The Classical Organ in Britain 1955—1974,* Positif Press, Oxford, England, 1975; William H. Barnes, *The Contemporary American Organ,* J. Fischer & Bros., New York, 1948; Ulrich Pisk, *A History of Musical Style,* Harcourt, Brace and World, New York, 1963; Friedrich Blume, ed., *Die Musik in Geschichte und Gegenwart,* Baerenreiter Verlag, Kassel, Germany, 1952—.

Contents

Preface

This volume is intended to provide the practicing church musician with information, largely historical, that may be helpful in addressing matters of contemporary practice in church music. In order that the promise of a useful church music practice in our time might be achieved, the challenges and possibilities of today need to be seen over against the practices and experience of the church at worship throughout its history. The intent of this volume is to help clarify that view for our own day. In that sense this is an eminently practical book.

Each entry is organized according to the following pattern: the term or topic; the development of the topic in essay form; a brief selection of further readings, guiding the reader to other material that may be helpful in further study of the topic; cross-references to related articles in this volume and to pertinent chapters in the companion *Handbook of Church Music (HCM)* that may profitably be read in connection with the topic.

The authors of the articles, identified by their initials at the conclusion of each article, are highly competent scholars in their respective fields. Brief biographical notes on each author are included elsewhere in this volume. It should also be pointed out that the "Readings" given at the conclusion of each essay refer the reader to further treatment of the topic, for the most part in English-language publications that are quite readily available. In only a few instances are references given to foreign-language publications.

It is assumed that one comes to a volume of this kind seeking specific information about a particular topic, not with the intent to read straight through from beginning to end. As a point of departure, one might begin with the articles grouped under "Church music history," "Hymnody," or "Theology of church music," proceeding through the cross-references to related topics.

The selection of key words and concepts that might be helpful to the practicing church musician today is to some extent, of course, arbitrary. Yet within the limitations of available space the attempt has been made to represent a broad spectrum of ideas, practices, terms, and topics with which the well-informed and knowledgeable church musician should be conversant. Many more key words might profitably be addressed. But that task must await another time, and, perhaps, another volume.

Carl Schalk
January 1, 1978

KEY
WORDS
IN
CHURCH
MUSIC

alternation practice

A musical practice of the later Middle Ages and Renaissance in which a liturgically related text (e.g., parts of the ordinary of the mass, hymns, canticles, sequences) was performed in such a way as to alternate between two musical forces, the one normally presenting the unison chant, the other a polyphonic setting.

The roots of this practice can be traced to the antiphonal singing of psalms (which came into the Western church c. 400 A.D. and is associated with the name of Ambrose), in which two parts of the congregation or two choirs sang alternate verses of the psalms. Alternating practice of a general kind can be seen (1) in the Romanesque and Gothic period's use of alternating solo voices and choir in Gregorian chant, and (2), with the development of organum, in the use of sections in organal style (most probably sung by a small group of solo voices) alternating with the unison chant sung by the choir.

With the fuller development of polyphony, the practice of alternating plainsong and polyphony was adopted for use in connection with the parts of the ordinary of the mass. The ninefold Kyrie, for example, could be performed in the following manner:

Kyrie	homophonic chant
Kyrie	polyphonic setting
Kyrie	homophonic chant
Christe	polyphonic setting
Christe	homophonic chant
Christe	polyphonic setting
Kyrie	homophonic chant
Kyrie	polyphonic setting
Kyrie	homophonic chant

Many popular vernacular hymns of the later Middle Ages (e.g., the Leisen) were sung in alternating fashion, the stanzas of the vernacular hymns sung by the people alternating with the traditional Latin sequence chants sung by the choir.

The alternation of plainsong and polyphony in the presentation of liturgical settings was common in the 15th century, and by the 16th century it was a normal procedure. Fifteenth-century composers who wrote music in this manner include Binchois (a Magnificat on Tone 3), Dufay (hymns, sequences, mass sections), Isaac (see especially the sequences in the *Choralis Constantinus*), Prioris (Magnificats on Tones 4 and 6), Martini (a Magnificat), and such 16-century composers as Palestrina (9 Masses, Glorias, Credos), Gombert (8 Magnificats), Festa (hymns, Magnificats), Morales (Office of the Dead, Magnificats, Salve Regina), and Victoria (Improperia, Magnificats). Normally the odd-numbered verses were set to the traditional plainsong, the even-numbered verses (sometimes called "second parts") were set polyphonically, although there are examples of the reverse procedure. Some 16-century English composers who wrote music in alternating fashion include Taverner (Magnificats), White (hymns, Magnificats), Tallis (hymns), Shepherd (a *Playnsong Mass for a Mene),* Byrd (the hymn *Christe, qui lux es et dies*), and Blitheman (a setting of the Te Deum found in the Mulliner Book; it alternates between chant and organ).

With the gradual development of the organ in the 15th and 16th centuries, new possibilities presented themselves for alternating performance that used the organ in conjunction with the choir:

> unison choir vs. polyphonic choir settings
> unison choir vs. unison or polyphonic organ setting
> unison choir vs. polyphonic choir settings

Hofhaimer's 5 organ versets on *Salve Regina*, for example, present settings for the odd-numbered verses of the chant melody. The tablatures of Fridolin Sicher and Hans Buchner's *Fundamentbuch* contain additional organ versets for alternating use. Attaingnant's publication of three organ books (1530) presents alternate verses for the Te Deum, Magnificat, and for 2 masses. Cavazzoni's Magnificat settings also present organ versets for the odd-numbered verses.

The Lutheran Reformation of the 16th century continued and enriched the alternation practice, the unison singing of the congregation now participating especially in the alternate singing of the de tempore hymn (Gradual hymn) sung between the Epistle and Gospel. The congregation, singing the unison chorales unaccompanied, alternated with a unison-singing choir (the schola), a choir singing polyphonic settings of the chorales (the *figural* choir), or the organ playing chorale settings (e.g., Scheidt's *Goerlitzer Tabulaturbuch,* 1650). Johann Walter's polyphonic chorale settings (*Geystliches gesangk Buchleyn,* 1524) and many works of the

Reformation composers like Michael Praetorius (especially the *Musae Sioniae*, 1605—10) were intended for use in connection with alternation practice.

The use of the organ in the liturgical service of the early Lutheran Reformation differed in no significant way from its use in the Roman service of the same period. In the Lutheran mass the organ participated in the Introit and alternated with the singing at least in the Kyrie and Gloria in excelsis. In Matins and Vespers the organ was used to alternate with singing in the responsories, the canticles (especially the Te Deum, Magnificat, and Nunc dimittis), and the hymns. The use of the organ in the Roman service at the time of Clement VIII (c. 1600) shows a similar practice in connection with the Kyrie, Gloria in excelsis, Offertory, Sanctus, and Agnus Dei.

The organ continued to function in presenting polyphonic settings or organ versets in the liturgical service into the 17th century. At the time of the Thirty Years' War, for example, the organ was often the only performer of polyphonic music in many services. While there are a few complete organ masses from the 17th century (e.g., Scheidt 1624, Frescobaldi 1635, Couperin 1690), organ compositions on Gregorian melodies were basically intended to be used in alternation with verses sung to the traditional plainsong by the choir (see, e.g., Scheidt's 9 Magnificats, *Tabulatura Nova* III, 1624), in which only the alternate verses are presented.

New developments in the 17th century contributed to the gradual decline of the practice of alternation in the liturgical service. Among these were the rise of the concerted style and the gradual loss of the cantus firmus in much of this music; expanding dimensions of musical compositions that made them no longer especially suited for use in connection with simple congregational singing; the decline of the school choirs; and the development of the practice of accompanying every stanza of the congregational hymns with the organ.

The recent rebirth of interest in the use of alternating practice in connection with hymns and liturgical forms can be traced to the revival of German church music in the early part of the 20th century and to the work of such men as Christhard Mahrenholz. In America, the recovery of the de tempore hymn in the Lutheran churches, together with the publication of much old and new music designed for use in alternating practice, have supported this revival. CS

Readings: Blume, F., "The Practice of Alternation and Organ Music," *Protestant Church Music* (New York, 1974); Gotsch, H., "The Organ in the Lutheran Service of the 16th Century," *Church Music, 67·1.*

See also: de tempore hymn; Leisen; organ, use in the mass and offices; sequence; HCM, II, III, IV, V

anthem

Originally an optional English-language choral piece in the Anglican Service. The term is now popularly used to designate the principal choral piece in the Protestant service.

England

The break with Roman Catholicism (1543) created a need for syllabic music with English text for the Service. Adaptations of existing Latin pieces followed promptly, and English pieces were composed shortly thereafter, those of Christopher Tye (1500—73) and Thomas Tallis (c. 1505—85) bearing a similarity to the Latin types. Renaissance anthems first were uninterrupted choral pieces; the addition of accompaniment made possible the inclusion of solo sections, and the verse anthem, e.g., *Christ rising again* by William Byrd (1543—1623), appeared as a variant. Baroque influences, in the form of Italian declamatory style and French dance rhythms, followed.

Development of the anthem ceased abruptly with the Commonwealth, when all choral practice was suspended, for the composers were supported by the Chapel Royal. The Restoration of Charles II (1660) brought new life to English church music through renewed support by the Crown. Matthew Locke (c. 1630—77) led in developing instrumentally accompanied anthems; Henry Purcell (1659—95) refined the cantata-anthem; and Henry Aldrich (1647—1710) introduced the music of Continental composers through his arrangements.

Anthem texts were taken from Psalms and other Scriptures, collects, religious poetry, and carols. Long occasional anthems for royal weddings, funerals, coronations, and major church festivals were not always adaptable to repeated use because of the subject or size. Nevertheless, lengthy works, such as the Chandos Anthems of G. F. Handel (1685—1759), deserve more than passing mention.

The foregoing types of anthems developed in the cathedral practice, but the 18th century saw a shift of interest toward the parish churches. Some few supported respectable programs in the cathedral manner, but many modified their aims to suit volunteer choirs, and country churches welcomed women singers since choirboys were lacking. A new, familiar type of anthem, imitative of the cathedral but less complex, began to appear from Jeremiah Clarke (c. 1670—1707) and William Croft (1676—1736); short, easy anthems for the parish-church singers were published by Henry Playford (1656—1720), William Knapp (1698—1768), and William Tans'ur (1706—83).

By the middle of the 19th century, inexpensive octavo publication had begun, and many more composers were attracted to its rewards. Only a few notable composers were attracted to the anthem; the bulk of the literature comes from those who limited their efforts to short religious compositions. John Stainer (1840—1901), Charles Villiers Stanford (1852—1924), Edward Bairstow (1874—1946), and Ralph Vaughan Williams (1872—1958) stand out.

America

Tune-books imported for the singing-schools included anthems among the simple psalm tunes. Fuguing-tunes were imported from England, combining with the parish style that was adopted by many early composers. The need for cathedral music did not exist, and the taste for that idiom therefore failed to develop strongly.

Beginning with Lyon's *Urania* (1761), anthems by native-born Americans began to appear, and within a decade William Billings (1746—1800), the first American composer to bring a national flavor to the genre, began to publish. His work remained in vogue for decades, and revival of interest is again apparent. Through the first two decades of the 19th century, American publications showed a mixture of native compositions, English anthems, and European pieces in arrangement. Among the compilers who perpetuated the English idiom were Daniel Bayley (c. 1725—99) and Andrew Law (1748—1821); they supplied a pattern on which many composers modeled their works. As taste and performing skills developed, a broader range of imports appeared, including works in the European classical tradition. William B. Bradbury (1816—68) and Lowell Mason (1792—1872) visited abroad and borrowed more pieces, including some from the romantic period. The veneration of European composers found a strong impetus in publications by these men, especially Mason. Choirs proliferated, and the effects of the music-education movement were felt in an upsurge of anthem writing. The development of the quartet choir, often professional, developed a taste and repertoire beyond the skills of amateurs. The generation of Dudley Buck (1839—1909) produced material adaptable to both levels, with quartets serving as solo groups in pieces of the verse-anthem type. The hymn-anthem, a simple choral piece based on a familiar melody and text, came into relatively common use.

The proliferation of composers, publishers, and anthem types after that time was so great that reference works and publishers' lists should be consulted for more information. EWi

Readings: Daniel, Ralph T., *The Anthem in New England before 1800* (Evanston, Ill., 1966); Routley, Erik, gen. ed., *Studies in Church Music*, a series (New York, 1964—); Wienandt, Elwyn A., *Choral Music of the Church* (New York, 1965); Wienandt, Elwyn A. and Robert H. Young, *The Anthem in England and America* (New York, 1970).

See also: motet; Service; *HCM,* IV

baroque instruments

With the birth of monody in the 17th century, a wide range of expressiveness was required of both voices and instruments. This was not unaccompanied monody, as in ancient Greek times, but accompanied. Originally the instrumental bass accompaniment was given to lute with chitarroni, or to harpsichord and bass viol, whose job was to accompany the melody throughout with chords; hence, the name basso continuo.

Only those instruments were kept that had a rather wide range and dynamic flexibility. All at once rackets, crumhorns, and shawms were dropped from common usage. The 17th century preferred a dominating color like the timbre of bowed instruments. Whereas wind instruments were preferred in the Renaissance, stringed instruments with their expressive potential were preferred in the baroque style.

Stringed Instruments

lute. The lute continued to be very popular during the 17th century. By the end of the 16th century, lutes with prolonged necks, called archlutes, were made in Italy. Another large type of lute, called the chitarrone, was often more than 6½ ft. long. The theorbo was a slightly smaller chittarone, one of whose pegboxes was placed above and to the side of the other. At the end of the century the lute was progressively abandoned as an accompaniment instrument and replaced by the harpsichord.

guitar. The Spanish guitar established itself more and more in Italy. From Italy it spread to France. It was smaller than the modern guitar, but its body was deeper. Its belly was adorned with a rose-shaped sound hole, and its strings were simply tied to a bridge glued to the belly.

mandoline. Another plucked string instrument, the mandoline, appeared at the beginning of the 18th century in Italy. It had four double strings and the shape of a lute with a relatively short neck.

harp. At the end of the 16th century, several attempts were made to convert the harp into a chromatic instrument by adding additional strings. One such harp was called the *arpa doppia.* In 1720 an Augsburg harp maker invented pedals that would sharpen one note and all its octave transpositions by one half step.

viola d'amore. The viols continued to be played during the baroque period despite the growing popularity of the violin. In fact, new members were introduced into their family. The viola d'amore, the same size as the modern viola, had six of seven ordinary strings plus seven sympathetic strings of copper, which were placed under the other strings and sounded only in sympathetic vibration.

viola bastarda. The viola bastarda had a longer body than the bass viol, and its tuning pegs were in a higher position. It also had sympathetic strings tuned in unison with the others.

lyra viol. This instrument appeared for the first time in England in 1600. It had sympathetic strings and was fairly tortuous in shape. It was used to perform divisions or variations on a ground bass.

viola de bordone. Also called baryton, the viola de bordone had six or seven gut strings and a very large number of sympathetic strings (between 7 and 44) all mounted on a sound box no larger than that of a small bass viol. The gut strings were stretched over a narrow neck, which was placed on a wider neck, behind which the metal strings passed. The metal strings either vibrated in sympathy or they could be plucked with the thumb of the left hand. The instrument was played in aristocratic circles through the time of Haydn.

bass viol. A seventh string was given to the bass viol at the end of the

17th century although most of the music of the period was written for the six-stringed viol.

violin. In general, the violin of the 17th century had a shorter bridge and neck than the modern instrument. Consequently, the strings were shorter. From its inception the violin was regarded above all as a solo instrument. By the second half of the century a virtuosic technique was demanded by many composers—double stopping, scordatura, playing in fifth and sixth position.

During the baroque era, the violin was held in a position slanting downwards, and the bow was held at a point further from the end than is usual today. The bows of that time were straight, sometimes slightly convex; their tips were pointed. The bow was shorter and lighter and facilitated a particular way of playing with an articulated or even phrasing. The hair of the bow was free and did not yet have to pass through a wedge; the tension was regulated by means of slanting teeth, which could not be adjusted to such fine degrees as are possible today.

The 17th-century Amati violins were full-bellied and their sound was less strong than that of modern instruments. The German Stainer violins were more arched than the Amatis and had more rounded sound holes. The Stradivari instruments displayed a unity of conception, masterly craftsmanship, and exceptional sonority.

viola. The viola was not as widely used as today. Many old viola were no more than 15 inches long. It was the alto of the violin family and was usually played by violinists.

violoncello. This instrument appeared for the first time during the latter part of the 16th century. For a long time it was the rival of the viola da gamba. The early cellos were probably played after the manner of the bass viol, the bow being held with the palm of the hand facing upwards.

violoncello piccolo. Bach sometimes called for a violoncello piccolo in his works. This instrument was 40 inches high and was like a five-stringed viola.

Wind Instruments

recorder. In the baroque era the recorder was made in three detachable parts. The joints between the parts were generally embellished with bone or ivory collars. The bore became narrower and more conical; the bevel-edge was closer to the mouthpiece and wider. These changes gave the instrument a more penetrating tone.

transverse flute. This flute also underwent changes. Like the recorder, it was made in three sections—in four after 1750. The bore became conical; the widest diameter was at the head end. The virtuosos of the 17th century used a flute in D with a key that was used to obtain D#.

musette (French bagpipe). The musette was extremely fashionable with the 17th- and 18th-century aristocracy. The instruments were lavishly decorated with needlework, pipes of ivory, inlays of precious stones, pompons, fringes, and ribbons.

oboe. The oboe originated in the mid-17th century. In contrast to the Renaissance shawm, it was made in three pieces; it had three keys, a narrow bore and smaller bell. The holes were not as wide; the double reed was longer and narrower and was held directly in the player's mouth.

oboe d'amore. This variant of the oboe appeared around 1720. It was larger and sounded a minor third lower than the oboe. It also had a pear-shaped bell. Bach liked its sonority and used it often in his works.

oboe da caccia. The oboe da caccia was simply an odoe d'amore that sounded a major third lower. Early examples had a flared bell, but later the bell was globular. About 1760 the tube was bent to facilitate manipulation, and from that time on it was called cor anglais (hence the name English, i.e., angle, horn).

double bassoon. Made of wood or metal and sounding an octave lower than the bassoon, the double bassoon was invented in Germany about the beginning of the 17th century. It was over 6½ ft. high.

clarinet. Denner (1655—1707) refined the French chalumeau (a single reed instrument with the mouthpiece enclosed in a cap) and created the modern clarinet. The name clarinet was given because the instrument's high register recalled the sonority of the trumpet (It.: *clarino*). Denner dispensed with the cap, so that the reed was in direct contact with the player's lips. The size and width of its bore was also reduced. The bell was flared to give it the shape of a trumpet bell. Denner made his clarinets in three sections, with collars of ivory at the joints.

French horn. The French hunting horn (*cor de chasse*) originally had been straight but now for practicality curled in on itself. It was given a narrower bore. French makers made these refinements in the first half of the 17th century, and when it was imported to England the instrument was given the name French horn. The horn was bent in two and a half circles during the reign of Louis XV and has remained that way. Since the horn was made of a single tube, it could produce only a limited number of notes—the fundamental and its own harmonics. This led to the invention of crooks around 1715.

tromba da tirarsi. This instrument was a slide trumpet that had a mouthpiece fixed into a long neck, on which the body of the instrument could slide. Bach used it in a number of his cantatas.

trumpet. A flat trumpet appeared in England about 1690. A slide inserted in the loop nearest the player enabled him to play certain semitones that produced the minor scale.

trombone. The trombone did not undergo any changes during the baroque era. It was first used in an orchestral score by Monteverdi in *Orfeo.*

Percussion Instruments

kettledrum. Very similar to the modern instrument, the kettledrum was bronze and was struck with a stick. The skin of the drum was attached with pegs.

carillon. The carillon, which had first appeared in Belgium, spread to neighboring countries, although its manufacture was often entrusted to founders from Flanders, Louvain, or Brussels. Any carillon of less than 50 bells was considered of little importance. The cylinders were activated automatically by a clock; often they had over 1,000 pins, which activated the mechanism that operated hammers for the corresponding bells. These bells were fixed in position.

In England the bells were suspended in the manner of ordinary church bells. There were no prefabricated cylinders that could play a given tune; instead, men activated the bells according to the change-ringing system.

orchestral chimes. Handel was the first to use orchestral chimes in his oratorio *Saul* (1738). The orchestral carillon consisted of bronze hemispherical sections scaled to different sizes and struck by the player with two mallets.

Keyboard Instruments

harpsichord. Flemish and French harpsichords were characterized by their two keyboards, the same set of stops as in the Italian harpsichord (one or two 8' stops and one 4' stop) but divided over the two keyboards. The body was rather deep and on the heavy side. The chromatic keys were usually in bone, while the diatonic keys were in black-tinted wood.

The German harpsichords were frequently shaped in a double curve: Z. Some also had a 16' stop.

In the 18th century, harpsichords were constructed with extended keyboards. Old instruments were enlarged by the addition of keys both in the high and low registers; this procedure was called "ravalement."

Chromaticism made more demands on the harpsichord. Since the "short octave" lacked F# and G#, it was devised to divide the first two black keys into two parts, each of which activated a different string. This octave was called the "broken octave."

clavichord. The clavichord became unfretted in the 18th century, i.e., each key had its own string. In order to give more volume to the lower strings in the two octaves of the bass, they were doubled with thinning 4-foot strings. Cloth dampers were also added. The largest range attained by the keyboard was five octaves.

hurdy-gurdy. In the 18th century the hurdy-gurdy suddenly became fashionable, especially in France. This was the result of the popularity of pastorales.

organ. The organ was modified in the 17th century by the addition of sweeter and softer stops that imitated the human voice or stringed instruments. The tremolo was also introduced. The stops were all calibrated according to their volume.

From the 15th century on in France, the pedal board was made of pull-downs, wooden strips connected to some of the manual keys so that they could be operated by the feet. At first the pedal boards had between 8 and 10 keys; later they had 32 to 35 keys. In the 17th and 18th centuries, the French pedal board abandoned the deep stops it had featured and used 8′ and 4′ stops in the tenor register. They returned to 16′ stops at the end of the 18th century. Between 1650 and 1750 the French organ usually would have a principal manual, called the *grand orgue*, using 16′ stops; a secondary manual, the *positif*, using the 8′ stops; and two small manual keyboards, the *recit* and *écho*. Some organs also had a keyboard called the *bombardé*.

The Germans adopted a pedal board with longer keys and closer spacing, whose keys could be played with the heel as well as the toes. The German pedal board of the 17th and 18th centuries was supplied with a 32′, 16′, 8′, and 4′ flue and reed stops. The German organ offered a greater diveristy of stops than the French organ. Stopped pipes were preferred to reed pipes. Transverse flute stops were featured. Distinctive and typical stops used in southern Germany were the 16′ violone, 8′ viola da gamba, and 8′, 4′, and 2′ salicional. The first five-manual organ was made in Germany sometime after 1629.

The Spanish organ divided its full stops into high and low registers and tended to place its clarion, trumpet, and bombarde pipes *én chamade* (projecting horizontally towards the inside of the church). Some Spanish organs had two pedal boards placed one above the other.

In both Italy and England the organ developed very slowly. The Italian organ had one manual and a primitive pedal board. Until 1536 English organs had only one manual and about six stops. After that time organs were made with two manuals and about 15 stops. It was not until 1720 that an English organ had a pedal board of only a few notes. ER

Readings: Bonani, Filippo, *The Showcase of Musical Instruments*, reprint of 1723 ed. (New York, 1964); Bragard, Roger and Ferdinand J. De Hen, *Musical Instruments in Art and History* (New York, 1967); Carse, Adam, *The Orchestra of the XVIIIth Century* (Cambridge, 1940); Donington, Robert, *A Performer's Guide to Baroque Music* (London, 1973); Sachs, Curt, *The History of Musical Instruments,* (New York, 1940).

See also: church music history, baroque; medieval instruments; Renaissance instruments

Biblical instruments

The Bible often speaks of various musical instruments. Instruments played an important part not only in the temple ritual but also in the court life of the Jewish kings and in the daily life of the Jewish people. Some of the more important of these instruments mentioned in the Bible or rabbinic sources are:

'asor (Heb.). A 10-stringed instrument, probably a zither-like instrument on a rectangular frame. The word 'asor means 10 and is used in Ps. 33:2; 92:3; and 144:9. The AV translates it "instrument of ten strings," the RSV (Ps. 144:9) "ten-stringed harp."

chalil (Heb., pl chalilim). A double-reed, oboe-like instrument probably made of cane, played at joyous festivities as well as at mourning rites. The use of from 2 to 12 chalilim is mentioned in connection with the second temple. It is mentioned in connection with the anointing of Solomon (1 Kings 1:40) but was apparently not used in the first temple. Mentioned also in 1 Sam. 10:5; Is. 5:12; 30:29; and Jer. 48:36, the chalil is translated aulos in the Septuagint, tibia in the Vulgate, "pipe" in the AV, and usually "flute" in the RSV.

chatzotzrah (Heb.). A trumpet-like instrument, the chatzotzrah is described by Josephus as a straight tube, "a little less than a cubit long," ending in a bell. It was used in pairs and was made of silver. A visual depiction of objects robbed from the temple by Titus is found on the arch of Titus, erected in Rome in 81 A.D., and includes two trumpets identical to those described by Josephus. Mentioned in Numbers 10:2, 8-10; 2 Kings 11:14; 1 Chron. 13:8; 15:24, 28; 16:6, 42; 2 Chron. 5:12, 13; 13:12, 14; 15:14; 20:28; 23:13; 29:26-28; Ezra 3:10; Neh. 12:25, 41; Hosea 5:8; and Ps. 98:6.

kinnor (Heb., pl. *kinnorim, kinnoroth*). A small harp or lyre referred to by the Greeks as the *kithara*. With a tone described as "sweet," it was probably made of ordinary cypress wood, with the strings made of sheep gut. At the time of the kings, precious metals were used as decoration and more exotic woods used in its construction. The strings were plucked with a plectrum, and the instrument was used in connection with singing. According to Josephus the number of strings was 10. The *kinnor* was associated with David. The Jews set it aside during the Babylonian exile. The Septuagint generally translates *kinnor* as *kithara* or *kinyra*, the Vulgate as *cithara*, the AV as "harp," the RSV as "lyre." The *kinnor* is mentioned in Gen. 4:21; 31:27; 1 Sam. 10:5; 2 Sam. 6:5; 1 Kings 10:12; 1 Chron. 13:8; 15:16, 21, 28; 16:5; 25:1, 3, 6; 2 Chron. 5:12; 9:11; 20:28; 29:25; Neh. 12:27; Job 21:12; 30:31; Ps. 33:2; 43:4; 49:4; 57:8; 71:22; 81:2; 92:3; 98:5; 108:2; 137:2; 147:7; 150:3; Is. 5:12; 16:11; 23:16; 24:8; 30:32.

magrepha (Heb.) The Hebrew name for the Greco-Egyptian water organ or *hydraulos*. The Mishnah (completed about the beginning of the 3d century A.D.) describes the *magrepha* in some detail as a complex instrument that could be heard from a great distance and could produce very many tones. Rabbinic sources differ, one source stating that there was no water organ in the temple, another stating that there was a *magrepha* in the temple.

The possibility exists that the *magrepha* was a primitive wind organ consisting of a row of 10 pipes (a sort of panpipe), each pipe having a number of holes, the complete instrument being capable of producing very many tones and used chiefly for signaling. An Alexandrian terra-cotta figurine from the 1st century B.C. shows such an instrument, the bottom of the pipes connected to a bag (or reservoir) connected to a bellows operated by the right foot. Such an instrument could hardly have been used in the temple worship except toward the very end of Israel's national existence. It is mentioned in Jewish literature only in connnection with the second temple.

mena'an'im (Heb.) Mentioned in only one passage of the Bible (2 Sam. 6:5), most likely a shaken instrument, similar to the Egyptian *sistrum*. The AV incomprehensively translates *mena'an'im* as "cornets;" the RSV uses the word "castanets."

nebel (Heb., pl. *nebalim*). A stringed instrument, most likely a vertical, angular harp, but larger than the *kinnor* and having a lower pitch and a louder sound. Josephus relates that it had 12 strings and was plucked with the fingers. Mentioned in 1 Sam. 10:5; 2 Sam. 6:5; 1 Kings 10:12; 1 Chron. 13:8; 15:16, 20, 28; 16:5; 25:1, 6; 2 Chron. 5:12; 9:11; 20:28; 29:25; Neh. 12:27; Ps. 33:2; 57:8; 71:22; 81:2; 92:3; 108:2, 144:9; 150:3; Is. 5:12; 14:11; Amos 5:23; 6:5, the *nebel* is translated as *nabla, psalterim,* and *kithara* by the Septuagint, *psalterium* by the Vulgate.

pa'amon (Heb., pl. *pa'amonim*). A small bell or jingle prescribed to be sewn to the hem of the high priest's robe. Mentioned in Ex. 28:33-34; 39:25-26.

tseltselim (Heb.). Associated with the *metziltayim,* both were apparently brass cymbals, two of a number of percussion instruments associated with Jewish temple worship. Both *tseltselim* and *metziltayim* derive from a word meaning "clash." *Metziltayim* are mentioned in 1 Chron. 13:8; 15:16, 19, 28; 16:5, 42; 25:1, 6; 2 Chron. 5:12, 13; 29:25; Ezra 3:10; Neh. 12:27. *Tseltselim* are mentioned in 2 Sam. 6:5; Ps. 150:5.

shalish (Heb., pl. *shalishim*). Used only once (1 Sam. 18:6, in the description of the women welcoming Saul after the battle against the Philistines), *shalishim* is variously translated, e.g., "triangles" and "three-stringed instruments." The word may also indicate some sort of dance. It is not found in the Talmud. Both the AV and the RSV translate it "instruments of music." Perhaps it does not refer to musical instruments at all.

shophar (Heb., pl. *shopharoth*). A ram's or goat's horn without a mouthpiece; produces only two harmonics (the 2d and 3d). The only instrument from early Hebrew history that is still a part of Jewish worship (used particularly on New Year's Day and on the Day of Atonement), it is chiefly a noisemaker and is associated as a signaling instrument with such Biblical accounts as the destruction of Jericho (Joshua 6), and Gideon and the Midianites (Judg. 7). The *shophar* is mentioned in Ex. 19:16, 19; 20:18; Lev. 25:9; Joshua 6:4, 5, 6, 8, 9, 13, 16, 20; Judges 3:27; 6:34; 7:8, 16, 18, 19, 20, 22; 1 Sam. 13:3; 2 Sam. 2:28; 6:15; 15:10; 18:16; 20:1, 22; 1 Kings 1:34, 39, 41; 2 Kings 9:13; 1 Chron. 15:28; 2 Chron. 15:14; Neh. 4:12, 14; Job 39:24,

25; Is. 18:3; 27:13; 58:1; Jer. 4:5, 19, 21; 6:1, 17; 42:14; 51:27; Ezek. 33:3-6; Hos. 5:8; 8:1; Joel 2:1, 15; Amos 2:2; 3:6; Zeph. 1:16; Zech. 9:14; Ps. 47:5; 81:3; 98:6; 150:3. The word *keren* (mentioned, e.g., in 1 Chron. 25:5) is sometimes equated with the *shophar*, although some (e.g., Rothmueller) hold that while the *shophar* was made from a ram's horn, the *keren* was made from a bull's horn.

toph (Heb., pl. *tuppim*). A small drum made of a wooden hoop and two skins, similar to the present-day tambourine, but without the jingling device. It was played almost exclusively by women among the Jews. The translation of *toph* in the AV is "timbrel." Mentioned in Gen. 31:27; Ex. 15:20; Job 21:12; Ps. 81:2; 149:3; 150:4; Judges 11:34; 1 Sam. 10:4; 18:6; 2 Sam. 6:5; 1 Chron. 13:8; Is. 5:12; 24:8; 30:32; Jer. 31:4; Ezek. 28:13.

'ugab (Heb.). An early Hebrew musical instrument, mentioned only four times in the Bible (Gen. 4:21; Job 21:12; 30:31; and Ps. 150:4); apparently a long, wide, vertical flute commonly associated with shepherds. Translated in the AV as "organ," in the RSV as "pipe." Elsewhere it has erroneously been translated as "panpipes." Together with the *kinnor*, the *'ugab* was one of the earliest instruments of the Jews. CS

Readings: Rothmueller, A., *The Music of the Jews* (New York, 1954); Sachs, C., *The History of Musical Instruments* (New York, 1940); Sendry, A., *Music in Ancient Israel* (New York, 1969); Stainer, J., *The Music of the Bible*, rev. ed. by Francis W. Galpin, reprint (New York, 1970); Werner, E., "Musical Instruments," *The Interpreter's Dictionary of the Bible*, III (New York, 1962), 469—476.

See also: church music history, Jewish; *HCM,* V

Caecilian movement

This term describes certain efforts in the 19th-century Roman Catholic Church to achieve musical reform in the liturgy. The need for reform was recognized early in the century and inspired timid efforts in the 1830s and 1840s, the reform movement itself gaining increasing momentum in succeeding decades. The movement had its beginnings in Bavaria but spread rather quickly to other German states as well as to countries outside Germany.

At the beginning of the 19th century, Roman Catholic church music, shaped by tastes formed during the 18th century and by practices in vogue even longer, urgently needed reform. The influence of opera resulted in a certain theatricalism that was very much in evidence. High mass, especially on festive occasions, had absorbed many elements from opera—florid solos, duets, choruses, and instrumental interludes. Furthermore, during the 18th century professional church musicians had more and more abandoned the church, turning instead to the opera and concert hall to make a living. With the exception of festive works commissioned for special occasions, church music was, for the most part, entrusted to second- and third-rate composers. It seems unlikely, too, that more than a few parishes could muster either the singers or the instrumentalists to perform the best "liturgical" music available at any time during the 19th century. Cries for reform came from everywhere. Even Richard Wagner (1813—83) very severely deplored and chastised the "trivial scrapings" in the church music with which he was familiar.

The court in Munich provided the right set of circumstances to initiate church music reform. Johann Kaspar Ett (1788—1847), organist at the court church, was commissioned by Ludwig I, king of Bavaria, to revive some of the masterpieces of the 16th and 17th centuries. The center of revival then shifted to Regensburg, where the guiding light was Karl Proske (1794—1861), who devoted most of his life to research, collecting manuscripts and editions of 16th-century sacred vocal music and making selections available in his *Musica Divina*. Franz Witt (1834—88), perhaps the most influential of all the Cecilians, founded the *Allgemeiner Deutscher Caecilienverein* in 1868, bringing together the various Cecilia Societies that had sprung up in Germany, Austria, and Switzerland. This General St. Cecilia Society was sanctioned by Pope Pius IX in a special brief on Dec. 16, 1870.

The society's goal—to supplant the tawdry and often pompous church music of the day with a more decorous and liturgical style—was to be achieved mainly by the restoration and revival of plainsong and classical polyphony. The ideal of the Cecilian movement was the old a cappella style, but Witt's reforms were broader in scope, embracing not only new a cappella music but also new works with either organ or orchestral accompaniment, not to mention vernacular hymns. Unlike their Lutheran contemporaries, German Catholics immediately put the revived music to use at mass and Vespers; for them the revival of old music was a means of worship reform as well as serving as the inspiration for reform-minded composers (Hutchings).

Alongside the names of Ett, Proske, and Witt, Michael Haller (1840—

1915), Ignaz Mitterer (1850—1924), and Gustave E. Stehle (1839—1915) should be mentioned.

The Cecilians were prolific, turning out a veritable deluge of compositions in a pseudo-16th-century style. Their cultivation of a *stile antico* was really only one side of the coin; the other was a rejection of contemporary currents in music. By cutting themselves off from the general musical development of their own day they were forced, rather awkwardly, to look elsewhere for the materials and models that would help them create a church style. Their compositions were largely "characterless" (Lang), written in a style that could hope for acceptance all over the world. This archaism produced many lifeless pieces of music, alienated and cut off from "the true sources of a living religious art" (Lang, Fellerer).

In fairness it should be pointed out that, although much Cecilian music was shallow and without much artistic worth, some masses and motets wore well and were admired, even treasured, by several generations of worshipers in Europe and in the United States. As the 19th century came to an end, the movement began to lose strength; formalism had proved to be poor soil for artistic vitality. Some of the Cecilians, among them Peter Griesbacher (1864—1933), began to write in a more contemporary idiom, using chromaticism and even the leitmotiv to breathe some new life into church music.

United States of America

The movement for church music reform was felt in the new world rather early in the 19th century. The first Cecilia Society was established by the Rev. J. Martin Henni in 1838 in Cincinnati, Ohio, a large German settlement. It was the same Henni who in 1844 became the first bishop of Milwaukee, Wis., and in 1856, along with the Rev. Joseph Salzmann, established St. Francis Seminary near Milwaukee. Because of an urgent need for parish organists and teachers, Henni and Salzmann planned, as an adjunct to the seminary, The Catholic Normal School of the Holy Family, which opened its doors in September 1871. In response to an appeal for faculty personnel, Franz Witt sent John B. Singenberger (1848—1924) from Regensburg to the Normal School. Singenberger arrived in St. Francis in 1873. An American Society of St. Cecilia was founded the same year; a magazine, *The Caecilia*, appeared a year later and was published without interruption until 1964.

As teacher, composer, and organist, Singenberger left a permanent mark on Catholic church music in the United States. It is estimated that the bulk of Catholic church musicians in this country during the last quarter of the 19th and the first quarter of the 20th century was educated at the Catholic Normal School in St. Francis, Wis. It comes as no surprise, therefore, that during the first half of the 20th century most of the music sung in Catholic choir lofts was edited or composed by the many followers of Ett, Proske, Witt, and Singenberger.

The American Cecilia Society grew rapidly, numbering over 5,000 members by 1900. It sponsored regular choral festivals (*Caecilienfeste*) and general meetings from 1873 to 1903. After 1903, the year of Pope Pius X's motu proprio *Tra le sollecitudini*, some of the responsibility for church music shifted to local, diocesan authorities. National leadership in church music reform was one of the purposes of a new organization, the Society of St. Gregory of America, founded in 1913, which began publication of *The Catholic Choirmaster* in 1915. The society was also responsible for the publication of the St. Gregory Hymnal in 1921 as well as lists of approved and nonapproved music, the "White List" and "Black List."

The two societies and their publications came upon hard times even before Vatican II, and in August 1964 the board of directors of the two church music societies met at Boys Town (Omaha), Nebr., and voted to merge into a single society—the Church Music Association of America. This group, chiefly through its magazine, *Sacred Music,* is carrying the spirit and many of the ideals of the Cecilian movement into the final quarter of the 20th century. EP

Readings: Ellinwood, Leonard, *The History of American Church Music* (New York, 1953); Fellerer, Karl Gustav, *The History of Catholic Church Music*, tr. by Francis A. Brunner (Baltimore, 1961); Hutchings, Arthur, *Church Music in the Nineteenth Century* (New York, 1967); Nemmers, Erwin Esser, *Twenty Centuries of Catholic Church Music* (Milwaukee, 1949); Wienandt, Elwyn A., *Choral Music of the Church* (New York, 1965).

See also: church music history, American; church music history, classic and romantic; theology of church music, 19th century

canonical hours

Canonical hours (hours of the canon or rule) are daily hours of prayer and, by extension, the prayer offices appointed for use at those times by clergy, the ascetics, and laity in churches of the West and of the East. Also known as the divine office, the agenda, or the hours, the canonical hours comprise the offices of Matins, Lauds, Prime, Terce, Sext, None, Vespers, and Compline. The book that contains abbreviated forms of these offices is called the Breviary, though in fact there are multivolume editions of it. Traditionally the canonical hours have appeared in two forms: the Roman Breviary for nonmonastic clergy, and the Monastic Breviary for ascetic orders such as the Benedictines

The eight-hour daily cycle was essentially complete by 529, when St. Benedict wrote the *Regula monasteriorum* for the monks of Monte Cassino. According to his plan the prayer offices were arranged in the following way (summer schedule):

Time		Office	Theme
1:00—2:00	a.m.	Nocturns of Matins	End Time
2:15—3:00	a.m.	Lauds	Morning-Resurrection
4:30—5:00	a.m.	Prime	Preparation for Day's Work
9:30	a.m.	Terce	Pouring Out of Holy Spirit
11:45	a.m.	Sext	Hardship of the Day
2:00	p.m.	None	Strength for Remainder of the Day
6:30	p.m.	Vespers	Reflection on the Day and on Creation
7:30	p.m.	Compline	Protection against the forces of darkness

Variations of this schedule depended on the times of sunrise and sunset.

Traditional Structures

First-century Christians apparently maintained the synagogal traditions of daily morning and evening prayer (*shacharith* and *arbith*, derivations of hours of sacrifice in the Jerusalem temple), and continued to use liturgical ingredients from these services (Luke 24:53; Acts 2:42; 5:13, 42). Christological worship elements were soon developed in the form of creedal hymns (1 Tim. 1:17, Eph. 5:14; etc.). In the early 3d century Tertullian (*De Oratione*, xxv) assumed a regular practice of morning and evening prayer for Christians in community and supported private prayer (introduced by the ascetics of North Africa) at the third, sixth, and ninth hours (Terce, Sext, and None). A similar practice is recognized in the Church Order of St. Hippolytus (Rome, c. 215), in which is also found one of the first systematic descriptions of these services, complete with the *Lucernarium*, a lamp-lighting ceremony of Jewish abstraction. Noticeable in this early development of the office is the double tradition of a "monastic" version (with emphasis on meditation, thoroughness, and amplification) and of the "cathedral" version (with a skeletal cycle of evening and morning, simplicity of performance, and richness of ceremony). The latter, definitely for parochial use, was overshadowed and transformed when the hierarchy elevated the monastic form as the ideal for 6th- and 7th-century Christians. From then on to the Council of Trent, where the production of the *Breviarum ex decreto . . . Pii V.,* 1568, was initiated, the history of the office is marked alternately by expansion (the introduction of the little office of the Virgin Mary, the office of the dead, increase of commemorations, psalms, hymns, and prayers) and by many attempts at reform. The 1568 Breviary incorporated many reform proposals and was supplanted only recently according to the recommendation of Vatican II.

Luther reacted both against the length and complexity of the office and against the imposition of regulations regarding its use. Yet he permitted his own prayer life to be shaped by the office throughout his life. In the *Formula missae* (1523) he recommended a reduction of the Matins' psalms to 3 (originally 12 to 18), sought continuation of the day hours, Vespers, and Compline, and urged the further use of the whole Psalter together with the *lectio continua* (the reading of the entire Scriptures). In his *Deutsche Messe* (1526) he recognized value in daily Matins and Vespers because the schoolboys, he thought, would be given an opportunity to read psalms and lessons both in German and in Latin. This didactic emphasis and a sheer lack of Lutheran breviaries have been cited as reasons for the downfall of the office among Lutherans. In spite of widespread disregard, some larger parishes maintained the daily Matins and Vespers well into the 18th century (as in Leipzig at Bach's time), while smaller parishes tended to use Matins only on Sundays, and Vespers on Wednesdays and Saturdays, the latter with a penitential turn. Revival efforts by Kliefoth, Loehe, and others during the 19th century led to several 20th-century American Lutheran versions of Matins and Vespers.

For Roman Catholics the directives of Vatican II have materialized in the *Liturgia Horarum* (The Liturgy of the Hours), a rendition of the traditional canonical hours that highlights Lauds and Vespers, combines

Terce, Sext, and None, transforms Matins to an office of preaching, retains Compline, and suppresses Prime.

Components

The core ingredients of the canonical hours are psalms, readings, canticles, prayers, and hymns. St. Ambrose is credited with introducing the hymn to the office, and Benedict was one of the first to fix it as a proper. Some offices have had appointed hymns (*Te lucis ante terminum* for Compline, for instance), while others, such as Lauds and Vespers, used a rotation of hymnody.

In the traditional monastic office the entire Psalter is distributed over a week's period, the majority parceled to the three nocturns of Matins (9 to 18 psalms) and to Vespers (6 psalms); in some versions, each psalm was followed by its proper collect. Psalmodic texts are used throughout the office as introductory material (versicles and antiphons) or as utterances of praise (the responsory).

Traditionally the entire Bible was read in a year, the largest portions reserved for Matins' nocturns during the winter months. The day hours were supplied with a very short selection called the *capitulum* or little chapter.

Biblical canticles came to be associated with specific hours and days: the Benedictus with Lauds, the Magnificat with Vespers, the Nunc dimittis with compline, and the Te Deum with Matins. In Lauds other canticles, such as Is. 45:15-20, were used on weekdays. Some versions of the canonical hours provided for additional New Testament canticles, such as Col. 1:12-20; Eph. 1:3-10; and Rev. 5:9, 10-12.

In the "cathedral" type of office free intercessions were summoned to supplement prepared litanies. Other responsive prayer forms were fashioned from psalm verses (later known as the suffrages) that were then concluded with collects and the Our Father.

Music

Especially in the "cathedral version," the canonical hours were customarily brought to life through the help of music. The Jewish practice of antiphonal psalm singing was taken over by Christians probably already in the 1st century, further developed, according to Socrates in his *Ecclesiastical History*, in the 4th century. The major non-Gregorian systems of chant display large office repertories (e.g., the Ambrosian *Liber*

Vesperalis), and Eastern morning and evening prayer hours have been elaborated musically ever since the pattern set at St. Sophia in the 6th century.

Within the Western tradition the common tones of the offices include the formulas for prayers, lessons, versicles, blessings, the Benedicamus, and psalms. The Benedicamus is somewhat unusual because it has seasonal musical variants; these are generally quite melismatic and have been troped as well as set polyphonically (especially by Renaissance composers). The eight psalm tones plus the *tonus peregrinus* have been used as recitative formulas (also, as was true for Vulpius, in four- and five-part arrangements), and as motivic elements in polyphonic music. Likewise, office psalms were favorite sources for through-composed settings (Dietrich, Walter, Lossius, Monteverdi, Mozart, *et al.*).

Changeable songs include antiphons to the psalms and canticles, as well as the responsories. Antiphons serve to unify, thematically and musically, and were intended for the larger worshiping group (choir or congregation). They were sung before and after psalmodic sections, sometimes after each verse, though in the Gallican rite they were frequently used independently. Similarly, the Roman Marian antiphons (such as *Alma redemptoris mater*) have come to recognition apart from their respective psalms, enjoying the attention of many composers. Of the responsories, the Greater Respond (Prolix), used traditionally at Matins, is the most florid and has inspired many composers.

The larger musical items from the office are the hymns and canticles. Most important of the latter are the Venite (Ps. 95) from Matins with its own formulary tones and special antiphons (Invitatory), the Magnificat from Vespers, also with its own tones, and the Te Deum from Matins. Traditional melodies, as well as the texts alone, have attracted a wide variety of composers (from Dunstable to Verdi). Luther's version of the Te Deum has enjoyed popularity through the polyphonic settings of Schuetz, Reda, and others. Penderecki's *Utrenja* is based on the total resurrection office (Eastern), a practice in line with Rhau (*Vesperarum precum officia*, 1540) and Monteverdi (*Vespere*, 1610). MB

Readings: Apel, Willi, *Gregorian Chant* (Bloomington, Ind., 1958); Brodde, Otto, "Evangelische Choralkunde," *Die Musik des evangelischen Gottesdienstes*, vol. IV of *Leiturgia* (Kassel, 1956); Dugmore, C. W., *The Influence of the Synagogue upon the Divine Office* (London, 1964); Goltzen, Herbert, "Der taegliche Gottesdienst," *Gestalt und Formen des evangelischen Gottesdienstes*, vol. III of *Leiturgia* (Kassel, 1956); Grisbrooke, W. Jardine, "A

Contemporary Liturgical Problem: The Divine Office and Public Worship," *Studia Liturgica*, VIII/3 (1972) and IX/1—2, 3 (1973).

See also: canticle; chant, Gregorian; psalmody, Gregorian; *HCM*, I, IV

cantata

The origin of the cantata (from the Lat. *cantare*, "to sing") may be traced to early 17th-century Italian monodies. The term first appeared in Alessandro Grandi's *Cantade et arie a voce sola* of 1620. From the 1630s to the end of the century thousands of cantatas were composed in Italy alone. Most of the early cantatas were for one or two voices and basso continuo. Some were nothing but recitatives, and others were nothing but arias; the majority, however, employed an alternation of recitative and aria. After 1700 the chamber cantata became standardized as a sequence of two or three *de capo* arias separated by recitatives. Important composers of the Italian chamber cantata include Luigi Rossi (1598—1653), Giacomo Carissimi (1605—74), Marc-Antonio Cesti (1623—69), Alessandro Stradella (c. 1645—81), and Alessandro Scarlatti (1659—1725). Outside of Italy the chamber cantata appeared principally in France. Significant composers of French cantatas include Marc-Antoine Charpentier (1634—1704), Andre Campra (1660—1704), Nicolas Clerambault (1678—1749), and Jean-Philippe Rameau (1683—1764).

Church Cantata

In Germany the chamber cantata was largely neglected in favor of the church cantata. Such works were not usually called church cantatas but *concerti* or *motetti*. Sacred *concerti* typically used Biblical or chorale texts and consisted of several movements, some using chorus, others using solo voices. Instruments not only accompanied the voices but were assigned independent movements such as sonatas or ritornellos. The earliest composers of sacred *concerti* in Germany include Heinrich Schuetz (1585—1672), Johann Hermann Schein (1586—1630), and Samuel Scheidt (1587—1654). Several important composers of later sacred *concerti* include Andreas Hammerschmidt (1612—75), Franz Tunder (1614—67), Matthias Weckmann (1619—74), Dietrich Buxtehude (1637—1707), Johann Pachelbel (1653—1706), and Georg Boehm (1661—1733).

The sacred *concerto* with its Biblical or chorale text gave way at the beginning of the 18th century to a reformed type of cantata with a freely constructed poetical text. The change to freer texts was accelerated in 1700 with the publication of cantata texts by the court poet of Weissenfels, Erdmann Neumeister (1671—1756). Neumeister cast his poetical texts into sections, each designed for recitative, aria, or chorale, thus providing the format for the solo church cantata of the late baroque period.

One of the first composers to use Neumeister's reformed texts was Johann Philip Krieger (1649—1725). Only one example of the reformed cantata by Krieger is available, but it demonstrates admirably the procedures of the Italian chamber cantata as applied to the German church cantata. Other composers who followed in Krieger's train include Johann Kuhnau (1660—1722), Friedrich Wilhelm Zachow (1663—1712), Georg Philipp Telemann (1681—1767), and Johann Sebastian Bach (1685—1750). The reformed church cantata typically consists of recitatives and arias for solo voice and continuo. Later innovations include the addition of a chorus, the introduction of a final chorale, the use of a chorale melody as a generative principle, and the employment of the *da capo* aria. Kuhnau was one of the first composers of the reformed cantata to include a closing chorale and to use a chorale melody in the beginning and closing choruses. All the procedures and techniques of the church cantata, however, were used and summarized by the most famous composer of church cantatas, Johann Sebastian Bach (1685—1750).

Church Cantatas of Bach

Bach composed nearly 300 cantatas, of which about 200 are extant. He used the term cantata for the works for solo voice and the terms *Stueck, Concerto,* or *Motetto* for most of the cantatas using chorus. He borrowed procedures from both the older sacred concerto and the reformed cantata. The early cantatas (1704—11) show the influence of Buxtehude, Boehm, Pachelbel, and Kuhnau. *Gottes Zeit ist die allerbeste Zeit* is perhaps the finest of Bach's early cantatas. During the Weimar period (1712—17) Bach began to use the reformed texts of Neumeister and Salomon Franck. Although Bach wrote a few cantatas during the Coethen period (1717—23), it was during the Leipzig period (1723—50) that Bach produced most of his church cantatas. Particularly the chorale cantata and the solo cantata attracted Bach during this time. After Bach the church cantata largely disappeared in favor of the oratorio. Many works bearing the title cantata are in fact short oratorios, often dealing with secular subjects. HM

Readings: Bukofzer, Manfred, *Music in the Baroque Era* (New York, 1947); Blume, F., "The Older Church Cantata" and "The Newer Church Cantata and J. S. Bach," *Protestant Church Music* (New York, 1974); Palisca, Claude, *Baroque Music* (Englewood Cliffs, N. J., 1968); Ulrich, Homer, *A Survey of Choral Music* (New York, 1973); Wienandt, Elwyn A., *Choral Music of the Church* (New York, 1965).

See also: church music history, baroque; concertato style; oratorio; *HCM*, IV

canticle

A canticle (from the Latin *canticulum,* "little song") may be defined as a hymnlike text derived from one of the books of the Bible other than the Book of Psalms. Such canticles are generally identified by the Latin incipit of the text.

Cantica majora

The greater canticles are those taken from the New Testament. They include the *Benedictus Dominus Deus Israel* (Luke 1:68-79), *The Magnificat anima mea Dominum* (Luke 1:46-55), and the *Nunc dimittis* (Luke 2:29-32). In the Roman rite the greater canticles are used in Lauds, Vespers, and Compline respectively. The traditional Lutheran usage suggests the *Benedictus Dominus Deus Israel* (Song of Zacharias) as an alternate to the *Te Deum laudamus* in Matins. It is proper on all Sundays in Advent and Lent and also for daily use at any time. In Vespers the *Magnificat* (Song of Mary) and *Nunc dimittis* (Song of Simeon) serve respectively as canticle and alternate canticle. The *Magnificat* is proper on all festivals, and the *Nunc dimittis* may be used at any time except the greater festivals. Like the *Benedictus,* the *Nunc dimittis* is particularly appropriate during Advent and Lent. Peculiar to the Lutheran liturgy is the use of the *Nunc dimittis* at the close of the Communion liturgy. Also suggested for occasional use in some service books are the *Beati pauperes* (Matt. 5:3-12) and *Dignus est Agnus* (Rev. 5:12).

The *Te Deum laudamus,* which is not from the Bible, is also generally considered to be one of the major canticles. In traditional Lutheran usage it is the canticle for Matins on Sundays and festivals. This canticle, along with the three major New Testament canticles, has received special attention on the part of composers throughout the history of music. Choral settings of the *Te Deum* range from plainsong to elaborate concerted works using chorus, soloists, and instruments.

A distinctive Lutheran version of the *Te Deum* is Luther's *Herr Gott, dich loben wir*, arranged for antiphonal singing, half-verse by half-verse. The Wittenberg church order of 1533 directs that the first half-verse was to be sung by the choir, and the second by the congregation.

Klug's Wittenberg hymnal of the same year includes a variety of canticles from the Old and New Testaments, set to simple Psalm tones. Among them is a four-part *Magnificat* set to the *tonus peregrinus*. (See Vol. 53 of *Luther's Works* for a transcription of this work.)

Later chorale or hymnic versions of some of the major canticles for congregation include: *Grosser Gott, wir loben dich* (Te Deum), *Mit Fried' und Freud'* (Nunc dimittis), and *Mein Seel', O Gott, muss loben dich* (Magnificat).

Cantica minora

The lesser canticles are taken from the Old Testament. In the Lutheran service books they include: *Audite coeli* (Deut. 32:1-4, 9, 36, 40, 43), *Benedicite, omnia opera* (apocryphal Song of the Three Young Men, from the Song of the Three Young Men added in the Septuagint to the Hebrew Daniel), *Cantemus Domino* (Ex. 15:1-2, 6, 11, 13, 17-18), *Confitebor tibi* (Is. 12), *Domine, audivi* (Hab. 3:2-6, 13, 18-19), *Exultavit cor meum* (1 Sam. 2:1-10), *Song of David* (1 Chron. 29:10-18), and the *Song of Hezekiah* (Is. 38:10-20).

In the Roman rite the lesser canticles are used in Lauds. In the Lutheran liturgy the lesser canticles may serve as alternates for the greater canticles. HM

Readings: Davis, H. Grady, "Canticles," *The Encyclopedia of the Lutheran Church*, ed. J. Bodensieck (Minneapolis, 1965), pp. 364—365; Leupold, Ulrich, ed., *Liturgy and Hymns*, vol. 53 of *Luther's Works* (Philadelphia, 1965); Reed, Luther D., *The Lutheran Liturgy*, rev. ed. (Philadelphia, 1947).

See also: canonical hours; HCM, IV

cantional, cantional style

Cantional style is the designation for a basically homophonic vocal style for settings of congregational hymn tunes, usually in four or five parts, written with the melody in the upper part, the accompanying voices proceeding in homorhythmic fashion. Its early development is associated with a practice found in the Reformed Psalters of the middle and later 16th century, a practice subsequently adopted and developed to a considerable degree by German evangelical church music. The cantional style (or chorale in *contrapunctum simplex)* represented the homophonic standard in the purely vocal church music of the period; it contrasted with the chorale motet, which represented the polyphonic standard. Collections of these settings were called cantionals.

This style of writing developed especially in the latter half of the 16th century particularly as a means of furthering participation in congregational singing. While there are examples of cantional-like settings as

Johann Walter, 1524

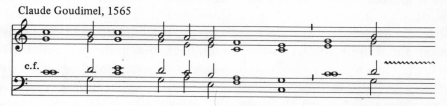

early as Johann Walter's *Geistliche Gesangbuechlein* (1524) and Georg Rhau's *Neue deutsche Geistliche Gesenge* (1544), the real impetus for the development of cantional style came from the Reformed psalters of the latter half of the

Claude Goudimel, 1565

16th century. Claude Goudimel's *Les pseaumes mis en rime francoise* (1565) contained simple four-voiced homophonic settings of the entire French Psalter with the melodies in the tenor; a second edition in the same year found the melody in the upper part. Lobwasser's widely used German translation of the French Psalter (1573) used Goudimel's settings and helped to prepare the way for the fuller development of the cantional style in Germany. The influence of Calvin's ideas concerning church music contributed to the movement in Germany in the middle and latter 16th century that sought a simpler religious service and emphasized greater participation in congregational singing. Several collections in the 1560s and 1570s that were important in these early developments were J. Heugel's settings for Burkhard Waldis' psalter (1555—70), Sigmund Hemmel's *Der ganz Psalter Davids* (1569), and David Wolkenstein's *Psalmen fuer Kirchen und Schulen, auf die gemeinen Melodien syllabenweise zu vier Stimmen* (1577, 1583). The two editions of Wolkenstein's collection clearly demonstrate one facet of the developing cantional style: the movement of the cantus firmus from the tenor to the upper part (in the first edition the melody occurs almost exclusively in the tenor; in the second edition over half of the melodies have moved to the upper part).

Lucas Osiander, 1586

It was for Lucas Osiander's *Fuenfzig geistliche Lieder und Psalmen* (1586) to clearly set forth and establish the basic characteristics of the cantional style. Osiander's title, "Fifty sacred songs and psalms arranged so, that an entire Christian congregation can sing along," not only suggests the relative failure of the older settings to lead in congregational singing, but most importantly establishes the general characteristics of the cantional style as a species of church music clearly differentiated from the chorale motet. Osiander's settings are quite purely homophonic, and consistently present the cantus firmus in the upper part, the individual voice parts proceeding in a homorhythmic style, the melodies, however, retaining their original rhythmic forms.

Following Osiander's example, the last decade of the 16th and early years of the 17th centuries saw a flood of cantional collections that were essentially *Gebrauchsmusik* for use in connection with congregational singing. These cantional settings were generally intended to be sung in parts by the choir, the congregation joining in the simultaneous singing of the melody, or as settings for choir alone, alternating with the congregation in the singing of the chorales. As the use of these settings spread, it was apparently not uncommon for instruments to play along with the choir, even occasionally supplanting the choir, while the congregation sang the melody. In later developments, the organ gradually assumed a role in which at first it joined in the accompanying of the singing by the choir and, by the later 17th century, ultimately replaced the choir, accompanying the congregation alone.

Generally speaking, the cantional collections were collections containing settings of the old traditional Reformation texts and melodies in *contrapunctum simplex*. They stand in contrast to two related types of collections also found in this general period: (1) collections in cantional style that contained settings of new texts and new melodies (e.g., collections usually titled as "Newe geistl. Gesg." or "Neue teutsche geist. Lider"); (2) collections based on the old texts and tunes but set in chorale motet style (e.g., Hassler's *Psalmen und Christliche Gesaenge . . . fugweis componiert*, 1607).

Among the early important cantionals, which reflected especially in their prefaces and subtitles the kind of congregational involvement envisioned by the composers, are: Andreas Raselius' *Cantionale oder Kirchengesaenge* (1588), which for the first time used the word "cantional" in connection with such a collection; Raselius' *Regenspurgischer Kirchen Contrapunct . . .* "mit 5 St. also gesetzt, dass jederman den Choral und unbekannte Melodey jedes Gesangs ungehindert wol mit singen kan" (1599); Georg Weber's *50 Geistl. Lieder und Psalmen* (1588), 4-part settings; Roger Michael's 4-part *Gebreuchlichsten und vornembsten Gesenge D. Mart. Luth. u. a.* (1593), in which "das neue Princip mit dem polyphonen Stilcharakter des alteren ev. Liedtypus in Einklang zu bringen"; Seth Calvisius' *Harmonia Cantionum Ecclesiasticarum* (1597), 4-part settings that continued through a 5th edition in 1622; Johann Eccard's *Geistl. Lieder auff den Choral* (1597), containing 55 5-part settings; Bartholomaeus Gesius' *Geistl. Deutsche Lieder D. Mart. Lutheri* (1601), 97 4- and 5-part settings with the melody in the upper part; Melchior Franck's cantional of 1602; J. Burmeister's *Geistl. Ps. D.M.L. u.a.* (1601), 4-part settings so arranged that "die gewoehnliche Melodey im Descant behalten und von der gantzen gemeine kan gesungen werden. Die andern drey St. aber von den erwachsenen Knaben und gesellen auffm Chor und wer sonst in der Kirchen zur Musica lust hat" (Zahn, VI, 98); and the *Hamburger Melodey-Gesangbuch* (1604), the work of J. Decker, Heinrich Scheidemann, and Jacob and Hieronymous Praetorius, one of the early collections to speak of the organ also accompanying the singing. ("Wenn solche christlich Gesaenge entweder die liebe Jugend auf dem Chor herquinkeliret oder auch der Organist auf der Orgel kuenstlich spielt oder sie beide ein Chor machen und die Knaben in die Orgeln singen und die Orgel hinwiederum in den Gesang spielet [als nunmehr in dieser Stadt gebraeuchlich], alsdann mag auch ein jeder Christ seine schlichte Laienstimme nur getrost und laut genug erheben und also nunmehr nicht als das fuenfte, sondern als das vierte Rad den Musikwagen des Lobes un Preises goettlichen Namens gewaltiglich mit fortziehen und bis an den Allerhoechsten reiben und bringen helfen.") Melchior Vulpius' *Kirchen Gsg. und Geistl. Lieder* (1604), 4- and 5-part settings, "also gesetzt, dasz sie nicht wohl koennen besser gesetzt werden und im Diskant den Choral richtig und eigentliche behalten," J. Jeep's *Geistl. Ps. und Kirchengesaeng* (1607/09/29), 62 settings, Gotthart Erythraeus'*Ps. und Geistl.Lieder* (1608), so arranged that "der Thon oder die in die jeder maenniglich, auch den gemeinen Mann, leichtlich moegen erkannt und gesungen werden," also belong to this early period.

With Hans Leo Hassler's *Kirchengesaenge, Psalmen, und geistliche Lieder . . . simpliciter gesetzt* (1608), 4-part settings of 69 melodies written for the Liebfrauenkirche in Nuernberg, we reach the high point in the development of the South German cantional. Hassler notes in his preface that the congregational singing to these settings "von der lieben gemeinen Buergerschaft mit sonderer Anmutung, christliche Lust und Eifer geschehe." In northern Germany the high point in the development of the cantional was reached at about the same time with the publication of

Michael Praetorius, 1609–10

Michael Praetorius' *Musae Sioniae* (Pts. VI-VIII, 1609—10). Both Hassler and Praetorius' publications stood significantly above their predecessors, Praetorius' work, particularly, being the most comprehensive chorale collection of its time. Both contained simple 4-part setting with the melody in the upper part.

The problem of the simultaneous singing of the chorale melody by both women and children and men (an octave lower) was addressed by Otto Siegfried Harnisch in his *Psalmodia nova. Simplex et harmonica* (1621) in which he placed the melody in both the upper and 2d tenor parts in which "die Melodey mit der Knabenstimme oben und auch mit der Mannstimme in der Octava unten ohne Dissonanz und Verletzung der Harmoney wohl mitsingen werden mag."

Some of the earlier cantional publications extended their influence through a number of editions; others were important only in their immediate localities. Among later publications that reflect the developing cantional tradition and should be noted are the *Cantionale sacrum* (Gotha, 1646—48), the *New Leipziger Gesangbuch* (Vopelius, 1682), and the *Grosse Cantional* of Briegel (1687).

The Reformed church in Germany largely continued to use the Goudimel settings together with Lobwasser's translation of the Psalter. New settings of the French melodies were attempted by L. S. Mareschall in his *Ps. Davids Kirchengsge. und geist. Lieder* (1594) and by J. Crueger in the *Psalmodia sacra* (1657/58) for the Reformed congregation in Berlin.

Johann Hermann Schein, 1627

With the publication of Johann Hermann Schein's *Cantional oder Gesangbuch Augspurgischer Confession* (1627), which included a figured bass, the development of the cantional begins to take a new direction, in which the use of vocal settings for accompanying congregational singing gradually comes to a conclusion and which, as the organ increasingly supplants the choir in accompanying congregational song, becomes the history of the development of the organ chorale-book. CS

Readings: Blume, F., "Beginnings of the Reformed Psalm Lied and the Origins of the Lutheran Cantional Settings, the Cantionales," *Protestant Church Music* (New York, 1974).
See also: chorale, vocal settings; church music history, Renaissance—the Reformation tradition; *HCM,* IV

cantor

Cantor was the Latin title given to the official in charge of the music of cathedral, collegiate, and monastic churches, and often the church-related schools. In the Middle Ages the English chanter or precenter was second in rank of the four principal dignitaries of the church. He had the first stall on the north side of the choir, for which reason the north side is called *cantoris* as contrasted with the *decani* choir on the south or deacon's side.

The duty of the German cantor, the English precentor, or French *maitre de chapelle* is to direct the musical part of the service and to intone psalms and canticles. He is in charge of the selection of the music and to see to it that it is properly performed, like the music director in an American church. In Germany the musical head of an educational establishment, with a choir-school or *Kantorei* attached to a church, was called the cantor, but he was also subject to a rector, the principal of the school

In selecting a cantor for a given position, the city council carefully investigated his educational qualifications, teaching experience, religious beliefs, and personal conduct. Even the credentials of a man like J. S. Bach were thoroughly examined. The deliberations of the Leipzig Council and their decision to offer the St. Thomas vacancy to Bach are well documented. A cantor hoping to secure a job needed more than teaching ability and specific musical qualifications. He was also required to commit himself to a certain doctrinal position. Therefore recommendations from men like Luther, Melanchthon, and Bugenhagen were most helpful.

Because of his dual role in the school and the church, the German cantor provided an important liaison between the clergy and the teaching staff. He carried full responsibility for the school music program, and he was the minister of sacred music in the life of the congregation. There are many testimonies to the fruitful cooperation of pastor and cantor in the areas of hymnody and liturgy. Some of the more notable ones were Luther and Walter at Wittenberg, Ludwig Helmbold with Joachim Burck and Johann Eccard in Muehlhausen, and Paul Gerhardt and Johann Crueger in Berlin.

Apart from his daily teaching duties and rehearsals, the cantor often found it necessary to write a practical method for music instruction, and sometimes was compelled to compose music for worship services of the new church when nothing appropriate was available. While these situations did not require a high degree of originality, a practical person was needed who could foresee the needs and then cope with them. He composed *Gebrauchsmusik* for special occasions and de tempore pieces for the church year.

The life and work of a cantor went far beyond the preparation and the performance of music for worship services. The cantor, because of his vocation, found himself closely attached not only to the church but to the community as well. As a responsible leader of the *Stadtkantorei* (city cantorei), an organization intimately concerned with the personal lives of its members, the cantor assumed important social obligations. He took a direct interest in the welfare of the *Kantorei* families, thus coming into close contact with the local citizenry.

The German cantor during the baroque period was continually in the public eye, not only at regular services, weddings, and funerals, but also at numerous important civic functions. In larger cities, he had the responsibility of dividing his singing forces among several churches on Sunday mornings, hoping to satisfy all concerned. It was also his job to recruit adults, usually former students or clergymen, for the performance of polyphonic music. Where a *Stadtkantorei* existed, he worked with carpenters, farmers, merchants—people from all walks of life. A city's musical life literally depended on his initiative and ability.

For all this, the Lutheran cantor viewed the use of his artistic gifts primarily as a summons from God to preach the Gospel. He did not consider himself an individual artist who was to receive honor and acclaim through his own doing. He regarded his work as existing only for the reason of purposeful union with God and the church. HN

Readings: Burney, Charles, *A General History of Music*, Book III, 1776, reprint (New York, 1957); Buszin, W., "Johann Walther, Composer, Pioneer, and Luther's Consultant," *The Musical Heritage of the Church*, Vol. 3 (Valparaiso, Ind., 1946); Schuenemann, G., *Geschichte der deutschen Schulmusik* (Leipzig, 1928).

See also: cantorei; decani/cantoris; *HCM*, IV

cantorei

Originally the term cantorei referred to a specific organization designed to meet the musical needs of a church or court. During the 16th century it began to be used in a much broader sense and was applied to various kinds of singing societies, school choirs, and instrumental groups, all of which were to play a fundamental part in the organization and development of the music program of the newly created Protestant church.

In the Middle Ages numerous *Kantoreien* were active in the cathedral towns and in the courts of the princes, where the music of the service

Medieval cantor and cantorei before a large choirbook.

played as vital a role then as it does in churches today. Choir schools were organized for the specific purpose of training singers in liturgical music.

One of the earliest institutions of this type was the Roman *Schola cantorum*, consisting of 12 professional singers, 12 students (boys), and two schoolmasters. It is believed that these papal schools were in operation as early as the fourth century, during the time of Pope Sylvester (314—336), and it was customary for the monks and singers trained in Rome to travel to distant cities to form additional choir schools. The results of this kind of missionary endeavor may be seen in the famous schools at St. Gall, Metz, and Reichenau, already in existence during the reign of Charlemagne, as well as in the English chantry schools and the French *Maitrise*. Martin Luther, visiting Rome in 1511, was deeply impressed when he heard such choirs sing the music of Josquin Desprez.

Forerunners of the 16th-century German cantorei date back to 733, when, under the commission of Boniface, a Benedictine monastery was founded in Fulda. The Magdeburg Cathedral School dates back to the year 1000 and was attended by Luther in 1497. At least 12 of the upper-grade students were in the choir for all regular services, including Matins, Terce, and Vespers. At the Spital cantorei in Nuernberg (1343) a special foundation for 12 choir students was established "for the purpose of

Cantorei with two choirbooks and two groups of singers from the *Concilienbuch* of Ulrich von Reichenthal published in Augsburg in 1483.

Cantorei from an illustration in Herman Finck's *Practica Musica,* Wittenberg, 1556.

greater service to God." To suit the need of the church, the hours for school exercises were carefully planned and often greatly curtailed, the claims of weddings, funerals, masses, and similar occasions being given preference over school studies.

Unlike *Kurrende,* who begged in the streets for food, the singers in the *Hofkantorei* (court cantorei) enjoyed good living conditions and were paid for their services. A pre-Reformation *Hofkantorei* vital to the cause of Lutheran music was that of the Saxon prince, protector and friend of

Luther, Frederick the Wise. Frederick's *Hofkantorei* was established in Torgau in 1491, but when the court moved to Dresden, Luther insisted that this city not be left without a cantorei. Torgau citizens, undoubtedly influenced by Luther's tract, established a cantorei in 1526 under the supervision of Johann Walter, Luther's musical adviser and a former singer in the Torgau *Hofkantorei*.

Within the *Schulkantorei* (school cantorei) were several branches, each of which had a particular assignment in the church music program. The *Schulchor*, for example, carried on the tradition of the medieval cathedral schools through the singing of Gregorian chant and unison hymns. Most towns also had a more select school choir, the *Chorus symphoniacus*, which specialized in the singing of polyphonic music. The *Chorus symphoniacus* consisted of select students from the upper grades and teachers or former students for some of the male parts. At times the lower voices were taken over by voluntary singers from the *Adjuvanten*, a society of local citizens interested in singing. It was through this type of cantorei organization that the Netherlandish music and the polyphonic music of the early Lutheran composers found its best vehicle of expression.

With the rise of Pietism and the Age of Enlightenment in the 18th century, the blossoming period of the cantorei came to an end. Today, in Germany, many singing societies, usually church-related, use the term as they seek to recapture the spirit of 16th- and 17th-century Kantoreipraxis. HN

Readings: Carpenter, Nan Cooke, *Music in the Medieval and Renaissance Universities* (Norman, Okla., 1958); Ehmann, Wilhelm, "Das Musizierbild der deutschen Kantorei im 16. Jahrhundert," *Musik und Bild* (1938); Held, Karl, *Das Kreuzkantorat zu Dresden* (Leipzig, 1894); Nettl, Paul, *Luther and Music* (Philadelphia, 1948); Nuechterlein, Herbert, "The Sixteenth-Century Kantorei and Its Predecessors," *Church Music,* 71·1.

See also: cantor; church music history, Renaissance—the Reformation tradition; *HCM,* IV

carol

The derivation of the word in uncertain, but it is generally accepted that originally a carol was a dance associated with song. Neither the religious significance nor the special association with Christmas are part of its original meaning.

Nonetheless, the earliest known carols are associated with religious words and come from the later Middle Ages. The best source for their study is Vol. IV of *Musica Britannica.* These medieval carols are virtually always written to the pattern known as "burden and stanza." The "stanza" is the narrative, sung by a solo or small group, while the "burden" is a chorus, sung by everybody, which preceded the first stanza and follows all the others. This corresponds to the form of the processional dance—a half-ceremonial, half-secular outdoor performance in the village street, where the dancers would move during the "burden," which they all sang, and stop or dance on one spot, while the "stanza," which continued the story, was sung by the song leader.

In addition to the dance form of carol (the "burden and stanza" pattern described above) is the ballad form of the carol, which simply tells a story from end to end (e.g., "The Cherry Tree Carol"). Often the "burden and stanza" form becomes merged with the direct "ballad" form by providing a chorus after each narrative stanza, but not a "burden" at the beginning. On the whole, the "burden and stanza" form tends to deal with Scripture and doctrine, while the "ballad" form very often slips over into mythology and legend.

The earliest examples, preserved in *Musica Britannica,* may well not be the oldest carols; for carol singing was at that time essentially an expression of popular religion. Nobody in the congregation sang in church, but they did sing out of doors at paraliturgical functions associated with the greater festivals. The written examples mentioned here are of a learned kind, with sophisticated harmony and counterpoint and probably represent a style of carol which at an early stage found its way back into church and was sung by the choir.

The music of carols was essentially simple and popular, and their texts were less dogmatic and more domestic and legendary than those of the church hymns. A well-known example is "The holly and the ivy"; a more developed and profound one is "Tomorrow shall be my dancing day."

It was the association between carols and outdoor or informal religion, together with the doubtful authority of their texts, that caused carols to be suppressed in the Puritan age in Britain, and the modern fashion of carol singing dates only from the 19th century. Many of our best-known English carols we owe to the researches of Davies Gilbert (1823) and George Sandys (1827), who traveled in the parts of England least affected by Puritan restrictions (chiefly Cornwall), collected by oral tradition a number of these songs, and later published them. Broadsheets, large song sheets with carol texts, became popular in London in the 1830s and "God rest you merry, gentlemen" first appeared in one of these.

In 1871 Bramley and Stainer published their famous *Christmas Carols New and Old*, including several pieces from outside England, and this coincided with the new folklore about Christmas that was so much promoted by Albert (1819—61), husband of Queen Victoria. The custom of holding a service of Lessons and Carols at Christmas originated in 1877 in the then temporary cathedral at Truro, Cornwall, and this in due course generated the world famous Christmas Carol service at King's College, Cambridge, which was instituted in 1918.

The danger of associating carols exclusively with Christmas and of the complete neglect of carols at any other season was foreseen and corrected in the *Oxford Book of Carols*, edited by Percy Dearmer, Martin Shaw, and R. Vaughan Williams (1928). The Preface to that work is essential reading for any who wish to study the subject, and its contents still provide a good conspectus of the international and wholly creedal significance of carols.

Many carol books have been published in the 20th century and the carol itself has undergone the modernizing processes noticeable in liturgy and hymnody; but essentially the difference between a carol and a hymn remains. The following verse, for example, appears in a well-known carol ("The Wassail Song") but would hardly appear in a hymn:

> Bring us out a table
> and set it with a cloth,
> bring us out a mouldy cheese
> and some of your Christmas broth.

ER

Readings: Musica Britannica, IV (London, 1956); Greene, R. L. *The Early English Carols* (Oxford, 1935); *Oxford Book of Carols* (London, 1928); Routley, E., *The English Carol* (London and New York, 1958); Routley, E., "Some Thoughts on the Carols of Advent, Christmas, and Epiphany," *Church Music*, 74·2; *University Carol Book* (London, 1961).

See also: hymnody, English; *HCM*, III, IV

Catholic pronouncements and decrees on church music

Under this title we include various directions from official sources that influenced or shaped the course of church music in the Western church.

Included are selected papal pronouncements (encyclical, apostolic constitution, motu proprio) as well as decrees of a council or Roman congregation (Council of Trent, Congregation of Rites).

Leo I, pope 440—461. The shift of influence in the early Christian centuries regarding both liturgical practice and music for worship was always from the East to the West. On the basis of a 7th- or 8th-century report that lists the names of popes who contributed to the formation of the Roman liturgy, it seems possible that Leo I was responsible for the first attempt to provide the Roman church with an annual cycle *(cantus annalis)* of chants of western origin.

Gregory I, pope 590—604. The role of Gregory in relation to the body of music that bears his name has been reinterpreted in recent times. It seems likely that under his direction the considerable repertory of melodies already existing in his day was organized, codified, and assigned to a definite place in the yearly cycle. It is possible that Gregory himself might have added some new music for feasts that he himself introduced.

John XXII, pope 1316—34. Living in exile in Avignon, John issued his well-known protest against some of the abuses that had made their way into church music. The decree of 1334, *(Docta sanctorum patrum)* singled out practices that distracted worshipers, "intoxicating rather than soothing the ears," or obscured the words and made unrecognizable the traditional chant melodies. Musical developments in the 13th century, especially the Gothic motet and the more earthy music of the troubadours, had exerted a strong influence on church music practices. Musical art as a whole was developing at a pace that the church found unacceptable. John's decree, calling for a return to older and simpler practices *(organum)*, sought in effect to establish a sacred or church style.

Council of Trent (1545—63). The Council heard many and grave complaints about the state of church music, especially the unintelligibility and neglect of the texts, the behavior and attitude of singers, and the intrusion of a secular spirit into church music through the use of tunes with profane associations as *cantus firmi,* as well as by the use of noisy instruments. Although the deliberations became very animated (some wanted to exclude polyphonic music altogether from worship), the decision reached in Session XXII (September 1563), did little more than recommend the avoidance of whatever conflicted with the dignity of worship. The composer of particular significance at this time seems to have been the Flemish Jacobus de Kerle (c. 1531—91), who was commissioned to compose music for performance during the services at the council. These works, written in a clear and moderate style, seem to have put council fathers at ease about the textual problems associated with complicated polyphonic music. In the final analysis the council made local bishops responsible for carrying out its thinking in specific matters of worship and music.

Benedict XIV, pope 1740—58. Encyclical letter *Annus qui*, Feb. 19, 1749. Benedict was primarily addressing the bishops of the Papal States when he asked for "decency and cleanliness" in all churches, and urged the avoidance of anything that might scandalize pilgrims to Rome during the 1750 Holy Year. This lengthy document cites many authorities, pro and con, on the use of choral ("figurative chant") and instrumental music in church. Singled out as abuses are the unintelligibility of the text in choral music as well as the worldly and theatrical use of instruments.

Pius X pope 1903—14. Motu proprio *Tra le sollecitudini* on sacred music, Nov. 22, 1903. In a very real sense Pius X summarized 19th-century ideals and efforts for church music reform. He wanted his instruction to be a juridical code of sacred music. He viewed sacred music as an integral part of the liturgy, as an aid to people in acquiring the Christian spirit from its first and indispensable source, namely, participation in the sacred mysteries. It follows that church music ought to possess the qualities that characterize the liturgy itself: holiness, beauty of form, and universality. Besides Gregorian chant and classical polyphony, modern music also has a place in worship, but must be chosen with greater care so as to avoid any hint of the theatrical style. Noteworthy also are the following regulations: soloists are permitted as long as they emphasize rather than monopolize the sacred text; women are not to be part of the choir because they cannot exercise a real liturgical office; instruments other than the organ may be used in worship, but never without the permission of the local bishop; pianos, bands, and percussion instruments are forbidden.

Pius XI pope 1922—39. Apostolic constitution *Divini cultus*, Dec. 20, 1928. Recalling the reform of sacred music envisioned by Pius X, Pius XI deplored the fact that in some places the motu proprio had not been fully observed. Understandably, he looked to seminaries for help and urged a thorough instruction in music and singing, especially Gregorian chant, for all students for the priesthood. Gregorian chant, classical polyphony, choirs, choir schools for boys, the human voice as *the* instrument of worship, the organ as an instrument of "extraordinary grandeur and majesty"—all receive high praise. Worshipers, Pius XI urged, should not be mere "silent spectators," but active participants by singing.

Pius XII, pope 1939—58. Encyclical on the sacred liturgy *Mediator Dei,* Nov. 20, 1947. This lengthy and important liturgical document—with its stress on worship by the entire Christian community, by the whole mystical body of Christ—makes a strong plea for congregational singing: "Let the full harmonious singing of our people rise to heaven like the bursting of a thunderous sea and let them testify by the melody of their song to the unity of their hearts and minds as becomes brothers and sisters of the same Father."

Pius XII encyclical on sacred music *Musicae sacrae disciplina,* Dec. 25, 1955. Pius XII wanted to throw new light on the 1903 legal code, but also had a vision of what sacred music—adapted to contemporary conditions and enriched—could mean to the mission of the church. Music, in fact, should make the prayers of the Christian community "more alive." Hymn singing receives much more attention than in previous documents; in fact, popular, vernacular hymns are recognized as powerful aids in worship. In a slight change from the moto proprio of 1903, stringed instruments receive special mention as possible helps in attaining the lofty purpose of sacred music. One thing, however, stands out above all others: for the first time in an ecclesiastical document church musicians are called "ministers of Christ the Lord."

Instruction of the Sacred Congregation of Rites on Sacred Music and the Sacred Liturgy. Sept. 3, 1958. The pastoral effectiveness of both the sacred liturgy and sacred music prompted this very lengthy document. Principles previously stated are interpreted more precisely with the hope that they can more easily be put into practice. The Instruction spells out in detail each and every aspect of participation in the mass. It carefully distinguishes the various kinds of sacred music. Its scope is broad and exhaustive, including such diverse subjects as the use of the organ and other instruments in worship, the use of such mechanical devices as tape recorders and film projectors, the transmission of liturgical services by radio or television, and even the matter of church bells. Liturgical roles are precisely delineated, including that of commentator. For the first time in an official document parish choirs may include women (i.e., where it is impossible to form a liturgical choir or schola cantorum in the historical sense). For the first time also an official document recommends a just wage for organists and choir directors. Finally, the Instruction envisions a broad program of education in sacred music and the sacred liturgy that begins in the Christian home and extends to the university level.

Second Vatican Council 1962—65. Constitution on the Sacred Liturgy, Dec. 4, 1963. One chapter of the constitution is devoted to sacred music. Chapter VI is a brief summary of key principles contained in previous documents. One slight shift of emphasis has unusual significance for the future course of church music. Pius X had stated very simply that sacred music is an integral part of the solemn liturgy; Chapter VI asserts that sacred song *united to the words* forms a necessary or integral part of the sacred liturgy. The pastoral bent of the constitution is evident from its recommendation that composers begin to provide "for the needs of small choirs and for the active participation of the entire assembly of the faithful." EP

Readings: Fellerer, Karl Gust., *The History of Catholic Church Music,* tr. by Francis A. Brunner (Baltimore, 1961); Fellerer, Karl Gust., "Church Music and the Council of Trent," *The Musical Quarterly,* XXXIX (October 1943); Lang, Paul Henry, *Music in Western Civilization* (New York, 1941); Seasoltz, R. Kevin, *The New Liturgy: A Documentation, 1903-65* (New York, 1966); *The Liturgy: Papal Teachings Selected and Arranged by the Benedictine Monks of Solesmes,* tr. by the Daughters of St. Paul (Boston, 1962); Wienandt, Elwyn A., *Choral Music of the Church,* with appendix containing the decree of John XXII (New York, 1965).

See also: Caecilian movement; church music history, classic and romantic; church music history, medieval; church music history, Renaissance—the Latin tradition; church music history, 20th century; *HCM,* I, II

chant, Anglican

The term "Anglican chant" denotes the harmonized chant that evolved from the medieval psalm tones of plainsong. It has been the characteristic manner of singing the psalms and canticles in the Anglican communion since the 17th century. In varying degrees it has also been used by almost all Christian churches as a means of musical recitation in four-part harmony of prose passages from the Psalms and other selections from the Bible.

For at least several centuries before the Reformation, perhaps as far back as the 11th century, two-, three-, and four-part harmonies or descants were improvised to the psalm tones. The practice in England is described, with examples for each mode, in Thomas Morley's *A Plaine and Easie Introduction to Practicall Musicke* (1597).

Ex. 1   Christ Church Tune

Written Anglican chants, in four-part harmony, date from the publication of *Short Directions for the Performance of Cathedral Services* (1661) by Edward Lowe and *Divine Services* (1664) by James Clifford. Both were attempts to recover the musical traditions that were lost during the days of the Puritan Commonwealth in England. The harmonization of Tone 1₄, with the plainsong in the tenor part is shown in Ex. 1. In William Boyce's *Cathedral Music,* I (1760) the plainsong was shifted to the treble and the whole falsely attributed to Thomas Tallis (c. 1505—85). In this form the chant has remained in constant use to the present time, the best-known example of a single chant. Chants such as this, repeating the music for each verse of the psalm, continued to be composed well into the 20th century.

Ex. 2   Matthew Camidge (1758—1844)

The recognized parallelism of the Hebrew poetry led 18th-century composers to write double chants for pairs of verses (Ex. 2). Perhaps because more music is involved, these double chants have since been the more popular of the two forms.

Some psalms, notably 1, 2, 39, 40, 41, 68, 76, 77, 93, 137, and 146 were written so that their verses fall into groups of three. Triple chants to

Ex. 3

R. Anthony Lee (b. 1937)

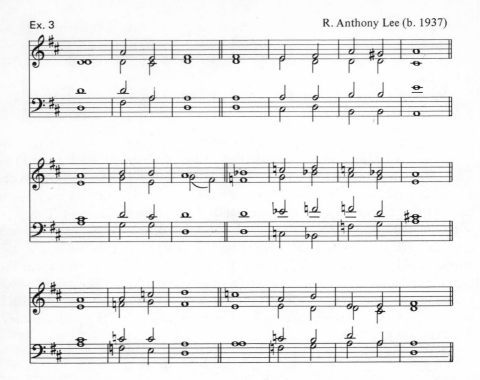

accomodate these psalms are first found in Sir John Frederick Bridge's *Westminster Abbey Chant Book* (1894). The rhythmic pattern for chanting cannot be varied, but 20th-century composers can use more modern harmonies. Such a triple chant is shown in Ex. 3.

Fitting words to music has always been a problem. When the words change from the traditional Latin to modern vernaculars, it is doubly difficult, for one has to unlearn the old as well as learn the new rhythms and stresses. Roman Catholic musicians are having to make the same adjustments today as Englishmen did in the mid-16th century. As long as the psalms were chanted primarily by professional choirs, words could be fitted to music by diligent practice. But with the Oxford Movement of the mid-19th century, many smaller, parish churches tried to chant the psalms with only amateur singers. This led to the practice of "pointing" the texts to show, by means of accents, asterisks, dots, syllables in heavy type, or bar-lines, how the words should fit the music. The first attempt at pointing was made in John Hullah's *The Book of Psalms with Chants* (1844). It took a number of decades to work out many of the problems. With the music of the chant and the pointed text on the same page, there was a tendency to read music more than words. The recitations were hurried and cadences drawn out, leading to the infamous "Anglican thump" on the first syllable after the recitation.

Good chanting reverses that pattern. It takes the recitation deliberately and keeps the same pace throughout. Strict musical rhythm must be avoided. Instead, the normal rhythm of speech should be cultivated. To hear a good choir chant the psalms at Evensong is often more moving spiritually than an anthem. Many a modern parish sings the chanted canticles as well as they do the hymns. LE

Readings: Bridges, R., "Chanting," *The Prayer-Book Dictionary* (1912); Ellinwood, L., "Anglican Chant: Past and Present," *Church Music,* 69·1; Ellinwood L., "From Plainsong to Anglican Chant," *Cantors at the Crossroads,* ed. J. Riedel (St. Louis, 1967); *The American Psalter* (New York, 1930); *The Oxford American Psalter* (New York, 1949).

See also: decani/cantoris; psalmody, Gregorian; *HCM,* IV

chant, Gregorian

What is usually referred to as Gregorian chant is known by a great variety of terms, among them the most common being plainchant, plainsong, *cantus planus* (Lat.), *cantus Gregorianus* (Lat.), and *Gregorianischer Choral* (Ger.).

It is doubtful whether Gregory the Great (c. 540—604) contributed to the liturgical music that bears his name. It is certain that he instituted a number of liturgical reforms during his pontificacy (590—604) that included the codifying and assembling of the chants then in existence. Many strophic hymns are attributed to him (e.g., *Audi benigne Conditor; Ecce jam noctis; Primo dierum omnium; Lucis creator optime*), yet it is more probable that he is the author of the lyrics rather than the composer of the melodies to which these hymns have been sung for many centuries. It is quite certain that he had more than a passing interest in the development of the daily office, since he founded many monasteries of the Order of St. Benedict, of which he was a member.

The history of Gregorian chant is conveniently divided into four basic periods. These are: (1) the period of formation, which extends from the beginning of the Christian era to the time of Gregory the Great; (2) the period of florescence from the 7th to the 13th century, when the great

Melodic Styles of Chant

Syllabic Chant

Portion of Sequence hymn, "Lauda Sion Salvatorem" *Liber Usualis,* p. 945

Neumatic Chant

Portion of Antiphon, "Laus Deo Patri" *Liber Usualis,* p. 914

Melismatic Chant

Portion of "Alleluia. Vidimus stellam" *Liber Usualis,* p. 460

scholas were established and the chant was widely disseminated throughout Europe; (3) the period of decline, with the rise of polyphony, beginning at the time of the Renaissance and extending to the 19th century; (4) the period of restoration, beginning about the middle of the 19th century, as the result of painstaking paleographic research in certain Benedictine monasteries, and extending into the 20th century, when Gregorian chant faces the problem of decreasing use because of certain liturgical developments in the Roman Catholic Church.

Authorities on Gregorian chant generally divide it into four basic categories: monolog and dialog; psalmodic; strophic; and commatic (through-composed). The three basic melodic styles of chant are syllabic (basically one note per syllable), neumatic (frequent use of several notes to a syllable), and melismatic (particularly florid melodies with many notes sung to particular syllables).

Monolog and Dialog

This category, together with the psalmodic compositions, is probably the oldest layer of plainsong and can trace its history to the liturgy of the synagog and, to a lesser degree, the Temple.

Monolog includes specific formulas for the cantillation of the Scriptural pericopes. In general, there are formulas for chanting the Old Testament (*Tonus Prophetae*), the Epistle (*Tonus Epistolae*), and several for chanting of the Gospel (*Tonus Evangelii*) at mass. Others include formulas for the chanting of the little chapters at the daily office. As previously indicated, they are derived from the Hebrew modes and tropes used for the cantillation of the Pentateuch (*Torah*), the Prophets (*Nebi'im*) and the Hagiographa (*Kethubim*).

Dialog may best be described as a chanted liturgical conversation between an officiant (celebrant, deacon, or subdeacon) and the congregation or choir. Such salutations as "Dominus vobiscum" (or "Pax vobiscum" in the case of a bishop) and its response "et cum spiritu tuo" are examples of dialog. The entire prefatory dialog culminating in the *Sanctus* is the most perfect example of dialog.

Psalmodic Chant

Psalmodic compositions, used for chanting the Psalter and other Scriptural canticles, are also derived from Hebraic antiquity. This category is discussed under the topic "Psalmody, Gregorian."

Strophic Chant

Strophic compositions came into the ancient church comparatively late and were coupled with the increase of gentile converts to Christianity. This was quite natural, since hymns and odes of the strophic type were quite common to Greeks and Romans alike in their pagan religious rites.

The strophic pieces are of two types, *monostrophic* and *polystrophic*. The former came into popular usage in the church toward the end of the 4th century primarily through the work of Ambrose of Milan (c. 340—397) who wrote many strophic hymns to combat the Arian heresy, whose adherents had used this form to further their false teaching concerning the divinity of Christ. His example was followed by many others who wrote in the same style and are classed as "Ambrosiani."

Strophic hymns are in meter, the most common of which is the iambic dimeter. They also have rhyme and are divided into strophes or stanzas. Those that are monostrophic make use of the same melody for every stanza.

With the rise of monasticism and the establishment of the canonical hours, hymn cycles for the whole church year were developed. It should be pointed out, however, that these hymns were sung at the offices and not at mass. Some of the important hymn writers, in addition to Ambrose and Gregory were: Aurelius Prudentius (348—c. 405), Caelius Sedulius (5th cent.), Venantius Fortunatus (531—609), Paul the Deacon (730—799), Theodulph of Orleans (760—821).

The polystrophic pieces came into being about the 8th or 9th centuries. These pieces were called sequences (a special type of trope) and were developed from the florid *jubilus* of the final vowel of the *Alleluia*. The practice seems to have originated in the Benedictine Abbey of Jumièges and was thought to have been brought to St. Gall by a monk who managed to flee from the monastery as it was being sacked by the Normans. The process, briefly, was that of adding strophes (usually couplets) to the *jubilus* melody, thus making it syllabic. As the sequence developed as a particular form, new melodies were composed. The reason for calling it polystrophic is that groups of melodies were set to pairs of verses, resulting in a pattern somewhat like *aa bb cc dd ee ff*, etc. Sometimes groups were repeated in the pattern *aa bb cc dd ee ff, cc dd ee ff, gg hh*, etc. Some also begin and end with unpaired verses and phrases: *x, aa bb cc dd . . . y.*

This form became very popular and spread throughout Europe. Probably the best-known and most prolific writer of sequences was Adam of St. Victor (d. 1192). The sequence was banned by the Council of Trent (1545—63), with the exception of four: *Victimae paschali; Veni, Sancte Spiritus; Lauda, Sion, Salvatorem;* and *Dies irae.* In 1727 the *Stabat mater* was reinstated. Probably the best known sequence is the *Victimae paschali*, from which the vernacular hymn "Christ ist erstanden" is derived as well as "Christ lag in Todesbanden." Unrhymed, it begins and closes with an unpaired phrase.

Commatic or Through-Composed Chant

This category represents the developed art form of the chant and thus probably the last to make its appearance. Most of the chants in the mass and office belong to this category. It can best be described as being freely composed, not limited to a repeated tune as in the case of the strophic compositions, nor to fixed formulae as in the case of the Psalms.

There are a number of processes by which these highly developed melodies came into being. At first, melodies were composed for specific texts and remained wedded to these texts down through the centuries to the present. In the course of time these melodies were adapted to new texts and eventually became melodic types similar to the *hirmoi* of Byzantine chant. For example, a comparison of the music of the Tract for Septuagesima Sunday (LU, p. 499) with that of the Tract for Quinquagesima (LU, p. 513) and the Fourth Sunday in Lent (LU, p. 561) will clearly show that this melody was adapted for these texts. It is not possible to tell which was the prototype.

No difference in text is involved, but it is interesting to compare the *Kyrie* of Mass IX (*Cum jubilo*, LU, p. 43) with the *Kyrie* of Mass X (*Alme Pater*, LU, p. 40). A comparison reveals a close relationship between the two. If we accept the latter as of the 11th century, the former, which is dated 12th century, is an adaptation of the latter.

More than 30 extant antiphons are based on the melody of *"Omnes de Saba venient"* (LU, p. 482).

That some melodies have clearly undergone ornamentation may be seen in a comparison of the melodies of the Kyrie in the *Missa orbis factor* (LU, pp. 46 and 85). The earlier version of the *Kyrie, orbis factor* (LU, p. 85) is the version that was sung in the 10th century. The later version (LU, p. 46) is that of the 14th to 16th centuries. In the latter example ornaments such as passing and neighboring tones have been added, making the melody more melismatic but, at the same time, causing it to lose much of its spontaneity and simplicity.

Kyrie fons bonitatis (LU, p. 19), an outstanding example of highly melismatic chant, was destined to become famous in some of the earliest examples of organ masses and to become the basis for one of the earliest examples of German vernacular hymns, the *Kyrie, Gott Vater in Ewigkeit,* which Bach used in Part III of the *Klavieruebung* and which has continued in use as a congregational hymn among Lutherans in many parts of the world. MAB

Readings: Apel, Willi, *Gregorian Chant* (Bloomington, Ind., 1958); Parrish, Carl, *The Notation of Medieval Music* (New York, 1957); Reese, Gustave, *Music in the Middle Ages* (New York, 1940); Suñol, Gregoria Maria, *Textbook of Gregorian Chant* (Boston, 1907); Wagner, Peter Josef, *Introduction to the Gregorian Melodies* (London, 1907); Werner, Eric, *The Sacred Bridge* (New York, 1959); *Liber Usualis* (New York, 1962).

See also: church modes; church music history, medieval; ecclesiastical Latin, pronunciation; mass; office hymn; psalmody, Gregorian; sequence; trope; *HCM*, IV

choir, history

The English term *choir,* along with its counterparts in other mainstream modern European languages (Ger. *Chor,* Fr. *choeur,* Ital. and Span. *coro*) derives through the Latin *chorus* from the Greek *choros.* Other languages tend to use only one term, with a modifier to indicate size, composition, or function of a given choral group. The English language uses two words, *chorus* and *choir.* In current English usage, *choir* tends to suggest a smaller group than *chorus;* the term *chorus* also suggests an organization devoted primarily to secular music, where *choir* suggests a group whose primary function is within the framework of the church service. Still other nuances in the use of these terms may be identified, but the distinctions are by no means clear cut.

The beginnings of the choral concept can be seen in the tragedies and comedies of the Greeks. The chorus for these Greek dramas, numbering from 12 to 24, sang in unison, probably with the support of a wind instrument, such as the *aulos.* The chorus functioned in the drama by commenting on the action as a representative of the people, expressing their hopes and fears regarding the unfolding action of the play. (Such commentary was also the means by which the poet expressed his personal convictions and opinions.) The music of these choruses was monophonic, and used the natural rhythms of the poetry. This fact, plus the general character of the performances, which included the important use of dance, suggests a kinship with all manner of folk ritual, pageantry, and celebration. Aspects of this early concept of choral singing may be seen later in the character, practice, and function of the plainchant of the Christian church.

From the time of the very early church until well into the Middle Ages, the predominant choral sound was that of male voices singing in unison. As early as the 4th century, with the establishment of the *schola cantorum,* plainsong was nurtured and cultivated in the church. After its reorganization by Gregory I (pope 590—604), the *schola* came to be regarded as the cornerstone of the Roman musical tradition. The singers of this choir school carried the tradition throughout Europe, teaching the chant and organizing more schools to insure dissemination of the music and the techniques of its performance. Boys and young men with good voices were much sought after, and they received a general and a musical education in these schools in return for their service as singers. The various choir schools throughout Europe, together with the *schola cantorum* itself were the training ground for most of the musicians who rose to prominence in the Middle Ages.

Gregorian chant was usually performed in antiphonal fashion, two choirs alternating with one another, or in responsorial style, in which a solo voice alternated with the choir. In spite of this variety of performance possibilities, it is clear that the unison texture of monophony presented a rather limited field of expression, even within the conservative framework of the church's liturgy. The answer to the limitations of monophony came in the development of organum, a development closely associated with the school of Notre Dame in Paris (c. 1200). It represents the beginnings of polyphony, the simultaneous combination of several voice parts. Polyphony was introduced principally as an adjunct to the responsorial style, in which the idea of a solo voice alternating with choir was amplified to include the notion of monophony juxtaposed with polyphony.

The introduction and first flowering of polyphony did not immediately mark the advent of polyphonic choral performance as we know it today. At the cathedral of Notre Dame, the chorus continued to sing in unison; the polyphonic sections of the responsoria were taken by soloists. It is clear that the centuries-old tradition of unison singing could not be altered immediately by great numbers of singers. Only a few—perhaps the best— were probably able to understand and negotiate the intricacies of the new style. True *choral* singing of polyphony—two or more singers to a voice part—had to wait until the 15th century for gaining the ascendancy. In his book *Studies in Medieval and Renaissance Music* Manfred Bukofzer cites as the first known piece of choral polyphony a *Credo* by Guillaume Legrant (fl. 1419). The manuscript is dated 1426. In the sections for choir, marked with the word *chorus*, the composer carefully placed the text under *all* of the three voices. (Often the text appeared under only one voice, suggesting instrumental rendition of the others.) There is also a discernible stylistic difference between the sections for soloists, written in more complex rhythms, and those for the chorus, which display a more chordal design. (See *Historical Anthology of Music*, ed. Davison-Apel, No. 56.)

Even as polyphonic choir singing became a reality, the size of choirs remained small, probably because of performance conditions in which, for example, all the members of the choir sang from a single large score, or *choir book*, around which they had to huddle; or because of the still bedeviling complexity of polyphony which required the very best singers—and they may have been in short supply; or simply because the *sound ideal* of the period preferred the transparent texture of the small ensemble. In any case, evidence shows that a choral body in the 15th century might have as few as eight singers, as in the miniature showing Jean Ockeghem (c. 1430—95) and his chapel singers, or as many as 24—the largest number employed in the papal chapel at that time. Church music and all forms of sacred music were probably performed with groups such as the above, with at least two singers to a part; secular music, on the other hand, tended to use singers as soloists, with only one to a part. As the notion of choral polyphony became increasingly established, as modality reached toward the peak of its potential, as composers gained ever greater skill in mastering the techniques of composition, choral polyphony, in the hands of such early masters as Ockeghem, Josquin Desprez (c. 1440—1521), and the two giants toward the end of the period, Giovanni Pierluigi da Palestrina (c. 1525—94), and Orlando di Lasso (c. 1532—94), reached sublime heights of expression.

As Caldwell Titcomb has pointed out about the performance of the music of this period, there was often a "large disparity between what a composer wrote and what the listener heard" (see *Choral Music*, Chapter 2, "From Ockeghem to Palestrina"). The composer was often also the conductor of his music and would be able to omit much from the score that would be worked out in rehearsal. Members of the choir usually had to supply the texts, for in the case of well-known texts from the mass, the composer might provide just the first word, leaving the rest of the textual detail to the performers. There were frequent and significant alterations of the notes themselves as the singers introduced *musica ficta*, particularly creating leading tones out of the subtonic notes that were original to the old modes. The music as written was apt to be subjected to all manner of embellishment, especially in the upper voice, and at cadence points. Since the music was not available in full score and did not have bar lines, the singer had to be a paragon of concentration in order to maintain the integrity of his particular part. As suggested above, music in the church at this time was performed by men together with boy sopranos or adults singing falsetto. As the 16th century progressed, *castrati* were increasingly employed.

Before we leave the Renaissance, a word should be said about the use of the choir in the music of the Reformation. Since it was Luther's intent to make the congregation an active participant in the Lutheran service, the position of the choir was somewhat altered. In the Catholic mass, the choir was always the main bearer of the liturgy—along with the celebrant. In the Lutheran service it shared liturgical responsibility with the congregation and the celebrant. The organ played an important role as well. The three elements of organ, choir, and congregation came together in the performance of the chorale tunes that were central to Luther's concept of the church service. Their participation was in "alternation," i.e. the various stanzas of the chorale tune were distributed among these three performing groups, the congregation singing in unison without benefit of accompaniment, the choir singing in parts, at times accompanied by the organ, and the organ improvising on a stanza of the chorale without the words being uttered. It is likely that the practice of alternation was responsible for the composition of many chorale settings of various types and the rise of the tradition of the organ variation that became so important in the baroque era.

The baroque era reflects the emergence and flourishing of instrumental music, but instruments played an important role also in the Renaissance. Choral singing in the Renaissance was more apt to be accompanied than not. (A cappella singing was simply not very prevalent—and did not become so until the 19th century.) Particularly in the period around 1400, during the emergence of the new polyphonic style, it was no doubt a real necessity to give instrumental support to singers, or replace singers with instruments, so as to keep performances intact.

Despite a rising interest in instruments and purely instrumental music, choirs and choruses maintained an important role in the new genres of opera and oratoria. In the early operas of the composers that came out of the Florentine Camerata (c. 1600), the chorus, functioning somewhat like the old Greek chorus, provided welcome relief to the monotony of the relentless recitatives. Even in the later, more sophisticated works of Monteverdi (1567—1643), the choral sections serve as important structural and musical pillars. Though in some areas of Europe, after the rise of the aria and the bel canto style of singing, there was some neglect in the use of the choir, this situation was not common everywhere. Heinrich Schuetz (1585—1672) wrote important works for choir, in many of which he employed a Venetian polychoral idea, *coro spezzato*, pitting one choral body against another (perhaps smaller) group. The importance of the choir to Johann Joseph Fux (1660—1741) may be seen in this, that in his opera *Constanza*, alongside 23 arias and a duet, he provided 16 choral movements.

A similar balance between solos, small ensembles, and choruses may be seen in the oratorios of G. F. Handel (1685—1759) or the Passions of J. S. Bach (1685—1750). In all of these works the chorus figures very prominently, which perhaps contributes to their continued popularity.

Amid all the changes that took place between the Renaissance and baroque periods, one important aspect was constant: choral groups remained relatively small. The *Kantorei* of Schuetz numbered about 26 singers; Bach could muster, at best, about 30. As Knapp has suggested, the choral sound desired was not massive, but rather emphasized clarity, balance, and clean performance (in *Choral Music*, Chapter 4, "Germany and Northern Europe before Bach").

In the crowning masterworks of Bach and Handel, polyphonic choral singing became a demanding art, requiring singers with highly developed musical skills. About this time women began to take their place in the church alongside men. Women had always been involved in the performance of secular music; a glance at any of the early paintings depicting musical subjects will turn up evidence of their participation in what might have been madrigal singing and the like. But Bach invited the wrath of the church fathers when, in 1706, he invited a young lady— probably his wife-to-be, Maria Barbara Bach—into the choir loft to make music. By 1716, however, Mattheson had presented a woman soloist in an oratorio performance in Hamburg and continued to make use of women's voices from then on, apparently without criticism. Certainly by the end of the century the sound of women's voices in church was widespread.

With the end of the baroque era, the declining interest in tonal counterpoint, and the growing interest in the orchestra as the leading medium of musical expression, the choir was forced into a secondary role. It continued as the important body in the performance of church music, but the vital connection with current musical styles was lost. A number of important choral works were written, such as Haydn's *Seasons* and the Mozart *Requiem*, but they were exceptions to the rule.

In the 19th century the orchestra grew in size until, by the end of the century, in the music of Wagner, Strauss, and Mahler, it had become a gigantic apparatus. When a choral group performed with an orchestra in the 19th century, it, too, had to be large to vie with the burgeoning instrumental body. It is not uncommon to read of musical events involving perhaps 200 singers and as many as 150 orchestra players. The delicate, subtle Renaissance and baroque sound was lost in the massive, overpowering spectacle of the romantic period.

One positive aspect of choral singing in the 19th century was the founding of singing organizations that encouraged amateur music making. In England such a group might be known as a Singing Society, or Oratorio Society; in Germany it might be called a *Singverein, Singakademie,* or *Liedertafel*. There were also a great many such groups devoted to literature for women's voices, or men's voices only. Many of these organizations are still active today and provide a pool of able singers for both church and secular musical activity in their communities.

Since World War I, musical research has begun to question the propriety of bigness for its own sake, and performances today often reflect a new awareness on the part of conductors as to the proper relationship of resources to musical style. Though there are professional vocal ensembles, particularly in resident opera companies or in state-owned radio stations in Europe, choral singing is primarily the province of the amateur. Therefore choirs and choruses represent a unique phenomenon in musical life; they also offer special challenges, particularly to the choral conductor. DJ

Readings: Blankenburg, Walter, "Chor," *Musik in Geschichte und Gegenwart*, II (Kassel, 1952), 1230—65); Bukofzer, Manfred E., *Studies in Medieval and Renaissance Music* (New York, 1950); Dart, Thurston, *The Interpretation of Music* (London, 1954); Jacobs, Arthur, ed., *Choral Music: A Symposium* (Baltimore, 1963); Young, Percy M., *The Choral Tradition* (London, 1962); Wienandt, Elwyn A., *Choral Music of the Church* (New York, 1965).

See *also:* alternation; cantional, cantional style; cantor; cantorei; chant, Gregorian; chorale; chorale, vocal settings; decani/cantoris; performance practice; polychoral style; Venetian school

chorale

The term is used to define two types of liturgical song. (1) *Choral* is the liturgical chant of the Roman Catholic Church, also called *cantus choralis,* Gregorian chant, plainchant, and plainsong. (2) *Chorale* is a hymn tune of the German Evangelical Church. *Chorale* is also a collective term used to denote both the text and the melody of German hymns, especially those of the Reformation era. The Lutheran chorale, both text and melody, is a unique combination of doxological praise and proclamation. This article deals only with the second definition.

Pre-Reformation Vernacular Hymns

Long before the Reformation the German people had begun to sing vernacular hymns. Some of these were based on sequences: the Christmas hymn *Gelobet seist du, Jesu Christ,* based on the *Grates nunc omnes reddamus*; the Easter Leise *Christ ist erstanden*, based on the Easter sequence *Victimae paschali;* and *Komm, Heilger Geist, Herre Gott*, patterned after *Veni, Sancte Spiritus*. These and other German hymns were sung at processions, pilgrimages, consecrations, celebrations of patron saints, and sometimes also at church festivals. Martin Luther (1483—1546) was well acquainted with these practices.

Because Luther had a profound understanding and appreciation of the doctrine of the universal priesthood of all believers (expressed, e.g., 1 Peter 2:9), he wanted the people to be as active as possible in the services of worship. In 1523 he wrote to Spalatin, "Following the example of the prophets and fathers of the church, we intend to collect German psalms for the people, so that through the medium of song the Word of God may remain among the people." For Luther, the congregational hymn on the lips of the people was the *viva vox evangelii*, the living voice of the Gospel. With this call for hymns, and his own subsequent contribution of 37 hymns, Luther became the father of evangelical hymnody.

Sources of Reformation Hymns

The sources of Reformation hymnody are varied. They include:

The Gregorian choral. The Gloria hymn of Nikolaus Decius (c. 1485—after 1546) "Allein Gott in der Hoeh' sei Ehr'" ("All Glory Be to God on High"), e.g., and Luther's *antiphona angelorum,* "All Ehr' und Lob soll Gottes sein" ("All Glory Be to God Alone"), are based on the *Gloria tempore paschali* of the *Graduale Romanum*. "Kyrie, Gott Vater in Ewigkeit" ("Kyrie, God Father in Heaven Above") is based on the Gregorian *Kyrie fons bonitatis*.

Latin office hymns. These include such examples as "Nun komm, der Heiden Heiland" ("Savior of the Nations, Come") based on *Veni Redemptor gentium* and "Komm, Gott Schoepfer, Heiliger Geist" ("Come, Holy Ghost, Creator Blest"), based on *Veni, Creator Spiritus, mentes* of Rabanus Maurus (c. 776—856).

Cantios. Latin unison hymns of the Middle Ages, of spiritual content, but not a part of the liturgy. Examples include the *Quem pastores laudavere,* which, together with the *Nunc angelorum gloria* and the *Magnum nomen Domini*, formed the Quempas Carol, and the macaronic carol *In dulci jubilo*.

Religious folk songs. Examples include "Nun bitten wir den Heiligen Geist" ("Now Let Us Pray to God the Holy Ghost"), "Gott sei gelobet und gebenedeiet" ("O Lord, We Praise Thee"), and "Wir glauben all an einen Gott" ("We All Believe in One True God"). These were one-stanza hymns that Luther "improved" and to which he added additional stanzas.

Contrafacta. These were, for the most part, secular songs that were transformed into sacred hymns. Two of the best known are (1) "Innsbruck, ich muss dich lassen," the lament of a lover who must leave the town where his loved one lives; it was transformed into a hymn of yearning for the heavenly Jerusalem, "O Welt, ich muss dich lassen" ("O World, I Now Must Leave Thee"); and (2) "Ich komm aus fremden Landen her" ("I Come from Foreign Countries"), which Luther transformed into the children's Christmas hymn, "Vom Himmel hoch da komm ich her ("From Heaven Above to Earth I Come").

Metrical versions of Psalms. Examples include: "Aus tiefer Not schrei ich zu Dir" ("From Depths of Woe I Cry to Thee"), based on Psalm 130; "Es wolle Gott uns gnaedig sein ("May God Bestow on Us His Grace"), based on Psalm 67; and "Ein' feste Burg ist unser Gott" ("A Mighty Fortress Is Our God"), based on Psalm 46. The preceding three are by Luther. "Nun lob, mein Seel, den Herren" ("My Soul, Now Bless Thy Maker"), based on Psalm 103, is by Johann Gramann (Poliander; 1487—1541).

Newly composed hymns. Examples include: "Christ lag in Todesbanden" ("Christ Jesus Lay in Death's Strong Bands") by Luther; "Es ist das Heil uns kommen her" ("Salvation Unto Us Has Come") by Paul Speratus (1484—1551); and "Herr Christ, der einig Gott's Sohn" ("The Only Son from Heaven") by Elizabeth Cruciger (c. 1500—35).

Luther and most of the hymn writers of the Reformation followed the Meistersinger tradition, in which the writer of the text and the composer of the melody were the same person. At the time of the Reformation, "to compose" did not necessarily mean to create something entirely new. Often a melody was adapted to fit a new text, or a new melody was created out of melodic fragments of an old melody, or of several melodies. Luther's "Christ lag in Todesbanden," a good example of this practice, is obviously based on the melody *Christ ist erstanden*. The tunes were chosen or composed to fit the character of the text, so that they, too, would contribute to the proclamation of the Gospel in accord with Luther's view that "Die Noten machen den Text lebendig" ("The notes give life to the text").

The Use of the Chorale

It is important to note how the chorales were used in the services and how they were sung at the time of the Reformation. In the *Wittenberg Gottesdienstordnung* (Order of Service) of 1533, e.g., there were the following possibilities for the singing of "Psalms" (chorales, vernacular songs): at the introit (as a substitute for the psalmody), except on festivals when Latin psalmody was still used; after the gradual and Alleluia on high festivals in alternation with the sequence; after the Latin Credo, Luther's "Wir glauben all an einen Gott"; after the sermon and following the Latin Da pacem, Luther's "Verleih uns Frieden gnaediglich" ("Grant Peace, We Pray, in Mercy, Lord"); at the beginning of the distribution in place of a versicle, or a collect by the pastor, a de tempore hymn; *sub communione*, that is, during the distribution, after the Latin Sanctus and Agnus Dei, "Jesus Christus, unser Heiland" ("Jesus Christ, Our Blessed Savior"), and "Gott sei gelobet und gebenedeiet" ("O Lord, We Praise Thee"); and after the distribution, the German Agnus Dei, "Christe, du Lamm Gottes."

During the Reformation era the hymns were sung in unison by the congregation without instrumental accompaniment. The singing was led and supported by the unison singing *chorus choralis*. Hence, the designation chorale, that is, unison liturgical song. Thus, according to the Reformation service orders, congregational singing was placed liturgically on the same level as the proclamation and prayers of the pastor and the liturgical music of the *figural* choir.

Early Chorale Publications

Luther's first hymn, "Nun freut euch, lieben Christen gemein" ("Dear Christians, One and All Rejoice"), was written in 1523 and appeared first as a broadside. The following year it was printed as the initial hymn in *Etlich christlich lider*, also known as *Achtliederbuch*, published by Jobst Gutknecht of Nuernberg, the first hymnal of the Reformation. It contained four hymns by Luther, three by Paul Speratus (1484—1551), and one by an anonymous poet.

The hymns in the *Achtliederbuch* and other early Reformation hymnals, such as *Das Erfurter Enchiridion, gedruckt zu Erfurt . . . 1524, Etliche Christliche Gesenge und psalmen/wilche vor bey dem Enchiridion nicht gewest synd, 1525, Das*

Klug'sche Gesangbuch, 1533, the *Schumann Gesangbuch* of 1539, and, perhaps, the most famous, *Das Babst'sche Gesangbuch*, 1545, with a foreword by Martin Luther, were published with text and melody only.

It should be noted that the early chorale melodies were in rhythmic form rather than in isometric form as in the harmonizations by J. S. Bach (1685—1750) and other collections of the period of Pietism.

The year 1524 also marks the beginning of musical compositions based on Lutheran chorales. In that year Johann Walter (1496—1570), Luther's friend and musical co-worker and the first cantor of the Lutheran church, published his *Geystliches gesangk Buchleyn*, which contained, in the main, polyphonic settings for three to six voices in the style of the old Flemish motet, with the melody in the tenor. Similar collections are *Newe deudsche geistliche Gesenge*, 1544, by Georg Rhau (1488—1548) and *Cantiones ecclesiasticae latinae . . . Kirchengesenge deudtsch*, 1545, by Johann Spangenberg (1484—1550). However, the involved polyphonic texture of the pieces in these collections precluded the possibility of congregational performance. In 1586 Lukas Osiander (1534—1604) remedied this situation in his *Fuenfftzig geistliche Lieder und Psalmen. Mit vier stimmen, auf Contrapunktsweise (fuer die Schulen und Kirchen im loeblichen Fuerstentum Wuerttemberg) also gesetzt, dass eine ganze Christliche Gemein durchaus mit singen kann* ("Fifty Spiritual Songs and Psalms. With four voices, set contrapuntally (for the schools and churches of the praiseworthy principality of Wuerttemberg) so the entire Christian congregation can sing along"), in which he placed the chorale melodies in the upper voice and supplied a simple homophonic accompaniment for the lower parts. This type of setting is referred to as cantional style.

Throughout its history the chorale has not only been the people's chief vehicle for praising God and singing the Gospel to each other, but it has also served as the basis and fountainhead of the great body of church music (simple chorale settings, cantatas, motets, Passions, oratorios, chorale preludes) beginning with Johann Walter's *Geystliches gesangk Buchleyn*, 1524, through the Bach cantatas, choral preludes and Passions, to Hugo Distler (1908—42), Ernest Pepping (1901), and Jan Bender (1909). EK

Readings: Ameln, Konrad, *The Roots of German Hymnody of the Reformation Era* (St. Louis, 1964); Blume, Friedrich, "The Period of the Reformation," *Protestant Church Music* (New York, 1974); Brodde, Otto and Christa Mueller, *Das Gradual-Lied.* (Munich, 1954); Buszin, Walter E., *The Doctrine of the Universal Priesthood and Its Influence upon The Liturgies and Music of the Lutheran Church* (St. Louis, 1946); Riedel, Johannes, *The Lutheran Chorale: Its*

Basic Traditions (Minneapolis, 1967); Zahn, Johannes, *Die Melodien der deutschen evangelischen Kirchenlieder,* reprint (Hildesheim, 1963).

See also: alternation practice; chant, Gregorian; metrical psalmody; office hymn; sequence; *HCM*, II, III, IV

chorale, vocal settings

Except for a few isolated examples, the history of chorale arrangement begins with the publication of the very first Lutheran hymnals in 1524. Martin Luther's *Achtliederbuch* and the two Erfurter *Enchiridia* of that year contained the texts and melodies of the newly constituted Protestant chorales, which immediately became the source material for a comprehensive body of chorale settings. Through the next two and one-half centuries a large number of chorale melodies were added to the original repertoire, most of which became material, in the hands of Protestant composers, for figural treatment. Johann Walter's *Geistliches gesangk Buchleyn* (1524) marks the first comprehensive attempt to clothe the new body of chorale tunes in polyphonic dress. From this time, through the late Renaissance and the period of baroque composition, Protestant composers fashioned from the chorale-tunes choral and instrumental works ranging from the miniatures of the chorale in *contrapunctum simplex* to the colossal creations of Praetorius and Bach.

Whereas in pre-Reformation times the plainchant had supplied composers with *cantus firmi,* the chorale now quickly usurped this position. Composers applied all the techniques and devices that were available to them by inheritance and contemporary development. Contributions in this respect were international. The whole art of Netherlands counterpoint, especially as crystallized in the motets of Josquin Desprez , Heinrich Isaak, and Ludwig Senfl, mark the starting point, to be followed by a thorough application of the principles of continuo, recitative, monody, and tonal counterpoint, of the concepts of the Venetian school, including echo effects, antiphonal singing, and polychoral writing, and finally the combination of choral and instrumental art in the concertato style. The systematic application of this international heritage resulted in the perfecting of many clearly differentiated forms in which the chorale took a prominent position. In the purely vocal music the chorale in *contrapunctum simplex* represents the homophonic standard, the chorale motet represents the polyphonic standard. The instrumental forms developed into the organ chorale, the chorale-fugue, variation, prelude, fantasia, and trio. The concertato forms, suggested by the accompanied motet, developed into the chorale concerto, the *Geistliche Konzerte*, and the solo and choral chorale cantatas.

The Cantional Setting

The chorale in *contrapunctum simplex* represents a type of *Gebrauchsmusik* that finds its strength in simplicity and utility. Arrangements in this category comprise harmonizations in four or five parts in which the chorale melody is maintained intact throughout as a connected *cantus firmus* in one voice. There is but slight, if any, imitative writing and the accompanying voices do not in any significant way partake of the subject matter of the chorale *cantus*. The need for these harmonizations was very great during the 16th and 17th centuries, when the new chorale melodies had to be taught to the congregations through the *Kantorei*. With the establishment of the organ as the leading instrument in the church, the constant introduction of new tunes, and the changes in musical style, the need was never really filled, and so composers periodically reset the melodies in *contrapunctum simplex*, either to make them more useful to the congregation or to bring them up to date.

Johann Walter's *Geistliches gesangk Buchleyn* (1524) marks the beginning of the chorale in *contrapunctum simplex* as well as the chorale motet. The differentiation of the two vocal species is unclear, the chorale harmonization appearing in a texture less simple and direct than developed, and the chorale motet less complex and polyphonic than is generally associated with this species. The two stand here very nearly on common ground to become more separated by subsequent composers. The chorale harmonization is generally simplified and adjusted to its use with the congregation, while the chorale motet becomes the real *figural* music of the *Kantorei*. Walter's settings maintain the durational accents of the early chorale melodies in the polymetric versions and he places the *cantus firmus* generally into the tenor in the tradition of his predecessors.

Lucas Osiander's *Fuenfftzig geistliche Lieder und Psalmen* (1586) are more purely homophonic and consistently present the *cantus firmus* in the uppermost voice. Osiander's title, "Fifty sacred songs and psalms set so, that an entire Christian congregation can positively sing along," reveals the failure of the older settings to lead the congregation effectively, and established the chorale in *contrapunctum simplex* as a species apart from the motet.

Hans Leo Hassler's two sets of chorale arrangements show the wide gulf that had by this time developed between the chorale harmonization and the chorale motet. The *Psalmen und christliche Gesaeng . . . fugweis komponiert* (1607) appeared first and marks a high point in Protestant chorale setting in polyphonic style. The *Kirchengesaenge, Psalmen, und geistliche Lieder . . . simpliciter gesetzt* (1608) is his contribution to chorale settings in simple style. His settings show a definite leaning away from modal toward tonal thinking.

At this same time Michael Praetorius was occupied with the publication of his monumental work on the chorale, the *Musae Sioniae* (1605—10). The work appeared in 9 volumes including chorale settings in 2 to 12 parts. Volumes VI—VIII (1609—10) enclose Praetorius' cantional, i.e., chorale settings in *contrapunctum simplex*. The work is of the first magnitude since it is the most comprehensive chorale book of its time.

Johann Herman Schein's *Cantional* (1627) and Samuel Scheidt's *Tabulaturbuch* (Goerlitz, 1650) mark the first attempts to make artistic arrangements of the chorales for the organ, to be used to accompany the congregation or to play them in alternation with the congregation and choir. Both composers show a decidedly advanced tonal vocabulary, and in Schein we encounter the figured bass. The process of rhythmic equalization of the chorale melodies began shortly after Scheidt's *Tabulaturbuch* and becomes general in Freylinghausen's *Geistreiches Gesangbuch* (1704).

Johann Balthasar Koenig's *Harmonischer Liederschatz* (1738) must be considered as the most important source for texts and melodies from the period of Pietism. It also shows all the changes that had taken place in the harmonization of the chorale and presents it in the form that J. S. Bach adopted for his harmonizations. Three hundred seventy-one chorale harmonizations of J. S. Bach were collected and published posthumously. They mark the greatest advance in the setting of chorale melodies and contain all the features developed by his predecessors. Bach's contributions to chorale harmonization lie, therefore, not so much in original technical features of composition, as in the infusion of an exalted spiritual fervor, derived from the text and affectively expressed in the music. Of course, he handled the harmonic vocabulary of his time with far greater resourcefulness and power than that of his contemporaries. By this time chorales were set exclusively in a tonal idiom, and even such strongly modal melodies as "Aus tiefer Noth" (Phrygian) were cast in a tonal harmonization by Bach. He used always the equalized isometric rhythm and the fermata to indicate the ends of text lines. Johann Friedrich Doles' *Vierstimmiges Choralbuch* (1785) marks the beginning of a long series of four-voiced choralebooks. The chorales are in isometric rhythm with bar lines and fermatas. From this time on such notation becomes the norm.

Four general trends are evident in the history of the chorale in *contrapunctum simplex:* (1) the cantus firmus moves from the tenor into the uppermost voice; (2) the harmonizations gradually pass from a modal into a tonal atmosphere; (3) the figured bass becomes an essential feature; and (4) the rhythm of the melody, originally polymetric, undergoes a process of equalization toward an isometric structure, where, eventually, one beat of rhythm is assigned to one syllable of text.

The Chorale Motet

The development of the Latin Scriptural motet as it had been crystallized by the Netherlands composers in the latter part of the 15th and early 16th centuries into the imitative treatment of successive portions of the text in a series of points, formed the vehicle for the chorale melody in the new chorale motet, whose inception must again be laid to Johann Walter in 1524. To this species belong only motets in which the chorale melody appears as an ingredient. The older motet, using Latin Scriptural texts and plainchant *cantus firmi*, was not abandoned by Protestant composers, but nurtured side by side with the newer species; the impact of the chorale melody became so strong, however, that among German composers the chorale motet assumed first importance from this time on. The species differs from the chorale in *contrapunctum simplex* in that the chorale motet generally displays a more polyphonic texture, cadences are likely to be dovetailed, imitation both rhythmic and melodic is a significant feature, canonic devices appear frequently, entries are likely to be fugue-wise, and the voices decidedly approach equality in importance. The history of the chorale motet displays many of the features of the internal changes that took place in the simple harmonization of the chorale, becoming, in addition, the medium for the projection of the resplendent Venetian polychoral style, as well as the progenitor of the chorale concertato through the addition of instrumental accompaniment, and one of the earliest forms to be bodily taken over into the realm of purely instrumental keyboard music as the organ chorale.

Johann Walter's *Geistliches gesangk Buchleyn* (1524) is our first source for the chorale motet. Although some of the settings are chorales in *contrapunctum simplex*, a good many are clearly of the chorale motet species, displaying features of Netherlands technique. Walter likes to use a strictly *cantus firmus* treatment, giving the chorale melody usually to the tenor voice in longer notes. Often the entries of the other voice parts are fugue-wise and the cadences dovetailed; the harmonic vocabulary is modal and the rhythm free and durational.

With the publication of Georg Rhau's *Newe deudsche geistliche Gesenge fuer die gemeinen Schulen* (1544) the first comprehensive collection of chorale motets by contemporary composers became available to the church. The work is of the first importance as a source of the early Reformation chorale motets. Of the 123 settings by far the greater part use the chorale. Composers represented include Resinarius, Bruck, Senfl, Hellingk, Ducis, Dietrich, Mahu, Stoltzer, and others. The collection is a mirror of the style movements of the 16th century in chorale motet writing. The style is retrospective in that much of the best strength of 15th-century culture is still alive in it. Resinarius, Senfl, Mahu, and Ducis appear as the representatives of contemporary ideals in Reformation music. Bruck and Dietrich point the way to the new style of the second half of the century, which found its fruition in Hans Leo Hassler. The Rhau composers were followed by Seth Calvisius, Gallus Dressler, Johannes Eccard, Johann Stobaeus, Leonhard Schroeter, Bartholomaeus Gesius, and Melchior Vulpius.

The emergence of Hassler as a motet composer of the first rank around 1600 reveals a considerable change in the treatment of the chorale motet. His settings show the influence exerted by the Venetian style, and the gradual retreat of the Netherlands style. With Hassler, the *cantus firmus* in long notes is completely missing, since all voices participate in the melodic contours of the chorale. A large number of 6- to 8-part settings appear and the 8- to 16-voiced pieces are really complexes of two, three, or four choirs, instead of a weaving of so many single voices. The appearance of the score is simple and compact, and the old polyphonic web with the many old-fashioned scale passages in the inner voices is conspicuously absent. His best-known contribution to the chorale motet is the *Psalmen und christliche Gesaeng auf die Melodeyen fugweis komponiert* (1607).

The prodigious activity of Michael Praetorius in the development of chorale arranging sets him out as one of the most prolific and imaginative composers of chorale motets. His settings, appearing in the *Musae Sioniae* (1605—10), are chiefly polychoral and his directions regarding their use, as well as his prefaces to the various volumes, give a good insight into the state of chorale motet composition in the early 17th century. Praetorius was one of the first to disseminate the new Italian manner; the fact that continuo, monody, and concertato style took such a rapid foothold in Germany is due largely to his efforts. Praetorius speaks of several methods he used in writing chorale motets: (1) fugue-wise; (2) in imitation of di Lasso, motet-wise; (3) in imitation of Marenzio, madrigal-wise. With Praetorius the chorale melody takes on a small amount of embellishment, is handled more freely, and enters into the polyphonic interplay of the parts. As with Hassler, the voices take on a certain degree of greater equality. Part IX of the *Musae Sioniae* contains Praetorius bicinia and tricinia, miniature chorale motets to two and three parts, where the chorale melody does not appear as a *cantus firmus* but rather in motival fragments.

The line of chorale motet development after Praetorius leads through the Thuringian masters and the contemporaries of Bach. Heinrich Schuetz, one of Bach's greatest predecessors, used the chorale but little in his works. The chorale motet finds cultivation rather among such masters as Johann Hermann Schein, Scheidt, Hammerschmidt, the two Ahles, Reinken, Pachelbel, Buxtehude, and the ancestors of Bach. Topf, Niedt, J. M. Bach, and Liebhold of the Thuringian group operating around 1700 present a style of chorale motet that shows the full influence of the developments of baroque musical thought and technique. The texture is contrapuntal, the vocabulary tonal, and the part writing quite instrumental in concept. The chorale melody and text is usually an added portion to a free text motet; it does not permeate the entire composition.

In a class by themselves stand the six motets of Bach. Most of them are more related to the chorale cantata than to the motet as developed by his predecessors. Four of them are for double chorus, one is for five voices (*Jesu, meine Freude*), and one is for four voices with organ (*Lobet den Herrn*). In some the chorale serves as the cornerstone, as in *Jesu, meine Freude*. Here the chorale appears four times in the upper voice, each time differently constituted. The motet contains 11 different settings, in some of which the chorale is somewhat hidden, so that the whole work counts as a chorale variation. The general style is Bach's customary: long notes are scarce;

short syllables, many notes to the beat, long coloraturas, sequential patterns are the rule. An instrumental concept underlies the treatment of the voices. The development of the motet after Bach is relatively unimportant. The significant works in this species are those of Brahms.

The Chorale Concertato and Cantata

Besides developing as an a cappella form, the chorale motet branched out into another species through the addition of instrumental accompaniment (concertato style). Beginning with the occasionally accompanied motets of Praetorius and Johannes Staden, the practice developed swiftly into the chorale concertato, the *Geistliche Konzerte*, and finally the cantata. The use of the continuo, from the start, becomes a distinguishing feature of the chorale concertato, which finds its first real flowering in Praetorius' *Polyhymnia caduceatrix* (1619), a collection of accompanied polychoral creations in the Venetian style of Gabrieli. Features of style prevalent in these works are the consistent use of multiple choirs, figured continuo, alternation of solo voices and ensembles, free handling of chorale melodies, introductory sinfonias, ritornelli, and a vague indication of the instrumentation.

The few-voiced concertato was especially cultivated by Johann Hermann Schein in his *Opella nova* (I, 1618; II, 1626) (*Geistliche Konzerte*). Schein's approach to chorale arrangement was highly subjective and the chorale tunes are handled with much freedom; the affective presentation of the words was Schein's chief concern, so that we find not only the chorale tunes intact as *cantus firmi* with the contrapuntal associates discoursing upon it textually and melodically, but often the tunes themselves are elaborated, rerhythmed, and decorated with ornamentations. In Part I of the *Opella nova* the instrumental support consists of *basso instrumento* (cello, fagott, posaune) and a figured *basso continuo*. Schein also included a few choral monodies in his *Opella nova*, in which a single voice handled both the *cantus* and its elaboration. As such, these are the precursors of the later solo cantatas.

The development from the chorale concertato to the chorale cantata engaged the attention of a great many of the German masters of the baroque period. The chief proponents included Matthias Weckmann, Franz Tunder, Christoph Bernhard Bach, Johannes Staden, and Andreas Hammerschmidt. Tunder's solo cantata (chorale) "Wachet auf" is set for canto solo with three violes and figured continuo. After an instrumental sinfonia of 13 bars the first strophe of the chorale is presented; the melody remains quite intact. The second half of the first strophe is treated more freely in a different rhythm. Occasionally the voice and instruments engage in dialogue and imitation. A repetition of the introductory sinfonia separates the first and second strophe, which is treated exactly as the first. Tunder's cantata for chorus "Helft mir Gott's Guete preisen" is an excellent example of the cantata *per omnes versus*. The text comprises six strophes of the chorale. Each strophe is set for different vocal and instrumental combination: (1) soprano solo, (2) duet for two tenors, (3) bass solo, (4) four-part chorus, (5) bass solo, (6) five-part chorus.

The immediate predecessors of Bach—Buxtehude, Zachau, and Kuhnau—show the last developments within the cantata before Bach adopted it as the great vehicle for his own religious expression. Buxtehude's "Ihr lieben Christen" brings a considerable amount of free poetic text into the framework of the chorale cantata, although the musical forms are not yet as inclusive as we find them in Bach; he restricts himself to choruses, solos, and duets as the media for the various movements. With Kuhnau the reform cantata is fully set up textually and musically. His "Wie schoen leuchtet" shows how close he came to Bach in cantata structure. Musical forms include choruses in four and five parts, a duet, several recitatives, several arias, and even a simple four-part harmonization of the chorale at the close.

With Bach the cantata was fully exploited. He composed five yearly cycles of which almost 200 are still in existence. Four generic types are distinguishable: (1) solo cantatas with recitatives and arias, (2) chorale cantatas in which a chorale in text and music is treated in manifold ways, (3) cantatas for chorus containing only choir settings with a few solo settings, (4) free cantatas, whose texts are composed of poems and Scriptural passages. Of these the chorale cantata, using the chorale both in text and melody comprise a large amount. Most frequently the melody is the cornerstone of a large fantasia, to reappear at the close in a simple four-part harmonization. Occasionally the chorale melody appears in the instruments as a *cantus firmus*. Whatever his method of treatment, the chorale permeates the greater portion of his output in this genus, so that the cantatas of Bach stand as the greatest essays in chorale arrangement. PB

Readings: Bukofzer, M., *Music in the Baroque Era* (New York, 1949); Blume, F., *Protestant*

Church Music (New York, 1974); van der Heydt, J., *Geschichte der evangelischen Kirchenmusik in Deutschland* (1932); Leichtentritt, H., *Geschichte der Motette* (Leipzig, 1908).

See also: cantata; cantional, cantional style; concertato style; motet; HCM, III, IV

church modes

The church modes provided the tonal bases for medieval chant and most of Western music until the end of the 16th century. Most specifically the term refers to the system of eight modes (ecclesiastical modes), or scale series of tones and semitones, developed to classify the melody patterns and to describe the tonal organization in Gregorian chant.

At first four modes only were described, corresponding to the white key scales starting and closing on d, e, f, and g, each having its own distinctive interval pattern. The starting tone, called the final (*finalis*), functioned as the central tone and was usually the last note of a melody employing the given mode. A secondary tonal center, identified as the dominant (*confinalis, tenor, tuba*), ordinarily functioned as a recitation tone. Because many of the chant melodies employed an octave range (*ambitus*)

Ex. 1

The Medieval Church Modes

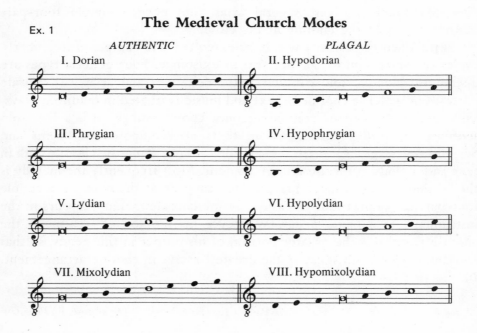

that would generally begin a fourth below the original or *authentic* mode, the system came to include four additional modes, the *plagal* or "derived" modes. The eight-mode system thus developed by the 11th century is illustrated in Example I, where the finals are shown as ⋈, and the dominants as ο; each mode is numbered according to medieval practice and identified by the nomenclature commonly used today.

The following characteristics can be noted:

1. The pairs of authentic and plagal modes share the same final. They differ in range and in the tone of the dominant.

2. The range of each plagal mode is a fourth lower than that of its respective authentic version.

3. In the authentic modes the dominant is located a fifth above the final, while in the plagal modes it is a third below that of the corresponding authentic mode (except that c is always substituted for b as the dominant—a condition that occurs only in Phrygian and Hypomixolydian).

It is sometimes helpful for the present-day student to relate the structure of the modes to the major and minor scales of the tonal system, although of course no such relationship existed in medieval practice. Thus the structure of Dorian is the same as natural minor, but with the sixth degree raised; Phrygian is natural minor with lowered second; Lydian is major with a raised fourth, and Mixolydian is major with lowered seventh. In Gregorian practice the octave ranges were sometimes exceeded by one or two notes at either extreme. The use, in authentic modes, of a tone to extend the lower range in preparation for a cadence *(subfinalis)* was most frequent. It is both historically and esthetically significant that the melodies of the chant determined the distinguishing characteristics of the modes, rather than the other way around. The melodic formulas invented for singing the psalms in the office (psalm tones) illustrate these characteristics most directly. There are eight tones, one for each of the modes.

The origin and early history of the modal system are somewhat obscure and subject to speculation. Earlier views which held to its origin in the Greek tonal system are not reliable, in spite of the (misapplied) use of the Greek names. Medieval theorists whose writings on the modes are extant already assume them as common knowledge. They identify them by numbers, using either Greek or Latin terminology or Roman numerals. Modern liturgical books use the Roman numeral classification, but the

Greek names, as they appear in Examples 1 and 2, are now used in most historical and theoretical writing.

The fully evolved form of the eight-mode system had been achieved by c. 1000. With the development of polyphony from the 12th century onward, modality went through a series of crises that became most acute in the late 16th century. Chromaticisms foreign to the regular characteristics of the modal scales were introduced into polyphonic textures, especially at points of cadence. These appeared first as accidentals to show semitonal raisings of the subfinal degree of the mode (the "leading tone," in terms of the major/minor system). Other accidentals were needed to notate modulations between related modes and to modify the melodic and harmonic tritone relationships between F and B (achieved by either B flat or F sharp). The prevailing polyphonic texture of Renaissance motets provided a natural ground for merging authentic and corresponding plagal modes, often using both at the same time and obscuring the distinction between them. Furthermore, the actual mode of a composition was sometimes equivocated. From a contemporary point of view, the practical way to determine the mode of a piece of polyphony is to regard the lowest note of the concluding sonority as the final (i.e., "tonic") of the mode in question. Constructing a scale on this note, and taking into account the possibility of a key signature, will identify the mode. A key signature beyond one flat (a B flat was used often to signify modes V and VI) suggests transposition, frequently necessitated by limitation of vocal range. Such generalized guidelines, however, should be qualified and used with precaution. For example, a composition in the Phrygian mode often ends with a sonority on its fourth degree, a chord on A replacing the final chord on E.

The frequent use of B flat in the Lydian mode and its occasional, though not exceptional, use in Dorian, suggested transposed scale patterns identical to those that might be constructed on C and A, the equivalent of major and minor scales in our modern tonal system. In an attempt to provide a theoretical accounting for these formations, a number of Renaissance theorists developed modal systems of 12 or more modes. The most noted of these was H. Glareanus, who, in his famous treatise, *Dodecachordon* (1547), identified and minutely described the white key scales on A (Aeolian and Hypoaeolian) and C (Ionian and Hypoionian) [modes IX and X, XI and XII in Example 2]. The mode located on B was identified as Locrian, but it and its corresponding plagal pattern were rejected as

Additional Church Modes
Identified by Late-Renaissance Theorists

Ex. 2

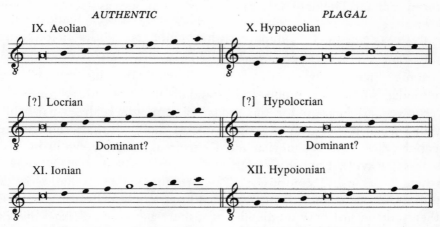

AUTHENTIC

IX. Aeolian

PLAGAL

X. Hypoaeolian

[?] Locrian

[?] Hypolocrian

Dominant?

Dominant?

XI. Ionian

XII. Hypoionian

impractical because of the inherent diminished fifth above the final. Ironically, Glareanus' book appeared at a time when the modes were already being transformed into something like the major/minor tonal system that prevailed after 1600.

Concepts of 15th- and 16th-century modality form the basic organization of the earliest Reformation chorale melodies. Luther and his contemporaries borrowed or adapted many of these tunes from preexistent German spiritual songs, secular melodies, and Latin (i.e., Gregorian) hymns. Except for instances of pentatonic usage (*Nun bitten wir den Heiligen Geist*), the chorale melodies of this era (c. 1523—50) use either authentic or plagal forms of the modes. Thus, e.g., *Christ lag in Todesbanden* is Dorian, *Aus tiefer Not* is Phrygian, *Ach Gott, vom Himmel sieh darein* is Hypophrygian, and *Gott sei gelobet und gebenedeiet* is Hypomixolydian. Even melodies whose pre-Reformation sources are not entirely evident, such as Luther's *Erhalt uns, Herr* (1543) and *Ein' feste Burg* (1528), should properly be identified as Aeolian and Ionian respectively. His setting of *The Litany* (1528) is a rare instance of the use of the Lydian mode. The earliest French Psalter melodies, e.g., *Donne secours* and *Les commandemens de Dieu*, are similarly modal in character, and the famous *Old Hundredth* tune, considering the historical context of its origin, is properly Hypoionian. After 1600 hymn composition gradually drew away from melodic modality in favor of the harmonic ingenuities of the major/minor tonal system. By ignoring their original modal character as far as possible, Bach, in his incomparable harmonizations, transformed the 16th-century chorales into exemplary pieces of early 18th-century major/minor tonality. Composers between Monteverdi and Debussy only rarely used the modes as a source of musical materials.

The use of modal idioms within generally tonal, polytonal, or pandiatonic contexts, as well as the free intermingling of melodic and harmonic characteristics of two or more of the several modes (panmodality), are techniques long standard in 20th-century composition. A renewed application for the modal system was realized early in this century when it was drawn upon as one of the several alternatives to the vocabulary of post-Wagnerian tonal chromaticism, especially by French (Debussy, Ravel), English (Vaughan Williams), Hungarian (Bartok), and Russian (Stravinsky) composers. The prominence of modality in 20th-century church music reflects continued musicological efforts to provide authenticity in not only medieval chant materials (the Solesmes and other editions), but also other historical repertories using the modes in either monophonic or polyphonic textures: Anglo-Saxon and French carols and folk hymnody (e.g., *King's Lynn, Deo gracias, Picardy*), Reformation-era chorales and French Psalter hymns (see above), 19th-century American spiritual songs as, e.g., in *The Southern Harmony* (1835) and *The Sacred Harp* (1844), and the whole repertoire of Renaissance polyphony. Idioms suggested by these and other primary sources have not only permeated the style of church music by composers as diverse as Ralph Vaughan Williams, Hugo Distler, Healey Willan, Jan Bender, and Fr. Joseph Gelineau, but have significantly influenced new liturgical and hymnic musical expressions such as those introduced in most recent American publications of worship materials. Panmodality is used in some of the most successful hymn tunes of relatively recent origin, e.g., *The King's Majesty*, with its felicitous combination of configurations from both Dorian and Aeolian patterns. RH

Readings: Apel, Willi, *Gregorian Chant* (Bloomington, 1958); Blom, Eric, ed., *Grove's Dictionary of Music and Musicians*, 5th ed. (New York, 1954); Crocker, Richard L., *A History of Musical Style* (New York, 1966); Grout, Donald Jay, *A History of Western Music*, rev. ed. (New York, 1973); Reese, Gustave, *Music in the Middle Ages* (New York, 1940).

See also: chant, Gregorian; chorale; church music history, medieval; church music history, Renaissance—the Latin tradition; church music history, Renaissance—the Reformation tradition; psalmody, Gregorian.

church music history, Jewish

Sources for a knowledge of music and instruments related to the life and worship of the Jews are limited almost exclusively to the references in the Biblical text and the Talmud. While Jewish tradition opposed artistic representation in the form of painting, sculpture, etc., nevertheless it is clear that music played an important role in Jewish life from the very beginning.

In Early Israel

Relatively little is known of Hebrew music in the period from about 1500 B.C. to 1000 B.C., before Israel was organized as a state. Toward the end of this period (the early years in Palestine) the Hebrews established local shrines (e.g., at Shechem and Shiloh) and undoubtedly developed religious lyrics and musical customs which formed a part of their early cultus. The number of musical instruments from this time mentioned in the Pentateuch are few: the *'ugab*, a long, wide, vertical flute of the kind often played by shepherds; the *kinnor*, a small lyre or harp used in connection with singing, the strings plucked with a plectrum; the *toph*, a small drum made of a wooden hoop with two skins, similar to the present-day tambourine, but without the jingling device; the *pa'amon*, a small bell or jingle, a number of which were sewn to the hem of the high priest's robe; the *shophar*, a ram's or goat's horn without a mouthpiece, still used in Jewish worship; and the *chatzotzrah*, a trumpet-like instrument used by the priests in pairs as a signal, described by Josephus as a straight tube ending in a bell. The first three were essentially instruments of the people used to accompany their songs; the last three were used more directly in the early stages of the developing Israelite religious cultus. In Biblical times, at least, Hebrew song was normally accompanied by instruments.

The Period of the Monarchy

Hebrew music entered a new stage (about the 10th century B.C.) with the adoption by the Jews of a monarchial system of government, the period of the kings Saul, David, and Solomon. During this time Israel developed a systematic musical organization as well as a professional class of musicians. Court musicians, both men and women, were supported by both David and Solomon. (Music at the Jerusalem court is reflected in such passages as 1 Sam. 19:9; 1 Kings 10:12; Amos 8:3; and Sirach 9:4.) David, himself a musician, founded an official group of musicians (chosen from the Levites) for the services of the temple that he hoped to build. David had the Ark of the Covenant brought to Jerusalem accompanied by a variety of singers and players (2 Sam. 6:15). He appointed a head musician (Asaph the chief, and next to him Zechariah) and assigned players to the various instruments (1 Chron. 16:5; 25:1-5). David must be credited with the general aspects of ordering the temple worship; Solomon generally adhered to the established order arranged by his father (2 Chron. 7:8; 8:14). During this period what was for all purposes an academy of religious music to provide music for the temple was established as an integral part of Jewish religious life.

The influence of foreign (esp. Egyptian) musical instruments and practice is also reflected in this period. (Solomon's wife, daughter of the Egyptian pharoah, is said to have brought with her "a thousand kinds" of Egyptian musical instruments. The relations established by the Israelites with Phoenecia in connection with providing for the building and furnishing of the royal palace and temple also brought the Hebrews into contact with different musical traditions and practices.) New musical instruments mentioned in the Biblical accounts of this period include: the *nebel*, most likely a large harp-like stringed instrument plucked with the fingers and having a louder and lower sound than that of the *kinnor*; the *'asor*, a ten-stringed instrument, probably on a rectangular frame; the *mena'an'im*, most likely a shaken instrument similar to the *sistrum*; and the *tseltselim* and *metziltayim*, brass cymbals. The term *shalishim*, probably the most disputed Hebrew musical term, and formerly thought to be triangles or triangular harps, perhaps does not refer to musical instruments. References in Talmudic literature to the *magrepha* (organ) disagree as to whether one was to be found in the temple; if one was used, it could hardly have been used until near the very end of Israel's national existence. With Solomon, who reigned with the pomp and splendor common to oriental courts of the time, came the great era of ritual music at both court and temple, 2 Chron. 5:12-13.

An important feature of temple worship and music was the singing of psalms. Special events at the court—such as the ascension of a new monarch, the enthronement of a new king or its anniversary, the king's marriage, his departure for war and his victorious return—undoubtedly called for special music (see the "royal psalms," e.g., 20; 21; 45; 72; 89; 110). Other types of psalms, such as psalms of praise (e.g., 145, 147, 148,, 150), psalms of petition (e.g., 44, 74, 79, 80, 83), psalms of thanksgiving (e.g., 30, 66, 116, 118, 126), and processional psalms (e.g., 24, 48, 95, 100) suggest the uses to which they were most probably put.

References to music in Jewish secular life include references to music in connection with feasting (Is. 5:11-12; Amos 8:10), harlotry (Is. 23:16), weddings (Jer. 7:34), funerals and mourning (Jer. 9:17-18; Amos 5:6).

Instrumental music as an aid to inspiration and prophetic ecstasy was favored during this period (2 Kings 3:15). In addition to singing and instrumental music, *mecholah* (dancing) was important in connection with religious ceremonies, although it apparently fell into disuse.

The Exile and Restoration

During the period of the divided kingdom the vocal aspects of religious music apparently increased in importance, the use of instruments being relegated more and more to accompaniment and to serving as signals in the religious ceremony. The Babylonian exile of the Jews (ended 536 B.C.) brought them under the influence of Babylonian music and orchestral instruments (see Daniel 3), and the effects of that sojourn on their music is reflected in Ps. 137:1-4. The return to Palestine and the restoration of the temple with its music (described in the books of Ezra, Nehemiah, and Chronicles) again made Jerusalem a vital center of religious and musical life, though on a scale more modest than in the time of David. During this period Ezra arranged for the first public recitation of the Pentateuch (Neh. 8).

The number of instruments used in the temple during this period is reflected in the Talmudic tradition (*Mishna Arakhin* II, 3; *Sukka* IV, V) and consisted of: two to six *nebalim*; a minimum of nine *kinnorim*, with an indefinite maximum; only one cymbal; and two to six *chalilim*. The total minimum number of instruments was thus 12 plus the addition of the two *chalilim* on 12 special festival days. Likewise the chorus consisted of a minimum of 12 adult male singers, the maximum being limitless. After five years of training a singer was admitted to the chorus at 30 and continued until he was 50. In addition some Levite boys were allowed to participate in the singing "in order to add sweetness to the song" (*Mishna Arakhin* II, 6; *B. Chullin* 24).

No written examples of Jewish chant or *cantillation* have come down to us from Biblical times. Recent research (esp. that of Idelsohn) has concluded that early Jewish chant was in free rhythm and was based on various stereotyped melodic formulas that could be adapted to the texts of the Psalter and Pentateuch. Thus melodic formulas, not fixed melodies, were characteristic of early Jewish chant. In this connection, the enigmatic headings of many of the Psalms (e.g., Ps. 8 "To the chief musician upon Gittith" which should rather be translated "To the chief musician, to be performed upon Gittith") more probably refers to the melody or the melodic formula to be employed, rather than to a specific instrument used to accompany the singing, as was formerly assumed. Some headings may suggest the use for which the Psalm was intended.

The practice of singing the Psalms responsorially, antiphonally (Deut. 27:14-26), in unison, or in solo form were all used. Simple single-word refrains ("Amen," "Hallelujah") were apparently used, also by the entire congregation. These practices, together with the use of basic melodic formulas for the singing of the Psalms, influenced the development of the early Christian chant.

After the destruction of the temple in A.D. 70, the use of instrumental music in Jewish worship passed into oblivion, vocal music being retained and transplanted into the service of the synagog. Also, by the beginning of the Christian era, Greek music had begun to penetrate into Palestine, much to the dismay of the majority of the Jews who sought to uphold the older traditions.

The Synagog

The synagog was of crucial importance in the continuing development of Jewish music. Established long before the destruction of the second temple in A.D. 70 (probably during the Babylonian exile), the synagog provided an opportunity for regular worship for those who could not take part in the temple worship, especially the Jews of the Diaspora. By the time of Christ the synagog was a well-established institution in which laymen held chief responsibility for the regulation of worship. The synagog did not use instruments, developing instead the vocal aspects of Jewish musical tradition. This abstention may have been a reminder of the past glories of the music of the temple; it may also have been part of the more general negative reaction to instruments (shared by the early Christian church fathers) fostered by the association of instruments with the pagan religious cults and the secular life of the times.

The vocal music of the synagog consisted chiefly in the intoning of the Psalms, the Pentateuch, and the prayers. While the cantillation of the prose Biblical texts was based on steretoyped melodic formulas (represented by signs called *ta'amim* (accents) written either above or below the lines of the texts), the prayers were freely improvised, often in highly virtuoso fashion, on the basis of traditional themes or melody types. It was to the *chazzan* (precentor or cantor) that the singing of the prayers was ultimately entrusted. The *chazzanim* were the chief carriers of Jewish ritual music through the 19th century, and were chosen chiefly for the excellence of their voices and their ability to improvise in connection with the prayers. Through the *chazzanim* the music of the synagog was transmitted orally for almost 1,000 years. (Earliest manuscripts containing Jewish ecphonetic notation date from the 9th century, although several such systems were apparently in existence from about the 5th century.)

Modern attempts to reconstruct the early Jewish musical tradition have been based on the assumption that the oral tradition of Jewish music preserved among the relatively isolated Jewish groups that have continued in existence will have retained the old traditions in relatively pure form. These groups included isolated Jewish settlements in Yemen, Iraq, Iran, the Jewish settlements in southwestern Germany, and those in eastern Europe.

In later centuries, orthodox Jews generally sought to retain the traditional musical practices, whereas more progressive groups tended to reflect in their music the styles and practices of the succeeding periods. (For example, instruments were introduced into some German synagogs in the 18th century; by the 19th century the cantor was eliminated, the organ was used, and Jewish hymns were written in German and set to German chorale tunes.) Jewish musicians who influenced the various developments in synagog worship include Salomon Rossi (1587—1628), Ahron Beer (1738—1821), Israel Jacobson (1768—1828), and Salomon Sulzer (1804—90). Among Jewish musicologists who have contributed to an understanding of early Jewish music A. Z. Idelsohn (1882—1938) and Eric Werner (1901—) are the most prominent. CS

Readings: Idelsohn, A. Z., *Jewish Music* (New York, 1929); Kraeling, C. H. and Lucetta Mowry, "Music in the Bible," *New Oxford History of Music*, I (New York, 1957); Rothmueller, A. M., *The Music of the Jews* (New York, 1954); Sachs, Curt, *A History of Musical Instruments* (New York, 1940); Sendry, Alfred, *Music in Ancient Israel* (New York, 1969); Werner E., *The Sacred Bridge* (New York, 1959); Werner, E., "Music," *The Interpreter's Dictionary of the Bible*, III (New York, 1962); 457—469.

See also: Biblical instruments; hymnody, Old Testament

church music history, medieval

The use of "medieval" (meaning: of the Middle Ages) to identify a period of music history suffers from the persistent and now meaningless question: middle of what? At the same time the term's imprecision encourages a confusing array of decisions regarding the period's temporal boundaries. The beginnings of medieval music are commonly understood to coincide with the beginnings of music in the Christian church, hence with Pentecost. Termination of the period is not so easily agreed to. Some historians are convinced that the Middle Ages extend either up to (Friedrich Blume) or into (Gustav Reese, with the fall of Constantinople, 1453) the 15th century. Others suggest an end to the musical period at 1400 or thereabouts (Albert Seay, Hugo Riemann, Jack Westrup, et al.), while a middle ground is reached by positing the 14th century as transitional (Paul H. Lang) or by suggesting two renaissances (Charles van der Borren).

This variety of definitions results from differing perceptions of the 14th century, particularly the events that led to the weakening clerical influence and control over the people of the church. Political maneuverings by Philip VI of France led to the "Hundred Years' War" (1337—1453) and to inevitable suffering. In the midst of the conflict the bubonic plague swept Europe, leaving behind people who either sought out the contrast of pleasure or looked for new and better fortunes with the church. The new "looking" piety, epitomized in the monstrance and supported by allegorisms, spawned an interest in the ordinary of the mass and prompted a rash of musical settings. Many people gave up on the leadership of the church: its record was marked by political foibles epitomized by the exiled pope at Avignon—this after a century that welcomed one of the greatest theological synthesizers of all time, Thomas Aquinas (d. 1274).

There were far-reaching musical changes during the 14th century. With the advent of mass settings the performance of polyphonic church music turned from an essentially solo rendition to an essentially choral one. The gradual liberation of the semibrevis (the smallest unit of time) from the dominating patterns of the rhythmic modes, begun already about 1230 by the theorist Garlandia and continued by Franco (1260) and Pietrus de Cruce (fl. latter half of 13th century) reached the critical point c. 1320, when Philip de Vitry recommended in his treatise *Ars nova* the equality of duple and triple meters. For centuries the tripartite construct had been extolled as trinitarian, and therefore preferred. Such a favored status needed to be relinquished, argued de Vitry, as he commented on the music of his time. This change in attitude reflected an emerging impatience on the part of musicians with ecclesiastical dicta regarding their craft. Jacobus de Liege, in his *Speculum musicae* of c. 1330, made a last attempt to defend the old; however, his efforts, together with the *Constitutio docta* (1324/25) of Pope John XXII, failed to halt the erosion of churchly influence and control.

Together these observations manifest an expanding, intoxicating mood of independence during the 14th century that heralds the birth of the Renaissance and signals, especially for church musicians, the close of the Middle Ages.

Early Christian Music

As the Jewish roots of early Christian liturgy continue to be uncovered, it is no surprise to discover that Semitic sources are also behind most early Christian music. The bulk of 1st-century church music is probably described in Eph. 5:19: psalms, hymns, and spiritual songs. Dependent as they were on the synagog, the early Christians probably used simple psalmodic refrains as responses to the solo chanting of psalms, likely heard Scriptural lessons cantillated (a kind of sung speech) and were encouraged to pray by recurring sung interjections such as Kyrie or Hosanna. For hymns early worshipers probably used Scriptural songs of praise or their paraphrases, singing through the texts with one or two notes per syllable. The earliest example of Christian music fits this category, the Oxyrhynchus hymn from the late 3d century. Spiritual songs or odes were textually parascriptural, musically more florid than the hymns, and possibly accompanied. The best example is that model of jubilation inherited from the synagog and the temple, the alleluia, which Saint Augustine in the 4th century already exalts as an ecstatic song without words.

The impact of Semitic influence on early Christian music has been brought to light by the comparative studies of Greek Byzantine, later Jewish, and (Western) Syriac music. For example, the Oxyrhynchus hymn, at first thought to be built from the Greek modes, now appears to have been constructed by the linking together of Syrian-inspired melodic formulas. These in turn display similarities to certain modes described much later by the theorists.

The compounding of melodic archetypes was a constitutional

procedure handed down by the first churches of Palestine, and then modified according to the individualities of local parish clusters. In the East the liturgies of the Syrian family (Maronite, Chaldeon, etc.) were ornamented with their own cult musics and especially with vernacular hymnody. Parochial musics were also developed for the Armenian, Egyptian, Byzantine-Greek, Byzantine-Slavic, and Melkite rites. The same kind of evolution occurred in the West; by the 5th century repertoires of liturgical music had come into being at Rome (Old Roman), at Milan (Ambrosian), at Benevento, in Spain (Mozarabic, of which only a handful of pieces are decipherable), and in France (Old Gallican, of which all original chants have disappeared).

Christian church music came into being only with great difficulty. For the first two centuries elaborate music was apparently viewed by the tiny clans of Christians as a luxury, and they were warned by the clergy (e.g., Clement) against its pagan influence. With the Edict of Constantine (313), however, liberty was granted to the church, and Christians were given a chance to sink roots into the surrounding culture. Many basilicas were opened, the liturgies were reshaped to fit their new settings, and the musicians set to work embellishing the chants and songs, particularly at Rome. In 382 Pope Damasus held a council in collaboration with Eastern bishops. Their presence in Rome resulted in Eastern influence on Roman liturgy and music. A half-century later, Celestine I (422—432) supervised the formation of the Schola Cantorum and gave its members the express tasks of composing and performing liturgical music. Leo the Great (440—461) continued this line of musical popes by providing for special music in the papal basilica.

Rome's rise to power—hierarchical and musical—was helped by the administrative separation of East and West in 395 and by the total papal control resulting from Justinian's death in 565. A few years later Gregory the Great (pope 590—604) reorganized the Schola Cantorum, and arranged to have the Roman chant collected and codified; the repertoire henceforth was known as "Gregorian Chant." Members of the Schola were sent throughout Europe (e.g., St. Augustine to England), local enthusiasts were given official recognition (Boniface in Germany, Pepin in France), and within four centuries these musical missionaries had succeeded in supplanting all the local flowerings of church music with the Gregorian versions, Spain being one of the last to capitulate. Monasteries at Metz and St. Gall, which even today house the many important manuscripts that trace this transformation of repertoires, developed as distribution centers for this retooling work.

Compositions and Composers

The paucity of extant music from the first seven centuries permits only tentative statements regarding musical practice among Christians. It can be assumed that most of the mass and substantial sections of the cathedral office were in musical form. For these first centuries, graduals, alleluias, antiphons, responsories, etc. probably underwent continual improvisatory revision and elaboration, though tempered by persisting oral traditions. No doubt a body of paraliturgical, more popular, songs existed for use in the home or for less formal liturgical occasions, such as funeral processions. Beginning with the 8th century the repertoire was expanded; added were: ordinary and propers for new feasts, hymns, nonliturgical religious pieces such as the conductus, metrical versions of the canonical hours, tropes, sequences, and liturgical drama. Outside of a few isolated pieces, actual examples of any of this music exist in sources dating from the 11th century or later. Earlier manuscripts—the earliest being from the 9th century—are simply not decipherable.

Anonymity surrounds most medieval music. Many of the hymns, sequences, and tropes have come down credited to St. Ambrose or to monks such as Notker, Tuotilo, and Adam of St. Victor. More recent pieces, such as the Notre Dame Organa and motets, appear in the manuscripts with the composer's names, especially those by Leonin (d. c. 1200) and Perotin (d. 1235). Because of their reputation theorists such as Hucbald (d. 930), Guido d'Arezzo (d. 1050), and Jean de Muris (d. 1351) were usually better known than most composers. Sometimes, as is true of Franco of Cologne and Philip d'Vitry, a composer was remembered both for his music and for his theoretical treatises.

Trends

The Quest for Unity

Because of their missionary impulses Christians were constantly confronting alien religious and philosophical systems. When rejection did not seem necessary, they often adopted and assimilated new ideas and views, subconsciously perhaps following their belief in the total lordship of Jesus. The quest for unity in thought and confession manifested itself in

Nicaea and other councils, in frequent commerce between Eastern bishops and Western leaders, and in the obvious dependence of the church fathers on secular learning. As the first great synthesizer, Boethius (470?—525) brought together the teaching of Plato, Aristotle, and Pythagoras by insisting that music was integral to the total structure of the world. Relying on the Roman view of education he gave music its customary penultimate importance on the ladder of learning (*quadrivium*): arithmetic, geometry, music, astronomy. Over these four, he allowed, theology and philosophy reigned supreme. Furthermore, he understood music to be audible number. Beauty, according to Boethius, resulted from intervallic ratios (e.g., octave=2:1), the simplest being the most beautiful. The principle of ratio prevails throughout creation, he claimed; experience of it is personally beneficial and is triggered by active involvement in music at three levels: *musica instrumentalis,* sounding music, both vocal and instrumental; *musica humana,* the balance which keeps together body and soul along with the emotions and moral will; *musica mundana*, the music of the spheres including the music of heaven itself. According to his view, music is cosmological—all-embracing, and integrally connected with morality. Later theorists, preserved this monolithic view of things. Cassiodorus (d. 580), Isidore (d. 636), and Rabanus Maurus (d. 856), each in his own way, stressed the unity of music with all there is. "Without music," said Maurus, "no discipline can be perfected." The hierarchical ranking, so typical of the Boethian system, was later clarified with the adoption of an ascending scale, a reversal of the earlier Greek arrangement.

Bringing observable musical phenomena into a reasonable system was a typical inclination of medieval musicians who, merging poetic interests with musical practice, availed themselves of modal rhythm—a system of six fundamental rhythmic patterns of long and short values—in order to provide a piece with perceptible structure. Nearly every theorist busied himself with explanations of consonance and dissonance in order to accommodate all the scale steps as his disposal.

Complete and controlled organization manifested itself also in musical form. In the 13th century, composers became fond of assembling the tenors (melodic foundations) of clausulae (self-sufficient polyphonic sections of larger pieces) and of motets by joining the pitches of the preexistent melody with a freely chosen rhythmic pattern. The collection of pitches and the rhythmic pattern need not be of the same length, that is, the melody might require two uses of the pattern in order to run its full course, or vice versa. When this technique, known as isorhythm, was put into practice, composers normally designed several repetitions of both melody and rhythmic pattern. Once these were fixed, the overall structure of the piece was established. The quest for unity subsided with the advent of the *Ars nova*, when music was pressed for its expressive qualities or was viewed as an equal partner with grammar, rhetoric, and dialectic (*trivium*).

The Development and Use of the Musical Trope

The golden age for the formulation of chant melodies was the 5th through the 8th centuries. Curtailment of chant composition came as the Roman repertoire was made normative for all of western Christendom. From then on established chants could be altered only by receiving a "commentary," or a trope, a practice in literary realms known as glossing. It was a favored compositional technique from the 9th to the 13th centuries.

Melodic elaboration, as a kind of troping, was common already in pre-Gregorian centuries, especially when melismas from one responsory were transferred to another. In the case of the Alleluia Verse, the melisma over the final syllable (the *jubilus*) underwent similar amplification. During the 10th century it was fitted with text, resulting in a self-sufficient piece soon separated and independently performed. It was not long before these textual-musical tropes were composed apart from any preexistent alleluia, and because they and their prototypes followed the alleluia in performance, they were all called sequence hymns. Later examples usually followed given poetic schemes.

Kyries, Glorias, and other sections of the mass that contained melismas were similarly troped. Vestiges of the practice appear in the titles of some Gregorian Kyries, e.g., the *Kyrie fons bonitatis* (known in its German translation as *Kyrie, Gott Vater in Ewigkeit*). In the East medieval hymnodists adopted the troping principle when they chose a model canticle (*hirmos*) which was to shape the multistanza ode called a *kantakion* (later, *kanon*). The whole process of clarifying or expanding on a model is particularly noticeable in the emergence of liturgical drama. Late 10th-century sources, such as the *Regularis concordia* of St. Ethelwold, contain imaginative dialogs and stagings in answer to that inquiry common to both the Christmas and Easter narratives: Whom do you seek? (*quem quaeritis*). As the troping impulse matured, replies to this question grew in size and complexity to become independent plays. The troping dramatists soon chose other Biblical stories and arranged to have some of their stories completely sung with instrumental accompaniment (e.g., *The Play of Daniel*).

Medieval musicians discovered that tropes need not always be arranged consecutively, but that glosses could be developed for simultaneous performance, resulting in many voices or polyphony. Western musicians were in part led to this discovery by an acquaintance with similar Eastern musical practices. Many origins have been suggested for polyphony; whatever proves true, improvised parallel motion (parallel organum) below an established chant is essentially a commentary, hence a trope. So is an organal gloss which moves in contrary motion (free organum). Both styles are described in one of the first treatises on polyphony, the 10th-century *Musica Enchiriadis*. Moving the gloss so that it becomes the highest voice (as is common in the 11th-century *Winchester Troper*) or giving it more notes (as was suggested by John Afflighem c. 1100) reflects greater independence on the part of the arranger, and when at Notre Dame the three-voice clausulae evolved to the motet, in which the gloss has received new text, the troping principle has come full cycle: the trope has been troped, or the preexistent authority has been freely constructed by the commentator himself.

As the age of the trope came to a close, musicians began to look outside of the church for creative inspiration, but also searched for new ways to express their musical allegiance to the faith. The prevailing solution was the use of chant fragments. At first these melodic pieces were rhythmically augmented to form pedal points over which other voices were made to weave a colorful fabric. Exquisite examples of this style are among the older motets (*Ars antiqua*) contained in the *Roman de Fauvel* (c. 1316), a lengthy poem with musical interpolations, and among the liturgical motets of Guillaume de Machault (1300—77), a French priest who, because of his evident interests in things nonecclesiastical, summarized the spirit of a new, postmedieval age (*Ars nova*). A century later chant fragments were employed as melodic generators for more of the voice parts, e.g., in the motets and masses of early Renaissance composers such as Guillaume Dufay (1400—74). While all of these works are yet tropes in a broad sense, they rather represent an artistic independence that at best incorporates a polite gesture acknowledging the past and that signals the close of the real age of troping.

The Growth of Sacred-Secular Awareness

The hesitancy with which the early church approached music reflects an understandable desire on its part to set up protection against antichristian influences. That fear of syncretism not only made it difficult for music to survive, but it made creditable those Jewish, Gnostic, and Neoplatonic arguments for worship in spirit only, that is, without audible voice. Patristic proponents of these theories anchored their versions of the disputation in the teaching of Jesus (John 4:23-24). Assimilations of this sort indicate some recognized conflict between church and culture in the first centuries of the church, but it is far less severe than that sacred-secular stylistic dichotomy brought about by the Council of Trent more than a millennium later. Rather, the ideal of inaudible worship is a survival attempt in a hostile environment, an attempt that was abandoned in the 4th century.

Post-Constantinian attitudes toward music derived from a non-apologetic interchange of what later generations would label sacred and secular. The conductus, or processional song, was prepared for use both within religious as well as nonreligious environs. Prototypes for the sequence hymn have been found in the then current secular "lai" as well as in the "rhythms"—sacred-secular songs of trochaic rhythm. In the 10th and 11th centuries, without serious objection, roving bands called Goliards developed a repertoire of songs that were combinations of old religious tunes and new secular texts, record of which appears in the 13th century manuscript, *Carmina Burana.* Free interchange of that sort was continued by the troubadours, trouveres, and Minnesingers. Religious folk songs, e.g., in the Spanish collection *Cantigas de Santa Maria* and the Italian *laudi spirituali,* show great similarities to the secular *Virelai.* Another favorite poetic form, the ballade (AAB) was taken over as the barform by the Meistersinger in the 14th and 15th centuries. It became a favorite structure for Lutheran hymnwriters.

Similar reciprocation of the religious and nonreligious was common to paraliturgical music, popular all across Christendom. In the East semireligious acclamations were employed by the faithful as the emperor processed to the church for worship. Coptic Christians developed a large repertoire of spiritual folk songs, and Abyssinian Christians distinguished themselves for their ecstatic ritual dancing. With this unified view of things composers in the late 13th century quite naturally set out to construct sacred motets from nonsacred tunes.

Less ordinary—and possibly insensitive—was the use of secular texts for upper voices in sacred motets. Love songs as tropes for graduals, for instance, surely irritated the less-open clergy as did the use of hocket (those hiccup-like broken phrases), setting up the case for quite explicit clerical interdicts (as that from John XXII in 1324). Whether or not ecclesiastical criticisms caused musicians to seek their fortunes at secular courts is not demonstrable; the fact that in the 14th century their output revolved more around secular interests helped to put distance between the church and culture. The effects of that, stylistically, would not be felt until after Trent, but the seeds for differentiation were sown by the close of the 13th century.

Medieval church music was the product of pioneering churchmen who were not afraid of trying to mate art and faith. They soon discovered that an affair with music would give birth to innumerable difficulties, many of which were left to succeeding generations. But the totality of the legacy, if the perspective of later generations is accurate, ultimately provided ample assurance that the marriage was worth perpetuating. MB

Readings: Fellerer, Karl Gustav, ed., *Geschichte der katholischen Kirchenmusik* (Kassel, 1972); Hughes, Dom Anselm, ed., *Early Medieval Music up to 1300,* Vol. II of *The New Oxford History of Music* (London, 1954); Reese, Gustave, *Music in the Middle Ages* (New York, 1968); Seay, Albert, *Music in the Medieval World,* Vol. I of *History of Music Series* (Englewood Cliffs, N. J., 1965).

See also: Catholic pronouncements and decrees on church music; chant, Gregorian; hymnody, Greek; hymnody, Latin; liturgical drama; mass; medieval instruments; motet; notation; sequence; theology of church music, early church fathers; trope.

church music history, Renaissance—the Latin tradition

As to the question exactly when, in Western music, the Renaissance was, a very good case could be made for the answer: "Continuingly." For music, in apparent contrast to literature and painting, experienced neither a hiatus nor a barren period during the 12th through the 14th centuries. Rather, this period saw the logical growth of such basic musical means as polyphony, mensural music, and expanded pitch resources (*musica ficta*); and of such important types as the motet, canon, and conductus. The spectacular flowering of music during the 15th and 16th centuries, the period most often called the Renaissance, would have been impossible without the legacy of such gifted 14th-century composers as Philippe de Vitry (1291—1361), Machaut (1304?—77), and Landini (1325—97)—to name only the best-known. In this article the Renaissance will be considered as starting about the time of the Council of Constance (1414—18), when, by settling the feud among rival claimants to the papacy and reestablishing the papal seat at Rome, it extended the mandate of the undivided Western church for a century—until the Protestant Reformation. The Renaissance will be considered as closing with the deaths, both in 1594, of Giovanni Pierluigi da Palestrina (b. c. 1525) and Orlando di Lasso (b. 1532), the last of the great composers within a tradition that had started almost two centuries earlier, with Guillaume Dufay (c. 1400—74) and his generation.

A number of historical events exerted a significant influence on the nature of church music in this period. The Council of Constance provided a century of reasonable stability for the Latin church. Until 1453 the continuation of the Hundred Years' War kept the French impoverished and the English embattled on the Continent. These invaders had military success until the 1430s, when their decline began. The Burgundians, led by Duke Philip the Good, were allies of the English in their prosperity and English composers, including, perhaps, Dunstable, must have influenced their Burgundian counterparts. Ultimately, Duke Philip, a member of the French royal, Valois family, returned to the French fold. Since the Franco-Flemish border region, part of the realm of Duke Philip, was to produce the majority of significant composers for several generations, its exposure to more "tuneful," harmonic English music was of major importance.

In 1477 the last Duke of Burgundy, Charles the Bold, died. His daughter-heir, Mary, soon married the son of the Holy Roman Emperor, bringing the Low Countries immediately under German domination. When the Habsburgs intermarried with the Spanish royal line, Spanish influence also became strong. These alliances were of great musical import, since through them the powerful Franco-Flemish musical tradition was widely disseminated. German and Spanish composers, along with Italians, became heirs after about 1520 to this great heritage. After the Protestant Reformation was established, the stream of Renaissance church music divided, with much of north Germany and England developing significant new liturgies for use in Reformed services. The Latin (Catholic) tradition was maintained in Italy, Austria and Bavaria, Spain, and for the most part in France. The Council of Trent, meeting between 1545 and

1563, helped codify and regulate future music in the Catholic tradition.

What should be considered "church music" in the Renaissance? Is music to be judged sacred by text alone, or also by certain musical traits? Until about the middle of the 16th century, the answer would seem to be text, since the practice of *contrafactum* (substituting sacred for secular words in preexistent music) was tolerated and used freely. A more circumspect answer was given ultimately by the Council of Trent. Although no specific directives were issued at Trent, a somewhat austere model for liturgical music emerges from the pronouncements, and this ideal embraced musical as well as textual qualities. The Tridentine ideal was promulgated for universal observance, in sharp contrast to the regional practices that had pertained earlier. Hence any judgment we make *now* about the suitableness for liturgical use of any given composition must take into account the time and the region of its origin. It should be added that the chanson-mass and the motet with paraphrased sacred text—to name two of the most questionable types—seem less improbable for liturgical use since Vatican Council II (c. 1964) with its sweeping changes and experiments. During the four centuries before that, the austere Tridentine tradition, reaffirmed in 1903 in a motu proprio of Pius X, definitely influenced everyone's judgment.

The remainder of this article discusses developments in Latin sacred polyphonic music as taking place within five generations of composers. Specific composers or works are discussed only as they epitomize or, in some cases, initiate developments of an age.

The Generation of Dufay and Binchois

The two men whose names designate this period represent the two types of musician the Franco-Flemish border region produced in profusion for well over a century. Gilles Binchois (c. 1400—60) spent his entire life in the Low Country domain of Duke Philip the Good and became the chief jewel of the prestigious Burgundian court chapel. But Guillaume Dufay (c. 1400—74) labored mostly far afield, spreading the taste for elegant northern polyphony to Italy in particular. He was the prototype of the peripatetic, influential Franco-Flemish musician of the next several generations.

At the beginning of this period, most sacred and secular music retained many of the traits of the 14th-century secular music, typically three-voiced in texture with a mellifluous, high, often florid upper part. The usual cadence was the *clausula vera* in the outer parts (a major sixth interval opening to an octave) with the third voice in the texture a fourth below the higher note in each sonority. The topmost part might drop to the note below before moving to its resolution, thus constituting the "Landini" or "Burgundian" cadence. Until about the middle of the 15th century, sacred music is found most often in the form of separate mass movements (occasionally paired, as in the Kyrie-Gloria), motets, hymns, and compositions based on Marian texts. If today we question the propriety of ascribing music so seemingly "secular" in sound to liturgical situations, we must recall that Binchois himself was a religious, presiding as one of Duke Philip's chaplains; and Binchois' own sacred music is typical of everything described above.

By the time of his maturity, Dufay had restored to his sacred music much of the seriousness and delight in elegant craftsmanship wanting since the heyday of the French motet in the 13th century. Although a chronology for Dufay's works is not yet firmly established (but see Charles Hamm, *A Chronology of the Works of Guillaume Dufay, Based on a Study of Mensural Practice,* Princeton, 1964), three Masses seem to be early works, since they share traits of music of Binchois and other Burgundians. Five other Masses show more progressive traits: four-voiced texture, use of *cantus firmus* as a framework for the polyphonic structure, and a lowest part tending to move by wider intervals, in anticipation of the "harmonic" bass parts of slightly later music. Dufay was instrumental in establishing the five-movement Mass cycle (Kyrie, Gloria, Credo, Sanctus, Agnus) as the preferred large-scale form, which musicians of future generations would use with such impressive results.

In summary, Binchois was a man of his time and environment; Dufay was a cosmopolitan who helped mold the future.

The Generation of Ockeghem

Johannes Ockeghem (Okeghem; c. 1420—95) differs from his slightly older peers in that his sacred music constitutes the greater part of his repertoire. Born and trained in the Franco-Flemish border region, he spent his entire creative life in the service of the kings of France: Charles VII, Louis XI, Charles VIII. The elegance of his compositions and his obvious delight in musical architecture mark him as heir to the French Gothic musical tradition. Ockeghem's Masses (about a dozen or more) use several fresh musical means. Several masses, for example, are freely composed,

Johannes Ockeghem with a group of singers.

that is they have no apparent *cantus firmus*. The best-known are *Missa Mi-Mi, Missa Cuiusvis Toni,* and *Missa Prolationum*. Each is based on a specific "learned" device: "Mi mi" designated the hexachordal names of the notes E-A as a lead-motive in the bass; "Cuiusvis toni" indicates that the music may be performed in any of the four original modes; and "Prolationum" refers to the increasingly complex canons that underline successive movements.

Of particular note is Ockeghem's Requiem, which appears to be the earliest surviving polyphonic setting of the Mass for the Dead (Dufay's Requiem, which has disappeared, may have been earlier.) The traditional plainsong, in the highest voice, is the basis for each of the movements. It should be noted that the Gradual and Tract use pre-Tridentine texts, "Si ambulem in medio umbrae mortis" and "Sicut cervus" respectively.

Two among Ockeghem's many gifted contemporaries must have special mention: Antoine Busnois (d. 1492) who, like Binchois, spent his entire career at the Burgundian chapel, helping to preserve its glorious tradition in the dismal times after the death of the last of the Burgundian dukes; and Jacob Obrecht (c. 1505) who was the only Hollander of the group, and whose music, only just now becoming better known, matches that of any master of the period.

The Generation of Josquin Desprez

Josquin Desprez (c. 1445—1521), a native of the border country, spent his active life mostly in Italy and France, serving with such distinction that, even in his own lifetime, his music was the model for all to emulate. It is the considered judgment of a large number of present-day scholars that Josquin is the one composer before Monteverdi who belongs in the ranks of the consummately great composers of all time. To his numerous and varied sacred works he brought, besides superb craftsmanship, genuine musical sensitivity that imparts a new expressiveness to all he wrote. The title of premier Renaissance composer, for many years tendered to Palestrina, has now been accorded almost by consensus to Josquin.

Josquin's gifted contemporaries are legion, but space permits mention only of Heinrich Isaac (c. 1450—1517). Isaac left his Flemish homeland to serve Lorenzo the Magnificent; ultimately he was court composer to Emperor Maximiliam I. Isaac's most important composition, the so-called *Choralis Constantinus,* has long been recognized as unique in being the first attempt after Perotin to set to polyphonic music the Proper of the Mass for the entire liturgical year. Recent research indicates, however, that the publisher, Formschneider, not Isaac, may have been responsible for the actual organization into a cycle of this music for the Mass Proper. Formschneider published the *Choralis Constantinus* in three books between 1550 and 1555. Probably only Book II merits the title, since it was apparently written in response to a commission from the Constance Cathedral. Books I and III are compilatoins of motets for the Proper written at various times during Isaac's lifetime. None of this detracts from Isaac's accomplishment nor from the quality of the music. Since the Council of Trent was deliberating when Formschneider's publication took place, it is possible that he anticipated Tridentine attitudes in making available this large body of music all based on traditional plainsong *cantus firmi.*

From the Death of Josquin to the Council of Trent

After the Protestant Reformation was well established in the 1520s, Latin church music lost much of its thrust; no longer did those who wrote

Emperor Maximilian (d. 1519) at Mass, from the woodcut by Hans Weiditz. Note the emperor kneeling at the right, Mass being celebrated, Paul Hofhaimer at the *Apfelregal* at the left, and the choir singing from a large choirbook at the right. (New York Public Library)

Masses and motets compose for a universal Western liturgy. The principal places that retained the Catholic liturgy were located in the German provinces of Austria and Bavaria, in Spain, which was linked to them by Habsburg marriages, and in Italy and France. The court chapel of Emperor Charles V was the most palpable link with the musical glories of the Dukes of Burgundy, Marguerite of Austria, and the Emperor Maximilian. Nicolas Gombert (d. c. 1556) was the most distinguished composer in the service of Charles V. He was joined by a number of gifted Spaniards and Franco-Flemings. In Venice, Adrian Willaert (c. 1490—1562) emplanted a taste for northern polyphony that bore splendid fruit with the advent of Andrea and Giovanni Gabrieli and other gifted Italians of the next generations. This was a time of conservation and of waiting.

After the Council of Trent

In this last generation of Renaissance composers, as was the case with the first one, two men epitomize the tendencies of the age. Palestrina (c. 1525—94), a native of Italy who spent most of his life in Rome, learned the Franco-Netherlandish contrapuntal style from his early teachers. That he learned his lesson well is attested by his own music, which might be described as a distillation of what had gone before, but shaped by the Tridentine ideal of sacred music. The special place among Renaissance composers long occupied by Palestrina came about through two practical circumstances: Palestrina's was the only Renaissance music widely known and available up to the 20th century; and his sacred music enjoyed a kind of official approval, reinforced by the Cecilian revival of the 19th century and confirmed by the gist of Pius X's motu proprio of 1903.

Another towering figure of the twilight of the Renaissance is Orlando di Lasso (1532—94), Low Country born (even now his portrait hangs in the town hall of Mons, his birthplace), but serving much of his active career at the Catholic court of Munich—conveniently removed from the inhibiting

Detail from the title page of the *Graduale Romanum,* Antwerp, 1599, depicting 11 singers with 4 instrumentalists.

effects of Tridentine decrees. Lassus was a far more individual composer than Palestrina and his sensitiveness to text nuance caused him to favor the motet, with its ever-varied text, over the Mass. Even so, Lassus wrote a profusion of sacred works of all kinds. His parody settings of the Magnificat are of particular interest. Lassus had a special penchant for "word painting," and his works abound in such forward-looking devices as chromaticism, bold leaps, dramatic pauses, and disjunct linear structure. Lassus is the last Netherlander in a line that began more than a century earlier, when Dufay and Binchois embarked on their fruitful, historic careers.

Readings: Hughes, Dom Anselm and Gerald Abraham, eds., "Ars Nova and the Renaissance 1300—1540," *The New Oxford History of Music*, III (London, 1960); Reese, G., *Music in the Renaissance*, rev. ed. (New York, 1959); Wangermee, R., *Flemish Music and Society in the Fifteenth and Sixteenth Centuries*, Eng. version by Robert Erich Wolf (New York, 1968).

See also: Catholic pronouncements and decrees on church music; contrafacta; hymnody, Latin; mass; notation; polychoral style; Renaissance instruments; Roman school; Venetian school

church music history, Renaissance
—the Reformation tradition

The theological basis for the music of the Reformation era is its medieval interpretation as *donum divinum ab initio mundi* (God's gift from the creation of the world). Adapting a common pre-Reformation heritage to their frequently interacting artistic aims, Protestant and Catholic musicians shaped a musical language, at once traditional and modern, and remarkably unified in form and style. Specifically Protestant elements, emanating from the spiritual thrust of the Reformation, are reflected in legitimized congregational participation on a broad scale (the Lutherans through the chorale, the Reformed through the psalm) and in the desire to cleanse the church from papist abuses (the Lutherans through alteration, reordering, and selection, the Reformed through radical abandonment of accustomed liturgical practice).

The latitude and extent of music's contribution to their respective movements were defined by the reformers. Although recommending "the singing of songs of praise," Zwingli, himself a highly educated musician, eliminated all music from the service. For Luther, on the other hand, music was the *ancilla theologiae* (the handmaiden of theology), ranking second only to theology as medium of Gospel proclamation. "Ich gebe nach der Theologie der Musica den naehesten Locum und hoechste Ehre."—*"Sic Deus praedicavit evangelium etiam per musicam."* Calvin, dismissing instrumental music as *puerilia elementa* ("childish rudiments," i.e., Old Testament concessions for which New Testament Christians have no further need), banning from the service choral polyphony and chanting at the altar, but introducing congregational psalms, holds the middle ground between Zwingli and Luther.

Music of the Lutheran Church

Martin Luther (1483—1546) was perhaps the single most creative and guiding force in the development of 16th-century church music. Although he considered himself only an amateur—he had tried his hand at polyphonic composition, was a passable lutenist and had a pleasant tenor voice—he was well versed in theory and showed a keen appreciation for the music of his time. Above all, he had the unfailing judgment and intuition of the true artist. The strength, simplicity, and instinctive

Title page of *Etlich Christlich lider* of 1524, the first Lutheran hymn book, containing eight hymns with five melodies, together with the first hymn text and melody "Nun freut euch, lieben Christen gmein."

rightness of his melodic treatment were complemented by an equally creative linguistic talent. These unique gifts were to produce the prototype of the Lutheran chorale.

The Lutheran chorale. Most of the 36 chorales ascribed with certainty to Luther were apparently written in the period 1523—24. The first Protestant hymnal, known as *Achtliederbuch* (Nuremberg, 1523—24), contains four of his chorales, three by Paulus Speratus and an anonymous two-part setting of "In Jesu Namen heben wir an." It was followed by a number of larger hymn books. The most important of these include the Erfurt *Enchiridion* (1524), Koepphel's *Deutsch Kirchenamt* (Strasbourg, 1525), the *Klugsche Gesangbuch* (first, lost edition, Wittenberg, 1529), and the *Bapstsche Gesangbuch* (Leipzig, 1545), all of which reached several successive editions. Illustrating the geographical spread of Lutheranism during this period are such other sites of hymnal publication as Breslau, Zwickau, Leipzig, Augsburg, and Zurich. Luther's direct or indirect influence in these various hymnals is reflected in a basic core of hymns, usually consisting of his own, in addition to chorales by "others among us," "by faithful Christians who have lived before our time," and of "Varia." A certain independence displayed by publishing centers in the South and the adoption of Michael Weisse's hymnal of the Bohemian Brethren (Jungenbunzlau, 1531) in Strasbourg (1534—36) and Ulm (1539) were quite consistent with Luther's intent.

This unified character of early Lutheran hymnody was somewhat diffused in the latter part of the century. Second-generation hymnals reflect a subtle shift of emphasis. The vacuum in leadership left by Luther's death, the uneasy peace of Augsburg, intra-Lutheran theological disputes (Philippists *vs.* Gnesiolutherans), and the dual threat posed by the Council of Trent and spreading Reformed influence effected a gradual tempering of evangelical militancy by humanistic, conciliatory sentiments.

Martin Agricola's *Sangbuechlein aller Sonntagsevangelien* (1541), Nikolaus Herman's *Sonntagsevangelien ueber das ganze Jahr* (1560), Keuchenthal's *Kirchengesaenge lateinisch und deutsch* (1573), and the comprehensive hymnals of Cyriakus Spangenberg (Eisleben, 1568), Johann Wolff (Frankfurt, 1569), Valentin Fuhrmann (Nuremberg, 1569), greatly enlarged editions of earlier hymnals, and many similar publications illustrate a trend toward encyclopedic compilations, often supplied with voluminous regional appendices and organized according to special designations (devotional, educational, children's songs).

Two pages from the tenor part book of Georg Rhau's *Neue deutsche geistliche Gesaenge...fuer die gemeinen Schulen* of 1544 showing melodies of motets by Stephan Mahu, Ludwig Senfl, and Balthasar Resinarius.

The instant popularity of the Lutheran chorale in church, home, and school is traceable to the surefootedness of Luther and of his collaborators in selecting, assimilating, and adapting preexistent texts and tunes in order to augment the relatively small stock of original chorales. They drew freely on pre-Reformation Latin hymns (a few of these Marian), some sequences, Latin or macaronic pilgrim, folk and school songs, German *Leisen*, and *Lieder* from such sources as Minnesinger, Meistersinger, Crusaders, and flagellant orders. Texts at variance with Lutheran theology were "improved in a Christian manner" and many Latin hymns were translated into a vibrant vernacular often requiring corresponding musical alterations. Finally, *contrafacta*—applied to tunes as well as texts—abound.

The polyphonic chorale and motet. "It is not my opinion that on behalf of the Gospel all arts should be trampled underfoot to perish. . . . Rather, I should like to see all the arts, especially music, in the service of Him who has given and created them," Luther wrote by way of authorizing the first edition of the *Wittenberg Geystliches gesangk Buchleyn* (Wittenberg, 1524; five successively enlarged editions, 1525—51). Containing 38 German and 5 Latin three- to five-part settings by his collaborator, Johann Walter (1496—1570), it inspired an impressive number of choral publications. Among these, the *Neue deutsche geistliche Gesaenge* (1544) of publisher-composer Georg Rhau (1488—1548), the *Concentus novi trium vocum* (1540) of Koenigsberg cantor Hans Kugelmann (d. 1542), and the *Geistliche und weltliche deutsche Gesaenge* (1566) of Dresden kapellmeister Mattheus Le Maistre (c. 1505—77) offer predominantly German chorale settings and motets, including the novel, specifically Protestant psalm motet.

Owing to the interconfessional nature and liturgical significance of Latin art music, Catholics and Protestants shared a large body of pre-Reformation and Reformation literature. Among the many manuscript and printed anthologies are Rhau's *Selectae harmoniae de Passione Domini* (1538), *Symphoniae jucundae atque adeo breves* (1538), *Officia Paschalia de Resurrectione at Ascensione Domini* (1539), *Vesperarum precum officia,* (1540) *Opus decem missarum* (1541), *Tricinia* (1542), *Sacrorum hymnorum liber primus* (1542), *Postremum vespertini officii opus* (1544), *Bicinia* (1545), and *Officiorum de nativitate, circumcisione, epiphania domini . . . tomus primus* (1545).

The German and particularly the Latin polyphonic repertoire of the Lutheran church owes its stylistic variegation—ranging from modified late medieval linearity to homorhythmic and homophonic Renaissance simplicity—to Luther's ecumenical attitude toward the arts and the musical profession. The long list of contributors includes, in addition to the aforementioned composers, such distinguished masters as the Netherlanders Isaac, Josquin, Lasso, Lupus Hellinck, Clemens non Papa, the German Catholics Stoltzer, Senfl, Mahu, Arnold von Bruck, the Lutherans Sixtus Dietrich of Constance, Balthasar Resinarius of Boehmisch-Leipa, and a number of minor composers.

Liturgical and performance practices. Luther's *Ordnung Gottesdiensts* and *Formula missae et communionis* of 1523 retain essentially intact the mass (cleansed of the *canon missae*), Matins, and Vespers. At first, Latin was used exclusively and congregational hymns were added (not substituted) in the mass only. With the publication of his *Deutsche Messe* (1526) he provided the further option of a German service. However, being primarily concerned that "it must be done in a manner furthering the Word," he consistently refrained from imposing specific rubrics. This flexible approach resulted in countless local and regional *Kirchenordnungen*. Lucas Lossius' *Psalmodia, hoc est Cantica sacra veteris ecclesiae selecta*, printed in at least four editions between 1553 and 1579 and prefaced by Melanchthon, attempts to order and clarify the accumulated liturgical materials. Characterized by great latitude of liturgical and musical practice, these orders of service reflected three basic options which, in turn, allowed for a variety of combinations: all-Latin, all-German, mixed-language services; congregational chorale(s) and/or selection(s) added to or substituted for Latin and German hymns or portions of recited liturgical prose.

Since the hymnals of the day were intended for pastors, cantors, and schools rather than for the people, unaccompanied unison singing of memorized congregational chorales was facilitated by school children distributed over the seating area of the church. The rhythmically complex tenor-*cantus firmi* of polyphonic settings ruled out their use as accompaniment by the choir. (Organ accompaniment did not develop until the 17th century.) Thus, Walter's caustic reference to "the wild, donkey-like braying of the chorale"—even assuming the possibility of simplified congregational tune versions—may be fairly accurate. However, the universal custom of singing all stanzas of a chorale encouraged lively *alternatim* practice involving choir and congregation. Meuslin reports *vicissim* and *alternatim* use of instruments, organ, and choir for congregational singing in Eisenach and Wittenberg as early as 1535. Limited soloistic organ participation may also be inferred from the relatively small number of chorale settings contained in 16th-century tablatures, which, with few exceptions, are arrangements of choral compositions. On the other hand, Bugenhagen's and Jonas' service orders peremptorily forbid the use of organs.

Congregational hymns in lieu of chanted or polyphonically sung ordinary portions of the service quickly became popular, particularly in small and rural churches. In city churches, German and Latin choral polyphony dominated Vespers and Matins, but proper and ordinary parts of the *Messe* were more equally apportioned between choir and congregation. Increasing Latinization and gradual infringement by choirs on congregational singing toward the end of the century may well have been subjects of concern to Lucas Osiander (1534—1604); his purpose in publishing *Fuenfftzig geistliche Lieder und Psalmen* (1586) was to "set them in such manner [homophonic four-part choral texture, *cantus firmus* in descant, i.e., "cantional" style] that an entire Christian congregation can sing along throughout." Stylistically a logical extension of the Huguenot psalm, this first modern *Choralbuch* signals the beginning of a new era.

Music of the Reformed Churches

Although Jean Calvin (1509—64) owed a certain degree of musical literacy to his humanistic education, he was not himself a practicing musician. His interpretation of music as "a gift of God," contrary to that of Luther, was dogmatically restrictive. In the preface to the 1543 edition of Marot's Psalter, he reasoned that "we must be the more assiduous in so controlling music that it may be useful to us and in no manner harmful . . .

as it has a secret and nearly incredible power to move our hearts." Narrowing the field of acceptable musical practice to singing only, he called for "songs, not merely sincere but also holy." To satisfy such requirements "no better songs" could be found "than the Psalms of David." The world should accept these "instead of the vain, frivolous, stupid, dull, foul, vile, evil, and pernicious songs used heretofore." Besides thus distinguishing between sacred and profane, Calvin also relegated sacred art music to the sphere of household devotions, reserving for the service strictly unaccompanied unison singing of vernacular psalms.

The French Psalter. The first Calvinist songbook, *Aulcuns pseaulmes et cantiques mys en chant* (Strasbourg, 1549) contained 19 versified psalms with 18 melodies, the canticle of Simeon, and a decalog hymn as well as a translation of the Apostolic Creed. Calvin had contributed the text versions of the two canticles, the Creed, and six psalms, Clement Marot those of the remaining 13 psalms. Theodore Beza, Calvin's second most important text collaborator, continued the briefly interrupted task of versification after Marot's death in 1544. Concluding a series of at least six partial psalter publications, the first complete Genevan Psalter (1562) was issued simultaneously in Paris, Lyon, Geneva, and several other places. By 1565 a total of 63 additional printings, presumably reaching every Calvinist household, had been distributed. This success, unique in the history of hymnals, is stylistically attributable to the close congruence between melody and freely flowing poetic word rhythm. Invariably syllabic, the eminently singable Genevan psalm tunes were forged from a small yet versatile core of predominantly modal and economically patterned poly- and isorhythmic elements by such melodists as Guillaume Franc, Louis Bourgeois, and Pierre Dagues. Owing, perhaps, to Calvin's rejection of secular *contrafacta*, only the more or less obvious Strasbourg origin of some 15 tunes is demonstrable to date. Most of the other tunes appear to be adaptations from Gregorian models and, possibly, later folk sources. In accordance with Calvin's *La forme des prieres* (1542), one psalm was to be sung with the aid of school children at the beginning of Sunday service. Later, psalm singing before and after the sermon was added in Sunday and midweek services.

Polyphonic Settings. The *Pseaulmes cinquante* (Lyons, 1547) of Louis Bourgeois (1510—61) was the first of many psalm collections designated for use in the home that were to be published in the two ensuing decades. The two outstanding contributors to this popular genre, Claude Goudimel

(1510—72) and Philibert Jambe de Fer (d. 1572)—both victims of the massacre of St. Bartholomew's Eve, were joined by Pierre Certon, Didier Lupi Second, Clement Janequin, Jacques Arcadelt, and others. Their simple homophonic settings featuring the Genevan melodies in the tenor of predominantly four-part textures are complemented by an impressive body of equally popular highly polyphonic three- to eight-part literature. Next to Bourgeois and Goudimel, Claude Le Jeune (1528—1600), Pascal de L'Estocart (1540—?), Lasso, and others explored and cultivated such forms as the sectional and through-composed psalm motet and the *chanson spirituelle*. Lastly, the degree of popularity that the Genevan Psalters achieved in French society during the second half of the century may be measured by the existence of several volumes of psalm intabulations for lute and related instruments, prepared by Gorlier, Brayssing, and other composer-arrangers.

Reformed Music in the Netherlands, Germany, and Switzerland. In the Netherlands, early Lutheran and Anabaptist Reform attempts were gradually absorbed by spreading Calvinist influence. Massive immigration of French Calvinist refugees, Guy de Bray's Geneva-inspired Belgic Confession (1561), the formation of secret synods, and the official adoption by the Dordrecht Synod (1578) of Petrus Dathenus' translation of the Genevan Psalter mark the northward expansion of Calvinism. The Dathenus Psalter eventually displaced the *Souderliedekens*—indigenous, pre-Reform vernacular psalm texts fitted to secular folk tunes—in spite of their popularity, which between 1540 and 1613 produced 33 mostly monophonic editions (among them, however, Clemens non Papa's three-part settings of 1556—57).

In Germany, Calvinism was able to exert equally strong influence only in the Palatinate, as evidenced by the Heidelberg Catechism (1563) and the Palatinate service order of the same year. Elsewhere, particularly in Southern Germany and Northern Switzerland, interpenetrating Lutheran and Reformed approaches are reflected in the polyphonic psalm collections by Johannes Heugel, Burkhard Waldis, and others as well as in Johann Zwick's *Neues Gesangbuechlein* (Zurich, 1540), the Bonn Gesangbuch (1550), and the various Strasbourg and similar hymnals. The Lutheran Koenigsberg scholar Ambrosius Lobwasser's translation of the Genevan Psalter (Leipzig, 1573) and Goudimel's harmonizations of 1565 attained countless printings into the 19th century.

Zwingli's Switzerland had abolished all music in the church. However, congregational psalm singing is reported as early as 1526 and 1527 respectively for Basel, reformed by Oecolampadius, and Dominik Zili's St. Gallen, where the first Swiss hymnal was to be published in 1533. In 1598, the first Swiss edition of Lobwasser's Psalter, a monodic edition, was printed in Zurich. Congregational singing in all of German-speaking Switzerland became customary only in the 17th century. Likewise, continental 16th-century Reformed church music did not entail the use of organ or other instruments, notwithstanding some isolated reports of organ playing preceding the service. GK

Readings: Blume, Friedrich, *Protestant Church Music* (New York, 1974); *Luther's Works,* American ed., vol. 53: *Liturgy and Hymns,* ed. Ulrich Leupold (Philadelphia, 1965); Pratt, Waldo Seldon, *The Music of the French Psalter of 1562* (New York, 1939); Grimm, Harold J., *The Reformation Era* (New York, 1973).

See also: alternation practice; cantional, cantional style; chant, Gregorian; chorale; chorale, vocal settings; contrafacta; hymnody, German; hymnody, Scandinavian; Leisen; organ, use in the mass and offices; Renaissance instruments; theology of church music, Reformers

Music of the English Church

As a result of Reformation influences, the music of the English Church changed only gradually from the Latin forms of the Sarum liturgy to the vernacular forms of the Anglican liturgy. Although the spirit of reformation had its origins as early as John Wycliffe (1329—84), the Reformation era properly encompasses the time-span between the Tudor King Henry VIII's break with the papacy (1534) and the publication of the Book of Common Prayer in its final form in 1662. Central to an understanding of the church music of this period, however, is a discussion of the Book of Common Prayer and the distinction between cathedral and parish music.

The Book of Common Prayer

The impulse for liturgical reform in England had its roots in a movement to provide a vernacular Bible for the laity. The Royal Injunctions of 1536 required that every parish possess a copy of Coverdale's translation of the Bible. With the accession of Edward VI in 1547 the pace of reformation was accelerated, and an English Order of Communion was issued by Royal Proclamation in 1548. The most important single event of the English Reformation, however, was the passage of the first Act of Uniformity in 1549, which directed that the *Booke of Common Praier,* published in that year, was the only liturgical book to be used throughout the realm.

Although Latin was permitted in the College Chapels, the first Prayer Book directed that elsewhere all of the liturgical texts, both sung and spoken, must be in English. If sung, such texts should be set syllabically, *i.e.*, "for every syllable a note." The first musical setting of the Prayer Book to exemplify these principles appeared in 1550 as the *Booke of Common Praier Noted* prepared by John Merbecke (c. 1510—85). A second revised edition in 1552, however, quickly made Merbecke's initial work obsolete.

With the accession of Mary I in 1553 the Prayer Book was repealed and Latin rites were restored in the English churches. When Elizabeth I came to power in 1558, a new Act of Uniformity was issued along with another revised version of the 1552 Prayer Book. The 1559 edition then served as normative until James ascended the throne in 1603. Noteworthy events in the Jacobean period include another revised Prayer Book in 1604 and the Authorized Version of the Bible in 1611.

Under Puritan rule the Prayer Book was banned in 1645, and it its place the *Directory for the Plain Worship of God in the Three Kingdoms* was instituted. It was not until the Restoration of Charles II in 1660 that the Prayer Book was again used in the English Church. A final 1662 version then served as the only official service book of the Church of England for the next 300 years.

Parish Music

Perhaps the main reason that Merbecke's *Booke of Common Praier Noted* (1550) was not immediately revised or imitated stems from the fact that congregational singing of the liturgy was antithetical to 16th-century cathedral practice. The English cathedrals had long enjoyed choir schools and trained choirs to provide polyphonic music for their services. The congregation did not participate musically. The reformers, however, stressed simple music and liturgy that the people not only could understand but sing. Their musical ideals then found expression much more readily in the parishes rather than in the cathedrals, and in metrical psalters rather than in liturgy.

Like the 16th-century Lutheran hymnals, the 16th-century English psalters served multiple functions in church, school, and home. Some psalters included texts only; some were cast in tune-text format; and others offered polyphonic settings with the psalter tune in the tenor, or later, soprano. Some were clearly designed for congregational singing; some were primarily intended for private use; and others were best suited to a choral-instrumental ensemble.

One of the earliest collections to include metrical psalm tunes was Miles Coverdale's *Goostly psalmes and spirituall songes* (1539/40). This collection, however, was banned by Henry VIII in 1546. The first complete English metrical psalter appeared in 1549, the year of the first Act of Uniformity. This collection by Robert Crowley also has the distinction of being the first to contain harmonized settings of the psalter tunes.

A much more modest 1549 collection, however, was destined to become the standard psalter for English Protestants. Authored by Thomas Sternhold the first edition contained only 19 Psalms. By 1562, however, the Sternhold and Hopkins psalter—*The Whole Book of Psalms*—contained all 150 Psalms in metrical verse set to 47 different tunes. The first harmonized edition of the Sternhold and Hopkins psalter was issued the following year, 1563, by John Day. Day's collection was only the first of countless publications issued during the Reformation era that incorporated words and/or music from the Sternhold and Hopkins psalter.

Collections not based on the Sternhold and Hopkins model were also produced during the Reformation era. Several are particularly noteworthy because they included hymns of the leading composers of the period. Archbishop Matthew Parker's psalter, *The whole Psalter Translated into English metre*, was printed in 1567 and included nine settings by Thomas Tallis (c. 1501—85). George Wither's *The Hymnes and Songs of the Church* (1623) is significant not only for its inclusion of hymns by Orlando Gibbons (1583—1625), but for the introduction of freely-composed hymns not drawn from the Psalms. The hymns of Henry Lawes (1602—45) appear not only in George Sandys' *A Paraphrase upon the Psalmes of David* (1636), but in *Choice Psalmes put into musick* (1648), a collection published by Lawes himself.

Cathedral Music

It was in the cathedrals rather than in the parishes that the monuments of English church music came into being. Services sung daily as well as on Sundays required not only trained singers but a wealth of choral literature in various forms. As the major institution requiring music, the cathedrals also required the services of the best composers of the period. Chief among the liturgical forms found in the works of the 16th- and 17th-century English composers were Services and anthems.

A polyphonic setting of the Communion Service was simply called a Service; likewise polyphonic settings of the canticles for Morning and Evening Prayer are known as Services. If, however, all three Services are composed as a related group in the same key, they are referred to as a Full Service. Services are further distinguished on the basis of musical complexity. A Service written in polyphonic style is called a Great Service. A Service written in homophonic, syllabic style is referred to as a Short Service. Major composers of Services include Thomas Tallis, William Mundy (c. 1530—91), William Byrd (1543—1623), Thomas Tomkins (1572—1656), Thomas Weelkes (c. 1575—1623), and Orlando Gibbons (1583—1625).

Although the English anthem is in many respects a musical counterpart to the Latin motet, the anthem is freer with respect to its liturgical usage. In early Anglican worship the anthem followed the third collect at Morning and Evening Prayer. By the end of the Reformation era two anthems were commonly sung at Morning and Evening Prayer, the second coming after the sermon. Although the anthem generally used imitative counterpoint, the text was usually set syllabically in keeping with Reformation principles of textual declamation. Toward the end of the 16th century a modification appeared in the form of the verse anthem. As opposed to the strictly choral presentation of the full anthem, the verse anthem contained solo sections that alternated with choral sections, the whole being supported by instruments or organ. Noteworthy composers of the anthem include Christopher Tye (c. 1500—73), Thomas Tallis, William Byrd, Thomas Tomkins, Thomas Weelkes, and Orlando Gibbons.

Lesser liturgical forms found among the works of the late 16th- and early 17th-century composers include Psalms, Preces, Responses, and Litanies. Initially adapted to Sarum melodies, these forms increasingly appeared in Anglican Chant format, especially for festival occasions. Some of the more prolific composers of Psalms, Preces, Responses, and Litanies include Thomas Tallis, William Byrd, Orlando Gibbons, and Adrian Batten (c. 1590—c. 1637).

The use of instruments in the worship services of the period 1549—1600 is problematic. Although countenanced at the Chapel Royal and the cathedrals during the reign of Elizabeth I, organs, for example, were banned and even destroyed during the period of the Commonwealth. The extant organ literature reveals forms that would have been useful primarily in Catholic services—plainsong arrangements, verses for hymn alternation, and verses for use in alternation in certain portions of the Mass. Only the organ Voluntary enjoyed a long period of development, primarily for use in the Anglican Service. HM

Readings: Fellowes, Edmund H., *English Cathedral Music*, 5th rev. ed. (London, 1969); Le Huray, Peter, *Music and the Reformation in England 1549—1660* (New York, 1967); Long, Kenneth R. *The Music of the English Church* (New York, 1971); Stevens, Denis, *Tudor Church Music,* 2d ed. (New York, 1966); Wienandt, Elwyn A., *Choral Music of the Church* (New York, 1965).

See also: alternation practice; anthem; canticle; chant, Anglican; decani/cantoris; hymnody, English; metrical psalmody; organ, use in the mass and offices; Service; voluntary

church music history, baroque

Baroque church music can be rather conveniently located in a period beginning with the conscious innovation of new styles around 1600 and ending with the death of J. S. Bach in 1750. The modern church musician finds baroque church music history instructive because it reveals a struggle much like that facing the church today, the struggle to come to grips with new, progressive forces in musical style and still remain faithful to an ecclesiastical heritage. Baroque church music may thus be seen as resulting from two factors: (1) the musical requirements of the various confessional traditions; (2) the development of style along new principles. Four major traditions may be defined: Roman Catholic, Reformed, Lutheran, and Anglican. It should also be noted that baroque music was not confined to Europe but found its way to the New World, especially in Latin American Roman Catholic music and in the simple church music (fuguing tunes) of the English colonies.

Baroque church music text, style, and sound reflect three major characteristics, all of which were shared by the music world of the time: *sensitivity to text, sensitivity to style,* and *sensitivity to sound.* First, it was sensitivity to the text that led Italian intellectuals of the late 16th and early 17th centuries, especially the Florentine camerata, to develop a style of music that would equal the power of expression they believed ancient Greek music once possessed. The principal forms reflecting this new feeling centered on the use of the solo voice in recitative and song. Second, the rise of the new style made composers sensitive to a divergence of styles. In its most basic form this divergence was the subject of a dispute between the Italian composer Claudio Monteverdi (1567—1643) and the theorist Artusi in the first decade of the 17th century. Monteverdi justified his use of bold dissonance by defining a "first practice" (*prima prattica*) and a "second practice" (*seconda prattica*), also termed respectively *stile antico—stile moderno, stylus gravis—stylus luxurians*. The point here is not so much the nature of the new style as the fact that composers recognized the existence of two styles and felt themselves free to compose in either one. This picture of baroque church music practice is not complete without remembering that the older polyphonic repertoire (*prima prattica*) coexisted with the newer music and may even have been more frequently heard. In Bach's time, older works from the 16th century remained in the Leipzig choir's library and were regularly sung according to long-standing custom. Third, sensitivity to sound manifested itself in the practice known as "concertato" style, the polychoral style, and the increasingly idiomatic use of instruments, especially by a Venetian school of composers associated with St. Mark's Cathedral under Andrea and Giovanni Gabrieli and later Claudio Monteverdi.

The Roman Catholic Tradition

The progress of baroque innovation through the European lands begins in the Roman Catholic South, especially Italy. Official church music was centered in the mass and the office as revised under the aegis of the Council of Trent (1545—63). Mass and motet composition continued to maintain some of the older polyphonic forms of the Renaissance, as seen even in the work of Monteverdi. The style of Palestrina was perpetuated by later generations and finally distorted into a mechanical method of polyphonic virtuosity. The expressive power of the newly discovered Florentine monody left its mark, however. One of the first examples of the new style occurs in the motets for 1-5 voices of Ludovico Grossi da Viadana (1564—1627), the *Concerti ecclesiastici* of 1602, transitional compositions employing solo voices in the new "concerted" style. In addition to such sacred monody, smaller compositions for the liturgy were also written with instruments and produced a repertoire of exceptionally ornate character.

Larger, ensembles, however, were influenced to imitate the massive effects achieved by Giovanni Gabrieli (c. 1557—1612) and Andrea Gabrieli

(c. 1520—86) in Venice. This produced a "colossal" style of church music by employing polychoral and concertato techniques. With these devices the composer could achieve contrasting effects by alternating the various musical forces included in the whole ensemble. Monteverdi's Vespers, for example, are music of such grandeur that they are still striking to the ear of the modern listener.

A somewhat different situation developed around a group of composers in Rome who adapted a more conservative style as opposed to some of the new techniques. They thus produced polychoral compositions for up to 10 or 12 separate choirs, such as the mass by Orazio Benevoli (1605—72) consisting of 50 separate voices parts, 16 vocal and 34 instrumental, written to dedicate the cathedral at Salzburg in 1628.

Later in the 17th century the nonliturgical *oratorio* (or *istoria*) became popular. Based on the singing of sacred songs *(laude)* in semiprivate devotional meetings in a prayer hall *(oratoria)*, the new form of music developed as a combination of baroque recitative, aria, and arioso. The oratorio was a narrative form based on Biblical or sacred stories, Old Testament subjects receiving particularly frequent attention. In this respect it was much like opera, except that oratorio more often included a narrator *(testo)*. A number of composers distinguished themselves in this form, although the best-known is Giacomo Carissimi (1605—74). Gradually the oratorio developed a fuller use of the chorus, the *aria da capo* of the opera, and the harmonic richness of the later baroque and reached an artistic peak in the Passion settings of J. S. Bach and the oratorios of G. F. Handel.

Organ music in baroque Italy was largely devoted to incidental music for the mass. Girolamo Frescobaldi (1583—1643) wrote toccatas full of dissonance and chromaticism to be played, for example, during the Communion. In addition, Italian composers wrote intonations, freely improvised preludes, or variations (again often improvised) on a Gregorian *cantus firmus*. Instrumental ensembles were developed in the sonatas or concertos written for the church. The city of Bologna is especially noteworthy for a well-developed style of instrumental music for processions or other civic-religious events. The *sonate de chiesa* (church sonatas) of Arcangelo Corelli (1653—1713) are so termed less for the particular style of composition they represented than for the fact that they were performed in the church.

Roman Catholic France found its music, with few exceptions, centered in the royal court at Paris; and its sacred music history can be traced in the works performed there, primarily during the reign of Louis XIV. The French motet developed as a piece for solo voices, instruments, and large choruses alternating in either large (*grand*) or small (*petit*) scaled compositions. The principal composers in the newer style were Henry Dumont (1610—84) and Jean Baptiste Lully (1632—67), the musical arbitrator of French tastes in mid-17th century. In spite of French resistance to Italian influence, the later motets of Michel-Richard Delalande (1657—1726) and the oratorios by Marc-Antoine Charpentier (1634—1704) show a fully developed use of harmonic color, luxuriant counterpoint, and instrumental idioms found in late baroque music.

The Reformed Tradition

The Reformed areas of Europe do not present nearly the same degree of music activity as found in the Roman Catholic South. This is due to the discouragement of any music in the liturgy except the singing of metrical Psalms. As a result, church music in Calvinist areas such as the Netherlands was largely restricted to the elaboration or variation of those Psalm tunes. Jan Pieterszoon Sweelinck (1562—1621) rose above these restrictions in his masterful variations for the organ and became the teacher of a whole generation of Northern European organists.

The Lutheran Tradition

The Lutheran North of Europe, primarily Germany, developed a very rich tradition of church music for two main reasons. First, Lutheran liturgical tradition preserved the full mass, purified doctrinally, and added to that the practice of congregational hymn singing. Second, orthodox Lutheranism insisted on openness to all styles of music as appropriate for the praise of God. There was, moreover, a strongly structured music institution, the *Kantorei*, within which church musicians could find security in the exercise of their craft.

The German baroque can be said to begin around the turn of the 17th century with the works of Michael Praetorius (1571—1621). His *Musae Sioniae,* in nine volumes published 1605—10, deals not only with simple four-part hymn settings but includes magnificent compositions in the style of the Venetian composers. This example was followed by a number of important Lutheran composers of the time, notably Johann Hermann Schein (1586—1612), Samuel Scheidt (1587—1654), and Hans Leo Hassler (1564—1612).

The outstanding influence during the 17th century, however, was Heinrich Schuetz (1585—1672), who consciously sought to reorganize German church music to include the newer types of music which he, in a manner typical of North European composers, had gone to Italy to study. In addition to the grandiose Venetian style, Schuetz skillfully inculcated the Italian sensitivity for the text into concerted music for the Lutheran church; in so doing, he ushered in a new treatment of Biblical and liturgical texts. He used chromaticism, expressive solo passages, and word painting to express the text rather than to present it objectively. In addition, Schuetz offered magnificent polychoral motets in his *Psalmen Davids* (1619), more conservatively styled motets in the *Cantiones sacrae* (1625), music for smaller ensembles in the *Kleine geistliche Konzerte* in several volumes (1636—39), and a German form of concertato style in the several parts of his *Symphoniae sacrae* (I-1628/29; II-1647; III-1650). Above all, however, Schuetz is remembered for his masterful settings of the Passions, written toward the end of his life, in a style that fused the older Gregorian tradition with the dramatic power of baroque style.

The choir of the Dresden court under Heinrich Schuetz.

At the same time that Schuetz and his contemporaries were fusing the older German Lutheran traditions with the newer Italian styles into chorale concertato and choral motet, composers such as Andreas Hammerschmidt (1639—75), Johann Hermann Schein, Johann Crueger (1598—c. 1662), and Georg Ebeling (1620—76) wrote music for smaller churches, sometimes following the older cantional style and including parts for one or two descanting instruments.

The chorale concertatos and motets in later periods of the baroque began to include more movements for soloists and instrumental ritornelli and bore the title "cantata." In the works of Dietrich Buxtehude (c. 1637—1707), Johann Kuhnau (1660—1722), Friedrich Zachow (1663—1712), and Johann Pachelbel (1653—1706) German choral music developed a background for the magnificent cantatas of J. S. Bach, which reflected the reform efforts by which Lutheran composers strove to assimilate the innovations of late baroque Italian opera. Such operatic elements included the *aria da capo*, the instrumental sinfonia, and the recitative.

Organ music was especially well developed in Germany. During the early baroque era the organ was used chiefly in alternation with the congregation in presenting the chorales, and in improvising on stanzas of the hymn or on alternate verses of such liturgical pieces as the Magnificat. One of the first collections of chorale music for organ is contained in Samuel Scheidt's *Tabulatura nova* (1620), which contained simple harmonizations as well as fugues and variations. Scheidt, as well as Heinrich Scheidemann (c. 1596—1663), Johann Christoph Bach (1642—1703), and others had used a style of variation learned from Sweelinck.

Toward the end of the 17th century two distinct schools of organists were recognizable. The North German organists centered around figures like Franz Tunder (1614—67), Nikolaus Bruhns (1665—97), Georg Boehm (1661—1773), Adam Reinken (1623—1722), and the great master Dietrich Buxtehude. This group developed the toccata to new levels of virtuosity, including in it fugue-like sections that would crystallize into the preludes and fugues of J. S. Bach. Chorale settings were used as preludes, for alternating stanzas, or in sets of variations and were given their most advanced form in this period. A Central German school (sometimes grouped with the South German Catholic organists) centered on the work of Johann Pachelbel. Pachelbel has left a large number of Magnificat fugues, chorale variations, and chorale preludes that are stylistically akin to the Italianate figuration of composers such as Georg Muffat (1645—

Illustration from Johann Gottfried Walther's *Musikalisches Lexicon,* published in Leipzig in 1732, depicting instrumentalists, organist, and a conductor of the period.

1704) and Murschhauser in Austria. All these influences converge in the works of Bach.

The Anglican Tradition

Anglican church music in the baroque period presents a rather checkered picture. This is due, in part, to English reliance on the older styles of music till well into the 17th century, the low esteem for music generated in the later 17th century, the restriction of hymn singing to Reformed Psalm settings, the dismantling of music establishments under the Puritan Commonwealth, and the lack of a strong native music tradition after the Restoration in 1660.

The composers of the Restoration who are worthy of note (e.g., Blow, Cooke, Humfrey, Locke, Purcell) are almost all associated with the Chapel Royal under Charles II and often received their training in France or fell under Italian influence. The principal forms of English church music are Services and anthems. A Service is a collection of settings of the canticles, Psalms, or other texts for worship, especially including Morning or Evening Prayer. Anthems are either "full" anthems (for the choir alone) or "verse" anthems (alternating sections for soloists and choir). Anthems are basically motets with English texts, although composers came to prefer a homophonic style for anthems. This is apparent in the works of the greatest English composer, Henry Purcell (1659—95), who exploited such textures by introducing harmonic dissonance and altered chords for expressive purposes. Instrumental sections were added to the anthems so that they began to approximate in form the disposition of movements of the German cantata. By the end of the baroque period, however, few major establishments of church music carried on a vital practice of the art. The best in the sacred repertoire was to be heard in the oratorios of composers like Handel, who produced masterpieces for commercial presentation on the stage. VG

Readings: Anthony, J. R., *French Baroque Music from Beaujoyeulx to Rameau* (New York, 1974); Blume, F., "The Age of Confessionalism," *Protestant Church Music* (New York, 1974); Bukofzer, M. F., *Music in the Baroque Era* (New York, 1947); Dearnley, C., *English Church Music 1650—1750* (New York and London, 1970); Le Huray, P., *Music and the Reformation in England 1549—1660* (New York, 1967).

See also: baroque instruments; cantata; canticle; cantional, cantional style; cantor; motet; organ chorale; Roman school; Service; theology of church music, Pietism and rationalism; thoroughbass

church music history, classic and romantic

Duration and general characteristics

The classic-romantic era, sometimes bifurcated for intensive investigation, is generally understood to have extended from about 1730 (a time characterized by the noticeable shift to gentle nuance and subtlety, by increased attention to melody, and by increased use of the so-called Sonata form as a structure of balance) to about 1910 (a transitional period marked by the death of Gustav Mahler in 1911 and the introduction of Igor Stravinsky's *Petrushka* in 1911). As a designation for an art period, "classic" was used already by Johann Christoph Schiller and Johann Wolfgang von Goethe. To denote truth, wholeness, and balance, the same characteristics were also recognized in music from that time, but the term was not used until much later.

E. T. A. Hoffmann (1776—1822) was one of the first to use the term "romantic" for music. For him and his contemporaries, it originally meant those characteristics common to a vernacular folk story that transpired in natural scenic locales and stressed the exotic.

The unity of the entire period developed not from perduring style characteristics, but from a prevailing attitude that was brought into existence, ultimately as a product of the Renaissance, by a reorientation of man's view of himself. The glorification of man and his artistic abilities led to the consideration of music, for the first time, as a thing existing for itself: art for art's sake. Jean J. Rousseau (1712—78) and other encyclopedists still held to the imitative task of music, but later representatives of the Enlightenment became convinced that the discipline of music needed to be unshackled from extraneous norms in order to liberate its natural beautiful simplicity, to be apprehended by the active participating listener. In this classic esthetic scheme meaning and emotion were not disregarded, but were valued as the next step beyond perception of melodic balance and form, a tenet illustrated by the gradual replacement of simultaneous contrast (baroque counterpoint) with consecutive melodic contrast (the multiple themes of the sonata). While the classicist reveled in the emotional experience derived from sheer musical logic, the romanticist was one who discovered that with effort and skill, the emotional experience could be predetermined and then imposed on the listener. The romanticist elevated the passivity of the listener and the mysterious powers of music. His awe for music's superhuman qualities gave the romanticist an accompanying fascination for the fantastic, the dim dark part, as well as a preoccupation with restlessness and longing.

Ultimately the history of church music during this time is a history of the church. Doctrinaire assertions from the enlightened and their spiritual children stressed people's self-declared liberation and challenged churchly supervision. Ecclesiastical reactions ran the gamut from a churchly partnership (J. J. Spaulding, 1714—1804, viewed reason as *the* gift of grace) to a belligerent assertion of clerical authority (Papal Infallibility doctrine of 1870). Every kind of churchly reaction has its musical counterpart, from concert oratorio to Caecilianism.

Throughout the period there is a crisscrossing of movements and countermovements. Within a span of 16 years, Franz Gruber wrote the popular folk song "Silent Night" (1818), the restorational *Prussian Agenda* appeared (1822), Giuseppe Baini published his epoch-making biography of Palestrina (1828), Felix Mendelssohn resurrected J. S. Bach's *St. Matthew Passion* (1829), Johann Christian Lobe condemned the fugue as worthless for the church (1831), and Franz Lizst issued his call for a new church music that was to be godly as well as political (1834). This kind of diversity characterized the whole era.

Reordering of the Church Music Practice

The church music enterprise during the classic-romantic era abounds with evidence indicating a fundamental transformation of traditional values. The purpose of church music was changing. At the middle of the 18th century, J. S. Bach still used the old formula: "To the glory of God and the recreation of my neighbor." Such sentiments were not very popular among his contemporaries. Newer views stressed the betterment of the individual's heart and the increase of his devotion and piety. The necessity for growth and piety was assumed; utopian societies, Kantian ethical imperatives, and Darwinian optimism were part of the age. Music helped to guide the soul towards its goal, toward the infinite. "In truth," says Jean Paul, an 18th-century literary figure, music's "accents are echoes, gathered by the angels from the joyous sounds of the second world" (Hesperus, 1795). Experience showed the person of the age that upbuilding of the spirit was generated by opera as well as church music. Hence, Doles (1790) recommended a lowering of the barriers between the two genres, a "lover of church music" five years later published a collection of Karl Ditters von Dittersdorf's operatic arias with sacred texts, and Johann C. Lobe (1852) extolled Etienne Mehul (1763—1817) as a better church composer than J. S. Bach. The aim of "beautifying worship" was concocted in this age, a logical and necessary step following the curtailment of traditional liturgical form among Lutherans. For Roman Catholics, the enhancement of the pious sentiment was a goal for the total observance of the mass; music's task, according to Charles Rosen (*The Classical Style*, p. 366), went from the expressive of previous eras to the celebrative, as the masses of Franz J. Haydn (1732—1809) and Wolfgang A. Mozart (1756—91) testify.

Redefinitions of the musical task led to a changing image of the cantor. The elevation of the musical art created frequent tensions in choir schools because administrators were forced into making choices between artistic excellence and theological training, a separation never before envisioned. Internal bickering was compounded by a growing feeling that the *Kantorei* was old-fashioned and its participants stiff and rigid. Most of the schools went out of existence by the turn of the century (Leipzig and Dresden being two exceptions), and the instrumentalists who were formerly employed for concerted church music sought out jobs with the popular city or military bands.

Set against this background, the cantor was forced to overcome his financial and professional handicaps (he was often held to be an equal with the custodian) by turning to supplementary nonchurch work. Prevailing values lent encouragement to this new self image, for genius and art were singled out to the gradual exclusion of dedication and calling. Mixing of musical duties, was of course not new. Court composers such as Orlando di Lasso (c. 1532—94) and Ludwig Senfl (c. 1492—1555) had always been challenged to write music for all kinds of occasions, but the difference rests in the fact that their later counterparts (e.g., Domenico Cimarosa, 1749—1801; Antonio Salieri, 1750—1825; Simon Mayr, 1763—1845) concerted their best efforts almost exclusively in the sphere of opera. When Richard Wagner (1813—83) became kapellmeister (literally, chapel master) at Dresden, the job meant for him chiefly the conducting and producing of opera.

The withdrawal of musical talent and energy from the church was often prompted by the termination of financial support; enlightened rulers, such as Joseph in Austria (1780—90), severely curtailed traditional support of the church and its activities. The impact of "Josephism" and similar programs was predictable: it pushed the professional church musician into more profitable enterprises. In Leipzig, one of J. S. Bach's successors at St. Thomas, Johann Hiller (1728—1804), busied himself with productions of minioperas (*Singspiel*). He also found it consonant with his task as cantor to write a *Stabat Mater* and other pieces not strictly Lutheran.

The French revolutionaries and their counterparts across Europe sought for the liberty and equality of all persons, and thereby provided motivation for the democratization of all culture including music. Already in 1782 Johann A. P. Schulz (1747—1800) promoted melodic formulas (*Volkstoen*) which he promised to be useful for writing truly popular (people's) music. The industrial revolution several years later yielded a technology to make possible the mass production of instruments and music. From then on, everyone could own and play a musical instrument. Instruction books abounded. Publishers found it beneficial by the middle of the 19th century to issue musical parallels to the art work of the Nazarenes and Pre-Raphaelites. Known later in the century as "kitsch," these pieces stressed the trivial, sentimental, and tasteless, so as to provide entertainment for the crowds of middle-class workers. As early as 1804 Karl F. Bahrot, a church musician, wrote an article calling for popularity in church music. But he merely urged what was already happening.

The last decades of the 18th century witnessed an influx of private hymnals as well as Friedrich Klopstock's *"Die Choere"* (1761), in which he upheld the ideal of a popular church music in a simple hymnic style. To that pattern composers came with the current hesitation to design anything too boisterous (the thin scorings unleashed the delicate sentiments), so the majority of Passions, cantatas, and motets during the century following Bach's death were in the uncomplicated style epitomized particularly by Carl H. Graun (1703—59) in his *Der Tod Jesu.* The dual criteria of simplicity and popularity also help to account for the flowering of spiritual folk songs from 1770 to 1850; J. D. Fach's "O du froehliche" and J. F. Mohr's "Stille Nacht" represent a phenomenon not unlike the grass-roots folklore of the very popular *Des Knaben Wunderhorn* (1805—08).

While the hymnic style was elevated, the fate of traditional hymnody appeared to be uncertain. Klopstock differentiated between a *Gesang* (hymn) and the *Lied* (song), recommending the latter as best for the common worshiper. According to his thinking, the *Lied* must move the heart of the hearer and contain religious teaching. Examples from the period show a preoccupation with nature and morality. Moreover, a contingent of poets set to work updating older hymns (e.g., "Ein feste Burg ist unser Gott/So sangen unsre Vaeter"). Texts were purged of linguistic, dogmatic, common-sense "embarrassments." Tunes were re-shaped to conform to an even but slow tempo ($\downarrow$ =m.m. 30). Triple meters were avoided as too dance-like. Chants for the pastor were re-notated for metered performance and were supplied with accompaniments, a practice common also among the Roman Catholics.

Decided stylistic changes also occured in organ composition. Among the advocates of simplicity there prevailed a bland hymnic style with little rhythmic or figurative interest. With the admirers of George (Abbé) Vogler (1749—1814) and of his pyrotechnical recital abilities, a more lively kind of organ writing was emerging as the music of the future. Vogler's imitations of the Manneheim orchestral style, use of expression devices, and design of unusual organ stops attracted the liberated seekers of the exotic and new, and influenced organ building for the remainder of the 19th century.

In Italy, France, and Austria Roman Catholic composers followed a course typical of Jacopo Perti of Bologna and of his student Padre Martini (1706—84), who numbered among his students both C. P. E. Bach (1714—88) and Mozart. While showing expertise in the baroque and late baroque styles (*stile moderno*), they continued the practice of writing also in a Palestrinian strain (*stile antico*). Others forged a path alongside contemporary opera, and created so-called number masses complete with *bel canto* arias (Niccolo Jomelli, 1714—74; Giovanni Paisiello, 1741—1816; and Tommaso Traetta, 1727—79). These pieces are barely known to the 20th-century listener, but they were logical outcomes of the era's ideals: church music that is popular, simple, celebrative, and uplifting. Together with the religious works of Haydn and Mozart, they may be viewed as predecessors of the concert masses of Hector Berlioz (1803—69), Johannes Brahms (1833—97), and Frederick Delius (1862—1934), works which are religious but hardly liturgical.

Emergence of a New Faith

Advocates of the enlightenment and romantic litterateurs suggested that their belief in art for art's sake was a part of a new faith that was an expansion of traditional Christian belief and an attractive alternative to the then-current Christian theologies and cults. As one of its chief doctrines, this new faith called for recognition of the godly apart from the usual ecclesiastical structures. "Nowadays, when the altar is trembling and tottering, when pulpit and religious ceremonies serve as subject matter for the mockers and skeptics, art must forsake the holy of holies, expand itself, and seek a stage for its magnificent manifestations in the world outside," wrote Franz Liszt in his 1834 essay on church music. He called for a new music that would be "humanistic," beyond the narrowly Christian, uniting both the theatre and the church. Merging the political and divine, and obfuscating certain entrenched notions of sacred and secular, disciples of the new faith set out to liberate music from within the walls of the churches and to accord all music its rightful divine status.

Rousseau laid the groundwork by elevating nature as worthy of man's adoration. Jean Paul invited the romanticist to seize eternity by losing himself in the infinity of beauty, while E. T. A. Hoffmann extolled music because it encapsuled the infinite. For prevailing restlessness and longing, romantics prescribed the quest for the infinite, a quest that would lead through mythology (hence Wagner) as well as traditional Christianity. Paul, Elijah, and Christ were appreciated by the romanticists as paradigms of eternal longing and fulfillment and were selected as fitting heroes for oratorio morality. The popularity of the Faust legend among romantic composers and *Paradise and Peri* by Robert Schumann (1810—56) reflect this preoccupation with the eternal.

According to the adherents of the new faith, their common quest was rewarded by momentary glimpses into the beyond. "The lyre of Orpheus opened the portals of Orcus," claimed Hoffman and with that he raised music to the level of a means of grace. Schopenhauer paraded it as a means of salvation; Ludwig von Beethoven (1770—1827), whom Schopenhauer championed, valued music's revelatory powers above all philosophy and wisdom, and for many romantics the ecstasy derived from its salvific powers was no better celebrated than in the finale of his 9th symphony, for them a paragon of a search fulfilled.

The new faith offered a new church. Its members consisted of those whose common search for the eternal through music cut across denominational as well as class lines. Truly ecumenical gatherings met in concert composed of both listeners and performers. Public concerts came to maturity during this era. Organized as early as 1725, the *Concerts spirituel* of Paris was one of the earliest concert series and significantly Pergolesi's *Stabat mater* was included in every year's fare after 1753. In Berlin, the *Singakadamie*—a performer's "parish" replacing the faltering Kantorei—presented public concerts after 1791. There were organizations such as the *Allgemeine Caecilienverein* (formed in 1868) and many little gatherings for amateur performers, particularly the male chorus, that also ventilated popular nationalistic and political loyalties.

Often these new worship gatherings appeared as displaced Christian services. In England, George F. Handel (1685—1759) established success with *Israel in Egypt* in 1739. His subsequent popularity in the concert hall was due to his acknowledged talent, but also to the moral grist he offered to the masses of evangelical opera-detesters. For the next seven decades his oratorios, particularly *Messiah*, and many others, such as Haydn's *Creation*, were performed in concert together with all the rituals of amateurism (truncated versions and barbarous crowds), sometimes even with homilies and offerings.

The search for the eternal went backwards as well as forwards. Out of it came a new tradition, formed not by teachers and theologians, but among other things from the musical practices of exotic Eastern cultures, forgotten heritages of Christian chant, and from pre-Christian myths of European nationalities. The *Dies irae* in its setting of the Requiem Mass appealed to the romantic's sense of the fantastic; this is why Berlioz tried to blast his way back to the medieval mind that conceived this Mass of the Dead. Giuseppe Verdi (1813—1901) and Charles Gounod (1818—93), among others, were also intrigued by the shuddering verities of the Last Judgment. Their Requiems are possibly borderline church music, as are the psalm compositions and *Missa solemnis* (1855) of Liszt.

Others, such as César Franck (1822—90) and Anton Bruckner (1824—96), offered clearer evidence of the attempts to produce liturgical church music. At the other end of the spectrum, Wagner activated the religious subconscious of his followers by resurrecting the ancient myths of Norse divinities. In his monumental *Der Ring des Nibelungen, Tristan,* and *Parzifal* he epitomized the faith of romanticism, and invited allegiance through intoxication, a formula which, when combined with 20th-century nationalism, was to have drastic global effects.

The new believers called forth their liturgies. Rubrics evolved for behavior in concert halls. Shrines were erected to house the religious experience; the rituals that developed at Wagner's opera house in Bayreuth attracted thousands of pilgrims, including such composers as Brahms, Bruckner, and Liszt. The new faith came to be served by a new clerical hierarchy. Though idolized as prophets, the composer class had to share religious honors with the increasingly popular traveling virtuoso— the new priests. Their technical capabilities—to the uninitiated thousands: hocus pocus—drew that awe and devotion previously associated with churchly personages.

In sum, the breadth of religious belief born in the enlightenment generated a gamut of religious music, from the Christian paraliturgical through the a-Christian to, perhaps, the antichristian. Throughout there are the marks of cultic music; this is why many viewed the unfolding of the entire classic-romantic musical enterprise as an integrated religious whole. Some were not so convinced; their hesitations led to a variety of pet programs and causes, but emanated from the common conviction that church people—Catholic and Protestant—could not court the cultural and political spirits of the day without reservation.

Reactionary Movements

Throughout the last half of the 18th century there were voices bemoaning the sad state of affairs in church music, especially in comparison with earlier years. Martin Gebhard, in his 1803 *Choralbuch*, warned organists against the use of favorite opera themes in public worship. Eleven years later E. T. A. Hoffmann observed that ever since Palestrina church music had experienced a steady downfall, so he advocated a rededication to "true" church music. Evaluations and reflections such as these were part of a larger religious revival, brought about by a resurgence of pietism, reactions against the enlightenment, and by attempts to regain hold on a long-lost pre-Napoleonic equilibrium, however idealized that might have been. But the real spark for renewal came from Klaus Harms, who in 1817, marking the anniversary of Martin Luther's Ninety-Five Theses, posted his own theses calling for reform and a return to the theology of the reformer.

From all sides, also from the backward-looking, thoroughbred romanticists, came the counsel to value the old as very helpful, useful, and worthy of imitation. For this reason, the American Lowell Mason advised the use of old church music, pointing out, to be sure, the "good taste" involved with such sympathy; in fact, the very term "old masters" is a product of this 19th-century mentality.

When King Wilhelm III was backing research into Reformation church orders in order to prepare for his *Agende* (1822), Roman Catholics were busy investigating 16th-century choral music in hopes of bringing to light that "true" church music hallowed already by the Council of Trent. In 1825, three years before Baini issued his monograph on Palestrina, Jacques Thibaut published a seminal book (*Ueber Reinheit der Tonkunst*) extolling the purity of the Roman choral style. In Bavaria, King Ludwig I commissioned Kaspar Ett to uncover the musical riches of the old masters. Dissemination of these works was aided by Karl Proske's multivolumed publication called *Musica Divina*. A movement came to life, one that erroneously advocated a cappella performance but quickly spread from

Bavaria to Austria, Switzerland, Belgium, Spain, France, England, and Italy, where the opera composer Gaspare Spontini (1774—1851) lent his influence to the crusade against operatic church music. Supporters banded together into local societies (Caecilian Societies, named after St. Caecilia, the patroness of music); they met for study and performance of the old music. Composers such as Edward A. Grell (1800—86), a Lutheran, and Heinrich Bellermann (1852—1903) attained great skill in imitating the pure Roman choral style, while Liszt (*Missa choralis*), Bruckner, and Joseph Rheinberger (1839—1901) were more successful in assimilating the tenets of the Caecilian promoters.

Caecilian influences were felt also among the Protestants. Karl von Winterfeld, who wrote a biography of Giovanni Gabrieli in 1834, suggested Johann Eccard (1523—1611) as the Lutheran counterpart for Palestrina. J. S. Bach's music was considered too concert-oriented, and it was argued that most could not be performed a cappella. While the a cappella aspects of the restoration movement had far-reaching effects in the influential collection of Ludwig Schoeberlein (*Schatz des liturgischen Chor- und Gemeindegesangs*) (1865—72), and in the compositions of Johannes Brahms, Otto Nicolai (1810—49), and Bernard Klein, some began to criticize its historicist narrowness. Friedrich Spitta complained that its adherents mistakingly included the chorales of Bach among the repertoires they were so zestfully promoting. Some years later, in 1897, Heinrich von Herzogenberg, student of Brahms, picked up the same concern and warned of prejudices held against the concerted music of Heinrich Schuetz and J. S. Bach.

Interest in the music of J. S. Bach had been generated years before. Johann Forkel published a bibliography of him in 1802, and in Berlin, Goethe's musical advisor, Friedrich Rochlitz, together with Carl Zelter, conductor and mentor for the *Singakadamie* developed extensive—albeit somewhat nationalistic—interest in Bach and his music, moving Felix Mendelssohn to engineer the "modern" performance of the *St. Matthew Passion* in 1829. Encouraged by this event, Johann Theodor Mosewius in Breslau mounted an effort to have the cantatas performed in church as well as in concert hall. The success of these ventures was due to increasing fascination with old music, but also to the religious readiness of people who were reacting to the enlightenment with a new Bible-oriented piety.

Mendelssohn's influence on the musical life at Leipzig and Berlin helped to create an atmosphere in which there was an ever-growing awareness of Bach's organ and vocal works. It was this understanding and devotion that was passed on by scholars such as Hugo Riemann (1849—1919) to his students, among whom was Max Reger (1873—1916), and by these late romantics to church musicians of the 20th century such as Karl Straube (1873—1950), Reger's friend and proponent.

In England the Oxford movement developed the kind of liturgical interest that invited a search for old musical treasures. Taking up the challenge, and being intent on restoring the old for practical use, John Stainer (1814—1901) and Harry Wooldridge (1845—1917) prepared anthologies of English medieval and renaissance music, while John Mason Neale (1818—66) set out to translate old Greek and Latin hymns for use in worship. Neale's work prompted similar ventures. In 1863 Catherine Winkworth issued her translation of German chorales and so set the pace for a flurry of hymn writing towards the end of the century.

French versions of the Cecilian movement centered in the establishment of several schools for formal study: Alexandre Choron's *Institution Royale* in 1817, Louis Niedermeyer's *Ecole de Musique* in 1853, and the more important *Schola Cantorum* founded by Vincent d'Indy in 1894. The faculty of the Schola dedicated itself to the improvement of church music by working with church musicians and clergy alike, maintained a late 19th-century Belgian-French tradition elevating the organ works of J. S. Bach, and became instrumental in the restoration of plainsong. However, the most significant work on the chant was done by the Benedictines at Solesmes. Their efforts at gathering, codifying, and editing manuscripts eventuated in the practical editions (e.g., *Liber Usualis*) used well into the 20th century, and in the motu proprio *Tra le sollecitudine* (1903) of Pius X, a papal summary and recognition of the aims of the Caecilian movement.

On German soil, similar investigations were made into the origins and history of Protestant church music. In 1819 Ernst Arndt issued his *Von dem Wort und dem Kirchenliede*, in which he called for the restoration of original hymn texts. That process was aided by the monumental collection of Philipp Wackernagel, *Das deutsche Kirchenlied* (1855—77). For the recirculation of rhythmic versions of chorale tunes, the *Kern des deutschen Kirchengesangs* (1844) of Friedrich Layriz was crucial—also for American Lutherans—as was the prolific work of Johannes Zahn, *Die Melodien der deutschen evangelischen Kirchenlieder* (1889—93). Broader historical work was provided by Salomon Kuemmerle in his *Enzyklopaedie der evangelischen Kirchenmusik* (1888—95).

All of these investigations represent significant contributions to the then fledgling discipline of musicology. Their enduring value beckons a broader recognition of the variety of substantial contributions made to the practice of church music during the classic-romantic period. Sometimes less usual diversions and detours that recurred throughout the era have deterred the 20th-century observer from accurate evaluations; it is time for clearer perceptions, unshackled from prejudice, that promise to yield the equipment for dealing with the church musical enterprise in the 20th century. MB

Readings: Blume, Friedrich, *Classic and Romantic Music,* tr. by M. D. Herter Norton (New York, 1970); Blume, Friedrich, *Protestant Church Music* (New York, 1975); Einstein, Alfred, *Music in the Romantic Era* (New York, 1947); Fellerer, Karl G., *The History of Catholic Church Music,* tr. by Francis Brunner (Baltimore, 1961); Hutchings, Arthur, *Church Music in the 19th Century* (New York, 1967); Riedel, Johannes, *Music of the Romantic Period* (Dubuque, Iowa, 1969).

See also: Caecilian movement; theology of church music, Pietism and rationalism; theology of church music, classic and romantic

church music history, 20th century

Two major cycles delineate the history of 20th-century music, the first beginning about 1900 and the second around 1950, both radically revolutionary in their implications. In the midst of these developments church music seemed to survive and often thrived, not only by exhibiting a predictable resistance to radical change but also by displaying a surprising resiliency and creativity in the face of challenges as profound as any encountered since the era of the Reformation.

The beginnings of 20th-century music overlap the closing years of the classic-romantic era by several decades, but historians cite 1900 as a symbolic date of the revolution that threatened to break down Western musical traditions as these had developed over the previous 600 years. The music of this century properly begins with that of the French composer Claude Debussy (1862—1918), who first challenged the musical language of the German romantic tradition most radically in the way he formed his melodies (long lines and mosaics made out of pentatonic, whole-tone, and modal diatonic scales), in his chords (structured for their color effect alone, without reference to functional successions of tonal harmony), in his use of noncyclic and a-periodic phrase and formal structure, and in his aesthetic exploitation of tone color, raising this element of music to a position of equality with melody and harmony.

The reach for freedom from the bounds and habits of functional tonality was apparent in the works of other composers, but was achieved most significantly and sensationally by Igor Stravinsky (1882—1971) in *The Rite of Spring* (1913). This violent and beautiful work lays its unique claim to historical importance in the way Stravinsky used the element of rhythm and defied traditional premises about patterned motion: in the unprecedented and ingenious use of polyrhythms, syncopations, and metrical counterpoints the traditional elements of rhythm and accent no longer depended on formal factors of melodic and harmonic tonal organization.

In the Austro-German tradition Arnold Schoenberg (1874—1951) carried forward to its inevitable development the vocabulary of post-Wagnerian chromaticism with the prophetic zeal of one sent to rescue German musical culture and assure its predominant role "for the next hundred years," as he said. In a series of works between 1900 and 1908 he came to realize that chromaticism could develop no farther along lines of density and complexity without completely negating the unifying force of tonality, and he was prepared to pursue this course as far as destiny would take him. It took him, somewhere around Opus 11 in 1901, into the chaotic regions of panchromaticism ("atonality," as it was labelled in derision) where no tonal center can exist and where the melodic and harmonic habits of functional tonality are but futile anachronisms.

The first revolution in 20th-century music was an accomplished fact by the beginning of World War I. In the decades that followed (c. 1920—45) composers continued to explore the newfound tonalities and nontonalities, in search of various syntheses that could replace rejected assumptions of the pre-1900 era. Schoenberg's synthesis was embodied in the 12-tone row principles he devised in the early 1920s as a simplification of the process of ascertaining "atonality." Stravinsky's synthesis was embodied in neoclassicism, the new tonal style and objective approach to form that characterized his music as well as that of many others after 1920.

The beginnings of the second historical cycle are discernible, in retrospect, around the year 1950, when three developments became evident: first, the compositional procedures of serialism (based on principles formulated out of Schoenberg's row techniques) were widely adopted by the younger composers after World War II as a means of rationalizing all the controllable parameters of composition. Second, new technologies enabled composers to use unprecedented means of musical sound production. As the potentialities of *musique concrete* and the various electronic means were explored it became clear that vast new fields had been opened with implications too far-reaching for one generation to realize. Third, the very principles of order that had come to be assumed in 800 years of Western music were questioned, challenged, and rejected by a number of the imaginative and inventive younger musicians. For composers such as John Cage (b. 1912) the very process of composition gave way to performer and composer improvisation in varying degrees of control, and to chance itself, so that the sounds of a piece of music were purposefully indeterminate and subject to momentary and ever-changing environmental circumstance.

Not all composers, either before or after 1950, participated in these discoveries. Some resisted the vocabulary of new music entirely, while others were selective and adapted certain nuances to their own needs. Although composers in the church especially seemed to be among the resistors and selective adaptors, it must be noted that not all composers looked upon the vocabulary of 20th-century music as antithetical or inappropriate for religious expression. Most notable among these was Stravinsky, whose *Symphony of Psalms* (1930) is one of the major works of his repertoire and, along with the *Mass* (1948), an example of his personal, neo-tonal, style. Almost all the large works of his final years, from the *Canticum sacrum* (1956) to the *Requiem Canticles*, use religious subjects and texts as well as his personal stylized adaptation of serial techniques. Schoenberg's opera *Moses und Aron* (1932) is perhaps his masterpiece, and his last completed work is a choral setting of Psalm 130. Among other composers who produced concert religious and liturgical works were the British, Vaughan Williams, Holst, Walton, and Britten; the French, Milhaud, Poulenc, and Messiaen; the Italians, Dallapiccola and Petrassi; the Americans, Ives, Sessions, Copland, and Thomson; and, among the post-1950 composers, Gyoergy Ligeti and Kryzystof Penderecki.

It should not be assumed that historical developments described here had nothing to do with church music, or that a composer who wrote no music for the church at all, such as Bartok, can ultimately be said to have no influence on the course of church music. The music of Bartok, just as that of Debussy, Stravinsky, Schoenberg, and Cage, constitutes an aspect of the first of two major challenges that have confronted music in the 20th-century church: *how to be in the 20th century*. How can church music, with its unique and varied sets of historical, denominational, and provincial presuppositions and functional habits, be a lively participant in the cultural developments of its time? The shape of church music has, of course, depended not only on its responses to the challenges offered by the changing language of contemporary music, but also the church's own response to other current phenomena such as the growth of ecumenism, the strains brought to bear upon the disciplines of theology by the demands of secularized culture, and the increased economic and sociological interdependence in all of society.

A second major challenge, wholly related to the first, is: *how to deal with tradition.* The disciplines of musicology and liturgiology, together with a concomitantly heightened sense of identity with tradition, have affected the course of 20th-century church music as profoundly as developments in the new music. Not only has tradition challenged church music, but the 20th-century church has called into question the validity and existence of tradition itself. Church music in the various times and places of the 20th century has responded to these major concerns in several ways.

The changing position of church music, both Protestant and Catholic, in Austro-German culture has comprised one of the more lively developments of the century.. It was this culture, which by no coincidence had fathered the musicologist, Guido Adler (1885—1941), that, soon after the turn of the century, began to draw close to a legitimate pre-19th-century church music tradition. The first movement toward the renewal of church music was initiated by the organist-composer Max Reger (1873—1916) and the organist-educator Karl Straube (1873—1950), who tried to restore church musicianship to the high artistic level it was presumed to have held in the preclassic era. The "back to Bach" movement took root in sheer reaction to the routine and platitudinous music making of the late 19th-century church. A complementary movement toward liturgical renewal rediscovered the worship service as the "heart and core of life of the church," as Oskar Soehngen put it. "Church music was no longer merely a piece of ornament and decoration for spiritual edification, but it again formed an integral part of the theological-musical makeup of the worship service." The movement toward reform in organ building, one of the "most amazing adventures and solid achievements of 20th-century music," (according to William Austin), was initiated by Albert Schweitzer (1875—1965) who, in 1909, sounded the call for restoration of instruments that were soundworthy of the greatest organ music of the past, by which he meant the organ music of Bach. The organ movement was to spread rapidly after 1920, so that by the middle of the century exemplary new instruments were being created by builders in Europe and America. Of equal significance, the ideals of church music renewal were embodied in new compositions by some of Germany's best young composers in the period between the wars, notably in the organ works of Johann Nepomuk David (b. 1895), in the choral and organ works of Ernst Pepping (b. 1901), and in the choral and keyboard pieces of the sensitive and original composer, Hugo Distler (1908—42). Traditional forms of church music, the chorale motet, the Gospel motet, chorale prelude, Passion and cantata forms, and formal procedures such as ostinato and contrapuntal variation (as opposed to the classical development procedures) were reinstated, all in a time when the neoclassic and neobaroque aesthetic was much in the air. Stylistically much of this music can be identified with the neo-tonalities of Stravinksy and Hindemith, but the works of Distler, for example, were seldom surpassed in terms of imaginative text treatment and idiomatic use of voices and organ. Other composers after Distler carried the renewal movement forward, among them Helmut Bornefeld (b. 1906), Hans Friedrich Micheelsen (1902—75), Siegfried Reda (1916—69), and Johannes Dreissler (b. 1921). For a time it seemed that German church music had learned how to deal with tradition and how, at the same time, to be in the 20th century. But the advent of 1950 and the postwar concerns of the avant-gardists soon touched off a crisis and the renewal movement came to be identified with reactionism and institutionalism. New church music, taking its roots in tradition, is no longer possible—so implied critics such as Theodor W. Adorno, pointing to the fact that new secular music (in the hands of post-Schoenberg serialists) had advanced far beyond the level of "modern" church music. And many of the younger composers, Reda and Dreissler among them, turned to serial composition in their choral and organ works. Others asserted their independence from regimentation by liturgical and "practical" church music considerations and declared themselves in favor of an autonomous church-related art unencumbered by the needs of the worship service. In 1958 Bornefeld declared, "I believe that the new church music will become more and more an affair of a small minority of intellectually independent persons." Among the few younger composers who seemed to resist this trend toward esotericism was Heinz Werner Zimmermann (b. 1933) whose music, with its characteristic rhythmic vitality, follows quite naturally in the line of pre-1950 renewal.

While church music in Germany may not yet have resolved its crisis of how to be in the 20th century, some of the most serious issues have been faced here more profoundly than anywhere else.

English church musicians of the first decade of this century, led by the examples of Parry and Stanford, became aware of the need for higher standards of professionalism in the church, so that both composers and performers of high craftsmanship were drawn into its service. Conspicuous among these was Ralph Vaughan Williams (1872—1958), whose first major contribution was to serve as music editor for the *English Hymnal* (1906). This publication, which became a model for later English and American hymnals, reestablished contact both with English polyphonic traditions of the Tudor period and with English folk song traditions whose tunes and idioms were appropriated into the service of a revitalized English hymnody. Vaughan Williams contributed not only a set of memorable and widely known hymn tunes (*Down Ampney, Sine nomine, Salve festa dies*), but continued a professional association with the church throughout his lifetime as an editor (*Oxford Book of Carols*, 1928, and *Songs of Praise*, 1926, 1931, both with Percy Dearmer and Martin Shaw), and as composer of hymn tunes, choral-and-instrumental anthems (*Old Hundredth*, 1953), and many larger works, among them the *Mass in G Minor* (1922), *Benedicite* (1930), and *Hodie* (1954). In a style that maintained an exceptional homogeneity throughout all his writing, he used neo-modal and neo-tonal scales absorbed from Tudor and folk hymn sources, together with techniques from early 20th-century French composers. His lead and encouragement enabled other eminent English composers, such as Gustav Holst (1874—1934), William Walton (b. 1902), Michael Tippett (b. 1905), and Benjamin Britten (1913—76), to contribute some of their best musical efforts to the church. Especially Britten, in such vocal works as the celebrated *Ceremony of Carols* (1943), *Noye's Fludde* (1958), and in the dramatic *War Requiem* (1962), has shown extraordinary ability to use the nuances of the English language in musical settings. English composers of chamber, symphonic, and operatic music have maintained an amiable relationship with the church without seeming to make stylistic compromises. A number of distinguished composers toward the middle of the century, such as Eric Thiman (b. 1900) and Herbert Howells (b. 1892), have composed almost exclusively for the church, developing and exploiting with good craftsmanship such characteristic forms as the hymn anthem and organ works based on familiar congregational tunes. Music such as that of Howells tended to affect a *rapprochement* between traditional and new musical styles. Developments after 1950 found English church music reacting quite differently from that in Germany. The *20th Century Folk Mass* (1956) by Geoffrey Beaumont (1904—70) represented a startling social rather than musical response to contemporary challenges. In its employment of an everyday style of pseudo-popular music, it symbolized the beginning of the whole movement of folk-pop hymnody that invaded the Western church and was taken up with enthusiasm by worship leaders in Europe and America. The movement was symptomatic of sociological and theological concerns of the church in the 1960s and early 1970s.

The late 19th-century tradition of French organ playing, of which Widor and Vierne were the masters, was carried into this century by Marcel Dupré (1886—1971) and his composer-organist pupils, Jean Langlais (b. 1907), Jehan Alain (1911—40), and Olivier Messiaen (b. 1908). Langlais is distinguished not only for organ works but also for contributions to choral and congregational music for the liturgy. Messiaen, the father of European avant-garde, post-1950, and one of the most original figures of the century, is also a professional church organist and continues to carry on a long and glorious tradition of organ improvisation and composition. A French composer who anticipated some of the concerns expressed in *The Constitution on the Sacred Liturgy*, 1963, was the Jesuit Priest Joseph Gelineau (b. 1920). In his search for a simple and usable vehicle for chanting psalmody in the vernacular, Father Gelineau translated the Psalms into modern French, following strictly the rhythm of the Hebrew texts. Using folk song patterns as models, he composed melodies of extreme simplicity, using a metric grid with a change of pitch on accented syllables only. The principles are effective and flexible, and the Gelineau psalm settings, first published in 1956, have received wider currency than perhaps any other liturgical compositions of the 20th century.

Church music in 20th-century America has been as varied and diversified as the churches themselves. The many traditions, both historical and parochial, with their ethnic, regional, and sociological contradictions, make a complex pattern. Certain generalities can be stated:

First, American church music in the 20th century has been concerned with tradition, or "traditions," in ways quite different from those in Europe. Musical traditions in American churches at the turn of the century were either practically nonexistent or, at best, very young, or borrowed

144

from various 19th-century Protestant American practices, or brought directly from provincial European ethnic sources. By the 1940s and 1950s some American churches were experiencing a liturgical and church music renewal vaguely comparable to that in Germany after World War I. This new, however tentative, identity with older traditions had profound effects on liturgical and hymnic repertoires in many places and influenced at least a few composers in the direction of traditional ideals.

Second, during the earlier years of this century composers of church music in America were not as concerned about using the newer 20th-century musical idioms as were composers after c. 1950. Some of the earlier composers used left-over 19th-century styles; others took the more academic and conservative English composers for their models. Not many composers were affected by the music of Debussy, and almost none by Stravinsky or Schoenberg.

Third, composers of church music in America today are employing all the historic forms of church music plus a few newly invented ones, and are using the whole gamut of available styles from neo-tonality and neo-modality to serialism, chance, and indeterminacy, *musique concrete* and all the varieties of electronic means, especially mixed media—electronic and live.

Fourth, much of the published church music written in the advanced styles of 20th-century composition is not widely used in worship services. This is important to note in a period of time when one of the major concerns of the church in the 20th century has been to involve the congregation more deeply in the acts of worship. Two significant developments since 1960, however, are symptomatic of this latter concern: (1) the widespread practice of many worship leaders to use folk-pop spiritual hymnody as a musical medium for evangelizing, and (2) the high professional quality of liturgical and hymnic resources designed for congregational use that have been developed in new publications of worship materials in most American denominations. RH

Readings: Austin, William W., *Music in the 20th Century* (New York, 1966); Blume, Friedrich, *Protestant Church Music* (New York, 1975); Hillert, Richard, "Sources and Sounds of the New Music," *Church Music*, 72·1; Routley, Erik, *Twentieth Century Church Music* (New York, 1964); Salzman, Eric, *Twentieth-Century Music: An Introduction*, 2d ed. (Englewood Cliffs, N. J., 1974); Schwarts, Elliott, and Barney Childs, eds., *Contemporary Composers on Contemporary Music* (New York, 1967).

See also: theology of church music, 20th century; church music history, classic and romantic

church music history, American

The development of American church music is marked by great diversity, due both to ethnic factors and denominational traditions. Church music developed slowly in the early colonies largely because of the very nature of colonial life: even today farming and fishing communities have little music apart from folksong. There were no professional musicians among the colonists, and under the influence of Puritanism, singing in church was limited to metrical psalmody, which had to be lined out for the most part.

The Early Years

By mid-18th century, the picture began to change. Sizable towns and cities, such as Boston, New York, Philadelphia, and Charleston, S.C., began, after three or four generations of development, to offer a livelihood to a few trained musicians. The prevalent musical illiteracy was relieved by the rise of singing schools which flourished for many decades, gradually following the frontier westward. Hymn tunes relieved the rigidity of the psalm tunes in all except the Presbyterian churches.

Although organs were not uncommon in parish churches in England by the end of the 17th century, Puritanism would have nothing to do with them in America. They were regarded as a papish device. They were also unfamiliar and expensive—hence suspect. So congregational singing was unaccompanied for many decades. It is still unaccompanied among the *Sacred Harp* singers and Primitive Baptist congregations in the southern states.

During the 18th century many Protestant congregations began to use other instruments (violoncello, flute, clarinet, oboe, bassoon, trombone, etc.) to support their singing. The violin was usually forbidden—that was the dancing-master's or devil's fiddle. These instruments were used increasingly until the mid-19th century when the reed organ or harmonium was introduced as a substitute for the pipe organ, still suspect in many churches.

Once singing schools were established, young people welcomed more ambitious music to sing than simple hymn tunes. New England composers led by William Billings (1746—1800), Lewis Edson (1748—1820), and Jeremiah Ingalls (1764—1828) composed a great many fuguing tunes and simple anthems that were included in the new tune-books. Beginning with James Lyon's *Urania* (1762), over 130 collection of tunes with settings for part-singing were published along the east coast before 1800. Singers usually had a rack in front of them along the gallery rail to hold their tune-books while they held their hymnbooks (with texts only) in their hands. Separate tune-books continued to be published in large quantities until the mid-19th century. As far as can be determined, the *Plymouth Collection* (1855), compiled by Henry Ward Beecher (1813—87) and his organist at Plymouth Church, Brooklyn, John Zundel (1815—82), was the first modern American hymnal to combine both words and four-part music on the same page.

The Quartet Choir

Further change came c. 1840 when a number of English and German musicians settled in the United States, and a stream of American music students began to return from their studies in Germany and to settle in the larger cities as organists and singers.

About this time the vogue for quartet choirs took hold, followed even in smaller towns and replacing the older choirs derived from the singing schools. The reasons were perhaps partly financial (business-minded church boards asked: If a mere quartet would suffice with their expensive new organs, why hire more singers?), and partly social (skilled soloists in the quartet often disliked being associated with less skilled amateur choirs). The quartet itself was often made up with soloists from the local opera house. Some churches, wishing to imitate English cathedral music, had two quartets facing each other so that they could sing as decani and cantoris. Not until the 1920s did the quartet choir die out. During its heyday almost all sacred music composed in the United States consisted of solos or duos with interspersed quartet passages. The often florid accompaniments were more pianistic than organistic in style, as in the works of Dudley Buck (1839—1909) and Harry Rowe Shelley (1858—1947). Interspersed with such anthems were frequent excerpts from the popular European masses and oratorios. Even operatic selections were sung to sacred words, e.g., the sextet from Donizetti's *Lucia di Lammermoor* to "Guide me, O thou great Jehovah."

Toward Reform

Reforms trace from Archibald Davison (1883—1961) and his work with the Harvard Glee Club after 1910. Turning from the silly glees, standard fare of most 19th-century college groups, he steeped his singers at Harvard and Radcliffe in the great contrapuntal masterpieces of the 16th century. In the Midwest, F. Melius Christiansen (1871—1955) exerted similar influence with his touring choir from St. Olaf College in Minnesota. Clarence Dickenson (1873—1969) established a School of Sacred Music in 1928 at Union Theological Seminary, New York City. Two years earlier the Westminster Choir College was founded in 1926 by John Finley Williamson (1887—1964). These and many other schools have provided trained leaders and singers in such quantity that no church today need suffer from poorly trained musicians or from the lack of musical taste as did most 19th-century churches. Composers like the Canadian Healey Willan (1880—1968) and Leo Sowerby (1895—1968) have written much music that was widely used and met the best standards of liturgical music. The great repertory of fine church music of all ages available on recording and tape, works sung by outstanding choirs from Europe and America, can now be heard in the most isolated communities and used as models toward which to strive in local church services.

Many larger churches introduced a multiple choir system providing, at least theoretically, for a development program of training for choir membership. A tendency prevalent particularly in many of the so-called nonliturgical churches in America, but which sometimes also affected choirs in the liturgical churches, has been the desire to spend much time preparing the music for special concerts apart from the regular worship services. Where there was a need for such concerts in their communities they served a purpose, but church choirs in America often forgot that they were church choirs first of all, and that their principal efforts were to be devoted to the musical and spiritual enrichment of the weekly worship. Unfortunately, the Bach revival of the 1930s while adding great music to the repertory, also did much to encourage such choir concerts.

Episcopal Church Music

In the Episcopal churches, music has followed a parallel, though more conservative, development to that described above. Metrical psalmody was used throughout the 18th century, with Anglican chant used wherever there was capable leadership. When bishops were consecrated after the American Revolution and the church's General Convention was organized, an official hymnal (texts) was adopted. By canon law, only texts from this hymnal, the Prayer Book, and the Bible may be used in Episcopal church music. The Hymnal of 1789 included 27 hymns with the entire New

Version of the metrical psalms. In 1826 the psalms were reduced to 124, with a number of newer paraphrases replacing some of the New Version, and the hymns were increased to 212. Since 1871 only a few metrical psalms remain, scattered among the authorized hymns. The prose psalms of Morning and Evening Prayer have been chanted whenever possible. The canticles have also been chanted unless the choir sang a setting of the Service.

From colonial times, churches like Trinity, New York City, St. Michael and St. Philip, Charleston, S. C., and Christ and St. Peter, Philadelphia, employed English-trained organists to lead their music. Boy choirs were developed as soon as possible. The influence of the Oxford Movement in the mid-19th century led to the use of fully choral services in such churches as Advent, Boston, Holy Cross, Troy, N. Y., Atonement, Chicago, and St. Paul, Baltimore. Although few ever attempted daily choral services, many of the larger, city churches provided a cathedral-style music service on Sundays. The 20th century has seen a cathedral system rise throughout the country where, in some of the larger centers, there are not only daily choral services but also choir schools for the better development of the voices and general education of their boys.

Roman Catholic Church Music

Roman Catholic church music in America began as French and Spanish missionaries taught the plainsong to their Indian converts. As Irish, German, Italian, and other ethnic groups came across the Atlantic, the church itself grew, but they brought little music with them. Bishop Fenwick of Boston stated in 1840 that there was no singing at all in two-thirds of the Roman Catholic churches in the country.

The first record of music is in the *Pennsylvania Packet* for July 10, 1779, which reported that a solemn *Te Deum* was sung at St. Mary's, Philadelphia, to commemorate the third anniversary of the Declaration of Independence. In 1787 the first music for the use of Roman Catholics in America was published in Philadelphia by John Aitken (*c.* 1745—1831): *A Compilation of Litanies, Vespers, Hymns, and Anthems*. The texts were largely in English, a few in both English and Latin, still fewer only in Latin, and two in German; the music was in one and two parts. Editions of 1791 and 1814 had music in three parts.

By the mid-19th century, the larger city churches in the East had quartets and mixed choirs that sang Haydn, Mozart, and Gounod masses with operatic soloists. Elaborate vesper services were frequent, using music that was far from liturgical much of the time. One notable exception was at the Church of St. Francis Xavier, New York City, where a boy choir flourished c. 1885 under the Reverend John B. Young, S.J.

German Roman Catholic churches in the Midwest fared better. Archbishop Henni of Milwaukee brought John B. Singenberger (1848—1924) to this country in 1873. The latter promptly founded a Caecilian Society which, with its magazine and annual conventions, spread the Caecilian reforms of the movement.

St. John's (Benedictine) Abbey, Collegeville, Minn., was an exception among American religious houses and seminaries. Founded c. 1850, by the early 1870s it was cultivating plainsong and polyphonic masses.

In the East, Nicola A. Montani (1880—1948) took up the cause for plainsong and better liturgical music, ably supported by Mother Georgia Stevens, R.S.C.J. (1870—1946) at the Pius X School of Liturgical Music. For three decades the Paulist Choristers of Fr. William Joseph Finn, C.S.P. (1881—1961), through their tours and subsequent radio broadcasts, showed what glorious liturgical music can be created whenever there is adequate financial and spiritual support by the clergy and hierarchy.

Unfortunately, since Vatican II much of this has been greatly jeopardized by the near total abandonment of the Latin plainsong and other rich literature of the past. LE

Readings: Davison, A. T., Protestant Church Music in America (1933); Ellinwood, Leonard, The History of American Church Music (New York, 1953, reprint 1970); Ellinwood, Leonard, "Religious Music in America," Religion in American Life, II (1961); Gilman, S., Memoirs of a New England Village Choir (1829); Gould, N. D., Church Music in America (Boston, 1853, reprint 1972); Nemmers, E., Twenty Centuries of Catholic Church Music, Chapter VI (Milwaukee, 1949); Stevenson, R., Protestant Church Music in America (New York, 1966); Ochse, Orpha, The History of the Organ in the United States (Bloomington and London, 1975).

See also: Caecilian movement; chant, Anglican; decani/cantoris; gospel song; hymnody, American; metrical psalmody

church music history, American Lutheran

A half century before Willian Penn set foot on American soil two Swedish vessels sailed up the Delaware River in March 1638, bringing settlers who founded the first permanent Lutheran congregations in

America. John Printz, governor of the colony in 1643, wrote that they followed the Swedish orders of worship and sang both the liturgy and chorales. Andrew Rudman, a pastor who came to the settlements in 1697, published the first Lutheran hymns in America. These were two hymn texts in a pamphlet that he wrote as a gift to the congregation of Gloria Dei Church (Philadelphia) on New Year's Day 1701. About the same time he published a second pamphlet containing six hymn texts. Rudman was a musician, and his diary records that he played a small spinet that he brought with him to America. We do not know when Gloria Dei obtained an organ, though an unauthenticated claim exists that an organ, viol, wind instruments, and kettle drums were used for the ordination of Justus Falckner, Nov. 24, 1703, the first Lutheran ordination in America. However, an organ did exist in the church around 1740. The congregation took its music seriously, since church records indicate that the fine for "untimely singing" during worship was six shillings. After 1750 the Swedish churches were eclipsed by the growing German congregations, but they still played a significant role as a stable Lutheran body that upheld musical and liturgical traditions.

The Dutch settlements at New York included another pioneer Lutheran congregation that tenuously existed as early as the 1650s, but it was only after 1700, when Justus Falckner became pastor, that the church was firmly established. During 1708 Falckner appended three Dutch hymns to a little instruction book that he wrote. In 1756 the New York congregation assisted in publishing the first full-size Lutheran hymnal to be printed in America in English—John Christian Jacobi's *Psalmodia Germanica* (London, 1722). New York Lutherans were leaders in supporting English as the language for worship, a fact which led to America's first original English Lutheran hymnal, J. C. Kunze's *A Hymn and Prayer-Book* (New York, 1795). Kunze was a son-in-law of H. M. Muehlenberg, patriarch of American Lutheranism. After the American Revolution, churches in and around New York prospered, and their musical life grew accordingly. A booklet, *Hymns of Praise*, published in 1792 by Zion Church of Athens, New York, when their church organ was rebuilt is an example of this musical life. Nine pages of this booklet contain texts for a festival service that uses several hymns from the *Psalmodia Germanica* as chorale concertatos for choir, congregation, soloists, and organ.

German immigration into the Philadelphia area around 1750 brought the first major flowering of American Lutheran music. Heinrich

Melchior Muehlenberg (1711—87) founded St. Michael's Church, Philadelphia, in 1742, and this congregation prospered and grew into the historic St. Michael's and Zion congregation, which played a major role in American Lutheran life for the next century. May 12, 1751, St. Michael's dedicated a 20-rank organ built by Johann A. Schmahl of Heilbronn, Germany, and shipped to America under the supervision of Johann G. Landenberg. In his widely quoted travel accounts Gottlieb Mittelberger claimed credit for bringing this organ to Philadelphia, but a letter dated Mar. 3, 1752, from Pastor Peter Brunnholtz of St. Michael's to church officials in Halle indicates that Mittelberger's claim is false. This fine organ provided the impetus for many festival musical services that used orchestral instruments in addition to organ and choir. Immigration was so great that St. Michael's dedicated a second and much larger house of worship, Zion, in 1769. Zion seated 2,500 persons and had the largest

Title page of Schmauk's *Deutsche Harmonie,* popular German-American chorale and anthem collection that enjoyed wide use in 19th-century American Lutheran churches. (Library of Congress)

seating capacity of any building in Philadelphia. In 1790 Zion dedicated an organ of three manuals and 34 stops—the largest instrument ever built by David Tannenberg, the famed Moravian builder. From 1790 to 1795 John C. Moller, a prominent early American composer, was head organist at Zion. One of his duties was to compose and perform festive new music on the first Sunday in Advent, Christmas, New Year's Day, Good Friday, Easter, Pentecost, and on at least three other days as requested by the ministers. J. H. C. Helmuth, the congregation's senior pastor at that time, wrote the texts for Moller's anthems and cantatas, and the head choir director and schoolmaster, David Ott, helped conduct the performances. Helmuth was a pianist, writer, and poet, and was on the committee (with H. M. and G. H. E. Muehlenberg and J. C. Kunze) that compiled the *Erbauliche Lieder-Sammlung* (1786), American Lutheranism's first synodical hymnal. Helmuth contributed at least 36 hymns to the various editions of

Choral setting of the first part of "Dort auf jenem Todtenhuegel," one of the most popular hymns by J. H. C. Helmuth, as found in Schmauk's *Deutsche Harmonie*. The melody or soprano is next to the bass; the tenor is in the top line. (Library of Congress)

this hymnal. In 1813 he guided publication of America's first Lutheran chorale book, which provided 266 hymn tunes for use with the hymnal. Until this time American organists had to depend on German sources to compile their own manuscript books to provide tunes for the hymnals, which rarely were printed with music. Despite a destructive fire at Zion, Dec. 26, 1794, and perennial language controversies, the congregation flourished. In 1819 Johann G. Schmauk became one of the church's schoolmaster-organists, and in 1824 he published his first collection of anthems and chorales, the *Sammlung religioeser deutscher Gesaenge*. In 1833 Schmauk published his *Deutsche Harmonie*, which became the standard anthem collection for German churches in eastern America for the next generation. It had a second, greatly enlarged, edition in 1847 and remained popular through its 25th printing in 1875. It contains 107 chorales and 143 anthems, including 20 by Schmauk. The other anthems are selected from European writers and the publications of Lowell Mason and the Boston Academy. The anthems are mostly for three or four voices and the soprano and alto often move in chains of parallel thirds and sixths as was popular at that time. Schmauk expected organists to improvise introductions and interludes, though a few pieces contain suggestions for an organ part.

By 1850 American Lutheran church music was developing in three main streams. First, there was a continuation of the older German-American practice, which maintained some sense of liturgy as well as traditional uses of organ and instruments, albeit in a 19th-century style. This older tradition experienced many interesting blends with other Protestant groups in the Midwest and rural Pennsylvania. One finds such tune-books as J. J. Fast's *Cantica sacra* (Hudson, Ohio, 1854) and T. R. Weber's *Pennsylvania Choral Harmony* (Allentown, 1844), both of which are bilingual and use shape notes. Shape notes in German tune-books date back to Joseph Doll's *Leichter Unterricht* (Harrisburg, 1810). Such tune-books often contain some New England fuguing tunes and American folk hymns as well as German chorales. In 1849 the *Deutsches Gesangbuch* became the official synodical replacement for the 1786 hymnal. However, like most hymnals it lacked music, and there was still need for chorale books such as those published by G. F. Landenberger in 1870 or J. Endlich in 1879. Landenberger provided his chorales with suggested *Zwischenspiele*, recognizing that many organists no longer were trained to play improvised interludes at the end of each phrase.

The second main stream by 1850 consisted of English-language churches. These churches drifted away from Lutheran tradition in both hymnody and liturgy. Even such official synodical hymnals as the General Council's *Church Book* of 1872 (the first edition with music) showed strong Methodist influence. Toward the close of the century various Lutheran musicians in English churches tried to revive interest in liturgy, usually with strong Anglican influences. This is reflected in Seiss and Engelmann's *Church Song* (Philadelphia, 1875), Knauff's *Music of the Service* (Philadelphia, 1871), and the services and introits by Emanuel Schmauk (New York, 1909 and 1912).

The third main stream in 1850 grew from churches established by the mid-19th century German and Scandinavian immigration into the Mississippi Valley. This brought a new influx of European practices, though at first there was little interchange with the older churches in eastern America.

American Lutheran music in the 20th century has been most influenced by three factors: publication of official hymnals with music, Lutheran higher education, and Lutheran publishing houses. Beginning in the 1870s hymnals were printed with music, and by World War I every major Lutheran body had issued such a hymnal. This tended to standardize the repertoire, especially as mergers created larger church bodies. Since the pioneering work of F. M. Christiansen at St. Olaf College it has become traditional for Lutheran higher education to emphasize music. This has created interest in Lutheran musical traditions and made Lutherans more aware of their heritage and how this heritage speaks to the modern world. The various Lutheran publishing houses have also made a significant contribution. Concordia and Augsburg are especially active in printing music. Concordia has published practical performing editions from great masters of the past as well as contemporary chorale concertatos, motets, and cantatas. The combination of improved training for today's church musicians plus the ready availability of good materials should mean that American Lutheran church music has a bright future. EWo

Readings: Wolf, E. C., "America's First Lutheran Chorale Book," *Concordia Historical Institute Quarterly,* XLVI (Spring 1973); Wolf, E. C., "Music in Old Zion, Philadelphia, 1750—1850," *The Musical Quarterly,* LVIII (Oct. 1972); Wolf, E. C., *Lutheran Church Music in America during the 18th and early 19th centuries,* dissertation, University of Illinois, 1960.

See also: hymnody, American; hymnody, American Lutheran

concertato style

Concertato style exploits contrasts and combinations of various instrumental and vocal timbres and groupings. The word *concertato* is the past participle of the Italian verb *concertare* which means to coordinate or unite in a harmonious ensemble a heterogeneous group of players or singers or both. The noun form of the verb is *concerto*, and this term was used in the 16th century and most of the 17th to refer to an ensemble of various instruments or voices or both, or compositions for such an ensemble. The present participle of the verb *concertare* is *concertante*.

The principle source for the idea of strife or contention in the concertato was Michael Praetorius who derived the term *concertato* from the Latin verb *concertare*, which means to contend or fight. The noun form of the Latin verb is *concertatio*, however, and not *concerto*.

In a concerto, harmonious cooperation is achieved among different musical performers. To *concert* then is to secure this cooperation, and a concerted composition or style is one in which this union occurs. The term is mainly used when the forces are diverse. The term concerto does not imply the use of soloists, although it often occurs in connection with them. However, there are examples of the terms *concertato* and *concerto* being used for ensembles of voices and instruments in which instruments merely double voices of a chorus.

Dual usage of these terms becomes pronounced in the middle of the 17th century and is continuous through the late baroque. Concerto is used as a generic term meaning motet or symphony and also to designate a subspecies as equivalent of *concertatio* where the parts contend with each other. Praetorius recognized a general class called *concerto* and also a species of music called *concertando*.

The concertato style originated in the polychoral works of the Venetian school and in the polyphonic madrigals of Monteverdi in the late 16th and early 17th centuries in which two or three voices or a solo voice were featured against the background of the ensemble.

The first sacred concertos were written for solo voices with basso continuo (Viadana: *Cento concerti ecclesiastici,* 1602). Contemporary with Viadana's works are the sacred concertos of Agazzari, Banchieri, and Croce. These works show the influence of the polychoral idiom combined with an independent bass line. In Florence, Cavalieri was the first composer to introduce the new concerted monodic style into the church.

However, sacred concertos for few voices are perhaps best represented in the early 17th century by the works of Monteverdi and Grandi.

The Masses of a number of Austrian composers (J. Stadlmeyer, C. Strauss, A. Bertali, J. Schmelzer, J. Kerll, H. Biber) reveal in this same period a gradually increasing use of concertato style mixed with traditional choral writing and with operatic elements. Later in the century, passages for one or more solo voices were sometimes included in choral movements. The Gloria and Credo were sometimes divided into separate sections set for solo voice, solo ensemble, or choir.

In many Masses, instrumental accompaniment was the rule. Masses were often set with short interludes for instruments between choral passages; brass ensembles and timpani gave a festive air; and sometimes bells were used in the accompaniment of a Kyrie. Such masses became known as "concertato Masses."

The concertato style was also used in motet compositions. Bukofzer uses the term "dramatic concertato" in speaking of these works based on texts from the Psalms or the Gospels—texts that receive subjective and dramatic treatment. The dramatic concertato was cultivated by composers who also wrote chorale concertatos, and especially by Heinrich Schuetz. His *Symphoniae sacrae* collection of 1650 includes 16 settings for a variety of solo voices with a single or double choir. Continuo and other instruments are used in all of these motets, and short sinfonie appear between the choral or solo passages.

Many Lutheran composers used this new style in chorale settings. Single verses of the chorale were composed alternately as duets, monodies, choruses, and ensembles with or without instrumental accompaniment. M. Praetorius, J. Schein, S. Scheidt, A. Hammerschmidt, and F. Tunder provided many examples of chorale concertatos. In the chorale concertato lie the beginnings of the later church cantata.

The concertato style appeared rather late in French sacred music. Henri Dumont was among the first to use the style in his *Cantica sacra* (1652). Later composers, e.g., Lully, used it almost exclusively.

The concertato never actually crystallized into stereotyped musical schemes. Bukofzer, howerver, recognized three general types of patterns that occur frequently. They are: (1) through-composed, (2) arch form, and (3) free rondo structure. ER

Readings: Arnold, Denis, "Giovanni Croce and the Concertato Style," *Musical Quarterly XXXIX* (1953); Bukofzer, Manfred F., *Music in the Baroque Era* (New York, 1947);

Palisca, Claude, V., *Baroque Music* (Englewood Cliffs, N. J., 1968); Samuel, Harold, "Michael Praetorius on Concertato Style," *Cantors at the Crossroads*, J. Riedel, ed. (St. Louis, 1967); Wienandt, E., *Choral Music of the Church* (New York, 1965).

See also: cantata; church music history, baroque; motet; polychoral style; Venetian school; *HCM*, IV

contrafacta

Contrafacta are vocal pieces that are created when a text other than the original is adapted to a particular melody; in the context of church music a contrafactum usually refers to the provision of a sacred text for a melody which is already popular with its own text (usually secular) whose popularity may be useful in propagating new doctrine and encouraging congregational participation in worship, although the reverse may also occur, or a new sacred text may also replace an earlier one.

As early as the 9th century the adaptation of new liturgical texts to other melodies from the chant repertoire can be detected (esp. in connection with feasts established at a later date). The melodies of a number of alleluias, antiphons, hymns, and sequences reflect this practice. In the 12th and 13th centuries the troubadors and trouveres of France adapted melodies from the liturgical chant repertoire replacing the sacred texts with secular vernacular texts (the melody of the sequence *Laetabundus*, for example, was used for at least two trouvere songs, and later for a German piece found in a 15th-century manuscript, as well as for a 16th-century Huguenot song.)

Examples of the general practice of contrafaction are numerous in the 15th and 16th century and may be seen in such widely divergent sources as the *canti carnascialeschi* (secular popular part-songs associated with the carnival festivities in Florence) fitted with sacred texts and sung as *laudi spirituali*. Particularly striking is the use of the same music for the carnival song "Visin, visin" and the lauda "Jesu, Jesu." In the 15th century such composers as Binchois (c. 1400—60), Busnois (d. 1492), Caron, and others did not hesitate to introduce chansons into the church in which a sacred text was substituted for a frivolous one, the resulting work being called a *saincte chansonette*. The motet *O Jesu fili David* by Josquin Desprez (c. 1450—1521), originally published in Petrucci's Canti B (1502) as "Coment peult haver joye," illustrates the procedure. Some of the chansons of Orlando di

Lasso (1532—94) became so popular that they were fitted with moralistic texts to replace the amorous ones.

In the religious songs of the various churches of the 16th-century Reformation many older secular melodies were adapted to religious words and retained for use in the church. The *Souterliedekens* (1540), for example, a collection of 159 monophonic psalm tunes set to the Calvinist psalter, consisted largely of melodies borrowed from the popular folk melodies of the time, mostly Dutch. The Lutheran church in the 16th century produced or adopted over 170 contrafacta for its use, the Reformed over 100, while the German Catholic church of the same period took up over 40.

The classic example of a contrafactum of the German Reformation church is Luther's children's song for Christmas *Von Himmel hoch da komm ich her,* based on the secular song "Aus fremden Landen komm ich her." Other examples of melodies originally associated with secular words and taken up by the church of this period include *Auf meinen lieben Gott* (originally "Venus, du und dein Kind sind alle beide blind"), *Herzlich tut mich verlangen* (originally "Mein G'muet ist mir verwirret, das macht ein Jungfrau zart"), *O Welt ich muss dich lassen* (originally "Innsbruck, ich muss dich lassen"), *O Herre Gott, dein goettlich Wort* (originally "Weiss mir ein Bluemlein blaue"). *Es ist das Heil uns kommen her* (originally "Freut euch, ihr Frauen und ihr Mann"), is an example of the association of a new sacred text with an older tune already associated with another sacred text, in this case an Easter hymn.

Not uncommon in the 16th century were collections of contrafacta in which the "best of the old German songs" were transformed into new Christian hymns: Wepse's collection of 1571 and Heinrich Knaust's *Gassenhauer, Reiter- und Bergliedlein, christlich moraliter und sittlich veraendert* of the same year are typical.

That there was little or no hesitation in adapting sacred texts to secular melodies in this period can largely be attributed to the fact that the distinction between sacred and secular music was vague, if not, for most practical purposes, nonexistent. This, coupled with the Reformation church's need for material to easily involve the congregation in its new activity of singing, led to the adoption of whatever melodies were available and at hand—in many cases folk and secular tunes from a variety of sources. In the centuries following, the musical distinction between sacred and secular music was more readily apparent, with a consequent decline in the general use of contrafacta by the church.

A more recent revival of the practice in the church of the 20th century has been the popular trend of fashioning religious texts for many of the secular folk songs of the time. This technique enjoyed special popularity in Roman Catholicism following Vatican II when the need for material easily grasped by congregations with little experience in singing was great. The skill and artistry with which most of these attempts has been carried out has usually left much to be desired. CS

Readings: Blume, F., "The Contrafacta," *Protestant Church Music* (New York, 1974); Boehme, F. M., ed., *Altdeutsches Liederbuch* (1877); Reese, G., "The Earliest Music of the Lutherans: The Role of Luther; Walter," *Music in the Renaissance*, rev. ed. (New York, 1959).

See also: chorale; church music history, Renaissance—the Reformation tradition

decani/cantoris

Originating during the Middle Ages the terms "decani" and "cantoris" refer respectively to the dean and cantor of an English cathedral. The dean was the presiding clergyman of the cathedral. Second in rank to the dean, the cantor or precentor was charged with the responsibility of supervising the performance of the service in general and of intoning the psalms and canticles in particular. During the cathedral services the dean occupied the first return stall on the south side of the choir or chancel; the cantor occupied the first return stall on the north side. Hence the terms "decani," or dean's side, as contrasted to "cantoris," the cantor's side.

As shown in the accompanying diagram, the singers in a typical Anglican cathedral were divided into two equal groups facing each other across the choir. Such an arrangement imparted a spatial dimension to antiphonal or responsorial singing. In an antiphonal Psalmody, for example, the two choirs alternated "decani/cantoris" either verse by verse or half verse by half verse. Performance practices of this type are, of course, typical of monastic practices everywhere in Europe during the Middle Ages. The nomenclature "decani/cantoris," however, is distinctively English.

The terms "decani/cantoris" are also observed in the cathedral music of the 16th, 17th, and 18th centuries. In the anthems and Services of this period, one frequently encounters the terms "decani," "cantoris," and "full" as performance directions. Certain sections of a work are indicated

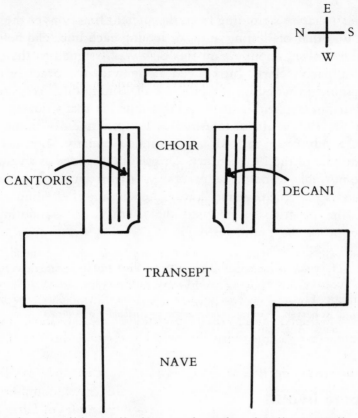

to be sung by the "decani" choir; others by the "cantoris" choir; and others by both choirs together marked "full." Since each choir was a complete SATB unit, works that required more than four parts necessitated a division of forces. For example, a five-part full anthem [SSATB] would engage the altos, tenors, and basses of both sides, but soprano I would be drawn from the "decani" choir and soprano II from the "cantoris." With the possibility of combining, contrasting, alternating, or dividing two SATB choirs, the composer of Anglican cathedral music had at his disposal a great deal of variety within the choral medium.

In the parish churches of the Anglican communion as well as in some non-Anglican churches the office of precentor or cantor was maintained with somewhat simpler functions. In the Presbyterian Churches of Scotland, for example, the precentor was supplied with a pitch-pipe to set the pitch for the singing of metrical psalms. Sometimes he was called the "uptaker of the Psalms."

Another practice stemming from the ancient functions of the precentor or cantor was that of "lining out," or having each line read before it was sung by the congregation. Again this task was assigned to the precentor, minister, or parish clerk. Introduced along with the practice of singing metrical psalms in worship, the practice of "lining out" received official status in Puritan England in 1644 and continued in many quarters until the middle of the 19th century. In America the practice of "lining out" was introduced at Plymouth in 1681 and continued in many American churches until the middle of the 19th century. Originally intended as an aid for those who were not able to read, the practice varied from reading one line at a time to reading an entire verse before the singing of the line or verse. In any case, the practice interrupted the literary, to say nothing of the musical, sense of the psalm. HM

Readings: Fellowes, Edmund H., *English Cathedral Music*, 5th ed. (London, 1969); Long, Kenneth R., *The Music of the English Church* (New York, 1971); Scholes, Percy, "Hymns and Hymn Tunes 8," "Precentor," *The Oxford Companion to Music*, 10th ed. (London, 1970); Wienandt, Elwyn A., *Choral Music of the Church* (New York, 1965); Wienandt, Elwyn A. and Robert H. Young, *The Anthem in England and America* (New York, 1970).
See also: chant, Anglican; cantor; metrical psalmody; *HCM, IV*

de tempore hymn

The name given to the chief hymn in the service on every Sunday and festival, so called because it fits the specific day and season in the church year. It is the hymn that responds most intimately to the dominant theme of the day, which is usually contained in the Gospel for the day. It is also called the "gradual hymn" (the preferred designation) because it was originally sung between the Epistle and the Gospel in place of the gradual. Other names are "Hymn of the Week" and "Hymn of the Day."

Proclamation and response determine the fundamental rhythm of everything that takes place in a Christian service of worship. In the synagog service each Scripture reading was followed by a psalm. This principle was also used by the early Christian church in its services. Thus the gradual psalm was sung after the first lesson, the Alleluia and psalm verses followed the Epistle, and, beginning perhaps as early as the 6th century, the Creed, as a sacrifice of praise, probably with reference to Heb. 13:15 ("Through him, then let us continually offer up a sacrifice of praise to God, that is, the fruit of lips that acknowledge his name" RSV), served as the response to the Gospel.

When Martin Luther (1483—1546) reformed the mass he retained the Latin gradual in its original form as a solo song of the cantor in his *Formula missae* (1523), the evangelical Latin mass intended for cathedrals, city churches, convents, and monasteries. However, in his *Deutsche Messe* (1526) he gave the gradual back to the people in the form of the congregational hymn. Many of the church orders of the Reformation era followed Luther's example. So it came about that already in the 16th century a fixed order of de tempore or gradual hymns for every Sunday and festival of the church year was established. While regional variations occurred in these listings, a remarkable uniformity was established. The various hymns were mainly chosen to fit the Gospel for the day according to the old standard pericope system.

With the substitution of a congregational hymn for the ancient gradual psalm the reformers created something entirely new. The congregational hymn was elevated to the same rank as the psalm in the mass. While in the mass the gradual psalm was intended mainly as adoring meditation, the gradual hymn in the Lutheran service had a more complex character. It certainly was intended as meditative adoration. But it was more than that. Just as the intrinsic character of all genuine church music is doxological proclamation, sung adoration, so also in the "singing and saying" through text and melody of the gradual hymn, the good news of the Gospel is proclaimed in song.

Although the de tempore hymn is mainly chosen according to the Gospel for the day, in many cases it also contains direct references to the Epistle. (See, for example, "Christ Jesus Lay in Death's Strong Bands," the de tempore hymn for Easter.) In addition, the special proclamation of the Sunday or festival is often bound up with the entire plan of salvation. In short, the de tempore hymn contains doxological proclamation, exegesis, exposition.

The gradual hymn series was in use in the Lutheran churches of Germany until the breakup of the old liturgical order under Pietism and rationalism. It was reintroduced in the Evangelical churches of Germany by Christhard Mahrenholz, Wilhelm Thomas, Konrad Ameln and others responsible for the preparation of the *Evangelisches Kirchengesangbuch* (1950). Similar "Hymn of the Week" plans are in use in the Lutheran churches of Holland and the Scandinavian countries, and in the evangelical churches of

Hymn of the Week Plan

First Sunday in Advent
    Savior of the Nations, Come

Second Sunday in Advent
    Lo! He Comes with Clouds Descending

Third Sunday in Advent
    Ye Sons of Men, Oh, Hearken

Fourth Sunday in Advent
    Oh, Come, Oh, Come, Emmanuel

Christmas Eve
    All My Heart This Night Rejoices

Christmas Day
    We Praise, O Christ, Your Holy Name

First Sunday after Christmas
    To Shepherds As They Watched by Night

The Name of Jesus
    O Blessed Day When First Was Poured

Second Sunday After Christmas
    From East to West, from Shore to Shore

The Epiphany of Our Lord
    How Lovely Shines the Morning Star

The Baptism of Our Lord
    Of the Father's Love Begotten

Second Sunday After the Epiphany
    The Only Son from Heaven

Third Sunday After the Epiphany
    O Christ, Our True and Only Light

Fourth Sunday After the Epiphany
    Seek Where Ye May to Find a Way

Fifth Sunday After the Epiphany
    O Splendor of God's Glory Bright

Sixth Sunday After the Epiphany
    From God Shall Naught Divide Me

Seventh Sunday After the Epiphany
    My Soul, Now Bless Thy Maker

Eighth Sunday After the Epiphany
    All Praise to God, Who Reigns Above

The Transfiguration of Our Lord
    O Wondrous Type! O Vision Fair

Ash Wednesday
    From Depths of Woe I Cry to Thee

First Sunday in Lent
    A Mighty Fortress Is Our God

Second Sunday in Lent
    Lord, Thee I Love with All My Heart

Third Sunday in Lent
    May God Bestow on Us His Grace

Fourth Sunday in Lent
    In Thee Alone, O Christ, My Lord

Fifth Sunday in Lent
    Let Us Ever Walk with Jesus

Sunday of the Passion (Palm Sunday)
    Ride On, Ride On in Majesty *or*
    The Royal Banners Forward Go

Maundy Thursday
    Jesus Christ, Our Blessed Savior

Good Friday
    A Lamb Goes Uncomplaining Forth

The Resurrection of Our Lord (Easter Day)
    Christ Jesus Lay in Death's Strong Bands

Second Sunday of Easter
    Ye Sons and Daughters of the King

Third Sunday of Easter
    With High Delight Let Us Unite

Fourth Sunday of Easter
    The King of Love My Shepherd Is

Fifth Sunday of Easter
    At the Lamb's High Feast We Sing

Sixth Sunday of Easter
    Dear Christians, One and All, Rejoice

The Ascension of Our Lord
    See God to Heaven Ascending

Seventh Sunday of Easter
    O Love, How Deep, How Broad, How High

The Day of Pentecost
    Come, Holy Ghost, God and Lord

The Holy Trinity
    Come, Holy Ghost, Creator Blest

Second Sunday After Pentecost
    Now Do We Pray to God the Holy Ghost

Third Sunday After Pentecost
    Hope of the World

Fourth Sunday After Pentecost
    All Mankind Fell in Adam's Fall

Fifth Sunday After Pentecost
  Lord of Our Life and God of Our
  Salvation

Sixth Sunday After Pentecost
  Come, Follow Me, the Savior Spake

Seventh Sunday After Pentecost
  Jehovah, You We Glorify

Eighth Sunday After Pentecost
  Lord of Glory, Who Hast Bought Us

Ninth Sunday After Pentecost
  One Thing's Needful

Tenth Sunday After Pentecost
  Our Father, Thou in Heaven Above

Eleventh Sunday After Pentecost
  Praise the Almighty, My Soul Adore Him

Twelfth Sunday After Pentecost
  My Soul, Now Bless Thy Maker

Thirteenth Sunday After Pentecost
  When in the Hour of Utmost Need

Fourteenth Sunday After Pentecost
  Thy Strong Word Did Cleave the
  Darkness

Fifteenth Sunday After Pentecost
  Jesus, I My Cross Have Taken

Sixteenth Sunday After Pentecost
  Lord of All Nations, Grant Me Grace

Seventeenth Sunday After Pentecost
  O Faithful God, Thanks Be to Thee

Eighteenth Sunday After Pentecost
  Salvation Unto Us Has Come

Nineteenth Sunday After Pentecost
  All Praise to Thee, for Thou, O King
  Divine

Twentieth Sunday After Pentecost
  I Know My Faith Is Founded

Twenty-First Sunday After Pentecost
  O Kingly Love

Twenty-Second Sunday After Pentecost
  In Thee, Lord, Have I Put My Trust

Twenty-Third Sunday After Pentecost
  Lord, Thee I Love with All My Heart

Twenty-Fourth Sunday After Pentecost
  Wake, Awake, for Night Is Flying

Twenty-Fifth Sunday After Pentecost
  In God, My Faithful God

Twenty-Sixth Sunday After Pentecost
  The Day Is Surely Drawing Near

Twenty-Seventh Sunday After Pentecost
  In the Midst of Earthly Life

Last Sunday After Pentecost
  At the Name of Jesus

St. Michael and All Angels
  Lord God, We All to Thee Give Praise

Reformation Day
  Salvation Unto Us Has Come

All Saints Day
  For All the Saints Who from Their
  Labors Rest

Thanksgiving Day
  I Will Sing My Maker's Praises

Switzerland. The "Hymn of the Week" plan presented in *Planning the Service* prepared by Ralph Gehrke (1961) for Lutheran churches of America using *The Lutheran Hymnal* was based on the *Wochenlied* plan prepared for the Evangelical Church of Germany.

A number of official and unofficial de tempore or "Hymn of the Week" plans are available for use in the Lutheran churches in America. The suggested listing in the accompanying chart is a revision of existing plans prepared by the author which is usable in churches using either the standard pericopes or the more recently available three-year lectionary. It is based on the traditional de tempore hymn plans of the Lutheran church, at the same time incorporating some material more recently available to Lutheran churches in America.

Method of Performance

From earliest days psalms were sung antiphonally in the church, that is, in such a way that two parts of the congregation or two choirs, often facing each other, sang alternate verses, thus inciting one another by the reciprocal, lively rhythm of alternate tension and relaxation. In a similar manner in the Reformation age, the gradual hymns were sung antiphonally by the unison singing congregation and a "partner." The "partner" was either a unison singing choir (the *chorus choralis*), a choir singing in harmony (the *figural* choir), the organ playing an organ chorale (such as the settings in the *Goerlitz Tabulaturbuch* [1650] of Samuel Scheidt [1587—1654]), or a brass ensemble. Thus the congregation was usually busy every other stanza. When it was not singing, its "partner" could bring into play the entire treasury of church music in order to unfold and interpret the melody, and thus illuminate the content of the hymn for the congregation. In this way genuinely artistic music became an organic part of corporate worship, and the congregation was drawn into the music making of the choir and organ, even as the choir and organ by their subjection to the *cantus firmus* of the congregation's hymn showed that they understood that they were not called to dominate the congregation, but rather to serve it in its worship. This is also the preferred method of rendition of the gradual or de tempore hymn today. EK.

Readings: Blume, Friedrich, *Protestant Church Music* (New York, 1974); Brodde, Otto and Christa Mueller, *Das Gradual Lied* (Munich, 1954); Gehrke, Ralph, *Planning the Service, A Workbook for Pastors, Organists, and Choirmasters* (St. Louis, 1961); Klammer, Edward W., "A New Approach to the Hymn of the Week," *Church Music*, 75·1 (St. Louis, 1975); Reed, Luther D., *The Lutheran Liturgy* (Philadelphia, 1947); Reich, Philipp, Konrad Ameln, and Gerhard Schwarz, *Das Wochenlied* (Kassel, 1952); Thomas, Paul, ed., *The Hymn of the Week*, 5 vols. (St. Louis, 1961).

See also: alternation practice; chorale; HCM, III, IV

ecclesiastical Latin, pronunciation

Ever since Pentecost the Christian church has used a multiplicity of languages. It also has had several "official" languages that were standard across a variety of cultures. The first of these "official" languages was

Greek, the language of the New Testament scriptures. At the end of the 2d century, as Mediterranean commerce increased and Roman influence became more dominant, the official language gradually shifted to Latin. It remained so for most of the history of the Christian Church, even through the Reformation, and since then has been the official language of the Roman Catholic church to this day.

All Latin is not alike, and it should be pointed out that ecclesiastical Latin is a special type with its own vocabulary, morphology, and syntax. It was developed and cultivated by the church as a kind of sacral language quite distinct from the street Latin spoken by the Roman citizens. As a result, ecclesiastical Latin became a kind of cultic speech which acquired an elevated, otherworldly sound that seemed appropriate to speaking or hearing "holy things."

The official language of the church was used for keeping records and for written communication, but these functioned primarily in silent reading. It was in the chant of the liturgy and in the motets and other attendant liturgical music that ecclesiastical Latin was most commonly heard. And it was here that pronunciation was of great importance. It was intended that the use of a single language should be an expression of the catholicity and unity of the church; but the pronunciation of the Latin became increasingly varied due to colorings from the native tongue of the speaker or singer, or due to lack of training or misunderstanding of the correct pronunciation. These variations actually altered the phonemic structure of the language. In addition there was an ever increasing number of variations creeping into the music used to present these texts.

Beginning in the 19th century and continuing into the 20th century there developed a strong desire for reform and restoration of the liturgy, and this included concern for both music as well as text. Documents associated with Pope Pius X (particularly the motu proprio *Tra le sollecitudini* of 1903, the decree of the congregation of rites of Jan. 8, 1904) called for this restoration and described its nature. These concerns are also reflected in the work of the Benedictine monks of Solesmes whose work (see esp. the *Liber Usualis* of 1934) has set the standard for both the performance of Gregorian chant as well as the pronunciation of ecclesiastical Latin.

Since Vatican II the restriction of liturgical language to Latin has been removed. But the liturgy is still often done in Latin, and there exists a rich heritage of chant, motets, masses, and other choral music that forms a large part of the repertoire of a variety of choral groups today. With a growing emphasis on correct performance practice, it is imperative that directors of choirs study carefully the correct pronunciation of ecclesiastical Latin so that their performance may also have phonological integrity.

One of the chief difficulties in achieving a correct pronunciation of ecclesiastical Latin is the changing of incorrect habits of the choir director or his singers. The most common error of this type is the sound associated with the letter *e*. It is frequently heard as the *a* in the word day, a mistake unfortunately promulgated by books that showed the wrong sound as the proper pronunciation (cf. Coward, H., *Choral Technique and Interpretation.* London, 1912). This approach presents the word *Credo* as KRAY-do. The second syllable of that word illustrates the other most common error, that of pronouncing the letter *o* as in the word *tone* instead of the word *song*. Actually each vowel in Latin should maintain its pure sound for its full length and not be colored by sounds which follow it, especially the sound of *r*.

Words that contain the letter *s* should be carefully watched so that the sound does not become voiced and thus shifted to the sound of English *z*. Singers whose native tongue is English will generally also tend to alter the sound of the letter *i* to the short sound of that letter (e.g., *tin*) especially for the Latin word *in* which is an English cognate. Words that end with consonant stops should be released passively so that there is no violent puff of air or extra sound after the word.

The syllables of Latin words must be carefully differentiated and not contracted or slurred together. Except for the diphthongs, each vowel must have its own distinct sound without blurring the connections between them. Thus *diei* (di-e-i) must have three clear syllables with a separate true vowel sound for each. The accentual stress of the syllables must be maintained for the sake of the rhythmic shape and flow of the music. Very often the music provides the accent for the text. In many cases, however, especially in music from the Renaissance, a knowledge of the proper syllable accent is necessary to reveal the microrhythmic structure of the music.

The accompanying chart shows the pronunciation of each of the graphemes of ecclesiastical Latin. TG

Readings: de Angelis, Michael, *The Correct Pronunciation of Latin According to Roman Usage* (Philadelphia, 1937); Gleason, Harold, *Music Literature Outlines*, Series I: *Music in the Middle Ages and Renaissance* (Rochester, N. Y., 1951); *Liber Usualis*, Tournai ed. (1950).

See also: Catholic pronouncements and decrees on church music; chant, Gregorian; church music history, medieval; office hymn; psalmody, Gregorian; sequence; trope; *HCM*, IV

Vowel Sounds

Vowel	Model word	IPA[1] symbol
a	father	ɑ
e, ae[2], oe[2]	red	ɛ
i, y	liter	i
o	song	ɔ
u	ruby	u

[1]International Phonetic Alphabet.

[2]If the e in these digraphs is marked with a diaeresis (aë, oë) then a syllable change occurs between the vowels and each gets its own sound.

au, eu, ay are treated as one–syllable diphthongs, and if they are extended by the music, the sound of the first of the two vowels is sustained.

u preceded by q or ng is sounded quickly like the English sound of w.

Consonant Sounds

Pronounced as in English:

b, d, f, k, l, m, n, p, q, v, ph

Slightly altered or variable:

j   is pronounced like initial y in English (may also be spelled with i)

r   is lightly rolled with the tongue

s   is like English s, but is slightly softened when between two vowels (see special case below under Variable)

x   is like English ks, but is slightly softened when between two vowels (see also special case under Variable)

z   is like English dz (lads)

ch   is like English k

With exceptions:

t, th   Normally like English t, but when followed by i plus another vowel and preceded by any letter except s, x, or t it becomes ts

h   Normally silent and omitted in pronunciation, but sounded like English h in the two words *nihil* and *mihi*

169

Variable:	before e, ae, oe, i, or y	IPA	before other letters	IPA
c, cc	ch(urch)	tf	c(ome)	k
sc	sh(op)	f	consecutive sounds sk	sk
g	g(inger)	d3	g(od)	g
			except before n, then the two letters are sounded ny (canyon)	nj
xc	ksh(friction)	kf	ksk (excuse)	ksk

Gospel motet

The polyphonic setting of a text taken from the Gospels of Matthew, Mark, Luke, or John. The genre flourished in Protestant Germany in the 16th and 17th centuries, when entire cycles of Gospel compositions were compiled to correspond to the assigned readings for Sunday and festivals of the Church Year.

Following the ancient Jewish practice of chanting Holy Scripture in public worship, early Christian services featured selections from the Old Testament and from the Epistles and Gospels of the New Testament. The Gospel was considered the chief of the lessons for each day of the developing Church Year, and its presentation was often accompanied by a significant ritual.

The longest of the assigned Gospel readings of the Church Year were the Passion accounts of the suffering and death of Jesus Christ, assigned to four days of Holy Week. In the 15th century the words of the "crowd" (*turba*) in the Passion were set to polyphony for performance by the choir, while the remainder of the text was still chanted. In the course of the next century many polyphonic settings of the entire Passion text were composed.

During the 16th century, Roman Catholic composers ranging from Josquin Desprez (c. 1440—1521) to Orlando di Lasso (c. 1532—94) wrote individual Gospel motets that were similar in character to other expressive motets of the age. Most of these Biblical settings were not a part of the conventional Proper or Ordinary texts of the Mass or the Office. Some were portions of other traditional liturgical texts, such as Office Responsories; some may have been composed for informal or private devotional services. It is not unlikely, however, that many were intended for use in Protestant services.

In his suggested model orders of worship (the *Formula missae*, 1523, and *Deutsche Messe*, 1526) Martin Luther made no special provision for the performance of a Gospel motet. In his Latin Mass of 1523 Luther naturally assumed that the Gospel would be chanted in Latin; in the German Mass of 1526 he specified a Gospel chant formula adapted to the German text. Luther's influence was strong in liturgical matters, and his followers supported his retention of the Mass and his encouragement of the optional use of a number of choral or congregational elements in the order, which led eventually to the choral performance of the assigned Gospel for the day. Although official regional orders of worship (*Kirchenordnungen*) published after Luther's time did not recognize the Gospel motet as such, its performance is established in part through the proliferation of its publication.

Most of the Gospel motets (*Evangelienmotetten*, sometimes called *Spruchmotetten*, "Bible-text motets") were settings of only a few verses, usually the essence of the message (called *Kernspruch*, "text-kernel"), often selected for their dramatic content or terse summary of a significant thought of the Gospel. From the internal evidence of chant formulas included in some collections of Gospel motets and from the observation that some of the texts of the motets are not complete in themselves, it may be assumed that the polyphonic motet was most likely sung in conjunction with either the Latin or German Gospel reading in the Lutheran service of the late 16th and early 17th centuries. (Reading, i.e., chanting of the Gospel in either or both languages was common in this period.) Following this assumption, the chanted Gospel would be continued at the appropriate point by the choir singing the verses of the polyphonic motet setting. At the conclusion of the motet the Gospel chant would be resumed.

Whereas individual Gospel motet compositions had appeared in the first half of the 16th century, several anthologies of motets for the Church Year were subsequently published, apparently intended for Protestant use, although consisting largely of works of Roman Catholic composers. One of the foremost examples of such collections was published in six volumes by

Montanus and Neuber in Nuremberg (1554—56). Perhaps such anthologies did not fully satisfy the worship needs of Lutheran congregations, for a generous outpouring of talent and energy soon gave rise to the birth of a new genre—Gospel motet cycles written by individual composers.

Publication of complete cycles of motets on German or Latin Gospel texts for the Church Year by Protestant composers seems to have begun in 1565 and continued until 1681. The composers of the major cycles, the date and language of publication, and the required performers follow:

COMPOSER	DATE	LANGUAGE	PERFORMANCE FORCES
Homer Herpol	1565	Latin	5 voices
Johann Wanning	1580, 1584	Latin	5—7 voices
Andreas Raselius	1594, 1595	German	5—9 voices
Friedrich Weissensee	1595	German	5 voices
Philippus Dulichius	1595, 1598	Latin	5 voices
Sethus Calvisius	1599	Latin	2 voices
Georg Otto	1601	Latin	2 voices
Georg Otto	1604	Latin	4—8 voices
Christoph Demantius	1610	German	6 voices
Volckmar Leisring	1611	German/Latin	4—8 voices, instr.
Melchior Vulpius completed by	1612, 1614	German	4—8 voices
Johannes Christenius	1621	German	4—8 voices
Thomas Elsbeth	1616, 1621	German	5 voices
Melchior Franck	1623	German	4 voices
Wolfgang Brueckner	1656	German	4—8 voices, instr.
Johann C. Horn	1680, 1681	German	4 voices, instr.

The fact that 29 editions of various Gospel motet cycles were published in 32 years (1594—1625) indicates the popularity of the genre.

The cycles generally contain settings of the Gospels for the Sundays and chief festivals of the Church Year. In keeping with the Lutheran calendar only Biblical saints are included and motets are assigned to three major festivals associated with the Virgin Mary. Thus constituted, the collections comprise a substantial body of choral literature, for the average size of the cycles amounts to more than 60 motets.

The style of composition characterizing the collections is that of a relatively conservative, imitative polyphony, although some composers (Vulpius, for example) wrote motets in a simple chordal style. Expressive writing does not dominate the collections, but is reserved for emphasis of dramatic words and phrases. Instrumental participation is indicated on title pages of three collections that contain no separate instrumental parts, while three others provide music for instruments in the concerted style.

Interest in the composition of motets on the unaltered Gospel texts waned as the popularity of poetic paraphrases of the Gospel increased. The declining interest in the singing of purely Scriptural texts coincided with the increasing influence of Pietism in worship services, and the development of the sacred concerto and the Lutheran church cantata.

A revival of interest in the singing of Gospel motets has resulted in modern editions of the complete German Gospel motet cycles of Vulpius, Raselius, and Franck, as well as the publication of individual Gospel motets by these and other composers of their age. Contemporary series of choral settings of Gospel texts in English have been undertaken by Richard Hillert, Jan Bender, and Gerhard Krapf. CM

Readings: Blume, Friedrich, *Protestant Church Music* (New York, 1974); Messerli, Carlos R., "The *Corona harmonica* (1610) of Christoph Demantius and the Gospel Motet Tradition," dissertation, University of Iowa, 1974; Moser, Hans J., *Die mehrstimmige Vertonung des Evangeliums,* I: *Geschichtliche Darstellung,* 2d enl. and rev. ed. (Hildesheim and Wiesbaden, 1968).

See also: church music history, Renaissance—the Reformation tradition; passion; *HCM,* IV

Gospel Song

The term gospel song refers to the religious song form that flourished in the United States during the revivals of the Reconstruction Era, beginning c. 1868.

The camp meeting, which began c. 1800 in Logan County, Ky., under Presbyterian leadership, soon spread to include Baptists and Methodists to the south and east, ultimately encompassing at least 14 states. With its spread also went the enthusiastic *camp-meeting song,* one of the chief antecedents of the gospel song. Camp-meeting songs are typified by simple, direct words that describe (1) the condition of the sinner and (2) his "being saved," matched with music derived from existing folk traditions. There is some evidence that these spontaneous songs were used in the great awakening of half a century before. Collections including Joshua Smith's *Divine Hymns, or Spiritual Songs* (1784) and Jeremiah Ingall's *The Christian Harmony* (1805) contain a few examples of camp-meeting songs.

Charles A. Johnson categorizes camp-meeting songs and hymns as follows: (1) *the religious ballad,* usually a solo voice presenting a personal witness to the "unsaved"; (2) *hymns of praise*, as in common practice from the previous revivals, the setting of classic English hymns of Watts, Wesley, Cowper, Newton, and other evangelicals to rousing, enthusiastic tunes. (Collections such as Henry Allison's *Hymns and Spiritual Songs* (1802), David Mintz's *A Collection of Songs—Usually Sung at Camp Meetings* (1809), Thomas S. Hinde's *A Pilgrim Songster* (1810) and John Wyeth's *Repository of Sacred Music, Part Second* (1813), contain some of these ballads and hymns: (3) *the revival spiritual*, texts based on phrases common to the language of the camp meeting, i.e., (question) "Who is going to the promised land?" (answer) "I'm bound for the promised land. Halleluia!" These responses and affirmations (choruses) freely used whatever music was at hand, and it is primarily here that the mingling of the folk music of Europe, Scandinavia, and England (including Scotland, Ireland, and Wales) with that of Afro-America begins.

Four important southern collections containing texts and tunes from camp-meeting times, as well as music from the "singing schools," are William Walker's *Southern Harmony* (1835), B. F. White's *The Sacred Harp* (1844), Hauser and Turner's *Olive Leaf* (1878), and C. H. Cayce's *Good Old Songs* (1913). *The Sacred Harp* (rev. 1971) is still in common use by Sacred Harp Singing groups in Tennessee, Georgia, Mississippi, and Alabama. Northern sources include Jonathan Leavitt's *The Christian Lyre* (1837) and Joseph Hillman's *The Revivalist* (1868).

As camp meetings gave way to "protracted meetings" of longer duration in more permanent buildings and grounds, we find the transition to the "camp meeting indoors," or the indoor revival and large assemblies.

With the founding of the Sunday School Movement in 1824 (The American Sunday School Union) there developed an organizational (as opposed to a denominational) need for a type of expression that Reynolds describes as follows: "The simple Sunday School songs found a warm welcome in those churches where the regular hymn singing had declined. . . lacking vitality and warmth. When educational standards were low and cultural advantages meager, the absence of a traditional (denominational) hymnody and the freedom and independence of local congregations all joined together to provide a fertile climate for the gospel song." Further, according to Benson, "the long series of Sunday School songbooks of George F. Root, William B. Bradbury, Asa Hull, Horace Walters, Silas J. Vail, Robert Lowry, William G. Fischer and others . . . developed a taste in the young for the lighter types of religious songs." (For a review of Sunday school texts, tunes, and sources, see Reynolds and Price's *A Joyful Song: Christian Hymnody.*)

In addition to the easy and catchy Sunday school songs are found the songs of national conventions of organizations such as the YMCA (founded London, 1844; Boston, 1851); "prayer and praise meetings" begun in 1873 by Eben Tourjee (1834—91), founder of the New England Conservatory of Music (1867) and chief organizer and conductor of revival choirs that served the needs of large throngs gathered in the Boston Tabernacle; the patriotic songs of the Civil War; the "living room music" typified by the genius of Stephen Foster; songs of the Salvation Army (founded London, 1865); and, of course, songs of the temperance movement.

All these antecedents combine to form the simplistic musical and rhetorical format that is at the center of the gospel song. If it is anything, the gospel song is functional, direct, enthusiastic, and abounding in musical generalization, the essence of popular music of any generation. (In the best sense, if you have heard one, you have heard them all!)

It is in the work of Philip P. Bliss (1838—76) that we can see in specific detail the gospel song as both the product and the embodiment of the Reconstruction Era Revival.

As writer-publisher, Bliss typifies the use of the newly opened copyright office in Washington, D. C. (1870). Previous to that time, copyrights were registered in the several districts of the individual states, making it almost impossible to enforce the 1831 copyright law. The effect of the centralization of copyright registration was to allow the publisher of the gospel song to have immediate and undisputed "right to copy," thus allowing only the owner to print and distribute without challenge from another publisher of the same style of music.

Bliss is also the first to use the term "gospel song" in reference to singing materials common to both the Sunday school and the revival. (*Gospel Songs, A Choice Collection of Hymns and Tunes, New and Old, for Gospel Meetings, Sunday School.* Cincinnati, 1874.) As Gealy points out, the title of this collection also begs the question of the distinction between gospel song and gospel hymns.

When Bliss joined with evangelist Major D. W. Whittle they established the combination of songwriter-publisher-evangelistic enterprise which became the hallmark of the succeeding revivals of Moody-Sankey, Alexander-Chapman, Sunday-Rodeheaver, and Towner-Torry. Beginning with Bliss, and excluding only the more recent revivals of Graham-Shea and others, most—if not all—"revivalism" directed, maintained, and recycled the gospel-song style through the means of exclusive copyright control. The direct effect of this was to bring into sharp contrast the music and words of traditional hymnody as found in the hymnals of the major denominations on the one hand, and the songbooks used in other than the main worship services on the other—which is to say that the gospel song became "the song" of recreation, education, and evangelism, and for many it still is.

Among the important names related to the development of the gospel song is that of Ira D. Sankey (1840—1908). Sankey found fertile ground for gospel songs in England as he worked in the revivals of Dwight L. Moody (1873). Returning to the United States, Sankey personified for a quarter of a century a certain integrity as a combination soloist-songleader, as opposed to others who performed more as master of ceremonies. Other poets of Reconstruction days' gospel songs include: Fanny J. Crosby (c. 1820—1915)—"Blessed Assurance"; Edward Mote (1797—1874)—"The Solid Rock"; Lydia Baxter (1808—74)—"Take the Name of Jesus With You"; Annie S. Hawks (1835—1918)—"I Need Thee Every Hour"; Will L. Thompson (1847—1919)—"Softly and Tenderly"; Katherine Hankey (1834—1911)—"I Love to Tell the Story"; Joseph Scriven (1819—86)— "What a Friend We Have in Jesus"; and Joseph H. Gilmore (1834— 1918)—"He Leadeth Me, O Blessed Thought." In more recent times the names of Charles H. Gabriel ("Since Jesus Came into My Heart"), B. D. Ackley ("If Your Heart Keeps Right"), and B. B. McKinney ("I Am Satisfied With Jesus") have been identified with the continuing tradition of gospel-song writers. The influx of black people into urban settings, according to Southern, stirred a new kind of gospel song performed in an improvisatory style with piano, guitar, and percussion. Thomas A. Dorsey

(b. 1899) is the name that symbolizes this Negro gospel music from its roots in the 1920s to the present. Somewhere between this urban "black" style and the rural "white" style of the 19th century is the productivity of the Philadelphia black Methodist preacher Albert Tindley (1851—1933), with its traditional identification of preaching with congregational song in the context of parish life and work. Although viewed by many as America's unique Religious song, it has at the same time been criticised as being inadequate in the explicit verbal proclamation of the social demands of the Gospel, that it has provided a much too friendly musical setting for words that express the life, death, and resurrection of Jesus Christ; and further, that this tradition, through its commercial grounding in exclusive copyright ownership, mass printing and distribution, as well as recordings, has recycled a one-time viable expression of a cause and event (the revival and revivalism) as *the* cause and event in each generation since Bliss and Sankey. CY

Readings: Benson, L. F., *The English Hymn* (Richmond, 1915); *Companion to the [Methodist] Hymnal,* F. Gealy, A. Lovelace, and C. Young, compilers (Nashville, 1970); Johnson, Charles A., *The Frontier Camp Meeting* (Dallas, 1955); Reynolds and Price, *A Joyful Song: Christian Hymnody* (New York, 1978); Reynolds, W. J., *Companion to Baptist Hymnal (Nashville, 1976); Jackson, G. P., Spiritual Folk Songs of Early America* (New York, 1937); *White Spirituals of the Southern Uplands* (Chapel Hill 1933); Yoden, Don, *Pennsylvania Spirituals* (Lancaster, 1961); Southern, Eileen, *The Music of Black Americans* (New York, 1971); Porter, Ellen Jane Lorenz, *Glory Hallelujah: The Story of the Camp-Meeting Hymns* (A publication of the Hymns Society of America; April 1978).

See also: church music history, American; church music history, American Lutheran; HCM, II, III, V

hymnody, Old Testament

The songs of the Old Testament are Israel's response to (a) the deeds the Lord performed in her history, and (b) the Word He gave through His servants. Many such songs are scattered throughout the Old Testament, e.g., the Testament of Jacob (Gen. 49), the Blessings of Moses (Deut. 33), the Song of Miriam (Ex. 15:21), the Song of Deborah and Barak (Judg. 5:3-31), David's Lamentation over Saul and Jonathan (2 Sam. 1:19-27) and over Abner (2 Sam. 3:33-34), the Last Words of David (2 Sam. 23:1-7), David's Thanksgiving for Victory (2 Sam. 22), the Song of Hannah (1 Sam. 2:1-10), and the Song of Habakkuk (Hab. 3).

However, most of Israel's sacred songs have been gathered in the Psalter, a sort of "hymnbook" for worship at the postexilic temple. Even though its final edition (3d century B.C.) presents the psalms as "literature" (divided rather arbitrarily into 5 "books:" Psalms 1—41, 42—72, 73—89, 90—106, and 107—150), easily discernible earlier collections such as the "Pilgrimage Psalms" (120—134) or "The Psalms of Korah" (42—49) indicate that the psalms had originally been written and collected for use in living worship, rather than for devotional reading as "literature."

But even earlier, these sacred songs had served to bring Israel's life experiences into the sharp focus of ultimate reality. For instance, whenever the community experienced catastrophe, whether famine or military defeat and the like, it appeared before the Lord with lament and petition, awaiting His Word (cf. Ps. 80). Whenever it experienced success, whether a bumper harvest or military victory, it appeared for worship with sacrifice and praise (cf. Ps. 124). Also individual worshipers, like Hannah in her distress over continued barrenness (1 Sam. 1), had expressed their laments in traditional prayers for hundreds of years before such oral laments came to be written down and collected in what we call "Psalms of Lament." Similarly, individuals who had experienced success and blessing, like the joyous mother of Samuel (1 Sam. 2), had expressed their praise in traditional prayers (and sacrifices, which were "acted prayers") for hundreds of years before such oral praise came to be written and collected in "Psalms of Praise." Such a background, extremely rich in the experiences of living and of worship, helps account for the fact that mankind has used and still uses the psalms to express its deepest experiences of ultimate reality. The emotional range of the prayer-psalms extends from dark lament through expressions of trust and petitions to ecstatic praise, which came to be the dominant tonality of Old Testament psalms. Even if a lament psalm begins on the dark note of lament, it changes and eventually expresses praise.

Three basic types of praying have resulted in three basic types of prayer-psalms: (1) lament-psalms, (2) praise-psalms, and (3) hymns.

Psalms of Lament ordinarily begin, after an Invocation, with the lament, fully expressed in three typical variations: the "I-Lament," complaining about personal suffering; the "They-Lament," complaining about "the enemy;" and a "Thou-Lament" complaining to the Lord about His apparent enmity. Expressions of trust and confidence (or a review of God's gracious acts in the past) often come next, before the petitions, which are usually expressed in three forms: (a) for God's presence ("Observe me"); (b) for God's intervention ("Heal me"); (c) against a triumph by the enemy. The Psalms ends with praise or, in the case of very dark laments, the vow to praise. 2 Chron. 20:1-23 vividly describes the drama out of which such psalms of lament arose. Ps. 13 is a typical "Individual's Psalm of Lament;" Ps. 80, a typical "People's Psalm of Lament." Variations include Psalms of Repentence (Ps. 51, 130) and Psalms of Trust (Ps. 23, 123).

Psalms of Praise, occasioned by marvelous rescue and usually accompanied by sacrifices of thanksgiving, are structured with two basic elements (often after an Introduction, consisting of either a brief summary or a statement of purpose): (1) the Summons to Praise ("Sing praises, O ye His saints"), originally addresssed to the people present in the sanctuary courtyard, and (2) the worshiper's Account of God's Rescue (traditionally stylized to include a look back at the crisis, and an account of the rescue: "I cried unto the Lord," "He heard me," "He delivered me"). A Conclusion expresses confidence or praise (Hallelujah! "Praise the Lord"). Typical examples are Psalm 124 (a People's Psalm of Narrative Praise) and Psalm 30 (an Individual's Psalm of Narrative Praise).

Hymns were accompanied by instrumental music, and sung regularly whenever God's people gathered for worship at set times, not only at crises or successes, when Laments and Praise were especially appropriate. Hymns are psalms of praise, but, instead of reciting God's deed (as Psalms of Narrative Praise do), hymns bring *descriptive* praise and delineate God's nature as not only the Majestic One, who is Creator and Lord of History, but also as the Compassionate One, who condescends to rescue the lost and to preserve those whom He has rescued. Ps. 113 is a typical Hymn. Variations concentrate on one or another of the themes common to the psalm-hymn (e.g., creation-psalms, like Ps. 8 or 104, praise Him as the Creator, whereas history-psalms, like Ps. 105, praise Him as Lord of History).

Besides these 3 basic types of Prayer-Psalms, the Psalter contains also Liturgical Psalms, Royal Psalms, and Wisdom Psalms.

Liturgical Psalms bring the words that once accompanied liturgical action. For example, Ps. 24 presupposes the annual procession in which the Lord's ark-throne was brought up Mt. Zion to its resting place in His temple throne-room. This represented a reenactment of David's first bringing "the Lord of Hosts," who sat invisibly upon the ark-throne, to his new capital city Jerusalem. This procession-psalm consists of three parts: (1) a hymn, presumably sung by the Levites as they moved in procession up the sacred hill, carrying the Ark, praising the Creator of the World (vv. 1-2); (2) an interrogation at the boundary line of the sacred precinct, to ascertain if the would-be worshipers were living in accord with the stipulations of the covenant and could be admitted to the sacred area (vv. 3-6); (3) an entrance song (vv. 7-10), sung antiphonally between a temple-acropolis guard inside and the oncoming procession as it was about to pass through the gate, whose dimensions were much too small for the gigantic divine Victor, "the Lord of Hosts," as He entered the temple-courtyard and the temple, where He would sit in state, to dispense His blessing and His Word to His people and to receive their prayers and sacrifices. Ps. 118 is also a procession-psalm, one in which the king played a key role, even reciting, as part of the liturgy, an Individual's Psalm of Praise. Pilgrimage Psalms are represented by Ps. 122; closely related to them are the Psalms of Zion, represented by Pss. 46 and 48.

Royal Psalms are those in which kingship—of the Messiah, or of reigning kings, or of both—is prominent. The promises rehearsed in them go back to the Lord's original promise to David concerning the everlasting and world-encompassing rule of his "house" or "seed" (2 Sam. 7). Psalm 2 reflects coronation ceremonies in which such promises are especially prominent. Such rites began with the anointing of the new king (henceforth called "The Anointed of the Lord," in Hebrew "the Messiah," in Greek "the Christ") by the high priest at the Gihon spring; the rites climaxed when the new king ascended to the throne of David, where he was officially adopted and proclaimed to be Yahweh's Son or Representative on earth and the recipient of the great promises made to David. Such royal psalms as Ps. 2, 72, 110, and 132 reflect such rites. Even after Israel had lost its political independence in the exilic age and flesh-and-blood kings had ceased to reign, these psalms continued to be used in worship, but now with reference to the expected final King of the end time, in whom the promises to David would really be fulfilled. Christians have considered these Messianic psalms fulfilled in Jesus of Nazareth, whom the Father elevated to the Messianic Throne at the Resurrection.

Wisdom Psalms stand, so to say, on the borderline between the Psalter and the Book of Proverbs. In fact such a "psalm" as Ps. 37 is really a loose collection of proverbs, each one full of the wisdom born and matured by life experience, like those of the Book of Proverbs. Wisdom Poems (usually contrasting the Righteous and the Wicked) are represented by Ps. 73, 1, and 119, the latter two having apparently once marked the introduction and conclusion to an early edition of the psalter at a stage in the development of the psalter when psalms were considered "devotional literature" to be read and heard like other poems from wisdom literature.

Research has been unable to reconstruct in precise and complete terms the worship out of which the psalms arose. Hence opinions are divided concerning the extent to which Israel's worship and its "hymnody" were similar to and different from that of her neighbors. What has become clear, however, is that ancient Israel did adopt certain formal elements such as particular poetic conventions (e.g., the Semitic poetic device of stating the same, similar, or contrasting, thoughts in parallel statements, the "thought-rime"). But it is also clear that, whenever she adopted such elements, she always also adapted them, integrating them into her monotheistic faith to express her covenant relation with the Lord. RG

Readings: Mowinckel, S., *The Psalms in Israel's Worship* (Nashville, 1962); Weiser, A., *The Psalms* (Philadelphia, 1963); Eaton, J., *Psalms* (London, 1967); Lamb, J. A., *The Psalms in Christian Worship* (London, 1962).

See also: Biblical instruments; church music history, Jewish

hymnody, New Testament

The New Testament writings attest both the content and the vigor of early Christian worship life. Here in generous frequency are excerpts of creeds, prayers, and eulogies, doxologies and benedictions, versicles and responses. Forming a significant portion of this liturgical bounty are "hymns" and "psalms" and "odes," or "songs" (Col. 3:16; Eph. 5:19).

Varied Terminology

The very use of diverse terminology such as this suggests that the early church encouraged a creative variety of musical and poetic expression in its corporate worship. Had the church sought to discourage such expression, the variety of terms would eventually have given way to a single term, by which we would now be able to define and delimit the "hymn form."

But instead of a crisp definition, the New Testament submits a succession of terms that its writers, like those in Judaism, appear to have used without differentiation. Philo, the Alexandrian Jew and contemporary of Jesus, refers to the Old Testament psalm collection as "hymns" (*Vit. Cont.* 25). The "hymn" sung by Jesus and his disciples at the conclusion of the Last Supper (Mk. 14:26; Mt. 26:30) was likely part of the Hallel (Pss. 114—118). In 1 Cor. 14:26 a "psalm" means a Christian song, perhaps newly composed. In Rev. 5:9 a distinctly Christian composition is called a "new ode," a term already used in the Old Testament Psalter (114:9).

Jewish Heritage

Though hymns were a significant and successful aspect of Greek religion (even prompting imitation by philosophical writers), there is no evidence that pagan Greek hymnody directly influenced early Christian worship. Since most of the earliest Christians had been members of Judaism and continued to worship in the temple in Jerusalem (Acts 2:46; 3:1; 5:12) and in the synagogs of Palestine and of the Diaspora (Acts 6:9; 13:14; 14:1; 16:16) after they became Christians, the most direct influence on their forms was exerted by synagogal antecedents.

Psalms from the Old Testament were a regular part of synagog services. There were psalms to be read on the different days of the week, psalms appointed for festival occasions, and there are indications that the 150 psalms were read consecutively over a three-year period on the sabbaths. Worshipers in the synagog were thus exposed to the psalm form and content. This form seems to have been the model for Christian hymns.

The Christian interest in Old Testament psalms is further illustrated by the fact that more than one third of the 300 Old Testament passages quoted in the New Testament are from the Psalms. Jesus had said that it was necessary to fulfill what was written about him in the psalms, as well as in the law of Moses and in the prophets (Lk. 24:44).

That Christians should write hymns in the psalm form is not unusual, since the production of psalms in Judaism continued after the completion of the canonical psalm book. One may adduce the apocryphal *Psalms of Solomon*, the "Song of the Three Young Men" inserted into the text of *Daniel*, the hymns in *Tobit*, the *Hodayot*, or Psalms of Thanksgiving, included among the Dead Sea Scrolls, and the hymn-writing activity of the Therapeutae described by Philo (*Vit. Cont.* 29).

Hymn or Poem?

The fundamental features of Hebrew poetry, as represented in the psalms, are *parallelismus membrorum*, a parallelism of thought in successive lines, and an accentual rhythm. A segment of poetry consists of two or three lines, each of which complements or balances its counterpart. Instead of an equal number of syllables, each line contains two, three, or sometimes four, word groupings, or sense units. The accent falls on the major words in the sense units. A variety of rhythms results from the combination of lines with either an equal or an unequal number of word groupings. Most Hebrew poems are divided into two or more stanzas.

Hymns in the New Testament are constructed in accordance with these stylistic features and are thus indistinguishable from poems. We have no absolute criteria for asserting that this New Testament poem or that is actually a hymn sung in early Christian worship. Probably only when a religious poem appears in an unmistakable liturgical context can it be called a hymn.

Occasions for Hymns

Like the Old Testament psalms, New Testament hymns were part of the corporate worship experience of the people of God. In the service, if an individual recites a "psalm," it is to be "for the common good" (1 Cor. 14:26). "Singing praises"—whether one has a specific hymn text in hand or not—requires the exertion of both spirit and mind (1 Cor. 14:15).

Col. 3:16 asserts that in demonstration of the "word of Christ" among them Christians are to "teach and admonish one another by psalms and hymn and songs." Such compositions are called "spiritual": wrought by the Spirit's help and used in the church, where the Spirit works. They are sung in heartfelt response to God's saving act in Christ. (See also Eph. 5:18-20.)

The content of New Testament hymns indicate that the celebration of the sacraments, particularly that of Baptism, was the occasion for the singing of many of these songs. Some hymns make use of baptismal metaphors, others contain creeds, which were baptismal in origin.

The Lukan Psalms

The most widely recognized examples of New Testament hymns are the canticles in Luke's infancy narrative: The *Magnificat* (1:46-55), the *Benedictus* (1:68-79), and the *Nunc Dimittis* (2:29-35). These psalms stem from the earliest community of Jewish Christians, before a specifically Christian theological language had emerged. They exhibit a sophisticated psalmography and have verbal and thematic parallels to the psalms in *Tobit*, to the *Psalms of Solomon*, and to *The Testaments of the Twelve Patriarchs*. Though they may have been originally written in Hebrew, these psalms in Luke are Christian, not Christianized: joy in fulfillment of God's promises pervades them.

Hymns in the Apocalypse

Among the hymn fragments recorded in the *Revelation of John* are 4:11, which praises the Lord as Creator; 5:9-10, specifically called "a new ode," which lauds the redemptive activity of the Lamb; 5:12, 13, which identifies the Lamb as worthy of honor; 11:17-18, which calls for the Lord, enthroned in power, to judge the world; possibly 12:10-12, which exults over the defeat of Satan; 15:3-4, called "the ode of the Lamb," which acknowledges the mighty deeds of the Lord; 18:1—19:4, lament and praise over the fall of Babylon; and 19:6-8, a hymn for the wedding of the Lamb.

Christological Hymns

In addition to the more easily recognizable hymns in Luke 1—2 and in the Apocalypse, there are passages in the New Testament letters that are hymnic in character and creedal, or confessional, in content. Phil. 2:6-11, which describes what is commonly called the Voluntary Humiliation of Christ, is seen to have six stanzas of three lines each. 1 Pet. 3:18c-19, 22 and 1 Tim. 3:16, because of similar content and order, are thought to have been based on a common original. Since the construction of 1 Tim. 3:16 is so compressed and lacks *parallelismus membrorum,* the 1 Peter passage is considered closer to the original hymn. (Notice the expressly baptismal nature of the intervening portion, 3:20-21.) Eph. 2:14-16 is composed of two series of parallel lines. Heb. 1:3 contains a three-line remnant of a hymn. Col. 1:15-20 has been analyzed as an essentially pre-Pauline two-stanza hymn 1:15-17 and 1:18-20. Also the prologue to John's Gospel, 1:1-18, which describes the preexistence of the Logos and his sojourn on earth, is thought to contain a hymn in verses 1-5 and 9-11.

On the basis of these seven hymns or hymn fragments, J. T. Sanders observes that the Redeemer's nature and activities have this pattern: (1) he possesses unity or equality with God; (2) he is mediator or agent of creation; (3) he sustains creation; (4) he descends from the heavenly to the earthly realm; (5) he dies; (6) he is made alive again; (7) he effects reconciliation; and (8) he is exalted and enthroned, the cosmic powers having become subject to him. The pattern is most evident in Phil. 2:6-11.

Other Hymn Possibiliites

Eph. 5:14, "Awake, O sleeper, and arise from the dead, and Christ shall give you light," is often considered a baptismal hymn because of its obvious rhythmical qualities and its employment of three baptismal metaphors. But because of the imperative at the beginning, the statement seems rather an invitation to the baptismal candidate to enter the life-giving water. Several passages—Tit. 3:4-7, which refers to the new birth in baptism; Eph. 2:19-22, which describes the oneness of the church metaphorically; and 2 Cor. 4:4-6, which refers to the saving light, which has illumined our hearts—by virtue of their baptismal images and balanced rhythm may be based on baptismal hymns which are now irrecoverable.

Eph. 1:3-14 and 1 Pet. 1:3-12, which have identical opening lines and contain similar vocabulary, may be based on a common original. The Ephesians passage has three stanzas each concluded by a refrain (6b, 12, 14). Similarly a common original may explain the resemblance between the statement in Rom 6:8 and the poetic lines of 2 Tim. 2:11-12a. Passages that declaim in poetic prose the saving activities of God in Christ (1 Peter 2:21-25; Rom. 3:23-25; Eph. 1:17-23; 2:4-7, 10; and Col. 2:9-15) may also have been based on existing hymns, but the case is not demonstrable.

Finally, it is possible that hymns were constructed by artfully combining quotations from Old Testament poems. Rom. 3:10-18 consists entirely of such quotations. Several other passages with poetic properties (1 Pet. 2:6-10; Rev. 1:7; 3:7; 4:8; 7:15-17; and 13:9-10) are similarly constructed. WWI

Readings: Delling, Gerhard, *Worship in the New Testament* (Philadelphia, 1962); Hunter, A. M., *Paul and His Predecessors* (London, 1961); Jones, Douglas, "The Background and Character of the Lukan Psalms," *Journal of Theological Studies*, N.S. 19. 1 (April 1968), 19-50; Sanders, J. T., *The New Testament Christological Hymns* (Cambridge, 1971).

See also: canticle; hymnody, Old Testament

hymnody, Greek

A statement now ascribed to Hippolytus of Rome (c. 170—236) and preserved by the 4th-century Christian historian Eusebius (*Eccl. Hist.*, V, 28) asks, "Who does not know about . . . all the psalms and hymns that were written by faithful Christians from the beginning, which sing of the Christ as the Word of God and treat him as God?" The statement focuses on two features of early Christian hymnody: its persistent presence from earliest Christian times and its confessional concern for the person of Christ.

Initially the noncanonical Greek hymns follow the poetic prose form of the New Testament hymns, using such Semitic characteristics as *parallelismus membrorum,* antithesis, and antiphony. Eventually Christian hymns come to be written in the ancient Greek meters, such as the anapaestic and the iambic. Longer hymns use such devices as acrostics to link strophes together and refrains sung by congregations or by choir in antiphonal response to a soloist.

Christological Hymns

Early in the 2d century Pliny (c. 62—114), the Roman governor of Bithynia in Asia Minor, wrote regarding the Christians in his province (*Epistolae,* X, 96): "quod essent soliti stato die ante lucem convenire carmenque Christo quasi deo dicere secum invicem" ("on a stated day they were accustomed to gather before daybreak and to sing responsively a song to Christ as to a god"). In the context of this oft-quoted sentence Pliny does not supply the specific content of the *carmen,* and since the expression *carmen dicere* may mean several things—"sing a song," "recite a poem," "utter a religious formula"—we are not sure what Pliny, as a non-Christian outsider, intended to describe. The value of his remark lies in its testimony to the Christocentricity of the particular *carmen* and to its alternating or antiphonal nature.

Ignatius of Antioch (c. 110), according to later opinion (Socrates Scholasticus, *Hist. Eccl.,* VI, 8), introduced antiphonal singing to Syrian Antioch, and from there the practice was said to have spread to other churches. But since antiphonal singing had long been a feature of synagog worship, Ignatius' role as innovator is doubtful. If there is any validity at all to the tradition, it is probably in its recollection of Ignatius' use of and interest in this type of musical composition.

In Ignatius' letters there are two passages that resemble New Testament Christological hymns in thought and construction. They are marked by an economy of words and by a paratactic balancing of antitheses. Both explore the paradoxes of God-made-man. The first is in his *Letter to the Ephesians* 7:2:

> There is one Physician,
> who is both flesh and spirit,

born and yet not born,
who is God in man,
true light in death,
both of Mary and of God
first passible and then impassible,
Jesus Christ our Lord.

The second is in his *Letter to Polycarp*, 3:2:

Wait for him who is above seasons,
timeless, invisible,
who for our sakes became visible,
who cannot be touched,
who cannot suffer,
who for our sakes accepted suffering,
who in every way endured,
for our sakes.

Several Christological passages in the apology *Ad Diognetum* (c. 200) are written in the poetic prose style of early hymns. In 7:2 Jesus Christ is called "the very artificer and Creator of the universe." The power and extent of his creative ability is then described in a series of carefully constructed modifiers artfully arranged in six groups of threes. *Ad Diognetum* 9:2 asserts the vicarious death of the Son and appends five briefly worded antitheses, e.g., "the just for the unjust," "the immortal for the mortal."

The concluding chapters of *Ad Diognetum* (11—12) are unrelated to the rest of the writing and are probably part of an Easter homily. Here (11:4-5) one encounters a section that may be divided into two strophes of comparable design:

This is he who is from the beginning:
he appeared to be new
and was found to be old
and is forever young
as he is born in the hearts of the saints.
This is he who is eternal:
through he is accounted a Son
through whom the church is enriched
and unfolding grace
is multiplied among the saints.

In an effort to influence pagan readers, the church of the 2d century compiled 14 books of didactic poems in hexameters that purport to be the oracles of the Greek Sibyl. They are an admixture of pagan, Jewish, and Christian material dealing with history, politics, and religion. In some Christian circles, however, these poems came to have the weight of Scriptural authority. Book VI contains a 20-line "Hymn to Christ" which "prophesies" his baptism in the Jordan and some of his many miracles. In Book VIII, lines 217—250 contain the celebrated acrostic poem constructed from the Greek letters of "Jesus Christ, Son of God, Savior, Cross."

Sacramental Hymns

An example of the use of the ancient Greek poetic forms in Christian hymnody appears in the "Hymn to Christ the Savior" with which Clement of Alexandria (c. 150—215) closes his *Paidagogos* (III, 12). Aside from the introductory lines, the hymn is composed in anapaests and consists mostly of metaphors for Christ, e.g., "King of saints," "Support of sorrows," "Eternal light, fount of mercy," sung in praise of the Shepherd by the lambs, or children, of the church, that is, the newly baptized converts. Clement's hymn, Christological in its focus, is sacramental in its original context, as were, quite possibly, most Christological hymns (e.g., *Ad Diognetum* 11:4-5).

It was the practice of the early church to admit converts into fellowship by means of a baptismal rite administered annually at the only festival observed by the church, Easter, the Christian Passover. The "Homily on the Pasch" by Melito, bishop of Sardis (fl. 175) demonstrates the typological interpretation of the Exodus Passover event in terms of the resurrection of Christ. The following hymn, ascribed to Melito, is probably a hymn for use at the Easter Vigil, as its use of nuptial imagery— long associated with baptism (cf. Eph. 5:25-27)—suggests:

> Hymn the Father, you saints,
> Sing to the Mother, you virgins.
> Let us hymn them and exalt them highly, you saints.
> Be exalted, brides and bridegrooms,
> For you have found your bridegroom, Christ.
> Drink of the wine, brides and bridegrooms.

Around the year 150, a group of 42 hymns appeared in a collection called the *Odes of Solomon*. Written by a single hand in a style reminiscent of Old Testament psalms, the odes are sometimes mystical, sometimes meditative, usually exuberant, always imaginative, and filled with metaphors and figurative language. They treat certain aspects of Christology, such as, the Incarnation (Odes 7 and 19), the Passion (28 and 31), the Cross (27), the Descent to Hades (17 and 22), the Resurrection (42). However, the recurring themes and metaphors of Baptism (e.g., enlightenment, in Odes 11, 15, 21, 25, etc.; milk for newborn babies, in 8 and 19; the Lord's planting, in 11 and 38; the seal, in 4, 8, and 42) recommends their probable origin in the context of the sacrament, perhaps as hymns to be sung by the newly baptized.

Gnostic Hymns

The Gnostic document *Pistis Sophia*, stemming from Egypt, c. 250—300, quotes five of the *Odes of Solomon*. This appropriation of Christian hymns by Gnostics, however, is not evidence of their failure to create their own hymnody, for hymn writing was a flourishing art in Gnosticism—in its pagan as well as in its near-Christian forms.

Since Christian Gnostics denied the validity of the Old Testament, including the Book of Psalms, they filled the void with their own creations. In style Gnostic hymns tend to follow ancient Greek poetic forms, however, rather than Semitic patterns. Bardesanes (154—222/3) is supposed to have written 150 hymns—a new psalter. The Muratorian Fragment, which lists the authoritative New Testament writings, c. 200 (?), rejects "a new book of psalms" written for the Christian gnostic Marcion. Valentinus (fl. 150) wrote a hymn entitled "Harvest," seven lines of which are quoted by Hippolytus (*Ref.* VI, 37. 7). Hippolytus also quotes (*Ref.* V. 10. 2 ff.) the "Naassene Hymn," which, except for the first three lines, follows the classic anapaestic meter. In this context one should add the two hymns contained in the 3d-century "Acts of Thomas": the "Wedding Hymn" in the first Act, and the "Hymn of the Pearl" in ch. 108—113. Also the apocryphal "Acts of John" from the 3d century contains a "Hymn to Christ."

Private vs. Corporate Hymnody

Partly to counterbalance the rich outpouring of Gnostic hymns, a steady production of hymns was maintained by the more orthodox hymnists. Two of these hymns have survived and are in current use. The evening hymn sung at the close of vespers in the Greek church, *Phos hilaron hagias doxes,* known in an English translation as "O Gladsome Light, O Grace," was attested as of unknown but ancient origin c. 375 by St. Basil (*de Spir. Sanc.* 29). A morning hymn, "Glory to God in the Highest," was accorded a place after the Kyrie in the Roman liturgy c. 500, though it is said to have been introduced into the West by Hilary of Poitiers c. 363. The ascetic writing *De Virginitate* (20), perhaps the work of St. Athanasius (295—373), quotes the opening lines of this hymn as well known to its readers. A variant, if not corrupt, form of the hymn appears in the 4th-century *Apostolic Constitutions* (VII, 47).

The earliest example of a Christian hymn with musical notation is the Oxyrhnchus Papyrus No. 1786, dating from the latter half of the 3d century. Except for the doxological formula, the hymn is in anapaestic meter. The broken fragment reads: "let not all God's (creatures?) be silent nor the brilliant stars hold back (?) . . . nor all murmuring rivers. As we praise the Father, the Son, and the Holy Spirit, all powers should join in harmony. Amen! Amen! Power, praise . . . to Him who alone gives all good things. Amen. Amen."

St. Methodius of Olympus (d. 311) includes near the end of his *Symposium* a hymn of praise sung by the virgins who escort the Bridegroom into the heavenly bridal chamber. This long hymn, written in iambic meter, has two important features. First, it is written in acrostic form: each of its 24 strophes begins with a letter of the Greek alphabet in order. Second, it uses a refrain, or *ephymion,* after each strophe. Though found here in a purely literary framework, both features reflect developing liturgical practice.

The Council of Laodicea (341—381) made several liturgical rulings, including the prohibition of the use of "private" psalms in church (Canon 59). The intent of the canon was to stop the flood of heretical hymns. Where it could be enforced it compelled hymn writers to base their hymns for corporate worship on Scriptural texts. It did not restrict the writing of poems for private use and circulation, however, for even Apollinaris (c. 310—c. 390), who became bishop of Laodicea c. 361, wrote private hymns as well as liturgical. The 5th-century historian Sozomen wrote of him: "Men sang his strains at convivial meetings and at their daily labor, and women sang them while engaged at the loom. But, whether his tender poems were adapted for holidays, festivals, or other occasions, they were all alike to the praise and glory of God" (*Hist. Eccl.,* 6. 25. 4/5). The Hymns of Gregory of Nazianzus (325—390) and those of Synesius, bishop of

Cyrene (c. 370—414), are so subjective and personal that they were probably never intended for corporate liturgical use.

From Canticles to Kanons

The Old Testament Book of Psalms, in use from the very beginning in the church, was supplemented at an early period by a series of Biblical odes, or canticles. The early 5th-century Codex Alexandrinus lists the canticles as follows: (1) The song of Moses after the passage through the Red Sea (Ex. 15:1-19); (2) The song of Moses before his death (Dt. 32:1-43); (3) The prayer of Hannah (1 Sam. 2:1-10); (4) The prayer of Isaiah (Is. 26:9-19); (5) The prayer of Jonah (Jonah 2:2-9); (6) The prayer of Habakkuk (Hab. 3:2-19); (7) The prayer of Hezekiah (Is. 38:10-20); (8) The prayer of Manasses (Apocrypha); (9) and (10) The Prayer of Azariah and the Song of the Three Children (apocryphal insert between Dan. 3:23 and 3:24); (11) The prayer of Mary (Lk. 1:46-55); (12) The prayer of Simeon (Lk. 2:29-32); (13) The prayer of Zacharias (Lk. 1:68-79); (14) The Morning Hymn: "Glory to God in the Highest." Four of these (7, 8, 12, and 14) did not remain in use in the Greek church and 11 and 13 were combined as one to bring the total to nine. The canticle was sung by a soloist. The people responded after each verse or two with a short refrain, or *hypopsalma*, taken from the first line of the canticle.

Another form of Greek hymnody is the *troparion*, short prayers in poetic prose inserted after each verse of a psalm. In the 5th century, when the *troparia* became longer and were composed in strophic form, they were sung only after the three to six last verses of a psalm.

A more developed form of hymn is the *kontakion*, which came into use in the 6th century. The *kontakion* consists of 18 to 30 *troparia* all structurally alike and ending with a refrain. The *troparia* are connected by an acrostic that is either alphabetical or spells out the title of the hymn and the name of the author.

Toward the end of the 7th century a new form, the *kanon*, made its appearance. The *kanon* is made up of nine hymns, each of which consist of from six to nine *troparia*. The nine hymns of every *kanon* are modeled on the pattern of the Nine Canticles. Whatever the occasion for the *kanon*, the first hymn of the *kanon* had to allude to the first Canticle (Ex. 15:1-19), and so in turn to all the canticles in all nine hymns. WWI

Readings: Baumstark, A., "Hymns (Greek Christian)," *Encyclopaedia of Religion and Ethics,* ed. J. Hastings, VII (New York, 1926), 5—12; Grant, Robert M., *Gnosticism: A*

Source Book of Heretical Writings from the Early Christian Period (New York, 1961); Hennecke, Edgar, and Wilhelm Schneemelcher, *New Testament Apocrypha*, English tr. ed. R. Mc L. Wilson, II (Philadelphia, 1964); Wellesz, Egon, *A History of Byzantine Music and Hymnography*, 2d ed. (Oxford, 1961).

See also: canticle; church music history, medieval; hymnody, New Testament; theology of church music, early church fathers.

hymnody, Latin

The development of Latin hymnody may be discussed within a framework of three major periods: (a) the 4th through the 9th centuries; (b) the 10th through the 16th centuries; and (c) the 17th century to the present.

4th—9th Centuries

It was not until late in the 4th century that Latin hymnody first began to flower. While the singing of hymns in the church was originally an Eastern development, these hymns were largely rejected by Latin Christianity, which found their mysticism and Eastern orientation unacceptable. The Psalms were the only hymns that the Western church knew.

With the steady decline of the Greek language in the West, the liturgy underwent the process of Latinization, which was complete by the beginning of the 4th century. There are extant examples of Latin Christian poetry by such writers as Commodius (mid-3d cen.). These, however, were not meant for congregational singing.

With the advent of the wave of heretical movements in various parts of the church came also the initial upsurge of song as a teaching tool. While in exile for four years in Asia Minor, Hilary of Poitiers (c. 310—366) became inspired to imitate his Eastern counterparts in the use of song against heresy and to promote orthodoxy. To Hilary is given credit generally as the first of the Latin hymnists. His *Liber Hymnorum* is lost, but fragments of his other works reflect a heavy, dogmatic style. His hymnody did not appeal to popular tastes and did not succeed in becoming a lasting part of the musical heritage of the church.

It is to Ambrose of Milan (340—397), a contemporary of Hilary, that the title "father of the Latin hymn" is universally accorded. The imperial troops of the Arian emperor Valentinian II were besieging the Milan cathedral because its bishop refused to turn his churches over to Arian heretics. According to Augustine, Ambrose rallied the faithful to the orthodox cause with doctrinal hymns composed in the most basic of Latin meters, the iambic dimeter. With these unrhymed but rhythmic expositions of the faith Ambrose won the day for the Scriptures and the doctrine derived therefrom.

The chief characteristic of Ambrose's style is its simple, popular meter. The rhyme scheme, however, is irregular, a feature of classical Latin poetry. Another feature of Ambrosian hymnody is its simple, direct style. Nearly all of Ambrose's hymns end with a doxological stanza, a reflection of his strong Trinitarian doctrine. Examples of hymns generally attributed to Ambrose include "Veni, Redemptor gentium," "Aeterne rerum Conditor," "Deus Creator omnium," and "Iam surgit hora tertia." Many other hymns written in a similar style are often attributed to Ambrose and are included in the body of material often referred to as Ambrosian hymnody. Credit for reforming the church music of Milan, and the establishment of antiphonal singing must surely be given to this great churchman.

The next influential figure in the development of Latin hymns was the great theologian, St. Augustine of Hippo (354—430). To his credit is the acrostic "Psalm against the Donatists," which was intended for congregational use. His poems are not numerous, nor do they imitate the simple Ambrosian style. However, Augustine's theological writings tell much about the life of Ambrose, as well as worship practices in the early church. Therefore he is invaluable as a source of information about hymnody. The legend that Augustine and Ambrose improvised the Te Deum on the baptism of Augustine is spurious. This hymn was probably already in use at the time.

Victory for popular song, however, was by no means universal. The Council of Laodicea (361) had forbidden, in an endeavor to check and eradicate the songs of heresy, any singing of hymns with non-Scripture texts. The Portuguese Council of Agde (506) went to the opposite extreme, ordering the singing of hymns daily at morning and evening. In 563 the Spanish Council of Braga adopted the Laodicean view. The Second Council of Tours (France) mediated, holding that—in addition to "Ambrosian" hymns—"there are yet some others worthy of being sung which have the names of authors, who were constant in the faith, prefixed." The position of the 6th Council of Toledo (can. 13) in the mid-630s ultimately became the rule for the Western Church:

For singing hymns and psalms publicly in the church we have the example of Christ and His apostles. Hymns are composed like masses or petitions, or commendations or laying on of hands, of which there are many, just as with prayers; let none of you for the future withhold hymns composed in praise of God, but let Gaul and Spain celebrate them alike. Those should be excommunicated who shall dare to reject hymns.

Entry into the Early Middle Ages showed hymns to be more popular than ever, particularly among the upper classes. An example is that of Prudentius (348—405), a younger contemporary of Augustine. His work, which marks the beginnings of the early Middle Ages, shows a blending of Christian beliefs with the classical poetry of the ancient world. His two collections of poems, the *Cathemerinon* and the *Peristephanon*, first written for literary purposes, were later incorporated into liturgical use. One of the hymns still used is the Christmas hymn "Corde natus ex Parentis."

Contemporaries of Prudentius are Paul of Nola (335—431), a lyric poet of whom little is known, and Sedelius (c. 450), the greatest hymnist of the 5th century. Two hymns of Sedelius still in use are "A solis ortus cardine" and "Hostis Herodes impie."

The most famous Latin poet of the 6th century was Venantius Fortunatus (535—609). Born in Italy, he spent most of his life at Tours in Gaul, later becoming Bishop of Poitiers. He was well versed in music and in the secular poetry of his day. Though much of the poetry of Fortunatus is lost, that which remains is elegant in style and largely liturgical in function. Hymns of Fortunatus in use today are such processional hymns as "Vexilla Regis" and "Pange lingua." Hymns such as these set the model for processional hymns of the coming era. They also served as literary models, displaying an elegant meter and a free rhyme scheme. The hymns of Fortunatus also mark the transition into the literary period of the Middle Ages.

Hymnody from the 8th century on was affected by two significant trends: the beginnings of the use of vernacular languages, and the impact of the literary and educational advances begun under the Carolingian kings. The establishment of church-connected schools and the gains in the educational system of the Gauls, promoted by Pippin the Short and Charles Martel, made itself felt in an increased interest in literature, and as a result literary figures increasingly attached themselves to the court.

The court was to have disastrous consequences for the first great poet of the court of Charlemagne. Theodulph (c. 821), Bishop of Orleans, primarily a secular poet and prose scholar, was employed as a legal emissary to the court of Charlemagne. Upon that monarch's death in 814 Theodulph became involved in political intrigue, and, while imprisoned, he wrote the hymn "Gloria, laus, et honor" which is still used.

The later Carolingian period is typified by the works of Rabanus Maurus (775—856), born at Fulda. A Benedictine monk, he was made Archbishop of Mainz in 847. Maurus was a noted scholar and is considered the first great German theologian. His poetic works demonstrate the loosening of the strict quantitative metric schemes of classical Latin. His metric system is governed instead by word accent and also by rhyme. A number of his hymns are still in use.

The period from the 4th to the 9th century reflects an expansion of the metrical systems used by Christian Latin poets—from the simple unrhymed iambic dimeters of Ambrose through increasingly complex metrical and rhyme schemes. Hymns had become part of the monastic communities' regular worship life. Here was a congregation that might rehearse the new material and thus put it into practical use. But with the increasing complexity of poetic and musical form, together with the decreasing use of Latin as the language of the people, the nature of the Latin hymn changed from a vehicle for popular expression to something reserved for the almost exclusive use of monastic communities and cathedral churches.

10th—16th Centuries

The period from the 10th through the 16th centuries continues the involved technical development of Latin poetry, including the rich development of such particular textual-liturgical forms as the trope and sequence. It also saw two new developments in regard to hymnody: the tendency to move from an objective to a more subjective and introspective approach in hymnic themes (although the former were not eliminated); and alterations or revisions of existing texts—usually with the intent of standardizing version for reasons of theological nuance—undertaken in Pius V's breviary reform in Counter Reformation times.

The 10th and 11th centuries also witnessed growth in the composition of tropes, textual additions inserted in the standard liturgical texts, and sequences, a hymn form which followed the Alleluia in the Mass. Though these forms had developed as much as two centuries earlier, it was during these centuries that they achieved a flowering into fully developed literary forms. Countless tropes and sequences were written to such an extent that they threatened to overwhelm the liturgy, a situation finally remedied by the Tridentine reforms of the 16th century.

The 12th century marked the climax of the Literary Period of hymnody. The century was a time of great philosophical and scientific growth, but at the same time it was also an age of religious fervor. Monasticism was at its height, Paris, in particular, mirrored the mood of the century. The city was filled with great churches and priests of various religious orders.

Among the great hymn writers of the 12th century was Bernard of Cluny. Very little is known of the life of this member of the Cluniac order, except that some time after his entry into the monastery in 1122 Bernard composed his great poetic work "De contemptu mundi." This poem, dedicated to the abbot of the monastery, Peter the Venerable, was some 3,000 lines long and was written in dactylic hexameter, a particularly difficult meter. The poem, with its familiar words "Hora novissima, tempora pessima sunt, vigilemus" is a contemplative one, a criticism of the evils of the world, at the same time demonstrating the literary skills developed by the 12th century.

A contemporary of Bernard of Cluny was Peter Abelard (1079—1142), one of the most brilliant thinkers of the Middle Ages as well as one of the most fascinating of historical figures. Abelard is the writer of numerous hymns, collected in his *Hymnarius Paraclitensis*, written for the abbey of the Paraclete. An example still used is the hymn "O quanta qualia." Abelard was best known for his scholastic works, but his poetic style is notable as well. His poetry is basically liturgical with a rather austere style. Many of his poems use trimeters, an unusual feature for Latin hymnody.

More famous than Peter Abelard was his arch rival, Bernard of Clairvaux (1090—1153). He took Cistercian orders in 1113 and two years later founded the abbey of Clairvaux. Due to the brilliance of his oratory and the magnetism of his personality, he became the most influential figure of his age, recruiting whole armies in the cause of the second Crusade with his eloquence. Intensely contemplative, Bernard was greatly opposed to the scholastic methods of Abelard, and brought about the condemnation of Abelard for heresy in 1141.

The poetry of Bernard is mystical and passionate. Nutter describes it in this way: "His love for Christ amounted to a deep and ardent passion that was unconscious of using terms of endearment not altogether becoming so divine a theme." The frankness of his poetry is almost embarrassing to modern readers, and proves difficult to translate into modern terms. However, the poetry of Bernard of Clairvaux had great appeal to the German pietists. The most famous examples of his poetry is his lengthy poetic study of the crucified Christ, "Salve, caput cruentatum," on which Paul Gerhardt based his hymn "O Sacred Head, Now Wounded," Other hymns of Bernard include "Jesus, the Very Thought of Thee" and "O Jesus, King Most Wonderful."

The later years of this period are noted for great writers and churchmen, but not for great hymnists. It is as though the religious excesses of the previous age had left not only the people but also poets rather weary. Moreover, reason had triumphed, and scholasticism was the order of the day. Prose was the more popular form of literature. Great theological works, and occasionally a hymn, were produced by such men as Thomas Aquinas (c. 1225—74).

Some hymns of Francis of Assisi (1182—1226) remain, but these are in early Italian and should not be considered as part of Latin hymnody. A slightly later example of hymnody is by Jean Tisserand (d. 1494), "O filii et filiae."

17th Century—The Present

By the beginning of the 17th century virtually the entire body of Latin hymnody had already come into existence. There remained but a handful of authors to arise in the succeeding centuries, and these chiefly in connection with the development of two French breviaries: Claude and Jean Baptiste de Santeuil for Cluny, Charles Coffin for Paris.

The greatest, and to some the most dastardly, event in Latin hymnody during this period was the breviary reform finalized by the last of the humanistic popes, Urban VIII, through four Jesuit "correctors" in 1632. Aquinas Byrns, quoting from Germing's *Latin Hymns*, notes:

It is a well-known fact that the Humanists in their extravagant admiration for the classical forms had little regard . . . for the splendid Christian poetry that had seen its golden age in the 12th and 13th centuries. Indeed, the classical revival was the death knell of Latin hymnody. . . . Radical changes were introduced into the existing hymns of the church. The ancient hymns of the Breviary, often irregular in their prosody, were to don the classic garb and be coerced within the laws of regular meter and Latinity. . . . Many of these compositions were, no doubt, improved in literary form, but what they gained in point of style they often lost in simplicity, in vigor, and nobility of thought. It must be admitted too that, whatever may be one's standard of Latinity, it was surely a risky thing to attempt to mend the compositions of a St. Ambrose, a Fortunatus, or a Prudentius. In view of these facts, for the further reason that modern scholarship justly regards the integrity of original texts, and particularly ancient texts, with a feeling akin to reverence, hymnologists are unanimous in condemning this revision.

With the abandonment of Latin as the language de jure for Roman Catholics today, it is chiefly through translations made in German and English that these Latin hymns continue to be alive. While it is true that, from time to time, English Romantists attempted to make Latin hymnody acceptable to Protestant England (chiefly through "Primers"), it was not until the Victorian era that English versions of Latin hymns became fully accepted through a notable spate of translations by Romanists and Protestants.

It is chiefly through these translations—directly from Latin into English or via another European language into English—that much of the best of the great Latin hymnic treasure has lived on in the church of the present century. It has also returned to its rightful singers, as Dom Britt notes:

> . . . last of all Rome admitted hymns into the Divine Office in the 12th century. It must not be inferred, however, that no hymns were sung in the churches throughout the West until they were officially recognized as part of the liturgical Office. From the days of St. Ambrose (d. 397) the singing of Latin hymns in the church occupied the same position that is now accorded the singing of hymns in the vernacular. This is true even of conservative Rome long before the 12th century. It might be recalled that Pope St. Gregory the Great (d. 604), himself a hymn writer of note, was . . . familiar with the *Ambrosiani* of the Benedictine Office which he sang daily. Nor is it conceivable, from what we know of his life, that as pope he should not have encouraged the singing of hymns in the churches of Rome.

Readings: Julian, John, ed., *A Dictionary of Hymnology*, 2 vol. reprint of 1907 ed. (New York, 1957); Raby, F. J. E., *A History of Christian-Latin Poetry from the Beginnings to the Close of the Middle Ages* 2d ed. (London, 1953); Britt, Matthew, *The Hymns of the Breviary and Missal*, rev. ed. (New York, 1924); Byrnes, Aquinas, *The Hymns of the Dominican Missal and Breviary* (St. Louis, 1943); Connelly, John, *Hymns of the Roman Liturgy* (Westminster, Md., 1957); *Papers of The Hymn Society of America*, (New York: ix, "Christian Hymns of the First Three Centuries," Ruth Messenger, 1942; xiv, "Latin Hymns of the Middle Ages," Ruth Messenger, 1948).

See also: Catholic pronouncements and decrees on church music; office hymn; sequence; trope

hymnody, German

In a strict sense the German hymn, as a popular religious lyric in praise of God, sung by the congregation, has its source in the German Reformation. But the beginnings of this hymnody are discernible in the centuries prior to the Reformation.

Pre-Reformation Models

Martin Luther (1483—1546), in a certain sense, was not an innovator. What he did was to give impetus, set the pattern, and allow the numerous types of pre-Reformation hymns to come into their own. There were available to him, for instance, the Latin sequence hymns and the Leisen hymns (German hymns with a "Kyrie eleison" refrain) that had developed around the 11th century. These are often referred to as the early form of the German congregational hymn. The rise of German nationalism over against the Roman papacy in the 13th century resulted in many vernacular hymns and songs. *Christ ist erstanden* was well known and became the pattern for other songs; *Nun bitten wir den heilgen Geist* was a favorite. There were sacred folk carols sung in connection with the liturgical dramas and mystery plays of the later Middle Ages, several of which were included in early Reformation hymnals. Furthermore, there were the one-stanza German antiphons, the Latin office hymns, the songs of the minnesinger and meistersinger. Not to be overlooked are the mystics of the 14th century, who, following the lead of Master Eckard (d. 1327), produced many songs of an inward, spiritual quality, voicing joy and personal love and union with the Redeemer. Already in the 15th century there appeared many translations of Latin church songs, among them a German version of the Latin credo, *Wir glauben all' an einen Gott* and of the Te Deum.

Thus, on the eve of the Reformation there was available to Luther and his colaborers a ready source of hymnody—liturgical, ecstatic, and devotional in character. It remained for him and his associates to rework and recast those hymns worthy of such endeavor and to use them, sternly disciplined and immensely powerful, in the cause of the pure Gospel.

The Lutheran Reformation

Martin Luther's efforts toward a German hymnody grew largely out of his concern for liturgical reform. As early as 1523 in his *Formula Missae* he bemoaned the lack of vernacular songs that the people might sing during the mass, and he encouraged German poets to compose evangelical hymns for this purpose. Thus, with Luther as their example, a host of hymn writers appeared to supply the want. Beginning in 1524 with the *Achtliederbuch*, many hymn booklets and hymnals appeared under the auspices of Luther, such as the *Erfurter Enchiridion,* the *Geistliches gesangk Buchleyn* (1524), the *Lufft Enchiridion* (1526), and Joseph Klug's *Geistliche Lieder* (1529). The *Geistliches gesangk Buchleyn* edited by Luther's friend and musical adviser, Johann Walter (1496—1570), the famous cantor at Torgau, was a collection of polyphonic motets designed for choir with the cantus firmus or melody in the tenor part. Twenty-four of the 38 hymns contained therein are by Luther, approximately two-thirds of his total output.

During the following 16 years other hymnals appeared by such men as Rauscher (1531), Klug (1535 and 1543), Schumann (1539), and Babst (1545). But these were for the most part reprints of Klug's 1529 collection to which other hymns were added. Babst's collection of 1545, with 120 hymns and 97 tunes, was the last publication that Luther supervised.

Luther's hymns, so far as their source is concerned, may conveniently be grouped into five categories. The Psalter furnished the immediate inspiration for the first group. The most celebrated and best known in this class are "A Mighty Fortress Is Our God," suggested by Psalm 46, and "From Depths of Woe," based on Psalm 130. Second, there are paraphrases of other portions of Scripture such as "Isaiah, Mighty Seer in Days of Old," based on Is. 6:1-4, "In Peace and Joy I Now Depart," and "Our Father, Thou in Heaven Above." Third, there are about 12 transcriptive translations of Latin sequences, office hymns, and antiphons. There is, e.g., the buoyant "Come, Holy Ghost, God and Lord" based on *Veni, Sancte Spiritus*, and "Now Praise We Christ, the Holy One" derived from *A solis ortus cardine*. The next group includes the pre-Reformation Leisen,

Two pages from *Geistlich Lieder* of 1545, the so-called Babst hymnal, considered the most representative German Lutheran hymnal of the 16th century. Contains a preface by Martin Luther and 129 hymns with melodies.

songs that Luther recast and revised, examples of which are "We Now Implore God the Holy Ghost," and "God the Father, Be our Stay." Finally, there are original hymns, e.g., that commemorating the burning at the stake in Brussels in 1523 of the Augustinian monks Heinrich Voes and Johann Esch, the first martyrs of the Reformation. Included in this category is also "Dear Christians, One and All, Rejoice," a clear and forceful expression of the whole plan of God's salvation for sinful mankind.

At first sight Luther's texts may strike one as being awkward and clumsy; they lack the artfully modulated diction, the subtle imagination, the metrical regularity one seeks in ordinary poetry. His speech is that of the people—idiomatic, penetrating, often coarse and rugged. It must be remembered that the rules of German poetry were not organized and standardized until the reform of Martin Opitz (1597—1639). Thus Luther's verse structure must not be considered in terms of long and short, weak, and strong, but his is a matter of counting syllables with every syllable receiving a strong accent and the accents often varying from line to line.

The flexibility of the plainsong melodies that Luther often adapted to his texts lent itself to the rhythm of speech. Furthermore, his tunes are polyrhythmic in nature. It was not until the 18th century that the isometric form with equal quarter or half notes supplanted the polyrhythmic form.

In line with the prevailing type of church music in his day, the majority of Luther's tunes are in the modal system of plainsong. Since the 16th century began to mark the transition from the modes to the major-minor system, some of his tunes strongly suggest major tonality.

Some of the great hymnists, inspired by Luther's example and closely associated with him in this early period, are Paul Speratus (1484—1551), remembered especially for his "Salvation unto Us Has Come," Justus Jonas (1493—1555), Elizabeth Creuziger (d. 1535), and Lazarus Spengler (1479—1534) with his "All Mankind Fell in Adam's Fall." Poets not immediately associated with him are Johannes Schneesing (d. 1567), especially esteemed for his "In Thee Alone, O Christ, My Lord" which, as someone has said, presents the Christian life in a nutshell, Johannes Mathesius (1504—65), whose "My Inmost Heart Now Raises" has enjoyed wide acceptance, and Nikolaus Herman (c. 1480—1561) with his "When My Last Hour Is Close at Hand." Herman created a type of hymn in which the more simple circumstances of the Christian faith are presented.

Many excellent hymns were first introduced in Low German, the language of northern Germany. Of these, two hymns, commonly ascribed to Nikolaus Decius (c. 1485—after 1546), became immensely popular as metrical settings of the ordinary of the service—"All Glory Be to God on High" and "Lamb of God, Pure and Holy."

The hymns of the Bohemian Brethren also enriched the treasury of German hymnody during this period, with Michael Weisse (1480—1534) as their foremost poet. And the interchange of hymns in the Lutheran hymn books and those of the Bohemian Brethren, numbering approximately 130, is noteworthy.

The hymns of this period breathe the bold, confident, and joyous spirit of justifying faith in its objective universality. They speak the great truths of salvation not in dry doctrinal tones or individualistic reflection but in the form of testimony and confession.

Developments c. 1577—1617

The productive period of hymnody in the Lutheran Church came to a close with the signing of the Formula of Concord in 1577, the event that gave final shape to its creed after violent doctrinal controversies. It was inescapable that these disputes should have their effects on subsequent hymnody. Dry, dogmatic, didactic, and oftentimes bombastic verses became the vogue; the poetic expression became weak and unyielding. However, there were still poets who produced an appreciable number of splendid hymns characterized by objectivity, childlike naïveté, and a general popular vein. Among such poets are Nikolaus Selnecker (1528—92) with his "Lord, Keep Us Steadfast in Thy Word," Bartholomaeus Ringwaldt (1530—99) with his "The Day Is Surely Drawing Near," Martin Behm (1557—1622) with his Passion hymns, Valerius Herberger (1562—1627), nicknamed the "Little Luther," with his "Farewell, I Gladly Bid Thee," and Ludwig Helmbold (1532—98), often called the "German Asaph," with his "From God Shall Naught Divide Me." There is also Martin Schalling (1532—1608) with his heartwarming "Lord, Thee I Love With All My Heart", and Philipp Nicolai (1556—1608), who wrote what are known as the king and queen of chorales—"Wake, Awake, for Night Is Flying" and "How Lovely Shines the Morning Star" respectively.

Developments 1618—75

Toward the end of the previous period the strong, confessional, objective character of hymnody began to wane. The objective faith is now brought into closer relationship to actual life situations, a fact evidenced particularly in the cross-and-comfort hymns. Two factors contributed to the character of the hymns of this period: inwardly, the sorrow and afflictions of the Thirty Years' War (1618—48); outwardly, the new activity in the realm of poetry, especially that of Martin Opitz, who introduced a greater purity of language and metrical regularity. The hymns of this period are therefore both rhythmically and poetically smoother and cleaner, softer and warmer in their theological content.

Johann Heermann (1585—1647) was the first to adopt the new rules of poetry. His hymns possess both the strong objective character of the Reformation period plus the clean poetic type of the present. His total output ran to some 400 hymns, of which the best are possibly "O Dearest Jesus, What Law Hast Thou Broken" and "O God, Thou Faithful God."

The poets of this period include such men as Heinrich Held (1620—59), Matthaeus von Loewenstern (1594—1648), and Martin Rinkart (1586—1649), who is especially known for his "Now Thank We All Our God." Then there is Johann Meyfart (1590—1642) with his "Jerusalem, Thou City

Fair and High," Josua Stegmann (1558—1632) with his "Abide, O Dearest Jesus," Josua Wegelin (1604—40) with his "On Christ's Ascension I Now Build," and Simon Dach (1605—59) with his "Through Jesus' Blood and Merit." Johann Rist (1607—67) stands next to Opitz in fame and productivity, having written about 680 hymns and spiritual songs, mostly, however, intended for private use.

With Paul Gerhardt (1607—76), the individualistic hymn begins to appear. Now the mind becomes more introspective. Sixteen of his 123 hymns begin with "I." Yet his hymns express the most beautiful and fervent faith; they are the finest in all sacred poetry and are probably next in importance to those of Martin Luther. This individualistic tendency continues also in Johann Franck (1618—77), who wrote one of the greatest of Communion hymns, "Soul, Adorn Thyself with Gladness."

The Age of Pietism: 1675—1750

The subjective tendency of the late 17th century gradually developed into the Pietistic Movement, a reaction against the so-called dry scholasticism, cold formalism, and dead orthodoxy of the time. Philipp J. Spener (1635—1705) gave direction to this movement, about the year 1670, in his efforts toward reviving a vital, living, and practical Christianity.

The hymnists of this period, to mention but a few, are Adam Drese (1620—1701), Wolfgang Dessler (1660—1722), Johann Rambach (1693—1735), Carl Bogatzky (1690—1774), Johann Freylinghausen (1670—1739), and Ludwig von Zinzendorf, (1700—60) who wrote over 2,000 hymns, most of which have been forgotten. Two of his better hymns remain in use—"Jesus, Thy Blood and Righteousness" and "Jesus, Lead Thou On."

Joachim Neander (1650—80), one of the great hymn writers of the German Reformed Church, may also be classed in this school. His "Praise to the Lord, the Almighty" is worthy of note.

Erdmann Neumeister (1671—1756) represents a reaction to Pietism in his dignified and evangelical "Jesus Sinners Doth Receive." The same may be said for Benjamin Schmolck (1672—1737), who wrote the tender baptismal hymn "Dearest Jesus, We Are Here."

Music also came upon evil days at the hands of Pietism. The spate of subjective, emotional, and sentimental hymn texts would not suit the sturdy, rugged chorale tunes of earlier days. Waltzlike triple meters became common. The old tunes became frilly and decorative. This is the very period in which J. S. Bach (1685—1750) lived and worked. By the time he arrived on the scene, Pietism had well-nigh done away with good church music, severely limiting the available hymnic resources.

Pietism's lack of intellectual strength left the field vacant for a movement generally known as Rationalism and in Germany as the Enlightenment. Now reason, science, humanism, and naturalism shook the very foundations of the Christian faith. Neither hymnody nor music was spared. The subtle process of revising hymns to suit the taste of the age caused the greatest harm. Originally perhaps well meant, this procedure gradually put the saving message of Jesus Christ in jeopardy.

Of the few poets worthy of note, but one brave name stands out, that of Christian Fuerchtegott Gellert (1715—69). His "Jesus Lives! The Victory's Won" is primitively apologetical.

Pietism's lack of interest in church music also extended into this period. It was the day of secular composers, opera, and the orchestra. The composing of tunes languished; the old tunes were further reduced to plodding, isometric forms; bombastic organ interludes flourished.

Efforts Toward Recovery

The confessional revival of the 19th century was a reaction against rationalism. In 1817 Claus Harms (1778—1855), archdeacon of St. Michael's Church in Kiel, reissued Luther's Ninety-Five Theses together with his own. In these he tried strenuously to arouse German Lutherans to the dangers of the "papacy of reason."

Revised liturgies and hymnals based on earlier models began to appear in the state churches of Saxony, Hannover, Baden, Brunswick, and other districts. Scholars produced extensive literature. Eduard Koch, (1809—71), Philipp Wackernagel (1800—77), and Ludwig Schoeberlein (1813—81) produced their significant volumes on hymnody and church music. Professors Friedrich Spitta (1852—1924), and Julius Smend (1857—1930) of the University of Strasbourg founded, in 1896, the *Monatschrift fuer Gottesdienst und kirchliche Kunst*, an influential liturgical musical periodical. The six-volume work of Johannes Zahn (1817—95) discussed nearly 8,000 chorale melodies with their variant forms.

Meanwhile Mendelssohn rediscovered the forgotten works of Bach; music leaders established choral societies, promoted church music conferences, and advanced the standards of music, thereby helping to quicken the entire church life.

This activity, certainly not without its crests and troughs, has continued to the present, both in Europe and America, in the realization that the German hymn in its long and often-time precarious history has exerted a tremendous influence on the development of both church music and music as an art, as well as on the Christian faith itself. FP

Readings: Ameln, K., *The Roots of German Hymnody of the Reformation Era* (St. Louis, 1964); Leupold, Ulrich S., ed. *Luther's Works,* vol. 53: *Liturgy and Hymns* (Philadelphia: 1965); Liemohn, Edwin, *The Chorale: Through Four Hundred Years of Musical Development as a Congregational Hymn* (Philadelphia, 1953); Precht, Fred, "The Historical Development of the Lutheran Chorale," *Church Music,* 66·1; Riedel, Johannes, *The Lutheran Chorale: Its Basic Traditions* (Minneapolis, 1958).

See also: church modes; church music history, Renaissance—the Reformation tradition; hymnody, Scandinavian; Leisen; office hymn; theology of church music, Reformers; theology of church music, Pietism and rationalism; theology of church music, 19th century

hymnody, Scandinavian

A discussion of hymnody in Scandinavia must take into account the fact that one is speaking about five different countries: Denmark, Finland, Iceland, Norway, and Sweden. Although there are points of common development in the history of hymnody in the five countries, there are also many points of difference, chief among which is that of language. Danish, Icelandic, Norwegian, and Swedish all have a common stem but have evolved into separate tongues with differing vocabulary, articulation, pronunciation, and feeling. Finnish is totally different from the other four in origin as well as in later development. In addition, there are differences of geography, custom, and piety, all of which have had effect on the evolution of hymnody.

Generally speaking, hymnody in Scandinavia had its beginnings in the Reformation era, but no account of it would be complete without at least mentioning the existence of a pre-Reformation hymnody. The Christian church had been active in the Scandinavian countries for half a millennium and the people had composed vernacular hymns there as they had in other countries. Most of these were private, liturgical compositions, but the people had also brought hymns into the mass by creating interlinear vernacular versions of sequences that were sung together with their Latin originals.

The singing of hymns in the Lutheran church has always been closely allied with Christian education. Traditionally, Lutheran children have learned hymns by heart, singing them in their homes, in school, and in confirmation instruction. This was especially true of the "core hymns" (*kjernesalmer*), that body of hymns that gave poetic expression to the central articles of the faith. In Scandinavian countries the state church system makes possible such instruction in the schools, but it is not as thoroughgoing today as it once was.

In the Reformation era the hymn singing was led by the choir or a precentor, who was a member of the congregation possessed of a strong voice and some musical sense. He led the singing by standing in front of the congregation or in the midst of it, sometimes using a melody instrument. Antiphonal singing between men and women was practiced in Finland and Sweden in the 17th and 18th centuries. When organs were first used their function was to play preludes, or intonations, to the tunes, occasionally alternating stanzas with the congregation (*alternatim*), but they did not accompany the singing. That function developed later. It was only in the large cities of Scandinavia that there were any organs at all. Small town and rural churches did not begin to acquire organs until well into the 19th century.

In rural churches hymn singing flourished as a purely vocal art, much of it memorized. Variants on hymn tunes appeared everywhere as imaginative precentors or other gifted singers added embellishments as they sang the tunes, giving rise to an extensive repetory of religious folk music. The isolation of many rural communities served to establish and preserve such practices.

Hymn collections as we know them in English speaking countries, furnished with four-part musical settings, do not exist in Scandinavia. There text and tune editions (called respectively, with varying spellings, *salmebok* and *koralbok*) are published separately, though some text editions are furnished with melody lines. Hymnals in the first two and a half centuries following the Reformation were provided with melodies. Beginning in the mid-18th century it became customary to publish a text edition for the people—who knew most of the tunes by heart anyway—and a harmonized tune edition for the organist.

Up until the 20th century, collections of texts and tunes were usually produced by individuals, pastors or organists, who functioned in the dual role of editor and creator, assembling and editing existing texts or tunes and writing new ones. The editor usually bore the cost of publication also, and made up for his outlay by selling the finished product. Most collections were conceived for home or school use. A few received official sanction and were authorized for use in the churches. The compilers of these publications were usually granted a royal "privilege" entitling them to exclusive publication and sales rights for a number of years. Congregations did not buy a supply of hymnals. Individuals bought their own and took them along when they went to church. In city churches in Scandinavia today one can usually find a rack of hymnals for visitors, but many members still bring their own copy.

The political situation in Scandinavia at the time of the Reformation was this: Norway and Iceland were both part of the kingdom of Denmark. Denmark continued to dominate the affairs of Norway until 1814, of Iceland until 1918. Finland was a part of the kingdom of Sweden in the 16th century. Sweden became an autonomous duchy under Russia in the 19th century and gained her independence in 1918. The history of Scandinavian hymnody, therefore, followed two broad lines of development, running more or less parallel with each other: on the one hand Danish/Norwegian/Icelandic, and on the other Swedish/Finnish. This remained generally true until the 19th century, when national interests began to assert themselves and the individual countries fostered their own hymnody.

Following is a listing of the landmark publications and editors from the Scandinavian heritage, beginning with the Reformation.

Hymnals and Chorale Books from the Danish/Norwegian/Icelandic Tradition

Claus Mortensen (Toendebinder; c. 1499—1575, *Thet Christelighe Messze Embedhe paa Dansche*, 1528. Actually a brief service book and hymnal, the service was modeled on Luther's *Deutsche Messe* and the Nuernberg Mass; Hans Tausen (1494—1561), *Psalme Bog*, 1553; Hans Thomissoen (1532—73), *Den Danske Psalmebog*, 1569. This became the standard hymnal in Denmark/Norway and was used for 130 years. It is regarded as the classic of all the Scandinavian Reformation hymnals. A companion volume for city churches where there were choirs was the *Graduale*, 1573, of Niels Jespersoen (1518—87), which contained traditional Latin proper and ordinary texts and music, as well as Danish. The last two volumes had their Icelandic counterparts in *Ein ny Psalma Bok*, 1589, and *Graduale*, 1594, of Gudbrandur Thorlaksson (1541—1627). Two Icelandic hymn collections

Title page of Hans Thomisson's *Den danske Psalmebog* of 1569, an early and important hymnal of Denmark/Norway, together with a page of music showing a translation of the *Kyrie fons bonitatis*.

preceded these publications, one by Marteinn Einarsson in 1555, the other by Gisli Jonsson (1515—87) in 1558. Thomissoen and Jespersoen were replaced by the *Psalmebog* and *Graduale*, both 1699, of Thomas Kingo (1634—1703). Latin texts and Gregorian tunes were not omitted. Kingo's book remained in use in Denmark/Norway, especially in rural congregations, for over 150 years. The following also appeared in the 18th century: Erik Pontoppidan (1698—1764), *Den nye Psalmebog* (modeled on Freylinghausen), 1740, and its musical companion, *Choral Bog*, 1764, by F. C. Breitendich (1702—75); O. H. Guldberg (1731—1808) and L. Harboe (1709—83), *Psalmebog*, 1778, and its *Choral Bog*, 1783, by Niels Schioerring (1743—98); N. E. Balle (1744—1816), *Den Evangelisk-christelige Psalmebog*, 1798, and its *Choral Bog*, 1801, by H. O. C. Zinck (1746—1832).

The chief hymnals in Denmark in the 19th and 20th centuries have been the *Roskilde Konvents-Salmebog*, 1855, *Soenderjydske Salmebog*, 1889, *Salmebog for Kirke og Hjem*, 1899, and *Den Danske Salmebog*, 1953. Chorale books of the same period were produced by C. E. F. Weyse (1774—1842) in 1838, A. P. Berggreen (1801—80) in 1853, Henrik Rung (1807—71) in 1857 and 1868, Chr. Barnekow (1837—1913) in 1878 and 1892, H. S. Prahl (1845—1930) and C. C. Heinebuch (1840—96), *Soenderjydske Choralbog* in 1895, V. E. Bielefeldt (1851—1909), *Melodier til Salmebog for Kirke og Hjem*, in 1901, *Den Danske Koralbog* in 1954 revised in 1974.

In Norway the chief hymnals in the 19th and 20th centuries have been M. B. Landstad (1802—80), *Kirkesalmebog* in 1869, E. Blix (1836—1902), *Nokre Salmar* in 1892; and *Landstads Salmebog*, revised in 1926. Chorale books in the same period: O. A. Lindeman (1769—1857) in 1838, his son L. M. Lindeman (1812—87) in 1877, *Koralbok for den Norske Kirke* in 1926. A revision of texts and tunes is in progress in Norway.

In Iceland the chief hymnals in the 19th and 20th centuries have been Magnus Stephensen (1762—1833), "Evangelical Hymnal" in 1801, *Salmabok* in 1886, revised in 1945 and called *Salmabok til Kirkju-og Heimasoengs*. Chorale books in the same period: Peter Gudjohsen (1812—77) in 1861, Jonas Helgason (1839—1903) in 1884, Sigfus Einarsson (1877— 1939) and Pall Isolfsson, *Salmasoengsbok til Kirkju-og Heimasongs* in 1936.

Hymnals and Chorale Books of the Swedish/Finnish Tradition

Olaus Petri (c. 1493—1552), *Swenska Soenger eller Wijsor* in 1526; Laurentius Petri (1499—1573), *Then Swenska Psalmeboken* in 1567, *Gamla Uppsala Psalmboken* in 1622 and 1645; Jesper Swedberg (1653—1735), *Then Swenska Psalmboken* in 1695 and its accompanying *koralbok* in 1697 by Harald Vallerius (1646—1716); J. O. Wallin (1779—1839), *Den Svenska Psalmboken* in 1819 and its musical companion, *Svensk Choralbok* in 1821 by J. C. F. Haeffner (1759—1833); *Den Svenska Psalmboken* in 1937 and its musical companion, *Koralboken foer Svenska Kyrkan* in 1939. A revision of both texts and tunes is in progress. The Lutheran church in Finland is bilingual, using Finnish and Swedish. Publications have had to take this into account. Finnish hymnals appeared in 1583 (ed. Jaakko Finno), 1614 (ed. Hemming of Masku), 1646 (ed. J. M. Raumannus), and 1701. In the 18th and 19th centuries two separate committees have produced the hymnals, in 1886, and in 1938 *Suomen Evankelisluterilainen Kirken Virsikirga*, the Swedish version appearing in 1943. Finnish chorale books, called *Koraalikirja,* appeared in 1909, 1939, and 1944.

Two musicians in the list above deserve special mention because the quality and character of the chorale books they published (not without opposition) were such that they placed a personal stamp on the hymn singing in their countries that lasted more than a century and still continues to be felt: J. C. F. Haeffner and L. M. Lindeman, who wrote the widely used tune *Kirken*.

The latter half of the 19th century and the first decades of the 20th witnessed a lively debate in Denmark, Norway, and Sweden over the rhythmic chorale. Chief among its proponents was the Dane Thomas L. Laub (1852—1927), who published several books on the subject, including a chorale book, *Dansk Kirkesang*, 1918, in which he used rhythmic versions of the Lutheran chorales and a simplified harmony. In Norway the members of this school were J. D. Behrens (1820—90), Otto Winter-Hjelm (1837—1931), and Per Steenberg (1870—1947), who published an alternate *Koralbok* in 1947. In Sweden the proponents of the rhythmic chorale were part of the society called the Friends of Church Song (Kyrkosaangens Vaenner). Leading figures were G. R. Noren (1847—1922) and J. T. Moren (1854—1932) who published a chorale book in 1922.

Two noteworthy publications, not mentioned above, deserve recognition: *Piae cantiones*, 1582, a Finnish collection of 70 Latin songs (ed. Jaakko Finno). It gained widespread use and has become a classic in its own right. A classic of a different sort is the *Passiusalmar* (Passion Hymns) 1666, of Hallgrímur Pétursson (1614—74). It continues to be reissued every few years. These hymns have been translated into other languages, and the chorale book of Iceland provides a special register for all 50 of the hymns.

In 1960 a pan-Scandinavian committee published *Nordisk Koralbok*, the purpose of which is to seek to establish a common practice in the editing of the Lutheran chorales in general use and to provide a source of such tunes for use in future hymn publications. GC

Readings: Cartford, Gerhard M., *Music in the Norwegian Church: A Study of Its Development in Norway and Its Transfer to America, 1825—1917,* dissertation, University of Minnesota, 1961; Moberg, Carl-Allan, *Kyrkomusikens Historia* (Stockholm, 1932); Schousboe, Torben, "Protestant Church Music in Scandinavia," *Protestant Church Music* (New York, 1974); related articles in *The Encyclopedia of the Lutheran Church,* ed. J. Bodensieck (Minneapolis, 1965).

See also: alternation practice; cantor; chorale; church music history, Renaissance—the Reformation tradition

hymnody, English

English congregational song was at first metrical psalmody, and the introduction of hymnody to worship was the result of influences outside the Established Church of England. Probably the earliest hymns sung in English worship were a number of eucharistic hymns by Benjamin Keach

(1673), a Baptist; but the first considerable contribution to hymnody was that of Isaac Watts (1674—1748) through his various publications (1705, 1707, 1715, 1719). During the 18th century hymnody expanded, mostly under the influence of the evangelical revival led by John Wesley (1703—91), whose brother Charles (1707—88) alone wrote nearly 9,000 religious poems, most of which can be called hymns. The Calvinist dogmatic stream was thus reinforced by evangelical warmth and fervour.

When hymnody came to England it had its music ready-made for it in the psalm tunes associated with the metrical psalters. Thus most early English hymnody was written in psalm meters; but the Wesleys had been subject to much German influence, and they introduced a great enrichment of meter, and therefore of style.

While hymnody remained officially forbidden in the Church of England until 1821, this law had become a dead letter long before that date, and evangelicals of all persuasions were singing the hymns of Watts, Philip Doddridge (1702—51), Charles Wesley, and their contemporaries.

A new era opened with the Oxford Movement, which is usually dated from 1833, the year of John Keble's assize sermon of July 14 and the beginning of John Henry Newman's publication of the *Tracts for the Times*. This reconstruction of Anglican piety and philosophy called for a revival of medieval liturgies and for a new body of liturgical hymnody, either translated from Latin and Greek sources or newly composed to provide a singing companion to the Prayer Book. So, after a very brief "romantic" period in the early 19th century that produced "Holy, Holy, Holy," "Brightest and Best of the Sons of the Morning", both by Bishop Reginald Heber (1783—1826), and "Ride On, Ride On in Majesty" by H. H. Milman (1791—1868), there followed a neoclassical period which produced hymns for saints' day, the Eucharist, morning and evening, and all the other occasions called for by the Prayer Book.

A tendency to mechanical platitude in this style of hymnody was energetically protested against by Robert Bridges (1844—1930) and Ralph Vaughan Williams (1872—1958) about 1900, and the result was a complete reconstruction of the ethos of English hymnody, not only in the provision of new words and music in a better style, but, perhaps even more, in the recovery for worship of poetry by 16th and 17th century poets who in their own day would have been forbidden to write hymns. This progress can readily be seen in a comparison of *Hymns Ancient and Modern* (preferably the edition of 1922) with *The English Hymnal* (1906), which represented the new scholarly protest. *Hymns Ancient and Modern*, first published in 1861 and still, in its fourth edition (1950), the most widely used English hymn book, shows comprehensively the strength and the weakness of the mid-19th century hymn explosion. But it should be noted that hymnody was during this period and by this very book enriched by the translations from the Latin and Greek of John Mason Neale (1818—66) and those of Catherine Winkworth (1827—78) from the German. Of the former, "Jerusalem the Golden" is a well-known example, and of the latter, "Now Thank We All Our God."

The first half of the 20th century saw much musical development, but little progress in texts beyond the standard reached by Bridges in his *Yattendon Hymnal* (1899); the most influential authors were Percy Dearmer (1867—1936) and G. W. Briggs (1875—1959). More recently there has been a vigorous revival of hymn writing, and the most sought-after English authors at present are Albert Bayly (b. 1901), Fred Kaan (b. 1929), Frederick Pratt Green (b. 1903) and Brian Wren (b. 1936). But alongside these, who are developing hymnody in its familiar form, though finding quite new subjects about which to sing, there are the informal songwriters, led by Syndey Carter (b. 1915) and Malcolm Stewart (b. 1926), who have developed, and indeed formed, a whole school of hymnody in a conversational style that sometimes, though not always, goes beyond the field of hymnody altogether.

The music of English hymnody has a more complex history than that of any other country, since it combines a 400-year span with a unique capacity for absorbing foreign styles. Any 20th-century English hymnbook contains music from other countries in a much higher proportion than that in which English music is found in non-English hymnals.

Broadly speaking the development of the English hymn tune from 1560 to 1900 shows the following styles:

1. The Psalm tune style before 1700, English and Scottish, of which the following is a typical example:

"Winchester Old"　　　　　　　　　　　　　　　　　　　　　　Este's *Psalter*, 1592

2. The 18th-century psalm tune and hymn tune influenced by the foreign styles (French and Italian) made current by the court music of the Restoration after 1660, and to be found preeminently in Purcell. The following, probably much older than its published date, is a good example (note the triple rhythm and dotted notes):

"Bishopthorpe"   1786

3. The evangelical style, coeval with style 2 but developing in a freer way through the expansion of meters and the development of choirs (originally formed of children in the orphanages founded under evangelical influence). The following tune, very well known in England and based on a secular melody, illustrates this: note the repetition of words required just before the end:

"Helmsley"   *Select Hymns with Tunes Annext, 1765*

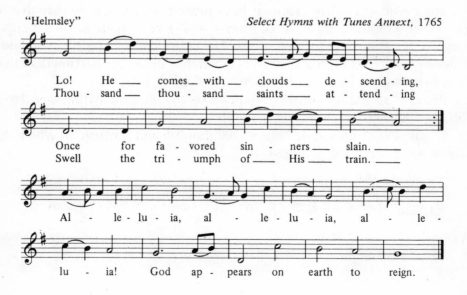

Lo!   He ____ comes__ with __ clouds ____ de - scend - ing,
Thou - sand ____ thou - sand __ saints ____ at - tend - ing

Once   for   fa - vored   sin - ners ____ slain. ____
Swell   the   tri - umph   of ____ His ____ train. ____

Al - le - lu - ia,   al - le - lu - ia,   al - le -

lu - ia!   God   ap - pears   on   earth   to   reign.

214

4. The "Anglican style"—associated with the new hymnody, whose best known source is *Hymns Ancient and Modern*, and whose best-known composer is J. B. Dykes (1823—76), who wrote this:

"Dominus regit me"
J. B. Dykes, 1861

The King of love my Shep-herd is Whose good-ness fail-eth nev - er;

I noth-ing_lack if I am_His And He is mine for- ev - er.

5. The neoorthodox style, associated with Ralph Vaughan Williams (1872—1958) and Gustav Holst (1874—1934), more austere, placing a primitive emphasis on rhythm and melody and less emphasis on harmony:

"Down Ampney"
Ralph Vaughan Williams, 1906

Come down, O Love di - vine: Seek Thou this soul_ of mine,

And vis - it it with Thine own ar - dor_ glow - ing.

O Com-fort - er, draw near, With - in my heart ap -

pear, And kin-dle it, Thy ho - ly flame be - stow - ing.

Tune from the *English Hymnal* by permission of Oxford University Press.

6. The folk-song style, also associated with the two composers above named, which fertilized English hymnody by reviving secular folk songs for hymns: the best-known in England is this (arranged by Vaughan Williams):

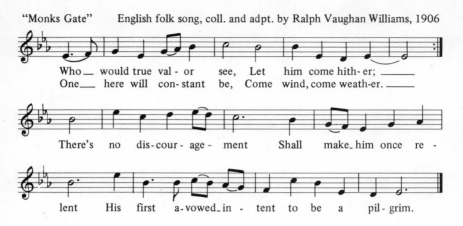

"Monks Gate"   English folk song, coll. and adpt. by Ralph Vaughan Williams, 1906

Who— would true val - or   see, Let   him come hith- er; _____
One— here will con- stant be, Come wind, come weath-er. _____

There's no dis- cour- age - ment   Shall   make_ him once re -

lent   His first a- vowed_ in - tent to be   a pil- grim.

Tune from the *English Hymnal* by permission of Oxford University Press.

This brings us to the contemporary period, in which we may note two deviations from the accepted style, as well as a development along traditional lines. The deviations are both in the direction of "popular" hymnody. One, associated with the Twentieth Century Church Light Music Group, founded by Geoffrey Beaumont (1905—71), uses the idiom of the large stage musical of the 1920s. The other, referred to above in association with Sydney Carter, specialized in "new-folk" styles, words and music often being written by the same person, the standard instrument for accompaniment being the guitar. The work of both kinds of composer is very readily accessible. Meanwhile the midstream composers continue to be active, and the best sources for their English works are *Hymns for Church and School* (London, 1964), *The New Catholic Hymnal* (London, 1971), and the *Church Hymnary* (London, 1973).

In most recent years the two most significant developments in England have been the new hymnody provided since 1964 for Roman Catholics and the advent of "supplemental" hymnaries—small books for new material to be added to existing hymnals, of which the most significant are *100 Hymns for To-day* (London, 1969), *New Songs* (London, 1969) and *Hymns for Celebration* (1974).

No attempt is made here to deal with Welsh hymnody, which is a separate subject. ER.

Readings: Benson, L. F., *The English Hymn* (New York, 1915); Frost, M., ed., *Historical Companion to Hymns Ancient and Modern* (London, 1962); Julian, J., *Dictionary of Hymnology*, 2 vols. (London, 1907); Routley, E., *Hymns and Human Life* (London, 1952); *The Bulletin of the Hymn Society of Great Britain and Ireland*, quarterly from 1936.

See also: church music history, Renaissance—the Reformation tradition; metrical psalmody

hymnody, American

The early colonists brought their metrical psalmbooks with their Bibles: Sternhold and Hopkins' "Old Version" to Jamestown and the Massachusetts Bay Colony, Ainsworth's psalter to Plymouth, and Datheen's Dutch psalter to New Amsterdam. A century later the Moravians and the Swedish and German Lutherans each brought hymnbooks in their native languages up the Delaware River. The Dutch, Moravians, and Swedes within a few decades turned to English translations, but the German Lutheran and Reformed congregations, supported by continued, fresh immigration, sang their hymns in German throughout the 19th century as they spread through the Midwest, joined by new Scandinavian groups.

Few New England colonists could read music; indeed there were very few tune-books available. So there arose the practice of "lining out" the metrical psalms. The parish clerk or deacon, seated at his own desk beneath the pulpit, would sing the psalm or hymn, pausing after each phrase or line for the congregation to repeat it after him, line by line through all the verses of the text.

With a very few exceptions, such as Old Hundredth ("All People That on Earth Do Dwell"), the "Old Version" texts were clumsy and ill-liked. So in 1640 a committee of New England clergy brought out the *Bay Psalm Book*, a fresh translation of the Book of Psalms into English verse and also the first book to be published in America. It was so popular that 27 editions were published in New England and 20 more in England before 1762.

In the meantime, the hymns of Isaac Watts (1674—1748) and of other poets made their way across the Atlantic, first to augment, eventually to displace all but a few of the metrical psalms. After the American Revolution, Watts' texts and those in the popular *Selection of Hymns from the Best Authors*, compiled in England by the Baptist John Rippon (1751—1836), were Americanized by various editors to remove references to England and its royal family. Watts' setting of Psalm 75, stanza 2, read:

217

Britain was doom'd to be a slave,
Her frame dissolv'd; her fears were great;
When God a new supporter gave,
To bear the pillars of the state.

For this, John Mycall (1750—1833) in his revision of Watts published at Newburyport, Mass., 1781, substituted:

America was doom'd a slave,
Her frame dissolv'd, her fears were great;
When God a right'ous council gave
To bear the pillars of the state.

Joel Barlow (1755—1812) made a second revision of Watts at Hartford, Conn., in 1785. The third and most successful was by the president of Yale College, Timothy Dwight (1752—1817), at New Haven in 1800.

The Great Awakening, begun by Jonathan Edwards (1703—58) at Northhampton, Mass., in 1734, was spread up and down the colonies by the preaching of George Whitefield (1714—70) between 1739 and 1741. Whitefield promoted the use of Watts' *Hymns and Psalms* as well as Wesley's *Hymns and Sacred Poems*. These hymns, from a Congregationalist and the founder of Methodism, were so popular in some conservative, Presbyterian circles that the resulting Great Psalmody Controversy raged for the next 100 years, splitting many congregations.

Baptists, whose theology needed more than metrical psalms and Watts, soon began to write their own hymns, which they adapted to popular melodies. One of the first was the Freewill Baptist Henry Alline (1748—84). Another prolific writer, the itinerant preacher John Leland (1754—1841), wrote:

Christians, if your hearts are warm,
Ice and snow can do no harm.

to encourage the fainthearted to be immersed for baptism in spite of wintry weather.

After the Revolution, when the western frontiers began to open up, the backwoods teemed with people in cabins and isolated farms. Few villages had settled clergy, so the Methodists organized "field meetings" and the Lutherans "grosse Versammlungen." The Second Great Awakening began in June 1800, led by the Cumberland Presbyterians in Kentucky under the McGee brothers and James McGready (c. 1760—1817). There was a sudden wave of frontier camp meetings where Baptist, Methodist, and Presbyterian ministers, black and white, worked side by side in the same groves with enormous crowds for days on end. The Cane Ridge meetings, August 6—12, 1801, had over 10,000 people in attendance constantly; the shouting and singing could be heard for miles. Hymns were "lined out" because of the scarcity of books. Refrains were added to older hymns for better mass singing. Thus a hymn like that of William Cowper (1731—1800)

> There is a fountain filled with blood
> Drawn from Immanuel's veins,
> And sinners, plunged beneath that flood,
> Lose all their guilty stains.

would have an extempore refrain added:

> Lose all their guilty stains,
> Lose all their guilty stains,
> And sinners, plunged beneath that flood,
> Lose all their guilty stains.

There were five basic types of camp-meeting songs. The *narrative ballad*, like that by Oliver Holden (1765—1844):

> When Jesus stood before the bar
> Of Pilate's judgement seat,
> The Roman prince a question ask'd,
> A question most discreet;

> What, Sir, is truth? (if thou canst tell)
> But silent He remain'd;
> For Jesus knew his heart full well,
> His pride was never stain'd.

> Had he desired the truth to know,
> He would have ask'd again;
> But many ask as Pilate did,
> Who never seek t'obtain.

> O may I never, never ask,
> Without a wish to have;
> And may I never cease to pray,
> Till Jesus deign to save.

The *experience songs,* like this by John Newton (1725—1807):

> In evil long I took delight
> Unaw'd by shame and fear . . .

The *mourners' songs:*

> Stop, poor sinners, stop and think
> Before you further go . . .

or

> Just as I am, without one plea . . .

The *martial songs:*

> I've 'listed in the Holy War
> To fight for life and endless joy . . .

And the *farewell songs:*

> Lord! when together here we meet,
> And taste Thy heav'nly grace,
> Smiles are so divinely sweet
> We're loath to leave the place.

or:

> God be with you till we meet again.

Back in New England, the Industrial Revolution roused the social consciousness of Unitarian writers like Edmund Hamilton Sears (1810—76), who wrote in his Christmas hymn "It Came upon the Midnight Clear" as stanzas 3 and 4:

> Yet with the woes of sin and strife
> The world has suffered long;
> Beneath the heav'nly strain have rolled
> Two thousand years of wrong;
> And man, at war with man, hears not
> The tidings which they bring;
> O hush the noise, ye men of strife,
> And hear the angels sing!
>
> O ye, beneath life's crushing load,
> Whose forms are bending low,
> Who toil along the climbing way
> With painful steps and slow,

Look now! for glad and golden hours
Come swiftly on the wing;
O rest beside the weary road
And hear the angels sing!

At the end of the 19th century, urban problems were marked by Frank Mason North (1850—1935) in "Where Cross the Crowded Ways of Life." The space age was introduced to hymnody by Howard Chandler Robbins (1876—1952)

And have the bright immensities
Received our risen Lord,
Where light-years frame the Pleiades
And point Orion's sword?
Do flaming suns his footsteps trace
Through corridors sublime,
The Lord of interstellar space
And conqueror of time?

The term "gospel song" entered the vocabulary as the result of successive collections of *Gospel Hymns and Sacred Songs* used between 1875 and 1891 by Ira D. Sankey (1840—1908) and other song leaders associated with the evangelist Dwight L. Moody (1837—99). One of the most prolific authors was the blind poet Fanny Crosby (Mrs. Alexander Van Alstyne, c. 1820—1915); others were George F. Root (1820—95), Edwin O. Excell (1815—1921), and Charles H. Gabriel (1856—1932).

Where the earlier camp-meeting songs had been sung to minor-mode melodies, the new gospel songs picked up the style of the popular songs of the Civil War era. Simple major-mode melodies, with the ever-popular refrain, were added to the older, still-useful, camp-meeting texts. With the exception of Fanny Crosby, most new writers composed both words and music. Whereas the older songs were largely sung in unison, the gospel songs had simple harmonies and rhythms that could be sung by quartets and choirs. Later, the use of some ragtime and jazz rhythms added more interest for the young people. Save for the words, popular sacred music was hard to distinguish from the secular.

The repertory continued to increase in the first half of the 20th century, spurred by the revival campaigns of Billy Sunday (1863—1935) and his song leader Homer A. Rodeheaver (1880—1955). Indeed, the extensive publication of gospel-song collections (as many as 50 per year), each with but a few new songs and many old ones from the public domain, became highly commercialized and profitable, little different from New York's Tin Pan Alley save in the places of publication.

Rodeheaver and his contemporaries used massed choirs and musical instruments to help lead the congregation in singing. They would begin to sing as much as an hour before the scheduled service, recapturing for the urban crowds something of the spirit and social significance of the frontier camp meetings. In the next generation, the meetings of Billy Graham (b. 1918) suffered greatly in their hymnody. The choirs and special groups did most of the singing. People had listened to radio and television so much they no longer sang. Community singing was a thing of the past. As a result the *Billy Graham Crusade Songs* were only a quarter of the size of the earlier gospel-songbooks, and new material consisted of a few refrains only.

Most American denominations bring out a new hymnal with each new generation. On the average, each one contains nearly 15 percent new material, both texts and tunes. There have been no prolific American hymn writers in the 20th century. Gospel songs have suffered greatly from a lack of inspiration. Yet, new hymns continue to be brought forth by each new wave of unrest, each new social and national problem. Since 1922 the Hymn Society of America has sponsored many competitions and projects to encourage the meeting of these needs. Most Americans know the contents of their hymnals as well or better than their Bibles. Congregational singing is better today than it has been since the early years of the Reformation. LE

Readings: Foote, Henry Wilder, *Three Centuries of American Hymnody* (Cambridge, Mass., 1940); Ellinwood, Leonard, "Religious Music in America," *Religion in American Life*, II (Princeton, 1961).

See also: decani/cantoris; gospel song; hymnody, American Lutheran; hymnody, English; metrical psalmody

hymnody, American Lutheran

The early Lutheran immigrants in America brought with them the hymnals of their homelands. Coming largely from Germany, the Lutheran settlers in American in the early 18th century used a variety of hymnals from the continent including, among others, Freylinghausen's *Geistreiches*

Gesangbuch of 1741, and the hymnals of Marburg, Wuerttemberg, Wernigerode, and Coethen.

The First Hymnals

The German Lutherans in Pennsylvania, under the leadership of Heinrich Melchior Muehlenberg (1711—87), prepared and printed the first Lutheran hymnbook in America, the *Erbauliche Lieder-Sammlung* of 1786. Compiled to replace the various hymnals brought to America by the German immigrants and to unify them in a single book, it became instead the first of many hymnals that reflected the changes in each new age. Muehlenberg's selection, taken largely from the Pietistic hymnody of 18th-century Germany, still retained a link with the normative core of confessional hymnody *(Kernlieder)* from Reformation times. Yet in his

Title page of the *Erbauliche Lieder-Sammlung* of 1786, the first Lutheran hymnal prepared and published in America, together with the title page and a page of music from its *Choral-Buch* of 1813 containing only melody and figured bass for the organist (Concordia Historical Institute and the Fuerbringer Memorial Library of Concordia Seminary, St. Louis, Mo.).

choice of hymns, Muehlenberg found the personal, subjective, or even mystical writings of such 17th-century hymnists as Paul Gerhardt, Johann Franck, or Johann Scheffler to be more compatible with his Pietistic orientation than the more objective, didactic, or narrative hymns of Martin Luther, Paul Speratus, or Justus Jonas.

As the hymn texts of German Pietism were transplanted to America, so was its music. The *Choralbuch fuer die Erbauliche Liedersammlung*, published in 1813 by St. Michael's and Zion congregations of Philadelphia, utilized the common musical coin of the day, the monotonous, dragging, isometric forms of the melodies popular in the latter 17th and 18th centuries. It contained only melody with figured bass.

Muehlenberg's hymnal was accepted and widely used, but it was readily apparent that continued use of German as the language for public worship and congregational song served only as a brake on those Lutherans who sought "boldly to adopt English in order to win America." The remarkable attempt of J. C. Kunze (1744—1807), Muehlenberg's son-in-law, whose *A Hymn and Prayer Book* of 1795 was the first English Lutheran collection of hymns prepared and published in America, and the less successful attempts of George Strebeck and Ralph Williston to compile adequate collections of English hymns were soon swept away on the currents of two theological movements whose influence on the course of Lutheran hymnody in America lingered for more than a generation. These two movements that rapidly displaced Muehlenberg's Pietistic confessionalism were rationalism, championed in America by F. H. Quitman (1760—1832), president of the New York Ministerium and disciple of Johann Semler, and unionism.

Rationalism and Unionism

Rationalism, trying to bring hymnody in line with human reason, brought Lutheran hymnody in America to its lowest point, a fact dramatically evident in Quitman's *A Collection of Hymns* of 1814. Quitman's *Collection* rejected completely the old *Kernlieder* and substituted hymns conforming to the "new thought" of the day. Quitman's rejection of the heritage of Reformation hymnody reflected his aversion to its vigorous confessionalism as well as the current conviction that translations were a hopeless exercise. His "improvements" brought the hymns of the church in line with a theology characterized by "its high Arminian view of human potentiality, its ethical moralisms, its sweetly reasonable descriptions of a benevolent deity, its criticisms of dogma." William Reynolds (1812—76), Lutheran scholar, teacher, and college president, noted 45 years later that there were few hymns in Quitman's volume "which a Unitarian . . . or a high Arian might not sing."

Quitman's influence extended to the General Synod's *Hymns, Selected and Original* of 1828, edited chiefly by Samuel S. Schmucker (1799—1873), chief proponent of "American Lutheranism, a movement which sought to place Lutheranism on a radically new confessional basis." Schmucker's hymnal, based largely on Quitman's work, added many hymns derived from the rising wave of revivalism, before which rationalism was gradually receding in the early decades of the 19th century. Frederick Bird, one of the significant American Lutheran hymnologists of the 19th century, characterized Schmucker's efforts as "Low Church and Broad Church . . . mixed into an agreeable compound, representing some of the worst qualities of both, with not much of the redeeming features of either."

Unionism, reflecting a parallel movement in Germany that led ultimately to the Prussian Union of 1817, exerted its influence particularly among the German Lutheran and Reformed groups who feared absorption in America and sought in various ways to preserve their identity. The use of "common hymnbooks" (*Gemeinschaftliche Gesangbuecher*) in these congregations, many of which gradually merged to form "union" churches, was often a most practical solution, since Lutheran and Reformed congregations often shared a single building for worship. In spite of their obvious weaknesses, "the omission of the classic hymns of the church and the insertion of weak and frivolous hymns," these "common" hymnbooks, the first of which was printed in 1817, continued to be a factor through most of the 19th century, for union churches were common and common hymnbooks were popular.

The Confessional Revival

Rationalism and unionism enjoyed success for a time, but both gave way before a rising tide of confessionalism that was to bring American Lutheran hymnody closer to the genius of its Reformation origins. The confessional revival's impact on hymnody centered in the movement to recapture and restore the original, unaltered texts of the old Lutheran hymns and to recapture the musical vitality associated with the original forms of the chorale melodies, forms displaced by the dull, plodding tunes of Pietism. The effect of the confessional revival on hymnody developed only gradually among those Lutherans who were the direct spiritual descendants of Muehlenberg. Rationalism and unionism had taken their toll, and recovery was a slow and lengthy process.

The return to a more Lutheran hymnody may be seen in varying degrees in C. R. Demme's *Deutsches Gesangbuch* of 1849, produced for the Pennsylvania Ministerium, and more noticeably in the General Council's *Church Book* of 1868 and *Kirchenbuch* of 1877.

More pronounced impetus to a revival of confessional hymnody was given by the immigrant groups that arrived in America in the late 1830s firmly committed to a strict confessional position. These were the Prussians under Grabau (1804—79), who later formed the Buffalo Synod, the Saxons under C. F. W. Walther (1811—87), who, together with the emissaries of Wilhelm Loehe (1808—72), formed The Lutheran Church—Missouri Synod, and several other groups already on the American scene. Their confessional position was immediately evident in the hymnody they espoused. To this period belong Grabau's *Evangelisch-Lutherisches Kirchengesangbuch* (1842), Walther's *Kirchengesangbuch* (1847), the Ohio Synod's *Gesangbuch* (1870), its *Evangelical Lutheran Hymnal* (1880), and several earlier volumes of English hymns produced by the Ohio Synod.

With few exceptions, the hymnody of the confessional revival was largely in the German language. Not until the turn of the century was the task of translation, summarily dismissed by rationalism in the early 1800s, again taken up in earnest. The various Scandinavian groups that had come to America brought with them their own unique heritage of hymnody, largely from the writings of Kingo, Brorson, Grundtvig, and others. Both German and Scandinavian immigrant groups, relative latecomers to America, were determined to transmit the hymns of the homeland to their children and began the task of translating their own heritage into English. To these times belong the *Evangelical Lutheran Hymn Book* (1889) of the General English Lutheran Conference of Missouri, the *Hymnal and Order of Service* (1899) of the Augustana Synod, *The Lutheran Hymnary* (1913) of the Norwegian groups, the *Hymnal for Church and Home* (1927) of the Danish Lutherans.

These early attempts at translations were often characterized by the awkward phrase, the doggerel rhyme, and the infelicitous handling of the language, yet the attempt was made. Charles William Schaeffer (1813—96), William Reynolds (1812—76), Jens Christian Aaberg, Carl Doving (d. 1937), E. W. Olsen, Paul C. Paulsen (1881—1948), Georg Alfred

Rygh (1860—1942), Oluf Smeby (1851—1929), Harriet Reynolds Krauth Spaeth (1845—1925), Matthias Loy (1828—1915), August Crull (1845—1923), and a host of lesser figures labored faithfully to adapt the languages of their homeland to the new situation.

The Movement Toward Consolidation

Meanwhile, building on the *Church Book* of 1868 and the cooperative endeavors that had led to the adoption of the Common Service in 1888 by the General Council, the General Synod, and the United Synod of the South, work began on a hymnal that appeared in 1917, coincident with the formulation of the United Lutheran Church, as the *Common Service Book and Hymnal.* This was the first of a number of hymnals to appear in the 20th century spawned by a new movement toward the consolidation of many Lutheran church bodies. Other examples were the *American Lutheran Hymnal* (1930), published at the formation of the American Lutheran Church (the former Iowa, Buffalo, and Ohio synods), and *The Lutheran Hymnal* (1941), published by the Synodical Conference.

By the middle of the 20th century Muehlenberg's dream of "one church, one book" seemed within the realm of possibility. Two hundred years of history brought decisive changes from earlier times. The language problem was settled; the movement toward organizational union reduced Lutheran churches to three larger bodies; and the confessional revival, in underscoring that the church's hymnody is in a special sense of the term a confessional proclamation, laid the foundation for a more adequate reclaiming of the hymnody of the Reformation. After 1958 most Lutherans in America were using either the *Service Book and Hymnal,* a joint endeavor of eight Lutheran bodies, published in that year, or *The Lutheran Hymnal* of 1941 published by the Synodical Conference.

With the formation in 1966 of the Inter-Lutheran Commission on Worship, which included for the first time representation from all major American Lutheran church bodies, work began in earnest on the preparation of common hymnic and worship materials for American Lutheranism. Beginning in 1969 a series of pamphlets of liturgical and hymn materials have been produced "for Provisional use" by the participating groups. CS

The following annotated listing contains some of the most important official German and English language Lutheran hymnals produced in America from Muehlenberg to the present.

German Hymnals

Erbauliche Lieder-Sammlung zum Gottesdienstlichen Gebrauch in den Vereinigten Evangelisch Lutherischen Gemeinen in Nord-America. Germantaun: Leibert & Billmeyer, 1786. The first German Lutheran hymnbook prepared and published by Lutherans in America. Largely the work of Henry Melchior Muehlenberg.

Choralbuch fuer die Erbauliche Lieder-Sammlung der Deutschen Evangelisch-Lutherischen Gemeinen in Nord-Amerika. Philadelphia: Zentler & Blake, 1813. The chorale-book for Muehlenberg's hymnal of 1786. Contained 266 settings consisting of melody (in isorhythmic form) and figured bass. The first Lutheran chorale book published in America.

Das Neu eingerichtete Gesangbuch. Second edition. New Market: Ambrosius Henkel and Co., 1812. An undistinguished collection of 249 hymns (the first edition of 1810 contained 246) prepared by Paul Henkel. Many of the hymns are by Henkel. Was apparently used by only a small number of congregations.

Das Gemeinschaftliche Gesangbuch, zum Gottesdienstlichen Gebrauch der Lutherischen und Reformierten Gemeinden in Nord-America. Baltimore: Schaffer & Maund, 1817. The first of a number of books prepared for joint use by Lutheran and Reformed congregations. Contained 494 hymns.

Evangelische Lieder-Sammlung, genommen aus der Lieder-sammlung und dem Gemeinschaftlichen Gesangbuch. Gettysburg: L. Johnson, 1837. Hymnal of the General Synod, this volume was derived in part from Muehlenberg's hymnal of 1786 and in part from the "common hymnbook" of 1817.

Deutsches Gesangbuch fur die Evangelisch-Lutherische Kirche in den Vereinigten Staaten. Philadelphia: L. W. Wollenweber, 1849. Largely the work of C. R. Demme, this volume was referred to as the "new Pennsylvania hymnal" and replaced Muehlenberg's hymnal of 1786.

Evangelisch-Lutherisches Kirchen-Gesangbuch. Buffalo: Gedruckt mit Georg Zahm's Schriften, 1842. Produced for the Prussian immigrants of the Buffalo Synod under the leadership of J. A. A. Grabau. Contained 491 hymns in both Latin and German. Many hymns from the Babst hymnal of 1545 were included.

Kirchengesangbuch fuer Evangelisch-Lutherische Gemeinden ungeaenderter Augsburgischer Confession. New York: H. Ludwig, 1847. Hymnal of C. F. W. Walther and the Saxon immigrants, it contained 437 hymns.

Gesangbuch fuer Gemeinden des Evangelisch Lutherischen Bekenntnisses. Columbus: Schulze & Gaszmann, 1870. Hymnal of the Ohio Synod containing 532 hymns.

Kirchenbuch fuer Evangelisch-Lutherische Gemeinden. Philadelphia: General Council Publication Board, 1877. German hymnal of the General Council. Contained 595 hymns.

Choralbuch mit Liturgie und Chorgesaengen zum Kirchenbuch der Allgemeinen Kirchenversammlung. Philadelphia: United Lutheran Publication House, c. 1879. Chorale book for the General Council's *Kirchenbuch*. Prepared by John Endlich, it furnished music for the liturgy and hymns, as well as choral selections.

English Hymnals

A Hymn and Prayer-Book: for the use of such Lutheran Churches as use the English Language. New York: Hurtin and Commardinger, 1795. The first English-language Lutheran hymnal published in America. Prepared by J. C. Kunze, son-in-law of H. M. Muehlenberg, it contained 220 hymns, 150 of which were translations from the German.

A Collection of evangelical Hymns, made from different authors and collections, for the English Lutheran Church, in New York. New York: John Tiebout, 1797. Prepared by George Strebeck for Zion Church in New York, the bulk of this hymnal contained hymns by Watts and Charles Wesley.

A choice Selection of evangelical Hymns, from various authors: for the use of the English Evangelical-Lutheran Church, in New York. New York: J. C. Totten, 1806. Prepared by Ralph Williston, Strebeck's successor at Zion Church, this hymnal also consisted chiefly of hymns of Watts, Charles Wesley, and other Evangelical writers.

A Collection of Hymns, and a Liturgy, for the use of the Evangelical Lutheran Churches. Philadelphia: G. & D. Billmeyer, 1814. Containing 520 hymns, this volume was largely the work of F. H. Quitman, leading exponent of the rationalistic tendencies of the day. With this hymnal, Lutheran hymnody reached its lowest point.

Church Hymn Book. New Market: Solomon Henkel's Printing Office, 1816. A collection of 347 hymns collected by Paul Henkel. This book had little effect on the general development of Lutheran hymnody in America.

Hymns, selected and original, for public and private worship. Gettysburg: Stereotyped by L. Johnson, Philadelphia, 1828. English hymnal of the

General Synod. Largely the work of S. S. Schmucker, it reflected a sympathy with the rising wave of revivalism. Was widely used.

Church Book for the Use of Evangelical Lutheran Congregations. Philadelphia. Lutheran Book Store, 1868. The hymnal of the General Council, it was largely the work of B. M. Schmucker and F. Bird. Was probably the best English-language hymnal that American Lutheranism had produced to this time.

A Collection of Hymns and Prayers for Public and Private Worship. Zanesville: Printed at the Lutheran Standard Office, 1845. An early hymnal of the Ohio Synod.

Evangelical Lutheran Hymnal. Columbus: Ohio Synodical Printing House, 1880. Hymnal of the Ohio Synod, this book contained 468 hymns. A music edition was published in 1908.

Hymnbook for the use of Evangelical Lutheran Schools and Congregations. Decorah: Lutheran Publishing House, 1879. An early English-language hymnal translated and edited by August Crull. Its use was encouraged by C. F. W. Walther among Lutherans of the Missouri Synod.

Evangelical Lutheran Hymn Book. Baltimore: Harry Lang, 1889. Published by the General English Lutheran Conference of Missouri and Other States, this book, prepared by August Crull, contained 400 hymns. It was the immediate forerunner of the first official English hymnal of The Lutheran Church—Missouri Synod.

Evangelical Lutheran Hymn-Book with Tunes. St. Louis: Concordia Publishing House, 1912. The first official English hymnal of The Lutheran Church—Missouri Synod. L. Herman Ilse and H. A. Polack were music editors.

Hymnal and Order of Service for Churches and Sunday Schools. Rock Island: Augustana Book Concern, 1899. (A music edition followed in 1901.) Text edition of 355 hymns serving the Swedish Lutheran immigrants. Music edition prepared largely by A. Ostrum.

The Hymnal and Order of Service. Rock Island: Augustana Book Concern, 1925. Later revision of the 1899 volume, contains 670 hymns. Music editor was E. E. Ryden.

Hymnal for Church and Home. Blair, Nebraska, Danish Lutheran Publishing House, 1927. Published by the Danish Evangelical Lutheran Synods in America.

The Lutheran Hymnary. Minneapolis: Augsburg Publishing House, 1913. Hymnal of the Norwegian Lutherans in America, the book contained 618 hymns. Music coeditors were John Dahle and F. M. Christiansen.

Common Service Book and Hymnal. Philadelphia: Board of Publication of the United Lutheran Church in America, 1917. The joint work of the General Synod, the General Council, and the United Synod of the South, which merged the following year to form the United Lutheran Church in America. Luther D. Reed was largely responsible for this volume.

American Lutheran Hymnal. Columbus: Lutheran Book Concern, 1930. Published concurrently with the formation of the American Lutheran Church (the former Iowa, Ohio, and Buffalo Synods). Emmanuel Poppen was chairman of the intersynodical committee.

The Lutheran Hymnal. St. Louis: Concordia Publishing House, 1941. Official hymnal of the Synodical Conference of North America, it contained 660 hymns. It was largely the work of W. G. Polack and Bernard Schumacher. Currently used by about one third of American Lutheranism.

Service Book and Hymnal. Minneapolis: Augsburg and others, 1958. Authorized by the eight Lutheran church bodies cooperating in The Commission on the Liturgy and the Commission on the Hymnal. Luther D. Reed served as chairman of the Joint Commission. Currently used by about two thirds of American Lutheranism.

Readings: Ryden, Ernest E., "Hymnbooks (Lutheran)," *The Encyclopedia of The Lutheran Church,* ed. J. Bodensieck (Minneapolis, 1965), 1072—90; Schalk, C., *The Roots of Hymnody in The Lutheran Church—Missouri Synod* (St. Louis, 1965); Smith, C. Y., *Early Lutheran Hymnody in America from the Colonial Period to the Year 1850,* dissertation, U. of Southern Calif., 1956; Spaeth, A., "Hymnody, Hymn-Books, Luth.," *The Lutheran Cyclopedia,* ed. H. E. Jacobs and J. A. W. Haas (New York, 1899), pp. 235—238.

See also: chorale; hymnody, American; hymnody, German; theology of church music, Pietism and rationalism; theology of church music, 19th century

Leisen

Sacred German folk hymns dating from the early Middle Ages that developed from the acclamation *Kyrie eleison* (hence the name Leise, or sometimes Kirleise) and retained the acclamation or some variant (e.g. Kyrioleis, even occasionally "Alleluia") at the conclusion of each stanza.

The Leisen played an important role in the development of congregational vernacular singing, a practice that, while not encouraged by the church (it was officially proscribed by a number of synods) was nevertheless tolerated at certain times and under certain circumstances. Historically, the Leisen are related to the acclamation of *Kyrie eleison*, a response in the mass that the people continued to sing even when other parts of the service had been taken over by the clergy and the choir.

Prior to Reformation times, Leisen were sung in processions, by pilgrims, at special religious occasions, and even occasionally at mass. A medieval diary from Danzig carries the following description of a religious procession: "Die pfaffin suze sungin / di glockin lute klungen / die leigen Laien ire leise / sungen di wegereise."

The oldest example of a Leise is the famous *Petruslied* from the 9th century, "Unser trochtin."

> Unser trochtin [Herr] hat farsalt [verleiben]
> Sancte Petre gewalt
> Daz er mac ginerian [erhalten]
> Ze imo dingeten man. Kyrieleison.

One of the oldest, and probably most important, of the Leisen is *Christ is erstanden*, which was inspired by the sequence attributed to Wipo c. 1050, the *Victimae paschali laudes*. It was widely known since the 12th century, a monophonic example dating from c. 1350, a polyphonic example from c. 1394.

Leisen were often associated with a particular festival of the church year, and in the later Middle Ages single stanzas of these vernacular hymns (sung by the people) alternated with the verses of the appointed Latin sequence (sung by the choir). The Easter festival joined the Leise associated with that day, *Christ ist erstanden*, with the sequence *Victimae paschali*; for Ascension *Christ fuhr gen Himmel* with the sequence *Summi triumphum*; for Pentecost, *Komm, heiliger Geist* with the sequence *Veni, Sancte Spiritus;* and for Corpus Christi *Gott sei gelobet und gebenedeiet,* sung by the congregation between the verses of the Latin sequence *Lauda Sion salvatorum* sung by the choir in procession on that day.

Other important Leisen include: *Nun bitten wir den heiligen Geist,* already known in the 13th century, and commended to be sung by the famous preacher Berthold von Regensburg, the people being permitted to sing after the choir had sung the Latin sequence; *In Gottes Namen fahren wir,* a pilgrim hymn known from the 13th century; and *Gelobet seist du Jesu Christ*, the people's response to the Christmas sequence *Grates nunc omnes*, the earliest source being a Low German manuscript from c. 1370.

During the 16th and 17th centuries Leisen enjoyed a widespread popularity, especially in connection with the high festivals of the church. Other Leisen popular during this period include the two Leisen related to the Ten Commandments, *Dies sind die heil'gen zehn Gebot* (based on *In Gottes Namen fahren wir*) and its abridged companion, *Mensch, willst du leben seliglich*; the burial Leise, *Mitten wir im Leben sind*; the Easter Leise, *Erstanden ist der heilige Christ*; and an original hymn of Martin Luther using the Leise form, *Jesus Christus unser Heiland, der den Tod ueberwandt*.

Settings in both familiar and contrapuntal style of these popular Leisen were composed by most of the important church composers of the 16th century such as Johann Walter, Hans Leo Hassler, and Michael Praetorius, CS.

Readings: Reidel, J., *Leisen Formulae: Their Polyphonic Settings in the Renaissance and Reformation*, diss., U. of Southern California, 1953; Reidel, J., "Vocal Leisen Settings in the Baroque Era," *Musical Heritage of the Lutheran Church*, V (St. Louis, 1959).

See also: church music history, medieval; church music history, Renaissance—the Reformation tradition; sequence; *HCM*, I, IV

liturgical drama

The liturgical drama of the Middle Ages, which flourished from the 10th to the 13th century, developed directly from the practice of troping. It was built on the latent dramatic action inherent in certain ecclesiastical rites and on the availability of dialoglike texts closely associated with the Easter and Christmas celebrations, the subject matter gradually broadening to include a wide variety of subjects from the Old and New Testaments. Texts were initially Latin, both prose and verse; soon, however, vernacular adaptations were also included. The music was ordinarily only a single melodic line derived from the melodies of Gregorian antiphons, sequences, hymns, secular music, but also incorporated original musical material. Most of the dramas concluded with a traditional chant appropriate to the ecclesiastical celebration. The melodies were most probably unaccompanied, although there is evidence that instruments were used, especially in the more elaborate productions.

Designations for the liturgical drama of the Middle Ages include a variety of terms such as *ordo, officium, processio, versus, historia, miraculum, misterium, ludus, repraesentatio, similitudo, planctus, play, spil, Visitatio sepulchri, de peregrino, Suscitatio Lazari,* and others.

The trope *Hodie cantandus* (often attributed to Tuotilo c. 900) represents an early dialog trope that led directly into the Introit for the Mass for Christmas. The first example of the more fully developed early liturgical drama is the Easter Mass trope *Quem quaeritis in sepulchro,* which appeared early in the 10th century and consisted of three sentences originally placed before the introit:

> Whom do you seek in the sepulchre, servants of Christ?
> Jesus of Nazareth who was crucified, celestial ones.
> He is not here, he is risen as he foretold; go, announce that he is risen from the sepulchre.

Simple forms of this dialog are found in manuscripts from St. Gall and Limoges; other examples with slight adaptations are found throughout Europe. The most important document showing the *Quem quaeritis* is the Winchester Troper, an Anglo-Saxon service book dating from c. 980. A detailed account of the performance of this Easter dialog is found in the *Regularis Concordia,* issued about the same time by Ethelwold, Bishop of Winchester (see Reese, *Music in the Middle Ages,* 194—195). Sometime in the latter half of the 10th century the Easter dialog was transferred from its position in the mass to the Easter Matins, where it achieved independence from the mass and where a greater opportunity for development of its dramatic aspects became possible. The *incipit* "Te Deum" is found at the conclusion of many of the dramatized versions, indicating the position it may have assumed in the structure of the Office.

The *Victimae paschali,* famous 11th century sequence with dialoglike passages, was incorporated into many of the simple singlescene Easter dialogs by the early 12th century. The addition of such scenes as the appearance of Peter and John at the tomb, the meeting of Jesus with Mary Magdalene in the garden, and the Thomas scene provided further opportunity for development. *Peregrinus* dramas, dealing with the Emmaus journey, are extant from the 12th century and were apparently performed as part of the Easter Monday Vespers.

A trope in dialog form of the introit for the 3d mass of Christmas Day,

Quem quaeritis in praesaepe, pastores, dating from the late 10th century, initiated a development similar to that of the Easter trope.

> Whom seek ye at the manger, O shepherds?
> Christ, the Savior, the infant Lord wrapped in swaddling clothes, according to the words of the angel.
> The child is here with Mary his mother, of whom long ago the prophet Isaiah spoke, prophesying: "Behold a virgin shall conceive and bear a Son"; and now as ye go forth say that He is born.
> Alleluia! Now do we know truly that Christ is born into the world; of whom let all sing, saying with the prophet:
> *Puer natus est nobis.*

Certain other scenes connected with the Christmas story, such as the shepherds as the manger, the journey of the Magi, the slaughter of the innocents, developed into independent plays.

Apart from an occasional use of the subject matter of the Passion story and the availability of an Ascension Day mass trope with obvious dramatic possibilities, there is little evidence that there was significant development of these subjects as liturgical dramas during the Middle Ages. The application of the idea of dramatic dialog to other portions of the Old and New Testaments, however, resulted, beginning in the 11th century, in such liturgical dramas as the "prophet plays," the "Plays of Daniel," the "Play of the Wise and Foolish Virgins" (the *sponsus* play), and others centering on such stories as the raising of Lazarus, the Conversion of St. Paul, Joseph and his Brothers, Esau and Jacob, legends of various saints (esp. St. Nicholas), and the Last Judgment.

The famous Fleury playbook, written in the 13th century at the monastery of Benoit-sur-Loive at Fleury, contains 10 music dramas and is an important source of music for the liturgical drama. Liturgical drama reached its peak in the 12th and 13th centuries and was increasingly characterized by the interpenetration of sacred and secular elements. Gradually the performace of these dramas moved from the sanctuary to outside the church, into the market place, and ultimately into the theater.

The development of the popular "mystery plays" of the 14th to the 16th centuries, dramatic representations of Biblical subjects, represent a development in which music was used only incidentally and in which the divorce from the liturgy was quite complete. They belong more properly to the development of European drama than as a further development of liturgical drama. CS

Readings: Bowles, E., "The Role of Musical Instruments in Medieval Sacred Drama," *Musical Quarterly* (Jan, 1959); Smoldon, W. L., "Liturgical Drama," *The New Oxford History of Music*, II (New York, 1955); Young, K., *The Drama of the Medieval Church* (New York, 1933).

See also: church music history, medieval; passion; sequence; trope

mass

The mass is the central ritual activity of the Christian church. It extends from the words of Jesus at the Passover celebration prior to his passion: "Do this to remember Me." The word itself is derived from the service's traditional dismissal formula "Ite, missa est" (Go, the gathering is dismissed), and is used as a label chiefly by Roman Catholics, but also by Lutherans and Anglicans. The service is also called Holy Communion, Lord's Supper, Holy Eucharist, or simply "Liturgy," the latter among most Eastern Christians. Style of celebration has led to a more specialized nomenclature: Solemn Mass *(missa solemnis)* presupposes participation from deacon (and, up to 1974, subdeacon) and the use of music and incense; Sung Mass *(missa cantata)* assumes the assistance of a server and the use of music; Solitary Mass *(missa solitaria)* refers to the private masses typical of the Middle Ages; and Read Mass *(missa lecta)* means a private mass in which the texts are simply read.

In the history of music, mass usually refers to grouped chant or polyphonic settings of the following mass texts: Kyrie, Gloria, Credo, Sanctus, and Agnus Dei. A *missa brevis* (short mass) is the grouping of Kyrie and Gloria (sometimes Sanctus).

Structure

The basic structure of the mass is discernible throughout its history: (1) the Preparatory rites, consisting of praise and confessional elements; (2) the Service of readings consisting of lessons from the Law, Prophets, Epistles, and Gospels, intervenient chants, homily, and intercessions; (3) the Service of Eucharist, consisting of thanksgivings and participation in the meal; (4) the Dismissal rite, or final prayers and blessings.

Among Roman Catholics the latest form of the mass is that which appears in the 1974 *Sacramentary*; this rite was approved by Pope Paul VI on April 3, 1969, but is based on a provisional predecessor that appeared in 1964. The most recent version is expected to be permanent. Before 1964 the mass was officially formulated according to the Missal of Pius V (1570), which incorporated the reforms emanating from the Council of Trent. A parallel sketch of these two rites (1570 and 1974) shows the consistency of overall structure.

The Mass

According to the Missal of Pius V	According to the Sacramentary
	1974
1570	*Entrance Song
I. Preparation	
	Invocation
Invocation	Greeting
Psalm 42	Confession or Kyrie
Confession	Supplications
Prayers for Absolution	
*Introit	Kyrie (if not used earlier)
Kyrie	Gloria in excelsis
Gloria in excelsis	(on Sundays and Feasts)
	*Collect
*Collects	
II. Service of Readings	*First Lesson
	*Gradual
	*Second Lesson
*Epistle	*Alleluia Verse
*Gradual and Alleluia Verse	*Gospel
*Gospel	Homily
Homily	Nicene Creed (Sundays and
Nicene Creed	Feasts)
	General Intercessions
III. Service of Holy Eucharist *Offertory and Offertory Prayers	*Offertory Song and Prayers

237

*Preface and Proper Preface	*Preface and Proper Preface
Sanctus	Sanctus
Canon (Eucharistic Prayer)	*Eucharistic Prayer
Our Father	Our Father
Agnus Dei	Agnus Dei
*Communion Prayers	*Communion Prayers

IV. Dismissal Rite

*Post Communion Prayers	Salutation
Ite, missa est	Blessing
Closing Prayer and Blessing	Dismissal
Last Gospel (John 1:1-14)	

*These elements change from service to service, depending on occasion or interest. Customarily they have been called "Propers"; the remaining sections are called the "Ordinary"; in a restricted sense the Ordinary has meant only Kyrie, Gloria, Credo, Sanctus, and Agnus Dei.

Scattered throughout both of these orders is a variety of antiphons, prayers, acclamations, versicle-response patterns, and specified actions that together provide actual use with particular color and mood. Often these less obvious details have affected the perception of the mass' basic structure, as happened, e.g., in the Middle Ages with the relegation of offertory actions to the priest alone. Such changes occurred frequently through the years, coincident, usually, with shifting understandings of the function of the mass.

During the first three centuries, before Christianity was legitimized, the celebration of the Lord's Supper was essentially a *domestic mass*, observed mostly in house churches. It consisted of elements from the first Eucharist combined with features of Jewish worship. Preparatory rites probably didn't exist, lessons were from the Law and Prophets, as well as from Epistles and Gospels, and the Service of the Word concluded with a dismissal of the catechumens, which emphasized the careful restrictions placed on membership. Because of the custom of improvisation, eucharistic prayers ranged from short to long, and displayed a prophetic quality. Dismissal rites were brief.

The move to larger buildings in the 4th and 5th centuries occasioned the *basilican mass*, a stage characterized by a switch to Latin as the liturgical language of the West, and by increased attention to the place of celebration.

That was prompted by a growing sense of the mass as a mirror of the heavenly liturgy, and achieved through a careful molding of liturgical text and movement. The rite began with a composed litany and introduced the Sanctus for the first time as a fixed element. Prayers were expanded and refined, and celebrative diction was achieved through the expanding sense of church year.

During the 6th and 7th centuries the eucharistic rite was modified through the introduction of courtly ceremonial. Originating at Rome, this *papal mass* was marked by increased use of incense, torches, and elaborate vestments, and was complemented with solemn movement music such as introits, offertories, communions, together with the earlier graduals and Alleluia verses (for Gospel processions), all of which consisted of verses chiefly from the Psalms. The regular use of Gloria in excelsis and Agnus Dei, which dates from these times, resulted from the then current preoccupation with divinely regal presence.

From the 8th to the 11th centuries local versions of the Western mass (especially the Gallican in France, and the Mozarabic in Spain) gave way to the Roman rite and its persuasive supporters. Meanwhile, formal aspects of the mass shifted to accommodate strains of personal piety (*sentiment mass*). Prayers were added for the priest's own meditation, and the service was concluded with a blessing, for the first time, rather than with an impersonal order to leave. Most notable among the innovations of this period was the practice of troping, a personal commentary on existing mass texts. Sequence hymns for instance, spun out the theme of the day, and the Nicene Creed—also new to the mass of this time—provided a commentary on the entire Service of Readings.

Subsequent alterations before the Missal of 1570 were more visual than structural. Growing illiteracy forced reliance on the other senses. Capitalizing on that need, the allegorists devised complicated interpretations of movements, colors, and actions in the liturgy by which people were left to perceive something of its meaning and form. Three periods of silence in the mass were to be taken as symbolizing Christ's three days in the tomb. This *dramatic mass* placed a premium on viewing the consecrated host and wine rather than on partaking of the Sacrament.

Unique structural variations resulted also because of the requirements of some special occasions. The extra ceremonies connected with Ash Wednesday, Palm Sunday, Good Friday, and Easter Eve gave new dimensions to the classic shape of the mass. Similarly, the Requiem mass (from the first word of the introit) called for the omission of the Gloria in excelsis and Credo, and its Alleluia verse was replaced by a tract which in turn was followed by the well-known sequence *Dies irae*.

Martin Luther's restructuring of the mass was prompted by his overall desire to unshackle the liturgy for fuller expression of the Reformation norm: justification by grace through faith. The first of his two major reforms was the *Formula missae* (1523), a Latin rite that was to accommodate vernacular hymns and a sermon. It came into being when Luther purged the existing rite of sacrificial phrases and notions, and removed most of the Offertory section together with the eucharistic prayer (Canon). He placed the Sanctus after the Words of Institution. Three years later (1526) he issued the *Deutsche Messe,* a simplified vernacular form with music designed to fit the German language. In this rite, prepared for the less educated, Luther displayed some of his less conservative tendencies, paraphrasing and replacing the Our Father, suggesting a division of the Words of Institution together with a double distribution. A comparison of the two rites shows their peculiarities.

Luther's Liturgical Orders

Formula missae	*Deutsche Messe*
1523	*1526*
Introit (whole psalm if possible)	Introit (psalm or hymn)
Kyrie	Kyrie
Gloria in excelsis	
Collect	Collect
Epistle	Epistle
Gradual and Alleluia (no sequence hymn)	Gradual Hymn
Gospel	Gospel
Nicene Creed	Nicene Creed (metricized)
Sermon	Sermon
Preparation of Elements	
Preface and Proper Preface	Paraphrase on Our Father
Words of Institution	Words of Institution
Sanctus	(Sanctus, Agnus Dei, or other hymns between divided Words of Institution)

Pax Domini
Agnus Dei
Communion Song
Collect   Collect
Benedicamus
Benediction   Benediction

The authorship of these two rites provided for their widespread influence on Lutheran liturgies for at least the next 200 years. Lutheran church orders, or liturgies, were produced for each local jurisdiction, and they were modeled on one or the other of Luther's productions. By the late 18th century his influence gave way to German rationalism as well as pietism. The effects of this were devastating. In the 1797 *Agenda* from Schleswig-Holstein, e.g., Holy Communion is an appendix to the regular service, and it is envisioned for use four to eight times a year. The service was to follow the pattern of the *Deutsche Messe* with emphasis on examination and exhortation. The historic propers were ignored, and what was left of the Ordinary appeared as metricized versions of the Gloria and Credo.

A somewhat different picture is presented by Heinrich M. Muehlenberg's liturgy of 1748, a rite prepared for American German Lutherans. His attempts at reconstituting earlier structures were complemented and expanded a century later by Wilhelm Loehe (*Agenda*, 1844); his mass bears many features common to Luther's work of 1523. Along the same lines but in English, the *Common Service* of 1888 (incorporated in the *Common Service Book* of 1917) helped to establish the 16th-century structural model for almost all Lutheran worship in America. The recent rite from the Inter-Lutheran Commission on Worship honors those traditions, but also displays similarities to the 1974 *Sacramentary*.

Music

Music for the mass falls into three categories: Common Tones, or the recitatives assigned to the minister and congregation; Propers, or those chants and settings usually given over to the cantor or choir; Ordinary, those pieces intended for the people.

The Common Tones

For the most part the common tones consist of reciting tones and of musical cadences that facilitate phrase and sentence punctuation. Those in the *Liber Usualis* (a collection of music needed for the pre-Vatican rite) are representative of the types of tones found earlier. There are formulas for prayers, prefaces, readings (Prophecy, Epistle, and several for the Gospel), blessings, confession, and for the Benedicamus. The tones for the Passions, the Our Father, and the Psalm tones also fall within this category, although the latter are sometimes used also for the Propers. A later practice, the *recto tono*, allows for some of these elements to be chanted on monotone.

There are fewer such common tones in the 1974 *Sacramentary;* it contains music only for the Prefaces, conclusion to the eucharistic prayers, the Pax Domini, and the blessings.

Most of the common tones continued to be used by 16th-century Lutherans. Together with Johann Walter, Luther prepared new versions of the lesson formulas, and, having unsilenced the Words of Institution, he suggested a tone also for them. Following a practice begun already with the 14th-century polyphonic settings of *Ite, missa est*, Lutheran composers created arrangements of the Our Father, the Pax Domini, the Communion psalm (111), the salutations, and the Words of Institution. Some of these were used in Leipzig at Bach's time. Though a concert piece, Bernstein's *Mass* also contains polyphonic settings of some of these recurring texts. Following the example set by Archer and Reed in *Choral Service* (1901), most 20th-century Lutheran rites have prescribed common tones for the pastor, in some cases created from new melodic formulas.

The Propers

The propers of the mass change from service to service. Those which have received the most musical attention are the introit, gradual, tract, Alleluia verse, offertory, and communion. When sung in chant form, the introit consisted of antiphonal psalmody interspersed with a melodic antiphon sung either by the people or later by the choir. Other people/choir (cantor) pieces are the offertory and communion, each built at first on the refrain/verse principle; later redactions have only the refrain (as in the *Liber Usualis*).

More contemplative and ornate are the traditional graduals and tracts. Their soloistic features are gilded with such musical developments as thematic repetition or variation. The Alleluias share many of these characteristics but are chiefly the result of the improvisatory impulse. In the Roman Catholic church the historic Gregorian chant versions of these propers have been replaced by the materials proposed in the 1974

Sacramentary. There no settings are prescribed for the revised texts of the introit (Entrance Song), offertory, or communion; in fact, provision is made for substitute songs. In practice the fixed texts of the gradual and Alleluia are sung to popular refrain-type psalm settings.

According to the *Formula missae*, Luther wished to perpetuate the Latin introits, graduals, and Alleluias. In his *Deutsche Messe* the introit was replaced by a German psalm and the gradual by a hymn. The Lutheran hymnic gradual (later *Hauptlied*, or sermon hymn) constituted an important structural change in the mass.

As the Latin mass lost popularity among Lutherans, most of the propers were no longer used. Renewal movements brought about restoration of the texts, as in the *Common Service Book* of 1917, and they were supplied with simple psalm tone settings or new chant formulas.

Leonin and Perotin (12th and 13th centuries) established a tradition of polyphonic arrangements for the propers—a tradition that was to be carried on in the 15th and 16th centuries by Isaac, Galliculus, Michael, Victoria, and many others. Erhard Bodenschatz's *Florilegium Portense* (1618 and 1621), a collection of polyphonic introit settings, was still used by J. S. Bach. Mozart and Bruckner kept the tradition alive, and there are contemporary collections by composers as diverse as Reda and Peloquin.

The Ordinary

In addition to the customary Kyrie, Gloria, Credo, Sanctus, and Agnus Dei, the sung ordinary includes the Our Father, the conclusions to the Eucharistic Prayer, the acclamations, and, among Lutherans, the offertory. The Kyrie is a remnant of litanic intercessions placed at the beginning of the mass structure. Some of its simple melodies reflect that ancient function. All parts of the ordinary, except the Credo, were sung by the congregation before the 9th century. The melodies were not written down. Later the choir alone sang these liturgical songs according to melodies that were increasingly ornate. The hundreds of new tunes were good raw material for the creative troper. Productions of this kind were extremely popular and continued in use even among the Lutherans (see Luther's "Kyrie, Gott Vater in Ewigkeit").

Settings of the five chief parts of the ordinary, including on occasion the *Ite, missa est*, were gathered together as a unit already in the 13th century. Polyphonic collections of the same type appeared a few years later; one of the earliest of these is the Tournai mass of c. 1300. Machaut's mass of c. 1350 is the first polyphonic mass by a single composer.

The mass structure was a favorite form for 15th- and 16th-century composers (among others, Dufay, Desprez, Senfl, Morales, Victoria, Palestrina, and de la Rue; Guerrero, and Orlando di Lasso for Requiem masses). Normal techniques of unification were the plainsong mass, in which each movement was based on the corresponding movement of a monophonic plainsong mass; the cyclical cantus-firmus mass, in which all movements were based on one and the same melody—a tune from liturgical or secular sources or one freely invented; and the imitation or parody mass, in which whole sections of preexistent compositions were borrowed or altered for the new piece. Occasionally masses were created without any previous model.

Among 16th-century Lutherans Latin chants of the ordinary were taken over without alteration, were translated into German, or were fashioned into hymns. Favorites among these hymns were the German Credo hymn "Wir glauben all' an einen Gott" and the Agnus Dei hymn "Christe, du Lamb Gottes." Because of these hymnic versions, Lutheran settings of the mass often consisted only of the *missa brevis* (so Walter, Paminger, Praetorius, and Ahle). Composers of subsequent periods continued to use this structure. Important predecessors of Bach's *Mass in B minor* were the concert masses of Gilles (Requiem), Biber, and Kerrl; the tradition of the orchestral mass was carried on by Hasse, Haydn, Mozart, Beethoven, Liszt, Berlioz (Requiem), Bruckner, Faure (Requiem), Janacek, Delius, and most recently, Bernstein. The Requiem mass of Brahms consists of texts freely chosen from the Bible, together expressing thoughts corresponding to the traditional Requiem.

In contrast to these concert productions, settings of the ordinary continue to be gathered for congregational use. The *Common Service Book* (1917), *Service Book and Hymnal* (1958), and *The Lutheran Hymnal* (1941) contain music by Tallis, Stainer, Ohl, Sowerby, and tunes from medieval plainsong and Scottish chant. Recent settings run the gamut of styles from pseudo-Gregorian to a variety of more popular and transient musical styles. MB

Readings; Blankenburg, Walter, "Der mehrstimmige Gesang und die konzertierende Musik im evangelischen Gottesdienst," *Die Musik des Evangelischen Gottesdienstes,* IV of *Leiturgia* (Kassel, 1961); Jungman, Joseph, *The Mass of the Roman Rite,* 2 vols. (New York, 1951—55); Reed, Luther D., *The Lutheran Liturgy* (Philadelphia, 1959); Robertson, Alec,

Requiem (London, 1967); Thompson, Bard, ed., *Liturgies of the Western Church* (Cleveland, 1961).

See also: chant, Gregorian; church music history, medieval; church music history, Renaissance—the Latin tradition; church music history, Renaissance—the Reformation tradition; sequence; trope; *HCM*, I, II, IV

medieval instruments

Practically no instruments from before about 1000 A.D. have survived. Investigation of instruments from this period is principally dependent on interpretation of art works of the time. Nearly all the instruments of medieval Europe came from Asia, from the southeast through Byzantium, from the Islamic empire through North Africa, or from along the Baltic coast.

Following instructions of the church, missionaries and bishops prohibited the use of instruments in worship. For this reason they were mainly used for secular activities. A few descriptions of certain instruments are found in the writings of the church fathers, but very often they are merely symbolic descriptions.

Stringed Instruments

lyre. (Ger.: *Harfe;* Welsh: *crwth*) A prominent instrument of the period, it consisted of a sound box with two supports joined together by a crossbar. Its strings were plucked before 1000 A.D.; after that time they were bowed.

harp. Ireland was the first European country to adopt this instrument, which, like the lyre, had plucked strings. In the early Middle Ages, it was small and had only one support, which served as a sound box; later a larger model supplanted it, and in the ninth century a harp was made with a curved anterior support; the upright rear support acted as a sound box.

dulcimer. Derived from the Persian santir, it is in the shape of a trapezoid, with the strings struck in the manner of a percussion instrument. It seems to have been used more in northern Europe than elsewhere.

psaltery. This instrument came from the East at the beginning of the 12th century. It had a variable number of single or double strings, which were stretched by means of pegs across the body and plucked. It could be triangular or square in shape. In its final form it became trapezoidal. The instrument was used mostly in southern Europe. With the addition of a keyboard it evolved into the spinet.

monochord. Originally intended for theoretical purposes, it soon was used as an instrument in its own right. It consisted of a long sound box, over which a string was stretched. Supporting the string was a movable bridge. Later several strings (up to 14) of different lengths were used on the same sound box and played with a plectrum.

tromba marina. (Ger.: *Trumscheit*) This instrument probably appeared in the 12th century. It had a long sound box in the shape of a narrow

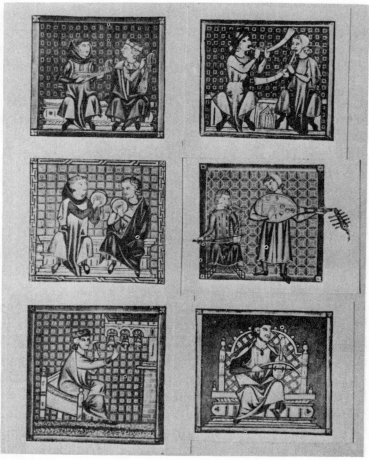

A variety of medieval instruments depicted in a late 13th-century collection of religious songs made by Alfonso X of Leon and Castile.

trapezoid, on the top of which was a neck. One fairly thick string passed over a bridge that had one leg against an ivory or bone plate embedded in the sound box. The bow was placed on the string between the player's hand and the scroll of the instrument. The left hand stopped the string only lightly, thus producing harmonics. The resulting sound was bright and brassy. The name of the instrument means "trumpet of the daughters of Mary," i.e., a trumpet used by nuns.

lute. This is another instrument from the East. It had a long neck and a pear-shaped body. It started out with three strings; later more were added. The strings were plucked with a plectrum while the instrument was held on the knees.

guitar. This instrument differed from the lute in that its back was generally flat and attached to the belly by splints. It was introduced into Europe from Arabia through Spain.

vihuela. The instrument developed from the *guitara latina* and had a flat sound box, a short neck that was bent backwards, and a pegbox that was mounted on an angle. There were three types: one kind played with a plectrum, one bowed, and the third played with the fingers.

fiddle. This name was used in the medieval era to designate any bowed stringed instrument. One type of fiddle was the lyra (not to be confused with lyre) with three strings. Another kind of fiddle was the gigue which usually had one string and a shape like a leg of ham.

rebec. Generally this instrument had three strings and was played with a very short, arch-shaped bow. It was principally used by minstrels because its harsh and penetrating sound was ideal for outdoor dances.

Wind Instruments

recorder. (Lat: *fistula anglica* (English flute), It.: *flauto dolce*, Fr.: *flute douce*, Gr.: *Blockfloete*) The vertical recorder possibly originated in England. It may be described as a beaked whistle flute, the upper end of which was stopped by a block or plug that left only a narrow flue to lead the breath towards the sharp edge of a mouth hole in the side. The bore tapered toward the lower end. It had a pale tone as reflected by its name.

transverse flute. Along with the recorder, this was one of the two main kinds of flute. It came to Europe by way of Byzantium in the 10th or 11th century. It was soon adopted by the Swiss and German peasants.

chalumeau. This French word could refer to any reed instrument. Reed instruments were used for outdoor or martial music.

shawm. This was an oboelike instrument with a conical bore and double reed. It had two to five holes and sometimes a bulge near the mouthpiece and near the bell.

bagpipes. The first mention of this instrument dates from the 9th century, but its history goes back to the Greeks and Romans. At first the instrument had no drones; the first one made its appearance in 1350, the second followed in 1400. A medieval variant of the bagpipe was the bladderpipe. It consisted of a blowpipe leading into a bladder, on another part of which were two reed pipes, one the chanter, the other the drone.

cor. This French word could designate a cowhorn, the cornett, or the oliphant. The cowhorn or the oliphant (made of elephant tusk) was used for martial music or hunting calls. The expensive oliphant was reserved for the nobility.

trumpet. This instrument was not so common. The metal trumpets were modelled on Roman *tubae.* They were slim and straight with a bell that was gradually widened due to the influence of Moslem trumpets. The French called this trumpet the *buisine.* These instruments were fairly expensive and so also belonged to the nobility. Another kind of trumpet was what the Italians called *trombetta.* It was smaller than the *buisine* and made of wood.

Percussion Instruments

Percussion instruments were very numerous in the Middle Ages. The *tympanum* was made of a hollow wooden body over which was stretched a skin; the skin was beaten with drumsticks. It seems they were used in pairs tuned an octave apart.

The instrument we call tambourine was called *timbrel* during the Middle Ages and was of Asian origin. Small bells, or in some cases small cymbals, were attached to the frame. At first it was played with a drumstick, later by the hands or knuckles.

The real medieval *tambourin* was a kind of drum. It was a fairly long narrow drum, and it was struck with one or two sticks. A similar instrument was the tabor. *Nakers* were small kettledrums, worn on the belt. Like the tympanum, they had definite pitch.

Other percussion instruments were the bell, the metal or glass plate, and the wood block. Gregory of Tours first used the bell in the sixth century to summon the faithful to worship. In the 12th century, monasteries owned bell sets, containing at least seven bells struck with hammers. During the 13th century, bells were first installed in church towers and belfries. Soon these bells were sounded mechanically by means of a cylinder with pins fixed to it that released hammers, which, in turn, struck the bells at fixed hours.

Bells were either forged or cast in the late Middle Ages. Up to the 13th century, bells were hive-shaped and struck on the outside. From the 14th century on they took their present shape and were usually struck by a mobile beater on the inside.

The first type of xylophone was the French *échelette*, made by tying together with cord a number of wooden blades in a strict order of diminishing sizes at a certain distance from each other. It was held at its upper (smaller) end, and the right hand struck the blades with some kind of beater.

Keyboard Instruments

harpsichord. Called *clavicembalo* for the first time in 1404, this keyboard instrument had plucked strings. A small piece of wood called a jack, at the farther end of the key, had a plectrum that plucked the string when the key was depressed. From the beginning of the 15th century, the harpsichord had a range of nearly four octaves (45 keys). The shape was similar to that of a harp placed on its side. The strings decreased in size from left to right and lay parallel to the keyboard.

clavichord. This instrument was mentioned for the first time in 1405 in a German poem. The strings are struck by a small tangent of brass attached perpendicularly at the farther end of the key. It continues to touch the string as long as the key is depressed.

hurdy-gurdy. This was an instrument with rubbed strings and a keyboard. It was also called *organistrum* or *symphonia* during medieval times. It could have a flat sound box like a guitar or a rounded one like the lute. A case with a pegbox at the top was fixed along the length of the sound box. Inside the case were tangents operated by keys on the outside. The strings, generally two tuned in unison, passed through the case ending in the pegbox. The strings were set in vibration by a rosin-coated wheel, rotated by a crank at the lower end of a sound box. Four larger strings, two on each side of the case, acted as drones. The sound was harsh and squeaky.

organ. The first church organ (either hydraulic or pneumatic) was built in 827 by the Abbot of Saint-Savin in Poitou. The noise of the bellows of ancient organs was extremely loud. After the 13th century, there were three different types: portative, positiv, and the large church organ. In the 13th century, keys, different registrations, separate ranks, and a modern system of transmission appeared. In 1306 the first pedal board was built. ERi

Readings: Bessaraboff, N., *Ancient European Musical Instruments* (Cambridge, Mass., 1941); Reese, G., *Music in the Middle Ages* (New York, 1940); Sachs, C., *The History of Musical Instruments* (New York, 1940).

See also: church music history, medieval; organ, history; Renaissance instruments.

metrical psalmody

Metrical psalmody is the term for the Psalms translated into any language in strophic form, resembling hymns, and thus adapted for simple congregational singing.

Metrical psalmody has its origin in the 16th-century Calvinist churches. The earliest metrical psalter is that of Strasbourg (1539) introduced in the time of Calvin (1509—64), and based on the psalms that a court poet, Clement Marot (c. 1497—1544) had translated into French meters. When Calvin moved to Geneva in 1541 he caused the psalter to be expanded, chiefly under the editorship of Louis Bourgeois (born c. 1510); 83 psalms, with tunes composed or adapted by Bourgeois, were completed by 1551. The full psalter, known as the *Genevan Psalter*, was finished in 1562 after Calvin's death. The psalter used 110 different meters for the 150 psalms. It was never revised, but its music is still to be found in all hymnals, its most famous contribution being the Tune *Old 100th*, set to Psalm 134 in the *Genevan Psalter*.

At almost the same time, a metrical psalter was developing in England from the psalms devised by Thomas Sternhold, a courtier, for young King Edward VI (d. 1547). Sternhold had only partially completed this work by the time of his death in 1549, but a team led by John Hopkins completed the work and it was published in 1562 as *The Whole Book of Psalms*, the same year that the Genevan Psalter was finished. Almost all the psalms in this version are in the meter of the English ballad (8.6.8.6). Many English psalters followed "Sternhold and Hopkins," including that of Ainsworth (1612) which was brought to America by the Pilgrim Fathers; but in the Church of England, which followed the Genevan custom of prohibiting for many generations any congregational song that was not psalmody, no other was authorized until 1696, when N. Tate and N. Brady issued their "New Version." Even then

Title page of *The Whole Booke of Psalmes* by Thomas Sternhold and John Hopkins, which first appeared in 1562, together with page showing the "Old Hundredth" psalm tune set to the words "All people that on earth do dwell." (Klinck Memorial Library)

the "Old Version," as Sternhold and Hopkins Psalter came to be called, remained the favorite, and was reprinted more than 300 times until the mid-19th century.

The first Scottish metrical Psalter was compiled in 1564, on the same metrical scheme as the English, but in an independent translation. It was revised in 1650, and, despite later attempts to modernize its language, it remains in that form in the worship of the Church of Scotland and all churches associated with it.

The only accepted modern version of the metrical psalter is *The Psalter* (1912), authorized for use in the Presbyterian Churches of the U.S.A.

Metrical psalmody is a distinctive feature of Calvinist churches, and therefore it is to be found in the minority Calvinist churches of 17th-century Germany, and is still revered in the Reformed Church of Holland.

Churches of Lutheran association have, following Luther's example, always preferred hymnody.

Metrical psalmody must be distinguished from hymns based on psalms. Of these the most celebrated are those of Isaac Watts (1715), and hardly less so, those of James Montgomery and of H. F. Lyte (who wrote "Praise, My Soul" as a version of Psalm 103) and those in the earlier German tradition of Martin Luther. But these are written with more freedom and less insistence on the precise rendering of every Hebrew word.

The music of metrical psalmody has always shown a vigorous capacity for survival, and psalm tunes from Geneva, England, and Scotland are now often used to carry hymns of any period and culture. Psalm tunes were in their day always sung in unison and unaccompanied; harmonized editions (Goudimel's at Geneva, 1565, Day's in England, 1563, being the first) were always unofficial and for use outside public worship. Nowadays the harmonies given are usually editorial. The most important sources for the music for English psalmody are the psalters of Day (1563), Daman (1591), and Ravenscroft (1621), and for Scottish Psalmody, the psalters of 1615 and 1635. ER.

Readings: Frost, M., *English and Scottish Psalm and Hymn Tunes* (London, 1953); Pidoux, P., *Le Psautier Huguenot* (Basel, 1962).

See also: church music history, Renaissance—the Reformation tradition; hymnody, English; HCM, III, IV

Moravian church music

The Moravian Church traces its ancestry back to John Hus (c. 1370—1415). The reverberations of his martyrdom on July 6, 1415, can be felt in the Western church to this day. He sought the removal from the church of those practices that he regarded as abuses, and he strove to recapture the pristine character and integrity of early Christianity. The Moravian Church also maintains its identity with the ancient "Unitas Fratrum," the Unity of the Brethren, whose history goes back to 1457 in Bohemia. A German sector of the "Unitas Fratrum" dates from 1478.

Hymnody in the Ancient "Unitas Fratrum,"
1501—c. 1620

The earliest known documentary basis for the history of hymnody in the Moravian Church is a Czech hymnbook printed without music in 1501 perhaps in Prague. (The Moravian Music Foundation, Winston-Salem, N. C., has a microfilm of the only known copy in the National Museum, Prague Sign. 25 F 3.) However, outstanding hymnologists have pointed out that members of the "Unitas Fratrum" throughout the 16th century never made proprietary reference to this very first of all printed hymnbooks. On the contrary, Bishop John Blahoslav (1523—71) in his *History of the Brethren* (Ms. fol. 112), refers to the year 1505 as follows: "The Brethren for the first time in 1505 had a large sized Kancional of sacred hymns printed." This Kancional of about 400 hymns was the first officially sanctioned hymnal of the Bohemian Brethren. No copy is known to exist; nor has a copy either of Brother Lucas' hymnal of 1519 or of the hymnbook edited by John Horn (Jan Roh) in 1541 been preserved. Perhaps the greatest of the Czech hymnbooks of the Bohemian Brethren was John Blahoslav's edition of 1561. Through numerous editions it was the most influential Czech Protestant hymnal up to the early part of the 17th century.

The history of hymnody in the German sector of the Unity of the Brethren begins with Michael Weisse's remarkable *Ein New Gesengbuchlen*, 1531, published in Bohemia for German-speaking congregations there. With its more than 150 items it was the largest German Protestant hymnbook of its time. It is rich in its adaptations from the vast hymnological treasures of the Middle Ages; for it includes many of the ancient classic hymns, Leisen in the folk idiom of the time, antiphons, and sequences with the prescribed music for unison singing. Weisse's *Gesengbuchlen* had a profound effect on Lutheran hymnbooks; for example, the second part of the *Babst Gesangbuch* of 1545 included 11 items from it. Before that, Luther had already appropriated Weisse's "Nun lasst uns den Leib begraben" in his *Begraebnislieder* of 1524. Through its many editions the *Gesengbuchlen* of Weisse exerted a direct influence on German Protestant hymnody far into the 17th century. The most voluminous German hymnbook of the Bohemian Brethren appeared in 1566. The ecumenical character of this work is revealed not only in a preface addressed to the "Reformed Evangelical Christian Churches of the German nation," but also in an appendix of over 100 hymns mostly of German Lutheran vintage. This hymnbook went through many editions up to the catastrophic annihilation of non-Catholics at the Battle of White Mountain in 1620, and the execution in Prague of Bohemian Protestant leaders on June 21, 1621. With the destruction of the Unity of the Brethren the vigorous growth of its Czech and German hymnody was halted.

There is no documentary evidence to indicate that the ancient Unity of the Brethren fostered any sacred music other than unison singing. The association of the polyphonic art with the Catholic ritual made figural music undesirable, whereas the singing of a single melody symbolized the concept of unity. The use of instruments, including organs, in the church service also lacks documentary confirmation. Even though unison singing was the norm, it would be erroneous to assume that all singing was in the simple strophic manner. The medieval sequences with their paired lines, the multisectional Kyrie tropes, and strophic verses with recurring refrains all strongly reflect the practice of responsorial and antiphonal alternation.

Hymnody in the "Renewed Unity of the Brethren," 1725—1784

With the emergence in the 1720s of the German Renewed Unity of the Brethren under Count Zinzendorf in Saxony, Germany, there appeared a proliferation of hymns down to the end of the 18th century. Zinzendorf published his *Sammlung geistlicher und lieblicher Lieder* in 1725, just three years after the founding of the Herrnhut community. But only about 30 of the almost 900 hymns are related to the ancient German Unity; otherwise the collection relies heavily on Freylinghausen's pietistic hymnbook of 1704. The first official hymnbook of the Renewed Unity appeared in Herrnhut in 1735. This book, with various editions and many additions, served the German Unity (also referred to as the German Moravian Church) for a half century.

After Zinzendorf's death in 1760, a thorough reevaluation of the thousands of German hymns from the previous decades took place. In 1778 a classic German Protestant hymnal, without music, was published with the title *Gesangbuch zum Gebrauch der evangelischen Bruedergemeinen*. The chief editor was Christian Gregor (1723—1801) who in 1784 brought out a companion *Choral-Buch*, which contained the melodies with figured bass for the organists. With these two monumental publications Christian Gregor placed the hymnody of the Moravian church on a firm basis.

Concerted Sacred Music in the Moravian Church, c. 1750—c. 1825

At the same time that the German Moravian Church reflected in its hymns the pietistic trend within the Lutheran Church, it also embraced the so-called orthodox attitude toward the generous use of concerted music for vocal-instrumental ensembles. The concept of a sacred cantata consisting of an intermingling of Biblical, chorale, and "new" devotional madrigalian texts had already been established by the Lutheran clergyman Erdmann Neumeister in the first decades of the 18th century. Such texts prescribed that the composers apply the techniques of secular opera and write recitatives, arias, and choruses. The German Moravian Church was well aware of this concept, for documentary traces of it are found in the archives of the Moravian Church, Bethlehem, Pa.

The sacred cantata, which had found a permanent home within the framework of the principal communion ritual (Hauptgottesdienst) in the Lutheran Church, apparently failed to find a similar place in the main liturgy of the Moravian Church. However, with Zinzendorf's encouragement, the Moravian Church developed a fairly elaborate calendar of ancillary observances that were marked by love feasts at which special concerted music was rendered. The music, either newly composed or adapted, was commonly referred to as the *psalm*; and the text, rendered by the liturgist, soloists, and chorus plus interspersed hymn stanzas for the congregation, was the *ode*.

The love feast, which emphasizes the bond of fellowship under the headship of Jesus Christ, is a non-Eucharistic experience that is nonconfessional in character. During the time that a repast, usually consisting of buns and coffee (or any other nonalcoholic beverage), is being consumed in the pews, the vocal soloists, choristers and instrumentalists render appropriate music. A love feast, which seldom supplants the main service of worship, may occur on a festival of the church year, on an anniversary in the history of the church, or on a Covenant Day for one of the *choirs*. In this context the term *choir* does not refer to a musical ensemble, but to a group of the local congregation's members organized according to a common age bracket, sex, or marital status. In a fully developed situation one will find choirs for little girls, little boys, older girls, older boys, single women, single men, married couples, widows, and widowers. Each choir is assigned an annual Covenant Day on which an especially prepared *psalm* (music) is sung to the *ode* (text) suited to the occasion.

It is impossible to state with documentary support when the custom of preparing special concerted music for love feasts began. Christian Gregor, who lived in Germany, states in his *Lebenslauf*, a type of autobiography, that in 1759 at the age of about 36 years he too began composing and compiling music for the love feast *psalms*. Some of Gregor's contemporaries and followers continued using the term in this sense. But toward the end of the 18th century the composers tended to write single works instead of composing and compiling multimovement *psalms*.

In addition to Gregor there are about 20 composers among the ranks of the clergymen and administrators of the Moravian Church whose names appear in the church's music archives of the second half of the 18th century and the 19th century. Of those who remained in Europe, Johann Christian Geisler (1729—1815) of Germany and Christian Ignatius Latrobe (1758—1836) of the English Moravian Church deserve particular mention. Others, such as Johann Friedrich Peter (1746—1813) and Johannes Herbst (1735—1812), were born and educated in Europe, but migrated to America and established respectable reputations as composers. John Antes (1740—1811) has the distinction of being the first of the Moravian Church's composers born in America. However, when he was 24 years old he went to Europe for his formal theological training. After serving as a missionary in Egypt, he went to England, where he lived out his life as a church administrator and composer.

The stylistic features of the music performed in the early American Moravian communities are those that are associated with the European, essentially German, expressive style *(empfindsamer Stil)* of the second half of the 18th century. The texture is predominantly homophonic. The straightforward diatonic melodies are supported by uncomplicated triadic progressions. One looks in vain for obscure chromaticism and remote modulations. The orchestra provides the overall framework of a composition: it has an introduction, it supports the soloist or chorus, it might have one or more interludes, and it finally rounds out the work with an instrumental close.

The period of greatest activity in the composition of sacred music in the Moravian Church lasted about 75 years. After about 1825 it is impossible to refer to a "school" of Moravian Church music composers. One does not find a second generation, though a few isolated names provide a thin thread of continuity.

The typical Moravian Church music composer was an amateur who directed his efforts toward the needs of a specifically local situation, and he judiciously operated within the known limitations of amateur performers. The thousands of handwritten copies of vocal and instrumental parts lie at the very heart of that rich treasury known as the Early American

256

Moravian Music Archives. Constant study and research under the jurisdiction of The Moravian Music Foundation provide deeper insights into a significant phase of church music that deserves greater recognition. EN

Readings: Blankenburg, W., "The Music of the Bohemian Brethren," *Protestant Church Music* (New York, 1974); David, H. T., *Musical Life in the Pennsylvania Settlements of the Unitas Fratrum* (Winston-Salem, N. C.); Fries, A. L., *Customs and Practices of the Moravian Church* (Winston-Salem, N. C., 1962); Nolte, E., "Sacred Music in the Early American Moravian Communities: An Introduction," *Church Music*, 71·2; McCorkle, D. M., *Moravian Music in Salem,* dissertation, Indiana University, 1958.

See also: church music history, Renaissance—the Reformation tradition; church music history, baroque; church music history, classic and romantic; church music history, American

motet

A term generally used to indicate an unaccompanied choral composition based on a sacred text for use in the liturgical service of Christian worship. The specific meaning of the word has varied considerably from its origin in the 13th century as a polyphonic extension of the Gregorian repertory.

The 13th-century use of the term derived from the addition of words (Fr. *mot*—"word") to the *duplum* or upper part of the *clausulae* of the Perotin period. The *duplum* with full text was called the *motetus*, from which the entire form took its name. The standard 13th-century motet, the most important of the early polyphonic forms, was normally set for three voices. The lowest part, or *tenor*, was taken from a melismatic Gregorian chant passage, except that it was presented in long notes, its rhythm following the strict patterns of one of the rhythmic modes. Each of the two upper parts, the duplum and triplum, followed its own distinct rhythmic pattern, usually a more quickly moving one, and often set to different Latin texts. Occasionally a French vernacular text was used simultaneously with a Latin text; toward the end of the 13th century secular texts sometimes intruded into one of the parts. In performance the tenor was either played by an instrument alone, or by an instrument doubling a vocal part. The 13th-century motet was essentially a polyphonic interpolation in the monophonic texture of the Gregorian chant to which it was related by means of its tenor. In general the text(s) of the motet sought to extend or

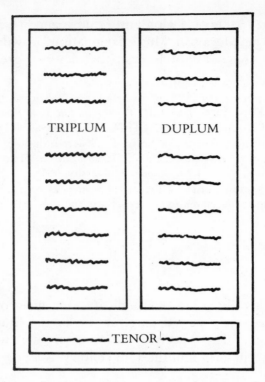

TRIPLUM   DUPLUM

TENOR

Typical arrangement of voice parts in a motet manuscript of the 13th century

reflect on the thought of the original text associated with the chant melody. The title of a motet is usually given as a composite of the *incipit* of each of the voices, for example: *O Maria, virgo davidica—O maria, maris stella—Veritatem*. In Sachs' words, the 13th-century motet could be "polyphonic, polyrhythmic, polytextual, and polyglot." Important collections of 13th-century motets are the Montpellier, Bamberg, and Las Huelgas codices.

The 14th century saw an increase in both the length and the rhythmic variety of the motet, the principle of isorhythm—the application of a reiterated rhythmic pattern or *talea* to the melodic intervals of a cantus firmus fragment or color—continuing to be applied to the tenor, and to a lesser degree to the upper parts. The use of isorhythm grew in complexity and finally dominated the 14th-century motet style; the technique continued to be used by some composers into the 15th century. An important source for these motets is the *Roman de Fauvel*, a literary work,

13th Century Motes

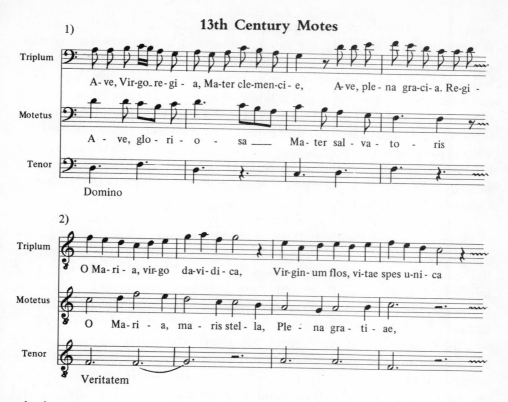

1)

Triplum: A-ve, Vir-go_re-gi - a, Ma-ter cle-men-ci - e, A-ve, ple - na gra-ci- a. Re-gi -

Motetus: A - ve, glo - ri - o - sa ___ Ma- ter sal - va - to - ris

Tenor: Domino

2)

Triplum: O Ma- ri - a, vir-go da-vi-di- ca, Vir-gin-um flos, vi-tae spes u-ni- ca

Motetus: O Ma- ri - a, ma - ris stel- la, Ple - na gra - ti - ae,

Tenor: Veritatem

which contained 33 isorhythmic motets among other musical compositions. Significant composers of isorhythmic motets are Guillaume de Machaut (c. 1300—77), Philippe de Vitry (1291—1361), John Dunstable (c. 1370—1453), and Guillaume Dufay (c. 1400—74).

Throughout the 15th century the motet was cultivated by the Flemish school of composers as a form for sacred music second only in importance to the mass. During this period the motet is characterized by: an increase in the number of vocal parts to from four to six; the gradual replacement of the longnote tenor cantus firmus by one characterized by an increasingly freer rhythmic treatment; the use of the same text in all parts; the practice of using only fragments of chant melodies; and the growing equality in importance of each of the vocal parts. Representative motet composers of the 15th century include Ockeghem (1430—95), Obrecht (c. 1430—1505), Adam von Fulda (c. 1440—1506), Heinrich Finck (1445—1527), Heinrich Isaac (1450—1517), and Pierre de la Rue (c. 1460—1518). Josquin Desprez (1450—1521) more or less established the practice of the imitative treatment of successive portions of the text, a practice generally regarded as typical motet style. By the latter 15th century Johannes Tinctoris (c. 1435—1511) could define the motet in his *Terminorum musicae diffinitorium* as follows: "A motet is a composition of moderate length, to which words of any kind are set, but more often those of a sacred nature." A mixture of sections of a motet in polyphonic style with other sections in familiar style is increasingly found in the 15th century. The use of familiar style together with the use of eight and more vocal parts ultimately laid the foundation for the Venetian polychoral motet style of the latter 16th century as practiced by such composers as Adrian Willaert (c. 1490—1562), Andrea Gabrieli (c. 1520—86), and Giovanni Gabrieli (c. 1554—1612).

In the early 16th century the motet spread rapidly throughout Europe: to Germany where the early Reformation composers developed especially the chorale-motet in which the new chorale melodies of the Lutheran Reformation appeared as *cantus firmi* (for example, the chorale-motets of Johann Walter), and free, non-cantus firmus motets set to various Scriptural texts (for example, the motets of Leonard Lechner and Johannes Eccard); to Italy, where the motet was exploited by Palestrina (c. 1526—94), the Gabrielis, Nanino, Anerio, Ingegneri, and others; to Spain, where the compositions of Victoria and Morales constitute a unique chapter in the history of the motet; to France, where Claude Goudimel and Regnart, among others, used the form; and to England, which saw the gradual transformation of the motet into the English anthem (see various works by Tallis, Byrd, Morley, Taverner, Gibbons, Bull, and others).

While the traditional 16th-century motet style was maintained down to the 18th century by such composers as A. Scarlatti, Durante, and Jomelli, this "older" concept of the motet gradually gave way in the early 17th century before the advent of the concertato style (which exploited the addition of instruments to the vocal texture) and the development of the solo motet (which used solo voices with instrumental accompaniment). Heinrich Schuetz' *Symphoniae sacrae* (1629, 1647, 1650) and Viadana's earlier *Concerti ecclesiastici* (1602, 1608) indicate the increasing difficulty in drawing a clear line of distinction between the motet and other forms of church music. In Italy the motet developed chiefly as a form for solo voices; in Germany it remained largely a choral form, reaching its highest peak of development in the six great motets of Johann Sebastian Bach. In the post-Bach period in Germany the motet declined in importance, becoming a vehicle for insignificant religious works by lesser composers.

In the 19th century the motet regained a small measure of its former prominence chiefly through the motet compositions of Felix Mendelssohn, Johannes Brahms, Franz Liszt, and Max Reger. The 20th century has seen a rebirth of the older chorale-motet and the freer non-cantus firmus motet forms in the works of such German composers as Johann Nepomuk David, Ernst Pepping, and Hugo Distler. Today the term motet is often applied to a wide variety of accompanied and unaccompanied choral compositions for use in the church. CS

Readings: "Motet," *Harvard Dictionary of Music,* 2d ed., Willi Apel, ed. (Cambridge, 1969); Hughes, Anselm, "The Motet and Allied Forms," *Early Medieval Music up to 1300,* vol. II of *New Oxford History of Music* (London, 1961); Wienandt, Elwyn A., "The Motet in the Middle Ages and Renaissance," *Choral Music of the Church* (New York, 1965).

See also: church music history, medieval; church music history, Renaissance—the Latin tradition; church music history, Renaissance—the Reformation tradition; concertato style; polychoral style; Roman school; *HCM, IV*

notation

The written symbolization of musical sounds. An ideal system of notation will use a concise, unambiguous, and visually clear set of graphic symbols that prescribe both pitch and duration, as well as the other properties of musical sound, and supply all necessary information for aural reproduction of the artistic phenomenon they are intended to represent.

Primitive societies do not use written musical symbolization, but pass on their music by rote process, which typically results in songs and dances undergoing more or less subtle changes from one generation to another. Western music has sought to develop a notation that will minimize the possibilities for such mutation and will preserve and communicate as accurately as possible the content of a musical composition.

The system of notation that developed in the West some 300 years ago is now understood and used by most societies that have been influenced by Western culture. Its genius lies in its capacity to designate both the intended pitch and duration (rhythmic) values of the sounds in any piece of music that employs conventional Western scales and tuning. The system is somewhat less than ideal in conveying other properties of musical sound such as intensity and color. These latter have come into greater artistic concern in much recent music, a development that has been reflected in newly invented symbolizations and some quite radical modifications of traditional notation.

The history of notation is one of slow transformation from generally complex and equivocal, although often ingenious, *polynomial* systems (in which one symbol is made to represent more than one possible relationship within its context, as in neumatic notation) to the basically absolute symbolizations of a *monomial* system (in which one symbol is made to mean one and only one thing, as in staff notation).

While the genealogy of modern notation stems from the Greeks and the early Christian era, various forms of notation were used by earlier and other, contemporaneous cultures such as the Chinese (as early as 1300 B.C.). In southern India the syllables of spoken language were used to notate musical formulas for Vedic chant, c. 700 B.C. These and many other cultures developed their own unique systems, usually polynomial in character. An ingeniously complicated polynomial system was that devised for the chant of the early Byzantine church.

Letter Notation

The Greeks of the pre-Christian era, as many cultures before them, devised systems of letter notation. The earliest of these, for instrumental music (c. 600—400 B.C.), was designed to show finger placement on string instruments (lyre, kithara), in a kind of tablature. This (polynomial) system employed a mixture of characters from the Greek and (probably) Phoenician alphabets, notating the letter shapes in various positions (upright, sidewise, reverse) to indicate special pitch inflections. Duration was sometimes shown by a metrical sign system based on multiples of a fixed unit. A later system, for vocal music (after 400 B.C.), used letters from the Ionic alphabet. This system developed into a complex set of symbolizations that ultimately comprised over 1,600 possible signs and interpretations. At least two other Greek alphabetical systems of notation were developed in the early Christian era.

Letter notation was used to some degree in systems throughout the era of early and medieval plainsong. These systems were essentially monomial, one pitch of the monophonic texture being represented by a single letter symbol. But they were also cumbersome and inefficient, and entirely incapable of showing rhythmic values. No single system came into wide or general use. One system was that devised by Boethius (d. 524), the most famous early medieval theorist, in which he adapted the Latino-Greek alphabet to the degrees of the scale. Others, such as Daseian notation of the 9th century, were little more than theoretical curiosities. Most of the famous names of medieval theory, Odo of Cluny, Notker, and Hucbald among them, contributed to the refinement and simplification of letter notation. Of special significance was the work of Guido d'Arezzo (d. 1050), whose reputation as an innovator is just short of mythical. His indisputable historical contribution was the introduction of the solmization names for the notes of the transposable hexachord. The much-cited hymn to St. John ("*ut* queant laxis *resonare* fibris," etc.), in which each line begins with the syllable for the successive degrees of the scale, was very possibly written by him as a specific mnemonic aid to teach the syllables he had devised. The system was an ingenious extension of the concept of letter notation. The flexibility and inherent pedagogical effectiveness of the sol-fa system are attested to by its nearly 1,000 years of utility. Another practical vestige of letter notation may be found in the pitch designation of Helmholtz (1821—94); A, a, a', a", etc., now generally used in musicological writings.

Letter and neumatic notation developed about the same time, but eventually the latter took precedence in the notation of plainsong. In some isolated instances, however, as late as the 11th century, the two systems were used together in the same manuscripts. Both contributed to the development of staff notation.

Neumatic Notation

The symbols of neumatic (probably from the Greek *neuma*, meaning a "nod" or "sign") notation were derived from the accent marks of Greek prosody. The two basic signs were the *acutus* (/), adopted to show rising pitch inflection, and the *gravis* (\ ), for falling inflection. These, together with other grammatical accent marks, could be combined to form composite neumes that represented slurs and extended melismas in a staffless notation that eventually developed into an efficient mnemonic guide for singers who were already acquainted with the basic chant melodies. The system was entirely sensitive to the nuances of medieval chant, although in their earlier forms the neumes were capable of indicating only vague and relative highs and lows of pitch, and, in spite of various attempts to provide a way of showing duration, their capacity to reflect accurate rhythmic values is a matter of legitimate historical dispute.

A slow and erratic developmental process, beginning c. 900, eventually brought this essentially polynomial system of notation to the threshold of a monomial system that used staff notation. Beginning around the 10th century the neumes were frequently placed above the Latin liturgical text in a manner that would visually outline the rise and fall of the melodic line. (See example of St. Gall ms.) It became evident that such diastematic or "heighted" neumes might be read even more accurately if a straight horizontal line were traced through the symbols to establish a fixed pitch. Once such a line was used as a point of pitch reference (at first f), inevitably another line (c') was added, then four and, somewhat later, five and six lines were used for greater graphic clarity. The fixed f or c', placed

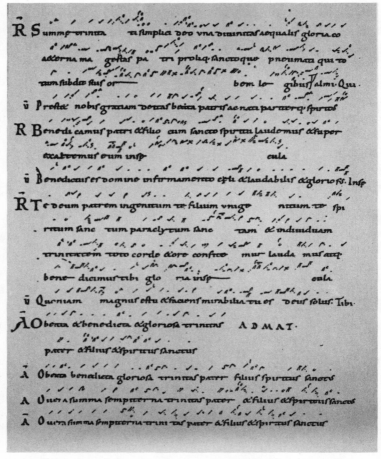

Examples of notation from a manuscript from St. Gall.

at the beginning of each system of horizontal lines (the *staff*), served as the first clef signs, from which our modern F- and C-clef symbols were derived.

Around 1200 another development, which came with the introduction of the quill pen in manuscript writing, radically changed the visual appearance of the neumes. This resulted in the rectangularly shaped notes and ligatures (polynomial symbols) usually associated with music of the Gothic period (See example of Perotin ms). This development, together with the introduction of the four-line staff, established plainsong notation in a form much the same as it still appears in Solesmes and Vatican editions

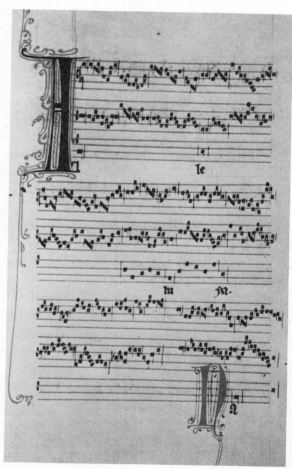

Example of notation from an *organum triplum* of Perotin.

of Gregorian chant. With the epochal introduction of staff notation the basic pitch of a note could be established by its position on the staff. There remained the equally challenging problem of inventing a complementary method of rhythmic notation.

Notation of Rhythm

As polyphonic textures became more complex the need for a clear system of showing rhythmic relationships became increasingly urgent. The rhythmic modes provided a tentative step toward this goal. They consisted of six patterned rhythmic schemes (all in the equivalent of modern compound binary meter, i.e.,$\frac{6}{8}$), employed in the texted parts of the 13th-century motets. At the same time the neume forms themselves began to assume independent rhythmic significance: by c. 1225 the long (*longa*, ▆) and the breve (*brevis*, ▪) and by 1250 the semibreve (◆). A proportional system of note division assumed "perfect" and "imperfect" forms: in the former the long was equal to three breves; in the latter the long was equal to two breves. Either two or three semibreves could be used in place of a breve. In time still shorter note values were introduced.

By 1260 Franco of Cologne advocated fixed rhythmic interpretation of the ligatures, independent of the rhythmic modes. This was the beginning of *mensural* notation, in which temporal relationships between notes were strictly prescribed, as distinct from the "unmeasured" rhythm of plainchant. The forms of early mensural notation were often inconsistent and highly varied (French and Italian practices differed significantly), and some proposed theories involved incredibly complex procedures. The division of the breve into as many as seven equal semibreves was introduced by Petrus de Cruce c. 1280. After 1300 the system of modal rhythm was abandoned as were strict ternary metrical restrictions. In his treatise, *Ars Nova*, c. 1320, Philippe de Vitry proclaimed the equality of duple and triple divisions of all note values and simplified the *mensuration signs* (incipient metrical signatures) that were used to distinguish between perfect and imperfect divisions.

About 1425 the squared-note forms began to appear in "white" notation, the black notes and ligatures of mensural notation now appearing as hollow outlines. Subsequently additional fixed values were devised in the form of black notes with stems and flags, on the "short" end of the scale of note values; these notes, except for their head shapes, now closely resembled the quarters, eighths, and sixteenths of modern notation. White

Example of notation from a motet of Josquin.

mensural notation accommodated most of the vast literature of liturgical and secular choral music of the Renaissance period (1450—1600). (See example of Josquin motet.)

The beginnings of music printing during the last half of the 15th century had the significant effect of slowing down the rate of notational change and served to standardize certain usages such as the five-line staff in instrumental music and the two-stave score in keyboard music (although some of the latter was also written in *tablature* notation). The late 16th century saw further standardization in the direction of modern notation. Triple mensuration was discarded, leaving only duple division between adjacent note values as the norm (e.g., $o = d + d$; $d = d + d$, etc.). With the introduction of rounded note heads and the general use of bar lines and metrical signatures, at least by 1650, notation became largely what it is today.

By the beginning of the 17th century a fully developed system of rhythmic notation, sometimes designated *orthochronic* (the term from the Greek *ortho*, "correct," and *chronos*, "time," is attributed to Jacques Chailley) had been largely realized. This (monomial) rhythmic system incorporated clear mathematical relationships within an orderly succession of duration values. The simple and essential characteristics of modern Western notation had been achieved: unequivocal pitch established by the position of the note on the staff, and unequivocal duration determined by the configuration of the note.

Notation in the 20th century

As in any living language, additions, changes, and refinements have continued to modify details of notation during the last 300 years. A number of standard practices were not fully developed until the 18th and even 19th and 20th centuries: the meaning of dotted notes; the use of key signatures and accidentals; consistent use of clef signs; and indications for tempo, dynamics, and articulation. Certain symbols, such as ornamentation signs in 17th and 18th century keyboard music, carried strong polynomial characteristics, with not only several different symbols used for the same ornament, but each symbol implying more than one possible interpretation. Such ambiguities fail to characterize an ideal system of notation. But the basic trend during this period has been toward precision and clarity.

Generally 20th century composers have tended to use the symbols of notation with a high degree of precision, simplifying where possible (e.g., notation of orchestral scores in C, enharmonic use of accidentals in nontonal contexts), elaborating and adding where necessary (e.g., signs for articulation and timbral effects, symbols for *Sprechstimme*). It is a tribute to the system that so revolutionary a work as Stravinsky's *The Rite of Spring* (1913) could have been, as it was, notated entirely within the conventions of standard practice.

Developments since 1950 have challenged the conventions of Western music notation as never before. Radical new concepts of rhythm and form, changed composer-performer relationship (the nature of the information a composer can be expected to provide in the score for the interpreter), the unprecedented esthetic significance assigned to the role of timbre (tone color) as an expressive element equal to rhythm, melody, and harmony, and the challenge to the very meaning of musical sound itself, have served to expose the limitations of standard notation, placing demands it was never meant to fulfill. These concepts require new methods of notation, of which there has been a highly variegated and abundant supply. For example, electronic music utilizes graphs and schematic drawings; *musique concrete* employs no notation at all, the sounds being placed directly on magnetic tape, ready to be heard; music of indeterminacy and chance use various forms: notation of approximate values of pitch and duration, spatial notation, drawings, graphs, and often simple verbal directives, which may be either vaguely suggestive or wholly explicit about the desired performance outcome.

The example from Penderecki's *Dies irae* (1967) illustrates a conservative and practical application of some of the new notational

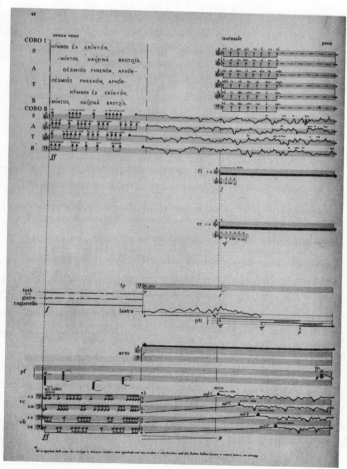

Example of notation from K. Penderecki's "Dies irae."

practices, especially as they pertain to the elements of duration and timbre: vocal effects such as whispering, speaking on indefinite pitches, vocalization at the highest possible pitch (↑), and nonsynchronized choral glissandos with vibrato, using improvised and rapidly fluctuating melodic patterns; and instrumental effects such as sound clusters in the flutes and horns (with definite pitches assigned to each instrument), a high cluster on the harmonium, pitch-percussive use of a cymbal on the piano strings, and rapidly vibrating and nonrhythmicized glissandi in the cellos and basses. As in many contemporary scores, the symbols of new notation have been combined with elements of standard notation. RH

Readings: Apel, Willi, *The Notation of Polyphonic Music, 900-1600*, 5th ed. (Cambridge, Mass., 1961); Karkoschka, Erhard, *Notation in New Music* (New York, 1972); Parrish, Carl, *The Notation of Medieval Music* (New York, 1957); Read, Gardner, *Music Notation: A Manual of Modern Practice*, 2d ed. (Boston, 1969); Stone, Kurt, "Problems and Methods of Notation," *Perspectives of New Music,* I (Spring 1963).

See also: tablature; performance practice

office hymn

Any one of the cycle of hymns designated for use in the canonical hours. Such a repertoire of hymns is associated mainly with the canonical hours as they existed in the medieval Latin church as well as in the practice of the Eastern churches.

Hymns for the canonical hours are used in matins (after the invitatory); in lauds (after the short lesson); in terce, sext, and none (preceding the Psalmody); and in compline (following the short lesson). The use of such a complete cycle of prayer is, of course, largely associated with monastic life; and it is in the monasteries and their books that the development of the office hymn must be traced. With very few exceptions, the Latin church excluded the use of hymns from the mass.

The primary sources of office hymns are the books produced for the monastic orders' observances of the hours of prayer called *hymnaries*. Hymnaries were not at all standardized but varied their contents according to local traditions, the requirements of the particular orders, and the sources available. For this reason, the repertoire of office hymns is comparatively large and varies considerably in the type of material appointed for various times of the day or for the various ecclesiastical seasons. In addition to hymnaries, office hymns may also be found in other books used in the observance of the hours. These include the breviary (used by the clergy), the so-called book of the hours (used primarily by laity), and Psalters. Psalters and hymn collections were in fact, often included in the same book.

The history of the office hymn must be traced back to the early church and its initial emphasis on psalm singing to the near exclusion of hymns. The early Western church apparently discouraged the use of hymns, since they were non-Biblical, privately composed texts. Hymns were first introduced extensively to the Church to counter the damaging influence of those composed and sung by a heretical Christian sect, the Gnostics. Orthodox hymns were thus primarily a product of the period beginning with the 4th century—a period that marks the beginning of monastic life. The monastic rule of St. Benedict (c. 480—c. 543) required the use of hymns in its cycle of prayer. Other monastic orders followed suit. Such required use of these hymns ensured their continued popularity and importance in Christian worship.

Separate hymn collections were developed for the various worship traditions in the Church. One of the most widely influential in Western Europe was an Anglo-Irish hymnary dating from the 7th century. Some early collections, such as those for the Mozarabic and Ambrosian rites, are still in use. These books formed the basis for the hymn collections used today in the Roman tradition. Most hymns from this early period were extremely simple in form, consisting of strophes of four lines each containing four iambic feet (the so-called "Ambrosian" form). The invention of this form is traditionally ascribed to Bishop Ambrose (340—397) of Milan, the "father" of hymnody in the Western Latin Church. In the Carolingian cultural florescence of the 9th and 10th centuries, hymn writers experimented once again with the poetic meters from the ancient classical world, thus expanding the types of hymn meters available to the church.

The first actual collection of hymns with music, the Moissac Hymnary, is a product of the 12th century. Since that time hymns have proliferated considerably. Except for matins and vespers, however, the idea of an "office" hymn became terminologically defunct in Protestantism—a fact which led to the loss of much of the ancient repertoire. In the 19th century, under the aegis of the liturgical and hymnological revival, Edward Caswall (1814—78) and John Mason Neale (1818—66) translated the Sarum and

Roman Catholic hymnals respectively. Thus the excellent, joyful hymns for the times of the day (e.g., Ambrose's "O Splendor of God's Glory Bright") or for the seasons of the church year (e.g., Rabanus Maurus's "Come, Holy Ghost, Creator Blest") have been preserved and revitalized for our time.

Modern sources for English translations of many of the office hymn are *The Hymnal 1940* (Episcopal) and Herbert Lindemann's *The Daily Office* (Concordia, 1965), which unfortunately makes no reference to any music for the excellent hymns assigned to all the times of the church year. The Latin texts and melodies of the office hymns are contained in *Liber Usualis*. VG

Readings: Britt, M., ed., *Hymns of the Breviary and Missal* (New York, 1936); Connelly, J., *Hymns of the Roman Liturgy* (Westminster, 1957); Lindeman, H., *The Daily Office* (St. Louis, 1965); Messenger, R., Various essays on the early monastic cycles of hymns, *Historical Companion to Hymns Ancient and Modern*, M. Frost, ed. (London, 1962); Pfatteicher, C. and D. Fitts, ed. *Office Hymns of the Church* (Boston, 1951); *The Hymnal 1940 Companion* (New York, 1951).

See also: canonical hours; hymnody, Latin; HCM, I, V

oratoria

Along with opera and cantata the oratorio arose during the early baroque period. Whereas the cantata flourished primarily during the baroque period, the oratorio and the opera enjoyed a long development well into the 20th century. Borrowing its essential elements from opera, the oratorio typically has a religious subject and includes recitatives, chorus, soloists, and orchestra, but omits costumes, stage sets, and dramatic action.

Baroque Oratorio

Early types of oratorio include the *rappresentazione* and the *historia*. The earliest example of the former is *Rappresentazione de anima e di corpo* by Emilio de' Cavalieri (c. 1550—1602). Written for the Congregation of the Oratory in Rome, the work was first performed in 1600. Unlike later oratorio, however, Cavalieri's work included costumes, dramatic action, and dance.

The *historia* is an extended work portraying a sacred story. The first great master of the *historia* in Italy was Giacomo Carissimi (c. 1605—74).

Old Testament stories (*Historia di Abraham et Isaac, Historia di Ezechia, Daniele, Jephte, Judicium Salomonis, Jonas*) served as libretti for Carissimi. Notable successors to Carissimi include Steffano Landi (c. 1590—c. 1655), Michel Angelo Rossi (c. 1600—c. 1660), Giovanni Legrenzi (1625—90), Alessandro Scarlatti (1660—1725), and Antonio Vivaldi (c. 1675—1741).

Carissimi's student, Marc-Antoine Charpentier (1634—1704), established the *historia* in France. Again Biblical stories (*Historia Esther, Filius prodigus, Judicium Salomonis, La Reniement de St. Pierre*) provided the libretti of Charpentier's works.

One of the early German masters of oratorio, Heinrich Schuetz (1585—1672), wrote two works entitled *historia*, one dealing with the Resurrection (1623) and one dealing with the Nativity (1664). Later German oratorio composers include Johann Sebastian Bach (1685—1750) and Johann Adolph Hasse (1699—1783). The oratorios of Bach, however, are large-scale cantatas rather than oratorios. The "Christmas Oratorio" consists of six cantatas to be performed during six celebrations of the 12 days of Christmas.

The master of the baroque oratoria was George Frideric Handel (1685—1759). Handel's oratorios were designed for performance in the theatre, especially during Lent, when operatic productions were forbidden. Whereas Handel's operas are in Italian, his oratorios are in English, and a majority of them are dramas based upon Old Testament stories (*Deborah; Esther; Israel in Egypt; Jephta; Joshua; Judas Maccabaeus; Samson; Saul; Solomon*). Others deal with mythological figures (*Hercules; Semele*); and some treat allegorical subjects (*Triumph of Time and Truth*). *Messiah* is unique among his oratorios in that its text embraces both Old and New Testaments, and is more meditative than narrative.

Classic Oratorio

The greatest master of the classic oratorio was Franz Joseph Haydn (1732—1809). Haydn's first oratorio, *Il Ritorno di Tobia*, was composed about 1774. It was not until after his extended visits to England, however, that Haydn composed oratorios on Handelian models. *Die Schoepfung* was composed in 1798 and is Haydn's most famous oratorio. Shortly after *Die Schoepfung* Haydn turned his attention to *Die Jahreszeiten*. Although other oratorios from the classic period might be cited, one other major work from the period should be noted—*Christus am Oelberg* by Ludwin van Beethoven (1770—1827).

Romantic Oratorio

The finest 19th-century oratorios were composed by Felix Mendelssohn (1809—47). His first oratorio, *St. Paul*, was completed in 1836 and was widely acclaimed. A second work, *Elijah*, was given its first performance in 1846 and has remained in the oratorio repertoire up to the present. Planned for the 800th anniversary of the Wartburg, *Die Legende von der heiligen Elisabeth* was completed in 1862 by the Hungarian composer, Franz Liszt (1811—86); a second oratorio by Liszt, *Christus*, was composed in 1873. Other notable composers of oratorio in the late 19th century include Hector Berlioz (1803—69) (*L'Enfance du Christ*), César Franck (1822—90) (*Les Beatitudes*), Sir Hubert Parry (1848—1918) (*Job, Judith*), Sir Edward Elgar (1857—1934) (*The Dream of Gerontius; The Apostles; The Kingdom*), and Horatio Parker (1863—1919) (*Hora novissima*).

20th-century Oratorio

Whereas the oratorio form largely retained traditional procedures through the 19th century, 20th-century oratorio is quite different in structure and function. Although it is not possible to discuss here the vagaries of 20th-century oratorio, the following are representative of the broad spectrum of oratorio-like works: *Gurrelieder* by Arnold Schoenberg (1874—1951), *Golgotha* by Frank Martin (b. 1890), *Le Roi David* and *Jeanne d'Arc au bucher* by Arthur Honegger (1892—1955), *Ezzolied* by Johann Nepomuk David (b. 1895), *Das Gesicht Jesajas* by Willy Burkhardt (1900—55), *Belshazzar's Feast* by William Walton (b. 1902), *A Child of our Time* by Michael Tippett (b. 1905), and *Dies irae* by Krzysztof Penderecki (b. 1933). HM

Readings: Jacob, Arthur (ed.), *Choral Music,* Baltimore, 1963; Scholes, Percy, "Oratorio." *The Oxford Companion to Music.* 10th ed. London, 1970; Ulrich, Homer, *A Survey of Choral Music.* New York, 1973; Wienandt, Elwyn A., *Choral Music of the Church.* New York, 1965.

See also: cantata; church music history, baroque; church music history, classic and romantic; church music history, 20th century; *HCM*, IV

organ, history

Antiquity—Early Middle Ages
(c. 400 B.C.—1100 A.D.)

The origin of the organ as seen from the Western concept of the instrument (wind supply, pipes, distributor, harness) predates the 4th century before Christ and occurred in the Near East from where it migrated through Arabian lands, Palestine, Syria, Byzantium, Greece, and Rome. The early development of the instrument exhibited three basic types: (1) the simple *pneumatic* organ, in which the source and regulation of wind was controlled by bellows or pistons; (2) the more complicated *hydraulic* organ, in which the source of wind was controlled by the flow of water; and (3) the *hydraulis,* in which the source and regulation of wind was also controlled by the flow of water. These instruments seem to have been very loud and used outdoors for civil and military processions, convocations, and similar secular purposes. Historians have sought an "inventor" but all claims are conjecture: Muristus, Aristotle, Ktesibios (c. 240 B.C.) and others, of which some contributed only basic concepts of pneumatics (Philo) and hydrostatics (Archimedes). Ancient organs are described in Hebrew, Syriac, and Arabian sources, and among such writers of Greece, Rome, and Byzantium as Philon (150 B.C.), Cicero (43 B.C.), Vitruvius (70 A.D.), Heron (150 A.D.), and Tertullian (222 A.D.). The forms of these instruments have been transmitted through ceramic and metallic reproductions such as the Carthage statuette and the Nero medallion. The descriptions of Heron (*Mechanics)* and Vitruvius (*De Architectura)* recognize bellows, pistons, regulators, conductors, valves, windchests, plinths (sliding keys), and pipes, all arranged to provide an operational instrument. A single example of such a system has survived in a Roman organ of antiquity (c. 230 A.D.) found in an archaeological dig at Aquincum in Budapest, Hungary, (1931). Shortly after the fall of Rome the organ disappears from recorded history for several centuries. In the East comprehensive translations of pertinent Greek technical writings into Arabic during the 9th century revivified the instrument as a significant part of the Muslim culture. In the West the presentation of an organ to Pepin, King of the Franks, by the Byzantine Emperor Constantine Copronymus in 757 A.D. launched the organ as an increasingly integral part of the Christian culture.

A modern restoration of a Roman organ from antiquity (c. 230 A. D.). An archeological find (1931) from Aquincum, in the western quarter of Budapest, Hungary.

Gothic Period (c. 1100—1400)

During the Gothic period the organ developed in two directions: comprehensive instruments such as those at Winchester and Halberstadt for use within the church; and small instruments such as portatives and positives for use in the home and certain social functions. The voices of the large organs were for the most part not selectively controllable (i.e., only the notes could be played selectively, not the stops); these operated consistently in gang as a bound corpus. Vestiges of this principle persisted well into the Renaissance (Netherlands.) Historical reports such as those of Wolstan and Praetorius describe them as producing violent, brutal, and piercing tonal effects. The small instruments possessed few ranks of delicately-voiced pipes. The portative (portable organ) contained either labial ranks or only reed stops (then, regal); the positives (stationary organs) contained several stops, selectively controllable. Both species found eventual resting places in the large church organ (the portative as the Brustwerk; the positive as the Rueckpositiv).

Left: Gothic organ (1380) in the St. Valeria church of Sitten, Switzerland (wooden bass pipes added in 1718). Metal bass pipes flank the central field.

Right: Gothic organ (1380) in the Old Cathedral (Capilla de Anaya) of Salamanca, Spain. Bass pipes form the center and the outer limits of the case; protective doors cover the facade.

Renaissance Period (c. 1400—1600)

By the beginning of the Renaissance (c. 1400—1450) the brutal character of the organ had greatly mellowed and different families or species of stops besides the simple principals began to emerge. Keys were reduced in size and increased in number, stop actions to facilitate selective registration appeared, and the gradual absorption of the small instruments (positives, regals) into the large organs marked the beginning of distinguishable tonal corpora and the eventual development of their various interrelationships.

During the Renaissance the organ made great strides toward becoming a comprehensive musical instrument of artistic stature. The various regions of western Europe developed organs that reveal distinguishing features, some of which were disseminated and assimilated. Organ building in Italy was dominated for nearly two centuries by the Antegnati family, whose instruments reveal a restrained and refined vocal character suited to their liturgical function in the church. The tonal corpora were restricted to principals deployed over the full tonal spectrum, plus some foundational flutes. The dispositions were modest (one manual corpus, attached pedal) but the selective control and registration of *all* ranks became an enduring characteristic.

Renaissance Netherlands took the lead in creating organs of note. Situated at a crossroad of commerce, their activity took on international character: they not only imported ideas from many countries but reexported them as well. The control entities were two manual corpora *(Hoofdwerk, Rugwerk),* the former of principals only in a bound disposition, the latter, of flutes and reeds selectively controllable. Enlargement resulted in the development of the *Bovenwerk (i.e., Oberwerk)* to contain the nonprincipal elements of the main organ, playable either from the *Hoofdwerk* keyboard or from a manual of its own. The pedal, attached to the *Hoofdwerk* keyboard, contained none or only a few supplementary stops. Several prominent schools developed in the Netherlands: Brabant (the Niehoffs), Utrecht (the de Swarts), Groningen (Agricola), and Gelderland-Overisjell (the Slegels). The Renaissance organ is described in Arnolt Schlick, *Spiegel der Orgelmacher und Organisten* (1511). Arthur Hill, *The Organ Cases and Organs of the Middle Ages and Renaissance* (1891) presents line drawings and descriptions of the organs and their cases from these periods.

French Renaissance organbuilders of the 15th and 16th centuries (Hestre, Henoque, Dabenest, Josseline, de Oliviers) developed these characteristics: a comprehensive main corpus *(Grand Orgue)* with full principal choir culminating in a rich crown structure, a substantial choir of gedackts and flutes revealing quint mutations and the Cornet, plus a group of reeds; a second, more modest corpus *(Positif;* one-half the size of the *Grand Orgue)* with a discreet selection of principals, gedackts, flutes, and reeds, plus occasional quint mutations; no pedal corpus, but occasional pedal stops chiefly at 8′ pitch and the customary attachment of the pedalboard to the *Grand Orgue* keyboard, with selected extensions downward to contra-F; the timid emergence of the *Echo* (a separate manual and chest fully or partly enclosed) having pipes only in the upper half of the compass; no *Oberwerk*, its contents and functions absorbed in the *Grand Orgue*; in general, selectively controllable voices rather than bound dispositions except for the Cornet. Some Renaissance cases are still in existence in whole or in part at LeMans (1531), Metz (1536), Amiens (1550), St. Bertrand de Cominges (1536), La-Ferté-Bernard (1501), and St. Maclou in Rouen (1542).

Baroque Period (c. 1600—1750)

Having inherited a distribution mechanism in the chambered spring and slider chests with key and stop actions, a harness adequate to route the key action through tracers, squares, backfalls, and rollers to various chest locations, a resource in labial and lingual pipes together with insights into their tonal properties, their interrelationships, and their deployment over a large area of the acoustic spectrum, and the requisite methods to produce and distribute the wind, the baroque builders stood on the threshold of an unprecedented development of the organ in sound and sight as an instrument of high artistic merit and significant social and ecclesiastical importance. In France the organ exhibited a four or five manual-and-pedal plan engaging most or all of the following: a *Positif* (principal plenum of moderate and narrow scales, gedackts and flutes of moderate and wide scales, mutations of the quint and tierce, a festive reed group) a *Grand Orgue* (more profuse tonal structure containing the same ingredients deployed over a wider range of the spectrum, plus the inevitable bound Cornet; a *Bombarde* (a festive reed group with a grand cornet); a *Recit* and an *Echo* (both solo claviers controlling a sparse selection of cornets and reeds); and the *Pedale*, ranging from the typical 8' Renaissance pedal of a few stops to more substantial layouts containing mostly gedackts and flutes at 16', 8', and 4', and a festive set of reeds.

French cases soon displayed a consistent shape: in the main organ, five round bass towers of pipes connected by four flat fields, all springing from a common impost, with a reflection in miniature of the same in the *Positif* (three round towers, two flats). French baroque builders of this period include Lefebure, Thierry, Clicquot, Isnard, and Andreas Silbermann. The foundational work by Dom Bedos de Celles *L'Art du Facteur d'Orgues* (1776—78) is a comprehensive exposition of the French baroque organ.

Stellwagen (1636/37) and others (c. 1500): small organ in the north transept of St. Jakobi, Luebeck, Germany. Renaissance case (two-dimensional facade, horizontal mouth lines) for main organ; incipient baroque case (three-dimensional facade, sloped mouth lines) for Rueckpositiv.

In northern Europe the baroque organ found its fruition in the "Golden Age of Organbuilding." The establishment of direct worship by the congregation through the singing of hymns and the liturgy during the Reformation soon provided a fertile soil for the cultivation of the organ as a necessary and effective vehicle. Among the north European baroque builders are such masters as Compenius, the Scherers, Bockelmann, Fritzche, Stellwagen, Arp Schnitger, Christian Mueller, and Gottfried Silbermann.

The organ of Arp Schnitger, as the archtype of the high baroque, has three, four, or five independent corpora (*Pedal, Hauptwerk, Oberwerk, Rueckpositiv, Brustwerk),* each an organ in itself, on which the voices are fairly equally distributed. The principal foundations (16′, 8′, 4′, 2′) are variously leveled and their bases differentiated in pitch on the several corpora. The crowns (Mixtur, Scharf, Zimbel) are clearly differentiated

Christian Mueller organ (1735/38) in St. Bavo church, Haarlem, Holland. High baroque case: three-dimensional facade, round towers, pointed towers, storied flats, and miniature reflection of the main case in the Rueckpositiv.

and evenly dispersed. Gedackt and flute foundations (16′, 8′, 4′, 2′) appear in all corpora and generally exceed the principals in number, while flute mutations are restricted to the quint and tierce, the former free (as 5⅓′, 2⅔′, 1⅓′) or bound (as Rausdequinte 2⅔′ and 2′), the latter bound only (as Sesquialtera 2⅔′ and 1³/₅′, Terzian 1⅓′ and 1³/₅′). The reeds appear in various groupings from 32′ to 2′ in the pedal and from 16′ to 4′ in the manuals, while all of the families (conical, cylindrical, fractional) are usually present and in mixed assortment. Cases (many still intact) follow the basic scheme of the "Hamburg Prospekt": a memberment to reflect the internal layout of the corpora (Hauptwerk in center, Oberwerk above,

Brustwerk below, divided Pedal on both sides; Rueckpositiv in front of the key desk and mounted on the gallery rail). The facade exhibits round pipe towers (center, outer extremes), pointed towers (in between) and flat fields (nine compartments in the main organ, five in the Rueckpositiv).

19th Century (c. 1775—1900)

Organ building in the 19th century was greatly affected by the invention and application of machine tools, and the predication of the art upon rather rigid mathematical foundations. Both of these conditions led to the eventual creation of very large instruments and the manufacture of the same in large quantities. Symptoms of these developments emerge in: the enlargement and improvement of the bellows to deliver a secure and steady wind under all conditions; an approach to pipe construction through mathematical scaling of all factors (thickness of metal, diameter, mouth-width, cut-up, etc.); precise craftsmanship extended to joinery and cabinetry within and without; refined devices for tuning and retaining the pitch of the pipes; aids to intonation (nicking, beards, ears, etc.) to guarantee flawless and uniform speech; and mechanical, pneumatic contrivances to aid in the manipulation of the instrument (pneumatic levers, crescendo movements, combination action, collectives, etc.) Foundational works on the organ that appeared in this century and had a very influential effect on the shop practice of the time as well as deep into the 20th century include Rimbault and Hopkins, *The Organ, its History and Construction* (1855), and J. G. Toepfer, *Lehrbuch der Orgelbaukunst* (1855).

Having played a subordinate role in the historical development of the organ in earlier periods, England (chiefly through Hill and Willis) took on leadership in the development of the romantic organ of the 19th century along with France (Cavaillé-Coll) and Germany (Walcker, Ladegast, Sauer, Schulze). Each country pursued distinctive paths in achieving the comprehensive instruments of the time. Building on the very modest foundations laid after the Restoration (1660) by Father Smith, Renatus Harris, John Snetzler, and Samuel Green, the organs of William Hill and Henry Willis (1821—1901) in mid-century (c. 1830—70) represented a vast expansion in the size and power of the instrument and exhibit characteristics which stamp them as of a different and new conception. The organ (as typified by Hill's St. George's Chapel, and Willis' St. George's Hall—both of Liverpool) has assumed a comprehensive girth of from 50—100 stops, the normal complement comprising from 40—80, deployed over four or five divisions (Great, Swell, Choir, Pedal, and Solo), the principalbases of which are differentiated by material, scale, and intonation rather than by pitch level. The aequal level often carries several "Open Diapasons," while crown structures—of generally meager disposed in choirs and contain orchestral imitators (Oboe, Clarinet, Trombone, Bassethorn, Ophicleide, Horn) as well as high pressure voices (Tube, Magna, Tuba Mirabilis) besides the more usual Contrafagotto, Trumpet, and Clarion. Aliquots appear only at the quint and tierce levels and the mixed voice concept is represented only by the Sesquialtera and Cornet. There is a generous supply of strings (Vioncelle, Gamba, Salicional) and a variety of echo voices (Dulciana, Vox Angelica, Suabe Flute) mostly at aequal pitch. The foundation pitches (8′, 4′, 2′) exhibit multiple stops at each level with the 8′ level favored. The concept of the continental Rueckpositiv or the English "chair" organ has disappeared along with that of contrasting and complementary tonal corpora. The Swell has become a large expressive division reiterating the ingredients of the Great on a lesser dynamic level but with greater emphasis on the reed chorus. The Choir is no more nor less than an accompanimental division having mostly background voices, while the Pedal predominates in grave bass voices (32′, 16′, 8′). The Solo organ presents an array of orchestral imitators (solo reeds) and the scorching high-pressure reeds indigenous to the period.

In France the romantic organ found its fullest expression in the work of Aristide Cavaillé-Coll (1811—99). His organs for Paris (St. Denis, St. Sulpice, Notre Dame, and St. Clothilde) clearly characterize his ideals: comprehensive symphonic organ embodying the color pallette of the orchestra in large measure; five or six divisions (Grand Orgue, Positif, Récit-expressif, Bombarde, Pedales, Grand Choeur); tonal ingredients that include the enlargement of the spectrum in the direction of gravity with the attendant grave mutations, extensive choruses of conical reeds, strings, célestes, echo voices, and overblown flutes; sonorous and bass-emphasizing pedals; compound voices of the Fourniture, Cymbale, Plein Jeu, and the Cornet; and physical layouts that use prodigious amounts of space for the chests, pipes, bellows, pneumatic levers, coupler actions, ventils, and the like. Literature for these instruments was created by the organists of the time: César Franck (1822—90), Camille St. Saens (1835—1921), Alexander Guilmant (1837—1911) and Charles Marie Widor (1845—1937) in the form of sonatas, symphonies, chorales, improvisations, and other examples of symphonic forms and styles.

20th Century

The organ of the 20th century has undergone a substantial metamorphose through the *Orgelbewegung*, which, initiated by Schweitzer (in 1906) and taken up earnestly in the North European countries at the Freiburg *Orgeltagung* (1926), found further development in America and England after World War II. In the earlier decades of the century the all-encompassing concerns dealt with the application of electrical energy to the harness and distribution system of the instrument: development and

Romantic organ by Henry Willis and Sons (1924) in Liverpool Cathedral, England. Divided organ placed into prepared pocket chambers near the crossing of the chancel and transepts.

refinement of electropneumatic action; emergence of the universal pitman chest; the adoption of increasingly higher wind pressures in order to secure effective response in the machinery; the consistent detachment of the console and its frequently vagrant location; the physical dismemberment of the instrument and its placement into prepared chambers lined with plaster or cement and often provided with constricted openings for tonal egress; and the development and application of a host of console aids for the player (super- and suboctave couplers, combination action, reversibles, crescendo and expression movements, etc.).

Such developments had a deteriorating effect on the tonal integrity of the instrument. Unification and duplexing of voices blurred the character of the ensembles and weakened the instrument in its vitals; augmentation of the pedal through borrowed stops and extensions reduced it to an impoverished existence; super couplers replaced mixtures and compound voices; the wind required high cut-ups in the mouth of the pipes and this reduced the harmonic content and made the pipes more fundamental (in effect, more colorless); mutations—largely borrowed from unison voices—failed to function and fell into disuse; the art of disposition atrophied to a point where most of the instruments became collections of favorite stops; voices were meekly differentiated by dynamic strength rather than by tone color. The instrument had done an about-face from the multiplicity of corpora to one corpus split into several divisions such as Great, Swell, Pedal, Choir, and Solo (ranging from 3 to 5 divisions in the order shown). Besides being excessively chambered the divisions suffered further annihilation through the overuse of swell boxes and expression louvers. In sum, the organ had become a large and unmusical machine, extremely insensitive to the touch and character of the organist's playing. Organs of this vintage were produced by such builders as Harrison and Harrison, Norman and Beard, Walker, Henry Willis and Sons of England; Walcker, Sauer, and Steinmeyer of Germany; E. M. Skinner, Moeller, Austin, Kilgen, Kimball, and Casavant of North America.

Into this state of affairs came the protestations of Schweitzer asking for a return to the more musical instruments of the great historical traditions, scaling practises based on the collective experience of generations, a return to the tone-channel slider chest, a mechanical harness for the key action, lower wind pressure to enrich the speech of the pipes, acoustically auspicious placement for unhindered propagation of the sound, and revivification of the aural advantages of the Rueckpositiv. The Freiburg

Beckerath organ (1965) in the St. Andreas church, Hildesheim, Germany. Modern instrument employing the corpus concept reflected in the memberment and facade of the case.

Orgeltagung took up the reform in earnest (1926) and in a considerably more penetrating fashion under the leadership of Mahrenholz and H. H. Jahnn, with Arp Schnitger and the north German and Dutch schools of his time as the emerging models for this *Orgelbewegung*. Besides the concerns of Schweitzer the movement promulgated also tonal design to fit the literature, clear and descriptive stop nomenclature, effective reincarnation of the corpus concept of the north German school, casing and facading

Modern American organ by Phelps (1974) in Hexham Abbey, Northumberland, England. Corpus concept is clearly enunciated by the memberment of the case and Principal postures in the facade.

which reflect the internal organization of the corpora, and the acoustically live conditions in the environs of the instrument. From the Freiburg *Tagung* until the present these principles have received more and wider acceptance and application. The Europeans who have become champions of the movement are Marcussen, Andersen, and Frobenius of Denmark; Flentrop of Holland; Beckerath, Schuke, and Ott of Germany; Metzler and Kuhn of Switzerland; Hammarberg of Sweden; Rieger of Austria; Harrison,

Walker, Hill, and Norman & Beard of England. In America the reform in various aspects has been cultivated by Holtkamp, Otto Hofmann, G. Donald Harrison, Schlicker, Fisk, Casavant, Brombaugh, and Phelps. PB

Readings: Andersen, P., *Organ Building and Design* (New York, 1969); Clutton, C. and A. Niland, *The British Organ* (London, 1963); Farmer, H. G., *The Organ of the Ancients* (London, 1931); Kraus, E., *Orgeln und Orgelmusik* (Regensburg, 1972); Ochse, O., *The History of the Organ in the United States* (Bloomington, 1975); Peeters, F. and M. Vente, *The Organ and its Music in the Netherlands 1500—1800* (New York, 1971); Williams, P., *The European Organ 1450—1850* (London, 1966).

See also: chorale; organ, literature; organ, use in the mass and offices; polychoral style; tablature; thoroughbass; voluntary

organ, use in the mass and offices

The principal role assigned to the organ in the mass and the offices until well into the 17th century was as participant in the practice of alternation (*alternatim praxis*), organ versets supplying the polyphonic music for alternate verses when the choral forces were limited to unison Gregorian chant. The all-important role that the organ fills today, the leading and accompanying of congregational singing of hymns, did not develop until the first half of the 17th century, or about 100 years after congregational singing became a significant feature in Lutheran worship.

The Organ in the Mass

The most common portions of the mass in which the organ participated were the five sections of the ordinary (Kyrie, Gloria in excelsis, Credo, Sanctus, Agnus Dei). Manuscript sources generally included versets for only one or two of the chants rather than the whole cycle. Even printed sources rarely included settings for all five parts. Organ mass movements were found in manuscripts as early as 1400 and were quite extensive in the Buxheim Organ Book and in the 16th-century tablatures of Hans Buchner and Johannes of Lublin. Other examples in that century are from the publications of Pierre Attaingnant (d. 1552) in France and from the works of the Cavazzonis, Marco Antonio (c. 1490—c. 1570) and Girolamo (c. 1520—c. 1560), and other Venetian composers. The early Lutheran church orders give ample evidence that the evangelical church includes this use of the organ among the musical practices taken from the pre-Reformation church and also applied it to the congregational hymn, but musical examples from Lutheran composers are restricted to later collections (Celle tablature, 1601; Petri tablature, 1611; Scheidt *Tabulatura nova,* 1624).

All movements of earlier organ masses were clearly based on the Gregorian chants, but several variants developed. In the three organ masses of Frescobaldi's *Fiori musicali* (1635) only the Kyrie chants are intended for alternation; the other movements are toccatas, ricercars, and canzonas whose titles indicate that they were to be played before, during, or after certain parts of the rite. The French organ mass of the 17th century (François Couperin [1668—1733], Nicolas de Grigny [1671—1703], and others), contained movements still intended for alternation, but with titles that indicated registration according to the French traditions. However, the corresponding Gregorian chant was not always clearly evident in each movement.

Not as well known as organ versets for the ordinary of the mass are those for certain of the propers. The Lutheran church orders and the tablatures of Hans Buchner (1483—1538) and Johannes of Lublin clearly indicate that the introit was often divided between the organ and choir (e.g., antiphon—organ; Psalm verse—choir; Gloria patri—organ; repeat of antiphon—choir). The various chants between the lessons (gradual/Alleluia) could have a similar performance. English composers particularly turned to the offertory for Marian feasts, *Felix namque,* so often that they gave it an independent existence. The French organ masses also included a piece of significant proportions entitled offertory, but this was not related to the melody of the proper.

Although it includes organ settings of the chorales of the *Missa brevis,* Bach's *Clavieruebung,* Part III, in no way merits the title organ mass sometimes given it in promotional materials for recitals, recordings, or publications. Influenced by the vocal chorale masses in 20th-century German church music, some composers have appropriately used the title organ mass for suites of organ chorales based on the hymn versions of the ordinary. A more significant 20th-century form of the organ mass was created by Charles Tournemire (1870—1939) in his *L'Orgue mystique.* Influenced by the Solesmes Gregorian revival and the requirement for French organists to improvise at certain points in the service, Tournemire provided a suite of five movements for each of 51 different Sundays: prelude for the introit, offertory, elevation, communion, and a terminal piece. Other French composers, such as Vierne, Langlais, and Messiaen, have written similar masses.

The Organ in the Offices

While there were organ versets in the 15th- and 16th-century sources for participation by the organ in antiphons (especially the Marian) and responsories, the chief role of the organ in the offices was related to the singing of the psalms, the canticles, and the office hymns.

A limited number of settings for the melody of the *Te Deum* are extant; those most accessible through excerpts in general anthologies are, for the most part, versets from the publications of Attaingnant. The German *Te Deum, Herr Gott dich loben wir*, was also frequently treated as an organ chorale.

The largest number of organ versets in the offices are designated for the *Magnificat*, because this text was chanted to eight different tones similar to the psalm tones (a ninth tone, the *Tonus peregrinus*, to which the German text was sung, was often provided with versets by Lutheran composers.) Settings of all eight (or nine) of the Magnificat tones can be found in the works of Attaingnant, Antonio Cabezon (1510—66), Hieronymus Praetorius (1560—1629), Jean Titelouze (1563—1633), Samuel Scheidt (1587—1654), and Johann Caspar Kerll (1627—93), among others. Some of these contain more versets than the six that would be needed for antiphonal performance of the Magnificat. It is likely that these were intended for lauds when the longer Benedictus would be chanted to the same melody. Organ versets intended for the chanting of the psalms are less numerous and tend to be restricted to earlier periods. HG

Reading: Apel, Willi, *The History of Keyboard Music to 1700*, rev. and tr. by Hans Tischler (Bloomington, 1972); Gotsch, Herbert, "The Organ in the Lutheran Service of the 16th Century," *Church Music*, 67·1, pp. 7—12.

See also: alternation practice; canonical hours; canticle; mass; organ, literature; organ chorale; psalmody, Gregorian; literature; *HCM*, I, V, VI

organ chorale

By strict definition a setting for solo organ of a tune for the German congregational hymn; used generically also for organ settings of tunes of other origins such as metric psalms and Latin, English, and American hymns. Historically such settings functioned as intonations for congregational singing, as organ versets in the practice of alternation, as independent organ contributions in the service, as instructive models for improvisation, and as recital music. The fact that the most widely used title for this genre, chorale or hymn prelude, suggests just the first of these functions is indicative of the lack of consistency in terminology by composers, editors, and musicologists.

A taxonomy of the organ chorale can be devised that will allow a more systematic organization of the various types. A basic distinction is that between chorales in which the tune is presented in its entirety in more or less a consistent manner and those in which it is not. Among the latter would be fugues or fughettas on the first phrase, generally used as intonations, and fantasias, in which the structure is more free and not subject to formal systemization. Most organ chorales belong to the former category and can be grouped according to the treatment of the cantus firmus and the accompanying texture. The cantus firmus may be presented with its phrases either conjunct or disjunct (separated by interludes), or the cantus firmus may be presented in its simple original form, in canon, or elaborated by figuration or agréments. The accompanying texture may be either contrapuntal or homophonic. If contrapuntal, the melodic material of the voices may be independent of the cantus firmus or derived from it either in simple or elaborated form. These accompanying voices may treat the material in a variety of ways: motivic counterpoint (as often encountered in Bach's *Orgelbuechlein*), canonic treatment, ritornello, motet style (in which each phrase of the tune is a point of imitation), fugal treatment, invention, trio, bicinium, or toccata. In homophonic textures periodic phrases related to or in contrast to the cantus firmus may introduce or occur between phrases of the tune. Chordal patterns, arpeggios, or toccata figurations may also be used with or between the phrases. The more extensive chorale partita or choral variations may be formed by a succession of settings, either as individual movements, or joined by link passages.

The earliest roots of the organ chorale are found in the settings of Latin hymns and German songs in such 15th-century tablatures as Paumann's *Fundamentum organisandi* and the *Buxheim Organ Book*. These roots continue most abundantly in 16th-century German tablatures (Schlick, Buchner, Kotter, Ammerbach, and many others); many of these are intabulations or transcriptions of known vocal models with the addition of idiomatic keyboard embellishments. Whether the others were original keyboard compositions or based on extinct vocal pieces cannot be precisely determined. Composers in such other centers of Europe as Poland, Venice (Cavazzoni), Spain (Cabezon), and England (Redford, Tallis), also contributed organ settings of Latin hymns.

In the baroque era only three non-Germanic composers provided additions to the repertoire. Titelouze published cycles of versets on 12 hymns; considering their date and other contemporary music they seem almost anachronisms. At the end of the century Grigny includes versets on five hymns in his *Premier livre d'orgue*, which contribute to his stature as the culminating figure of French baroque organ music. Of greater historical significance is Sweelinck, whose variations based on the vocal polyphony of his Netherland forebears and the keyboard techniques of the English virginalists established him as one of the most important of the precursors of the baroque organ chorale composers.

Sweelinck's greatest influence on chorale composition came through his many north German pupils. Besides circulating copies in manuscript of Sweelinck's works, his pupils continued further development of the variation principle in their own compositions. Chief among these were Heinrich Scheidemann and especially Samuel Scheidt whose *Tabulatura nova* (1624) contains more chorale variations than any other collection of the 17th century. The longest chorale settings of the period are the three large-scale motets by Michael Praetorius. In his publications Praetorius adds to the organ repertoire by suggesting performance on the organ of his vocal chorale bicinia and tricinia. In the second half of the century north German composers continue the development of the large chorale fantasy and of the shorter chorale setting with embellished cantus firmus. The latter type was particularly mastered by Diedrich Buxtehude and Nikolaus Hanff. The variation undergoes a transformation with Boehm whose chorale partitas, chiefly *manualiter*, include textures more typical of stringed keyboard instruments. Boehm also introduces French agréments and the ritornello structure of the aria into the chorale literature.

Except for the remarkable published set of 40 variations on *Vater unser* by the south German J. U. Steigleder, central Germany is the other locale in which the organ chorale comprises the major portion of the works of many composers. Examples of the more common types are provided by a set of 44 chorales by Johann Christoph Bach; a phrase from the title, "zum praeambulieren," indicates their function as intonations for congregation singing. In this type the structure is very simple, a fughetta on the first phrase(s) or minimal imitative treatment of many or all of the phrases. The most prolific composer of organ chorales, Johann Pachelbel, belongs to central Germany in cultural rather than geographic terms. He generally treated the cantus firmus in even note values in soprano or bass accompanied by figurative counterpoint with each phrase preceded by fore-imitation in diminution. Another type, peculiar to Pachelbel, preceded such cantus firmus treatment with a chorale fughetta on the first phrase. Other composers who contributed similar types include Friedrich Zachau, Johann Buttstett, and Nicolas Armsdorff.

As is the case with so many other forms, the organ chorale in the 18th century is dominated by the works of J. S. Bach. In five collections he presents all the possibilities of chorale treatment inherited from his forebears together with several new types. The *Orgelbuechlein* (c. 1717) with a title page indicating a pedagogical purpose, displays models of motivic counterpoint, canons, embellished cantus firmus, and especially of the aesthetic relationship between texts and organ music. A collection of transcriptions of cantata movements published c. 1746 shows the application of the ritornello principle to the contrapuntal structure of the chorale. Earlier the published *Clavieruebung,* Part III (1739), in which the chorales of the *missa brevis* preceded those of Luther's catechism, had included examples of such ritornello treatment as well as the highest development of motet, fugal, and other imitative treatments of the chorale. The Eighteen Chorales, revisions of earlier works for publication near the end of Bach's life, contained further development, especially of the embellished chorale in combination with motet and ritornello treatment. A specialized demonstration of Bach's contrapuntal skill is found in the Canonic Variations on *Vom Himmel hoch* (1747).

Although most of Bach's contemporaries and pupils wrote organ chorales, two stand out. His relative and associate in Weimar, Johann Gottfried Walther, not only collected and preserved the organ works of earlier composers, but also produced a corpus of chorale settings whose variety and general quality place him second only to Bach in this genre. Bach's favorite pupil, Johann Ludwig Krebs, wrote works based on the style of his master but also composed chorales in a texture first used by Georg Friedrich Kauffman—a trio for the organ with the cantus firmus assigned to a solo wind instrument.

In the 19th century a few composers are noted for their treatment of the chorale. Three of Felix Mendelssohn's sonatas are based on chorale themes. Johannes Brahms' *Eleven Chorales*, his final compositions, approach

Bach's both in their contrapuntal workings and in their musical aesthetics. Two other organ composers, transitional figures leading into the 20th century, bring the romantic treatment of the chorale to its climax—Sigfrid Karg-Elert and Max Reger; their chorales, both the short settings and the long fantasies, combine contrapuntal, harmonic, and chromatic complexities with their adaptations of baroque forms.

The German organ chorale of the present century was particularly influenced by various neoclassic attitudes such as the revival of interest in early music, the organ reform movement, and the renewed interest in music in the liturgical life of the church; leading composers would include Hugo Distler and the circle of pupils and followers of Distler who dominated German church music in the middle years of the 20th century. More advanced influences, particularly serial techniques, can be seen in the recent organ chorales of Johann Nepomuk David.

Outside of Germany organists of the past century have written compositions on hymn and chorale tunes partly influenced by the great interest in baroque music and partly to meet the demand for sacred *Gebrauchsmusik*. Typical composers who added extensively to this repertoire would be Flor Peeters (Belgium), Alec Rowley (England), Healey Willan (Canada), and Leo Sowerby (U.S.A.). HG

Readings: Apel, Willi, *The History of Keyboard Music to 1700*, rev. and tr. by Hans Tischler (Bloomington, 1972); Arnold, Corliss Richard, *Organ Literature: A Comprehensive Survey* (Metuchen, N. J., 1973); Blume, Friedrich, *Protestant Church Music* (New York, 1974); Keller, Hermann, *The Organ Works of Bach* (New York, 1967); McConnell, Harlan, "The Sixteenth Century German Keyboard Chorale," *Church Music*, 75·1, pp. 14—22.

See also: church music history, Renaissance—the Reformation tradition; church music history, baroque; organ, literature; *HCM*, V

organ literature

The history of organ music may conveniently be divided into three periods. The first of these extends to the end of the 16th century and is marked by the emergence of the basic genres of the literature. The second period, the 17th and most of the 18th centuries, coinciding approximately with the baroque era, is the golden period of the organ. The third period, since c. 1800, is a period first of more isolated contributions and then of a few national renaissances of organ music.

To 1600

In the first period one of the principal activities of organists was to provide music for the services and offices of the church. One of the functions required was to play intonations that would set the pitch and modality for chants or polyphonic music. Preludes that would serve this function are found in the three great 15th-century tablatures (Ileborgh, Paumann, and Buxheim); they consist primarily of scale passages over sustained notes with occasional chordal textures. While this type of short prelude continued into succeeding centuries in most of Europe, the development of the more substantial toccata in Italy introduced the most important free form of the following periods. Of particular importance for the succeeding development was the introduction by Claudio Merulo 1533—1604) of imitative sections that relieved the monotony of scales-and-chords texture and allowed the evolution of longer toccatas.

The important precursors of the fugue had their origins in 16th-century Italy, especially in Venice. The canzona, either an intabulation of a French chanson or a newly composed piece imitating it, was characterized by a lively treatment of successive sprightly themes. While a similar derivation of the ricercar from the motet has been frequently suggested in the past, the ricercar has now been shown to be of independent origin. It was a well-worked-out imitative treatment of a few themes of a more restrained nature. Similar to the ricercar was the Spanish tiento of Anonio de Cabezon (1510—66). Since these imitative forms had no special exclusive function in the church, many were intended as much for the harpsichord or clavichord as for the organ. Similarly, secular song variations and ostinato settings for keyboard may not belong to organ literature proper, although there is evidence that Sweelinck gave daily recitals in his Amsterdam church for the town merchants before they opened the stock market that would have provided an occasion to use such compositions on the organ.

1600—c. 1800

The organ music of this era developed its forms and styles in various national schools. The culmination came in the works of Bach that represent a fusion of the styles of the principal schools.

Italy

Although composers in various parts of Italy continued the development of the forms originated by the Venetians, Girolamo

Frescobaldi (1583—1643) achieved preeminence through the printing of eight different collections of keyboard music. His imitative pieces offer solutions to the problem of bringing some unity to the multisectional ricercar and canzona. His toccatas are most imaginative, combining harmonic and tonality changes with a great variety of short toccata figurations; they were to be played, according to one of his prefaces, with considerable use of rubato.

France

A large number of printed collections entitled *Livre d' orgue* or *Pieces d' orgue* present the repertoire of 17th- and 18th-century French composers. Intended primarily for the mass and the offices, but including also suites of pieces in the various tones, this music is characterized by extensive use of the ornamentation of the clavecinists and by titles that indicate texture (récit, dialogue, echo, trio) or registration (plein jeu, basse de trompette, tierce en taille, récit de voix humaine). Of a more popular nature were the variations by many composers on sacred or secular Noëls.

Spain and Portugal

The tiento continued to be the primary form used by the Iberian composers in the 17th century, but it was no longer limited only to imitative treatment. Sections could also have considerable keyboard figurations in either bass or treble that would have been played on the *trompeta real* peculiar to that region's organs. Other textures found in the tientos included toccata and antiphonal writing. Principal composers are Francisco Correa de Arauxo (born c. 1576) and especially Juan Cabanilles (1644—1712) whose tientos present the greatest variety of styles and forms.

England

The forms used by English organ composers had little in common with those from the continent except for antiphon and Latin hymn settings. While the early 17th-century composers continued the interest in the imitative fancy and fantasia as the basic imitative forms, the title "voluntary" became dominant in the organ music of succeeding generations. The typical 18th-century voluntary by such composers as John Stanley (1713—86), William Boyce (1710—79), and John Travers (1703—58) was in two movements (occasionally four), the first slow, the second fast. The movements frequently included indications of registration desired (diapason, flute, trumpet, cornet, vox humana, echo). The texture of some voluntaries suggests plenum registration as they are really the English equivalent of the continental prelude and fugue. The organ concerto with orchestra introduced by George Frideric Handel (1685—1759) led to the cultivation of this genre by other English composers. The English organ had no pedal and much of the writing called for only two (or occasionally three) manual voices; any edition that suggests the use of the pedal or supplies harmonic "filling" between the outer voices is not to be trusted as authentic.

The Netherlands

The only major composer in the Low Countries was Jan Pieterszoon Sweelinck (1562—1621). Contact with the music of English composers enabled him to introduce the keyboard techniques of the virginalists to the continental toccata and variations. His fantasies, monothematic with many sections and countersubjects, were large-scale, but unified imitative pieces. Those fantasies labeled "echo" introduced the technique of achieving antiphonal contrast by manual changes. Sweelinck's successors were not of his own country; because of his many pupils from North Germany he is generally considered the founder of the organ tradition of that region.

Germany

Besides the organ chorale, the *north German school* is particularly noted for the development of the north German toccata (also titled prelude and fugue or toccata and fugue). The preludes of Heinrich Scheidemann (c. 1596—1663) in which opening and closing chordal or figurative textures frame a middle section that is either sequential or fugal, contain the germ of this genre. The more extended fugal sections of Jacob Praetorius (1586—1651), the use of livelier fugal themes as in the canzona, the substitution of toccata figuration for the chordal textures, and the emergence of virtuoso writing for the pedal organ not found elsewhere in Europe lead to the large compositions of Dietrich Buxtehude (1637—1707). In these the basic structure was an alternation of toccata and fugal sections with the first toccata section long enough to stand alone and the fugal sections related by thematic variation. In the next generation Vincent Luebeck (1654—1740), Georg Boehm (1661—1733), and Nicolaus Bruhns (1665—97) contributed to the toccata literature.

The organ chorale dominated the activity of the *central German school*. The preludes and fugues were primarily short intonations. More substantial were the pedal-point toccatas and the independent fugues of Johann Pachelbel (1653—1706).

Two representatives of the *south German school*, Hans Leo Hassler (1564—1612) and Christian Erbach (1570—1635), composed a large number of toccatas, canzonas, and ricercars. In 1624 Johann Steigleder (1593—1635) published his *Ricercar Tabulatura*, containing 12 ricercars of striking originality. The Italian traditions of Frescobaldi's time were cultivated in German areas by his pupil Johann Jacob Froberger (1616—67) in toccatas and various imitative forms. Further development of the toccata is found in the works of Johann Caspar Kerll (1627—93); Georg Muffat (1645—1740) was the first south German composer to make extensive use of obbligato pedal for contrapuntal bass lines in his toccatas.

J. S. Bach (1685—1750)

Bach's organ compositions may be grouped into three periods, although there are some works that seem transitional or have characteristics of adjacent periods. The first period, ending about 1709, was devoted primarily to works that show the heritage from the central Germans (organ chorales) and from the north Germans (toccata-prelude and fugue) with the demands on pedal and manual virtuosity. The second period, the Weimar and Coethen years, began with the transcription for either organ solo or harpsichord and orchestra of Italian violin concertos and the writing particularly of imitative pieces based on Italian models. The great toccatas-preludes and fuges of this period show a juxtaposition and fusion of north German and Italian stylistic elements. Bach's works in the last period which begins with the move to Leipzig in 1723 included the great organ chorales, the trio sonatas, and the last five great preludes and fugues, which are the culmination of baroque organ music. In these "ritornello" preludes Bach adds the tensions of the concerto grosso principle to his earlier styles.

Bach was an isolated figure whose works were regarded as being out-of-date already during his lifetime. His only successors were his son Wilhelm Friedemann (1710—84) and his favorite pupil Johann Ludwig Krebs (1713—80). Mozart (1756—91) expressed great interest in the organ, but left only two large fantasias for an automatic musical clock organ and 17 sonatas for organ with instrumental ensemble.

Since 1800

During the 19th century the composers who continued to provide the functional music needed by organists were of minor stature. But several major composers did make significant contributions to the literature: Felix Mendelssohn (1809—47), three preludes and fugues and six sonatas originally commissioned as voluntaries; Franz Liszt (1811—86), three lengthy pieces requiring virtuoso manual and pedal technique and much music of modest scale intended for the church; Johannes Brahms (1833—97), early preludes and fugues and 11 organ chorales. Among the composers whose career centered about the organ would be Joseph Rheinberger (1839—1901), who wrote sonatas and concertos. But it was Max Reger (1873—1916) whose works represent the peak of German romanticism for organ and combine an interest in contrapuntal writing and historical forms with chromaticism, rich harmonies, and an orchestral approach to the instrument.

The most continuous line of organ composers of the past 100 years has been in France. This school began with the development of an organ of symphonic character by Cavaillé-Coll (1811—99) and the works of César Franck (1822—90) that used symphonic principles to exploit the possibilities of this organ. From Franck French organ music continues on two paths. The one produces concert music, primarily symphonies; leading composers were Charles Marie Widor (1845—1937) and Louis Vierne (1870—1937). The other is concerned with liturgical music and music with a religious program; composers include Charles Tournemire (1870—1939) and the highly innovative Oliver Messiaen (b. 1908). Many composers wrote in both categories; Marcel Dupre (1886—1971), Maurice Duruflé (b. 1903), Jean Langlais (b. 1907), and Jehan Alain (1911—40).

Closely associated with the German reforms in organ building that began in the 1920s are a large number of German composers who were active in Protestant vocal music of the period and who show strong neoclassic attitudes and a reaction against the bombast of some of the late Romantic organ music. These include Ernest Pepping (b. 1901), Hans Micheelsen (b. 1903), Helmut Bornefeld (b. 1906), Hugo Distler (1908—42) and Siegfried Reda (1916—68). Not connected with this school, but displaying neoclassic tendencies with superb craftmanship are the sonatas and concertos of Paul Hindemith (1895—1963).

Two native-born but European-trained musicians can be credited with founding the American organ tradition as virtuoso performers, composers, and teachers—John Knowles Paine (1839—1906) and Dudley Buck (1839—1909). Among the many American composers of the 20th century, one in particular should be singled out as most prominent in providing works for concert and service use, Leo Sowerby (1895—1968). HG

Readings: Apel, Willi, *The History of Keyboard Music to 1700,* tr. and rev. by Hans Tischler (Bloomington, 1972); Frotscher, Gotthold, *Geschichte des Orgelspiels und der Orgelkomposition,* 2 vols. (Berlin, 1934); Arnold, Corliss Richard, *Organ Literature: A Comprehensive Study* (Metuchen, N. J., 1973); Keller, Hermann, *The Organ Works of Bach,* tr. Helen Hewitt (New York, 1967).

See also: alternation practice; chorale; mass; organ, history; organ, use in the mass and offices; organ chorale; tablature; thoroughbass; voluntary

Passion

The narratives of the Passion story *(Passio Domini nostri Jesu Christi)* were read or recited in more or less dramatic fashion as early as the 4th century. Such a recitation with interspersed choruses is noted by St. Gregory Nazianzen (d. 389), and Augustine (d. 430) uses the words "solemniter legere" in connection with the Passion story (Sermo 218,1; *Patrol. Lat.* XXXVIII, 1084).

By about the 8th century the Passion story was apparently recited in a speaking voice, with the words of Christ, however, sung to plainsong. In the course of the Middle Ages liturgical practice assigned each of the four Passion narratives to a particular day of Holy Week: the Matthew narrative to Palm Sunday; Mark to Tuesday of Holy Week; Luke to Wednesday of Holy Week; and John to Good Friday. By the 12th or 13th century the procedure had become more elaborate with three distinct roles emerging in the presentation of the passion story: the narrator or evangelist *(Chronista)*; Christ (Christus); and the crowd and/or other minor characters in the story *(Turbae Judaeorum* or *Synagoga).* The three roles were differentiated both by the voice range chosen to represent each one as well as by the manner in which each was performed, the words of Christ in the lowest range and at a slow tempo, the words of the crowd at the highest range and at a faster tempo, the narrative in a middle range and at a normal tempo. Durandus (d. 1296) directs in his *Rationale divinorum officiorum* that the words of Christ should be sung with sweetness, those of the Evangelist in the formal Gospel tone, and those of the "most impious Jews" in a loud and harsh manner. It seems that these three roles were first performed by a single voice using its various registers, the assignment of the three roles to different individuals not appearing until about the 15th century. In general the texts were sungs to relatively simple plainsong formulas (Passion tones), with particular melodic formulas for beginning and ending each part, for questions, and for the introduction of the words of Christ by the evangelist. (Examples of these formulas from 18 13th—16th-century manuscripts are found in *MGG*, X, 891—892). The narratives of Matthew and John assumed a somewhat more elaborate character, due no doubt to the greater importance of the days to which these Passions were assigned in the life of the church. A more expressive melody was often used in connection with the words, "Eli, Eli, lama sabachthani." The definitive version of the Passion tones was prepared by Guidetti and published in Rome in 1586.

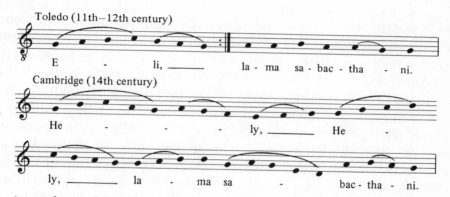

As early as the 10th century, manuscripts of the Passion story appear with cue letters, often written in red, indicating portions of the text assigned to the three principal roles. The table below indicates the most common use of these letters.

	about 10th cent.	later liturgical books	about 14th cent.
Evangelist or narrator	c(celeriter=quickly)	m(media)	C(Chronista)
Christ	t(tenere, tarde=slowly)	b(bassa)	I(Christus)
Crowd	a(altus) or s(sursum=high	a(alta voce)	S(Synagoga)

Polyphonic settings of the Passion history reflect two general practices: (1) that of setting only the *turba* or crowd choruses in polyphony, the remaining parts being sung in plainsong (this style is also known as the "scenic" or "dramatic" Passion); and (2) that of setting the complete Passion history text in polyphony (also known as the motet Passion).

The earliest extant examples of polyphonic Passions are from England (MS Egerton 3307) and reflect the first of these practices and date from the middle of the 15th century. These two early examples (one according to St. Matthew, the other St. Luke) set only the sections for the *Synagoga* polyphonically, and are apparently intended for performance by three solo voices, the remaining parts apparently intended for plainsong rendition (see Grove, IV, 579). Other examples from the latter part of the 15th century include those found in the Modena codex Est. lat. 454/55 (c. 1480) an English Passion (St. Matthew) *a* 4 by Richard Davy in the Eton MS (c. 1500), see *MB*, XII, 112-34), and others by Claude de Sermisy (c. 1490—1562), Orlando di Lasso (c. 1532—94), Jakob Reiner (c. 1560—1609), Giovanni Asola (d. 1609), Tomás Luis de Victoria (c. 1535/48—1611), Francisco Guerrero (1528—99), and William Byrd (1543—1623).

The use of the vernacular in the "dramatic" Passion settings as well as use of a simpler homophonic style may be seen especially in the early Lutheran setting by Johann Walter (St. Matthew, 1530), as well as in the works of other Lutheran and Catholic composers such as Antonio Scandello (1517—80), Jacob Meiland (1542—77), Bartholomaeus Gesius (c. 1555—c. 1613), Thomas Mencken (1550—1620), Samuel Besler (1574—1625), Melchior Vulpius (c. 1560—1615), Otto Siegfried-Harnisch (d. 1630—), Christian Schultze-Deilitzsch (1653), and Christian Flor (1667).

Paralleling the development of the dramatic or scenic Passion was the motet-Passion style, in which the entire text was presented in polyphonic fashion. This approach, which allowed greater musical elaboration but with less obvious dramatic character, can be seen in the Passions of Jacob Obrecht (d. 1505), Johannes Galliculus (c. 1520—50), Ludwig Daser (d. 1589), Vincenzio Ruffo (b. 1554), Cypriano de Rore (1557), Joachim a Burgk (1568), composer of the first motet Passion in the German vernacular, Jacob Regnart (1540—1600), Bartholomaeus Gesius (c. 1555—c. 1613), Orlando di Lasso (c. 1532—94), Leonard Lechner (1594) whose setting is thought by many to be the finest of surviving motet passions, Johannes Steurlein (1576), Johannes Machold (1593), and Christoph Demantius (1631) whose expressive use of the new harmonic techniques of the period is striking. In the early examples of the motet Passion the liturgical plainsong is usually retained as cantus firmus, a practice that declined and was sometimes altogether abandoned in the later examples. The motet-Passion type of Antoine de Longueval (Johannes a la Venture), who was active c. 1509—22, is noteworthy in that it is apparently the earliest attempt to combine the four Passion accounts into a single one, a practice that made possible the centering of attention on the seven words of Christ from the cross, a procedure especially developed in the years following.

With the 17th century we begin to see the application of all the dramatic devices of the baroque period applied to the Passion history settings in varying degrees: recitative, aria, the use of orchestra, together with a freer use of the Biblical text. Composers demonstrating these new tendencies include Thomas Seele (1599—1663), Thomas Strutius (d. 1678), and Johann Sebastiani (1622—83). The greatest figure of this period was Heinrich Schuetz (1585—1672) whose *Sieben Worte Jesu Christi am Kreuz* is an outstanding example of the new approach. Schuetz' other four settings of the individual Passion accounts, written at the close of his career, revert to a more conservative, austere style, alternating solo voices for the parts of the Evangelist and Christ with polyphonic choruses singing the words of the *turba*.

About 1700 the use of the Biblical text was increasingly abandoned in favor of freer texts of rhythmed paraphrases in the more sentimental and allegorical style of the day. Two Passion texts were especially popular, those of Chr. F. Hunold-Menante and B. H. Brockes. The latter text was used by many composers, among them Keiser, Telemann, Handel (St. John, 1704, and *Der fuer die Suenden der Welt gemarterte und sterbende Jesus*, 1716), and Mattheson. Keiser's *Der blutige und sterbende Jesus* (1704) and his later *Traenen unter dem Kreuze Jesus* (1711) reflect the more theatrical nature of these settings.

J. S. Bach's St. John Passion (1723) and especially his St. Matthew Passion (1729) represent a return to a more dignified style. Both use the Biblical text as the basic narrative, together with free poetic texts (from Brockes in the St. John Passion, from Picander in the St. Matthew Passion). Portions of a St. Mark Passion by J. S. Bach remain (in the *Trauer-Ode*, 1727), and a St. Luke Passion listed in an early catalogue of his works has been rejected as spurious.

Other passion settings of the 18th century, by such composers as Johann

Kuhnau (St. Mark, 1721), C. P. E. Bach (1787, 1788) Karl Heinrich Graun (*Der Tod Jesu,* 1755), and Joseph Haydn (*Die sieben Worte am Kreuz*, 1785), reflect the increasing overlapping of the Passion setting with that of the oratorio, as do such 19th-century examples of Beethoven (*Christus am Oelberg,* 1803), Spohr (*Des Heiland's letzte Stunden,* 1835), and Perosi (*La Passione di Jesu Christo,* 1899).

More modern Passion settings include those of John Stainer (*Crucifixion,* 1887), C. L. Williams (*Gethsemane,* 1892) and Arthur Somerville (*The Passion of Christ,* 1714). Twentieth-century passion settings include those of Hugo Distler (*Choral passion*), Hans Friedrich Micheelsen, K. Thomas, Ernst Pepping, Siegfried Reda, Felicitas Kukuck, and Krzysztof Penderecki. CS

Readings: Abraham, Gerald, "Passion Music in the Fifteenth and Sixteenth Centuries," *The Monthly Musical Record* (Oct.—Nov. 1953); Adams, H. M., "Passion Music Before 1724," *Music and Letters, VII* (1926); Smallman, Basil, *The Background of Passion Music* (London, 1957).

See also: church music history, medieval; church music history, Renaissance—the Reformation tradition; church music history, baroque; motet; *HCM, IV*

performance practice

Performance practice (*Auffuehrungspraxis*) refers to the study of how music of a particular era was understood and performed. This information aids today's performers in recreating music of the past so that it reflects the composer's artistic requirements and expressive intent. Until recently, scholars have not included the past two centuries in their research, but it is now apparent that performance techniques from 1750 to about 1920 are by no means thoroughly understood and should, along with earlier music, be included in studies on performance practice.

Among the problems dealt with in this area are those of historical context and style, notation, ornamentation, improvisation, instrumentation and use of voices, articulation (fingering, bowing, tonguing, breathing), registration, dynamics, tempo and its fluctuation, rhythm and its alteration, *musica ficta, basso continuo,* and scholarly editing.

A number of these problems involve musical notation itself. One such area deals with the transcription of obsolete notations of the Middle Ages and Renaissance into modern equivalents. The most controversial issues

Ex. 1

Louis Couperin (d.1661), "Prélude re mineur," from *Pièces de Clavecin*

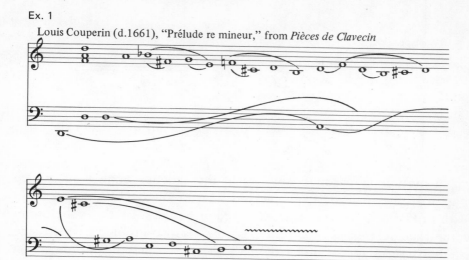

deal with (1) the question of transcribing proportional metric signs and note values into modern symbols or retaining the originals (most scholars now favor the latter) and (2) the question of adding *musica ficta* as determined by solmization of the hexachords, text, and nature of the modes. During the baroque era, several problems of performance also stem directly from the notation: the intensification of dotted notes in, for example, the French Overture; the French tradition of *notes inégales*, in which notes that are written equally are played unequally in certain situations; the realization of the unmeasured prelude, which, unlike other pieces in free rhythm (toccatas, fantasias, recitatives), was not written in proportional notation (Ex. 1). The resolution of the notation is left to the performer.

Improvisation and ornamentation constitute another field of inquiry. Italian diminutions (16th—18th centuries) and French *agréments* (17th—18th centuries) are frequently added to both vocal and instrumental music. The salient features in the construction of Renaissance music are: a leading voice that descends by a whole step to the cadence tone (½ step in a Phrygian cadence); an ornamental voice that forms suspensions, introduces *musica ficta* when necessary and ornaments cadences; and an accompanying voice or voices that fill in the *concentus* (tones sounding together at any given moment). *Musica ficta* and appropriate ornamentation must be added by the performer to the ornamental voice. Examples of improvisation and

Ex. 2

a) Cadence
   tremblement missing

b) Supplied
   by performer

c) Performed

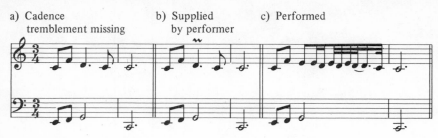

ornamentation in baroque music are: the cadence *tremblement*, which is obligatory in all music from the last quarter of the 17th century to the death of Handel, whether it is indicated or not (Ex. 2); the embellishment of the final section of a *da capo* aria; the realization of the *basso continuo*, whether figures appear under the bass line or not; and the improvisation of missing parts in the texture of a piece. For example, the two long chords at the end of the first movement of Bach's *Brandenburg Concerto* No. 3 should be improvised upon, and the *fermata* in keyboard sonatas of the 18th century, classic as well as baroque, should be embellished.

Another basic area of study is instrumentation and the use of voices. Modern performance practices are often far removed from those of previous eras. For example, most music for voices from earlier periods was not "choral" music in the modern sense. The use of a single voice to each part, a *sine qua non* of all madrigal performances, may also be safely applied to most polyphonic music from the 11th to the 14th centuries. Ensembles were usually not large. The papal choir in the 16th century ranged from 24 to 36 singers (many were smaller), and Bach's Leipzig choir consisted of from 12 to 16 singers plus at least an equal number of instrumentalists. The normal size of an 18th-century symphony orchestra was from 30 to 35 players, not the large forces usually used today.

Instrumental and vocal sonorities also need investigation. For example, female voices were not heard in churches until the end of the 18th century (1800 in Leipzig), and the type of voice production, that of the extremely agile *bel canto*, is all but lost today. Modern flutes were not in use at all until the 19th century. In Bach and Handel, the plain name *flauto* invariably meant recorder, and the transverse flute (*flauto traverso*) was a soft-toned wooden instrument.

All of these items and many more fall under the general area of investigation called performance practice. NJ

Readings: Dart, T., *The Interpretation of Music* (New York, 1963); Donington, R., *A Performer's Guide to Baroque Music* (London, 1973); Donington, R., *The Interpretation of Early Music* (New York, 1963); Jenne, N., "An Introduction to Baroque Performance: Practice and Sources," *Church Music,* 70·1; Vinquist, Mary and Neal Zaslaw, eds., *Performance Practice: A Bibliography* (New York, 1971).

See also: choir, history; church music history, Renaissance—the Latin tradition; church music history, Renaissance—the Reformation tradition; thoroughbass; *HCM,* IV, V

polychoral style

A style of antiphonal composition that incorporates two or more distinct groups of vocalists and/or instrumentalists into a unified ensemble. The groups may be identical or they may contrast with each other in pitch, timbre, type of constituent parts, or placement for performance. Typically, two or three groups alternate in performance by phrases, at times echoing, at times varying or extending material before combining to perform together. Overlapping of phrases and combining of forces achieves sonorous effects, particularly as cadences are approached. While instrumental participation may be assumed in most polychoral performance, whether specified or not, the introduction of the *basso continuo* and of concerted instruments became an important dimension of the polychoral style early in the 17th century.

Polychoral practice seems to have developed from two sources: liturgical chant and imitative polyphony. The singing of liturgical chant in alternation is particularly evident in the performance of psalms, canticles, and litanies. In Gregorian chant groups often answer individuals (responsorial chant) or groups answer groups (antiphonal chant). As liturgical polyphony developed, one chanting participant was often replaced in the alternation scheme by a choir or an organ performing polyphonic settings. The second source appears in 15th-and 16th-century polyphony with the increasing identification by composers of pairs or groups of voices in polyphonic imitation of other pairs or groups of voices for purposes of contrast and variety. Josquin Desprez (c. 1440—1521) and other Netherlandish and Franco-Flemish composers of the 15th and 16th centuries developed and expanded the style to a high degree of perfection. The practice was continued throughout the latter part of the 16th century by most of the masters of imitative polyphony, culminating in the works of di Lasso, Victoria, and Palestrina, which display numerous areas of choral contrast between various combinations of singers.

Italian sources indicate that as early as the second half of the 15th century two choirs would alternate in the singing of phrases of hymns, a practice called *coro battente* or *coro spezzato* (broken choir). In the period between approximately 1510 and 1520 Fra Ruffino Bartolucci d'Assisi set psalms for two four-voice choirs; Francesco Santacroce (c. 1478—1556) continued the practice in his psalm settings for divided choir written about 1524.

At an early date French composers contributed works displaying polychoral characteristics. Jean Rousée (early 16th century) wrote a "Regina coeli" (1535) for two equal, mixed four-voice choirs, and Dominique Phinot wrote five motets for two choirs of four voices each in

The Cathedral of St. Mark, Venice. The two choir (organ) galleries are beyond the transept crossing, on either side of the chancel, above and just beyond the screen stretching across the chancel entrance.

1548. Claude Goudimel (c. 1514—72) wrote a "Credo" for two choirs in 1564.

The appearance in Venice in 1550 of *Salmi spezzati* (Broken Psalms) by Adrian Willaert (c. 1490—1562) ushered in the development of polychoral composition at St. Mark's, where it was to find a uniquely hospitable environment. Using the architectural advantage of twin galleries above and to the sides of the high altar, Willaert wrote for two four-voice choirs that sang in alternation and in combination. Andrea Gabrieli (c. 1510/20—1586) enhanced the unfolding tradition with such works as "Deus misereatur nostri" for three choirs of distinctive range and timbre (SSAT-SATB-TTTB). But it remained for Giovanni Gabrieli (c.

Excerpt from "Magnificat"   Giovanni Gabrieli

Source: Arnold, Denis, ed. *Giovanni Gabrieli: Opera omnia* in *Corpus mensurabilis musicae*, XII, Rome, 1965–, IV, p. 133.

309

1555—1612) to develop the artistic and expressive potential of the idiom to its highest level. Giovanni specialized in impressive, yet sensitive, polychoral writing for as many as five contrasting choirs of voices and instrumental composition. The justifiably renowned "In ecclesiis" for three "Magnificat" for three choirs). While most choral performances were supported or reinforced with various instruments in this period, Giovanni Gabrieli often specified instrumentation in polychoral works and exploited ever greater contrasts of timbre, pitch, and size of component groups within the ensemble. He also applied polychoral principles to purely instrumental composition. The justifiably renowned "In ecclesiis" for three disparate choirs of voices and instruments is a jewel of particular brilliance among the works of a composer who added many gems to the crowning glory of Venetian music that was the polychoral style.

Other Venetian composers followed the leadership of these great masters, notably Giovanni Croce (1557—1609) and the eminent Claudio Monteverdi (1567—1643). In 1594 Croce published the first known example of a printed organ bass for double-chorus. Adriano Banchieri (1567—1634) of Bologna published a similar example in 1595.

Roman Catholic composers of traditional polyphony were not unaffected by the growing popularity of the Venetian style, although they seem to have approached the idiom with some caution. Three of the leading masters, Orlando di Lasso (c. 1532—94), Giovanni P. da Palestrina (c. 1525—94), and Tomás L. de Victoria (1535/48—1611), wrote some divided-choir compositions (particularly motets), but these generally did not approach the inherent grandeur and freedom of the works of the Gabrielis.

Other composers incorporated polychoral techniques into their basically contrapuntal style: Ascanio Trombetti (1544—90), Orazio Vecchi (1550—1605), Ruggerio Giovanelli (c. 1560—1625), Giovanni M. Nanino (c. 1545—1607), Giovanni Gastoldi (d. 1622), Steffano Bernardi (c. 1576—d. before 1638), and Juan P. Pujol (1573—1626).

An offshoot of both the Roman school and the Venetian polychoral school was the so-called "colossal baroque" style, which emphasized masses of sound produced by multiple choirs and instruments within a polyphonic texture, rather than the clarity and brilliance of contrasting ensembles. Representative composers of this style who utilized certain polychoral techniques are Tiburzio Massaini (before 1550—after 1609), Vincenzo Galilei (c. 1520—91), Domenico Allegri (c. 1585—1629), Paolo

Agostini (c. 1583—1629), Virgilio Mazzocchi (d. 1646), Antonio M. Abbatini (1595—1680), and Orazio Benevoli (1605—72).

The polychoral style of writing soon spread across Europe, and nowhere was it adopted with greater enthusiasm than in German lands. After a tentative beginning in the hands of Johann Walter (1496—1570) and Leonhart Schroeter (c. 1532—c. 1600) in publications of 1566 and 1571 respectively, the development of polychoral writing in Germany was nourished by the works of three giants: Hans Leo Hassler (1564—1612), Michael Praetorius (1571—1621), and Heinrich Schuetz (1585—1672).

Hassler, who thoroughly absorbed the polychoral style while he

Title page of Michael Praetorius' *Motectae et Psalmi Latini* depicting several choirs of voices and instruments.

studied in Venice, reflected this influence in his Latin motets (1591, 1601), a Mass (1599), and Psalms and German hymns (1608). Michael Praetorius wrote an immense number of polychoral chorale and motet compositions for a variety of *ad libitum* combinations of voices and instruments. For example, his *Polyhymnia caduceatrix et panegyrica* (1619) contains 40 multi-stanza chorale settings for as many as six choirs of voices and instruments. His instructions for performance, found in copius forewords and performance rubrics, suggest a dazzling array of polychoral possibilities. Praetorius in particular delineates the function in performance of the *Chorus pro capella* (large ensemble of singers), the *Coro favorito* (ensemble of solo singers), and the *Chorus instrumentalis* (ensemble of instrumentalists). Heinrich Schuetz brought German polychoral writing to its artistic pinnacle, most notably in his *Psalmen Davids* (1619) and in other single Psalm settings.

Other German Protestant composers utilized polychoral techniques in some of their writings: Balthasar Resinarius (c. 1485—1544), Leonhard Paeminger (1495—1567), Georg Otto (c. 1550—1618), Johannes Eccard (1553—1611), Leonhard Lechner (c. 1553—1606), Adam Gumpelzhaimer (1559—1625), Friedrich Weissensee (c. 1560—1622), Hieronymus Praetorius (1560—1629), Philippus Dulichius (1562—1631), Andreas Raselius (c. 1563—1602), Christoph Demantius (1567—1643), Christian Erbach (c. 1570—1635), Johann H. Schein (1586—1630), Samuel Scheidt (1587—1654), Daniel Lagkhner (later 16th c.—after 1607), Johannes Bach (1604—73), Andreas Hammerschmidt (1612—75), Johann R. Ahle (1625—73), Johann M. Bach (1648—94), and Johann P. Krieger (1649—1725).

Roman Catholic composers in southern Germany and at the Imperial Court in Vienna also used polychoral techniques: Christian Hollander (c. 1510/15—1568/69), Philippe de Monte (1521—1603), Jacob Vaet (1529—67), Blasius Amon (c. 1560—90), Jacob Regnart (c. 1540—99), Gregor Aichinger (1564—1628), Christoph Strauss (1575?—1631), Georg Poss (c. 1570/75—after 1637), Johann H. Schmeltzer (c. 1623—80), Johann K. Kerll (1627—93), Heinrich I. F. Biber (1644—1704), and Antonio Caldara (c. 1670—1736).

Venetian influence was felt in other lands: Wacław Szamotułczyk (1524/26—1560) introduced polychoral writing into Poland and his countrymen Mikołaj Zielénski (fl. c. 1611) later wrote compositions requiring as many as three choirs. Jacobus Gallus (Handel, 1550—91) of Prague wrote extensively for multiple choirs in his monumental *Opus musicum* (1586—91). In Holland Jan P. Sweelinck (1562—1621) wrote some works for divided choirs. Jean-Baptiste Lully (1632—87) and Marc-Antoine

Charpentier (1634—1704) of France used divided-choir writing in some of their choral works. Juan B. Comes (1568—1643) and Juan Cererols (1618—76) developed the tradition in Spain, and from Spain the Venetian influence even extended to colonial Mexico, where a polychoral Magnificat by the Spanish Bernardo Peralta (d. 1632) was performed, and where Juan G. de Padilla (c. 1595—1664) wrote extensively for two and three choirs.

The English choral tradition of a divided choir seated on *decani* and *cantoris* sides of the chancel did not develop into a true polychoral style. Instead, in English practice singers on either side of the chancel sing phrases in alternation, combining at times without increasing the number of parts. Composers representative of this tradition are Thomas Tallis (c. 1505—85), William Byrd (1543—1623), and later, John Blow (1649—1708), and Henry Purcell (1659—95).

Major composers of the later baroque era contributed occasional examples of divided-choir writing, but the practice never achieved its former significance. Four of the six motets of Johann S. Bach (1685—1750) as well as portions of his *St. Matthew Passion* and the *Mass in B minor* are for double chorus. George F. Handel (1685—1759), Alessandro Scarlatti (1660—1725), and Leonardo Leo (1694—1744) all contributed to the genre.

Occasional examples of polychoral writing appear in the works of preclassic and classic composers, such as J. Michael Haydn (1737—1806), Samuel Wesley (1766—1837), and Wolfgang A. Mozart (1756—91).

In the 19th and 20th centuries examples of polychoral writing can be found in the works of J. Friedrich Schneider (1786—1853), Anton Bruckner (1824—96), Johannes Brahms (1833—97), Gustav Holst (1874—1934), Ralph Vaughan Williams (1872—1958), Horatio Parker (1863—1919), Randall Thompson (b. 1899), and Benjamin Britten (1913—76). CM

Readings: Abraham, Gerald, ed., *The Age of Humanism (1540—1630)*, vol. IV of *New Oxford History of Music*, ed. J. A. Westrup *et al.* (London, 1968); Apel, Willi, ed., *Harvard Dictionary of Music*, 2d ed., rev. and enl., (Cambridge, Mass., 1969); Messerli, Carlos R., "Polychoral Music, Michael Praetorius, and the Fifty Days of Easter," *Church Music*, 73·1 (Spring 1973); Reese, Gustave, *Music in the Renaissance*, 2d ed. (New York, 1959); Samuel, Harold E., "Michael Praetorius on Concertato Style," in *Cantors at the Crossroads; Essays on Church Music in Honor of Walter E. Buszin*, ed. Johannes Riedel (St. Louis, Mo., 1967); Woerner, Karl, *History of Music*, 5th ed., tr. and supplemented by Willis Wager (New York, 1973).

See also: alternation practice; canticle; chant, Gregorian; church music history, Renaissance—the Latin tradition; church music history, Renaissance—the Reformation tradition; concertato style; decani/cantoris; Roman school; thoroughbass; Venetian school; HCM IV

psalmody, Gregorian

Gregorian psalmody traces its origin to the synagog of the pre-Christian era. It may conveniently be grouped into four basic types: simple psalmody; solemn psalmody; introit psalmody; and ornate psalmody.

Simple Psalmody

Applicable to all types is the basic structure of psalmody, which is governed by the external feature of this genre of Hebrew poetry. This feature, known as parallelism, usually divides each verse of the psalm into two parts and thus produces the following division of the musical phrase: Tenor (reciting tone)—Mediant Cadence—Tenor—Final Cadence.

Ex. 1   *Simple Psalmody without Antiphon*

The above example of simple psalmody is also known as direct psalmody and is used when no antiphon precedes or follows.

When an antiphon precedes the first Psalm verse the first Tenor is preceded by an introduction that leads from the antiphon to the first verse of the Psalm. In addition, the first half of the verse may use an inflection known as the flex. This inflection is used only when the first half of the Psalm verse is quite long and has a suitable punctuation break. The nature of the flex will be seen in the chant of the tones themselves. Thus the pattern of a verse with both these features will be as follows, bearing in mind that the intonation is only used for the first verse: Intonation—Tenor—(flex)—Mediant Cadence—Tenor—Final Cadence. An example of simple psalmody with antiphon may be found in the *Liber Usualis*, p. 372.

Ex. 2   *Simple Psalmody with Antiphon*

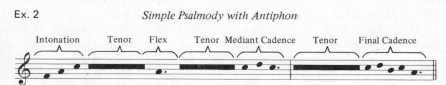

Solemn Psalmody

Solemn psalmody follows the same essential plan as that just described in simple psalmody with the slight difference that the intonation is repeated for each verse, the mediant cadence is slightly more ornamented, the final cadence, however, remaining the same as in simple psalmody. Both simple and solemn psalmody belong primarily to the Office. Solemn Psalmody, however, is reserved for the chanting of the New Testament Canticles (*Magnificat, Benedictus,* and *Nunc dimittis*) especially on high feast days such as the Nativity.

Introit Psalmody

Very closely related to the simple and solemn renditions is one that belongs strictly to the psalms used in the mass propers. This is known as introit psalmody. Nearly all the introits of the mass are based on psalm texts, the antiphon portion of the introit usually being one single verse which is often not the first but rather one of the internal verses of the psalm. Following it, the first verse is sung to the tone proper to it, followed by the lesser doxology (Gloria Patri) and then the repetition of the antiphon itself. Since the antiphons of the introit are somewhat melismatic, it would be in keeping stylistically that the psalm tones themselves be more ornate both as to intonation and cadences. That this is actually the case can be seen from the example of the introit for the mass of the day at Christmas together with *Gloria Patri* to be used with it (LU, p.408 and 15).

Ornate Psalmody

Also belonging to the classification of mass psalmody is the highly melismatic kind of solo chant called ornate psalmody and found particularly in the tracts. The tracts are used only in the penitential season of Lent and in Masses of the Dead to replace the Alleluia and verse which are as a rule very melismatic in style. They are always written in either the Second or the Eighth mode and characteristically employ many of the same segments of melodic formulae.

The Psalm Tones

There are eight regular psalm tones that reflect the characteristics of the mode to which they belong. The specific characteristics of the psalm tones are given in the accompanying chart. For example, Tone I has *la* (a) as its Tenor and this is also the so-called melodic dominant of the mode. Three of its final cadences (there are 10 in all—see chart) end in *re* (d) which is also the *finalis* of the mode. Its range (ambitus) stays well within the limits of the range of the mode. Tone II has *fa* (f) as its Tenor and this is also the so-called melodic dominant of the mode. Its only final cadence is *re* (d) which is also the *finalis* of Mode II.

The complete Psalm Tone formulae with the variant endings are on pp. 113—117 of the 1962 edition of the *Liber Usualis*. The Solemn Tones are on pp. 213—218 of the same volume. It is suggested that the reader refer to them in using the chart that follows. The chart will be helpful to the reader in understanding the structure of each psalm tone. The following notes will explain the scheme used in the chart. The numerals used indicate the steps of the scale: 1 indicates the step "do" or c; a figure with a dash through it (7̶) indicates Bᵇ; figures in parentheses (6) indicate an auxiliary note

THE FORMAL-FUNCTIONAL SCHEME OF GREGORIAN SIMPLE PSALMODY

Intonation	Tenor	Mediant Cadence	Tenor	Final Cadence
This is functionally the means by which the tenor, or reciting note, is reached smoothly after the ending of the antiphon.	The reciting note is always the dominant of the mode. If the text of the first half is long there may be a flex which is always a Major 2d, except in Tones 2, 3 5, and 7.*	This is actually a decoration of the midway point. It is based on a system of preparatory and accented syllables.	Free recitation on the dominant always without a flex, regardless of length. It is always the same note as in the first half except in the *tonus peregrinus*.	As a rule the final cadence descends, but its function is in genral to return to the beginning note of the antiphon. Each tone except 2, 5, and 6 has alternate endings.

Tone				
I	4 5 6	6	7̶ (6) 6 5 (6) 6	6	10 possible endings
II	1 2 4	4	5 (4) 4	4	3 1 2
III	5 6 1	1	2 (1) 1 (1) 7̶ 6 1	1	5 possible endings
IV	6 5 6	6	5 6 7̶ (6) 6	6	two possible endings
V	4 6 1	1	2 (1) 1	1	2 (7̶) 7̶ 1 (6) 6
VI	4 5 6	6	7̶ (6) 6 5 (6) 6	6	4 5 6 5 (4) 4
VII	1 7̶ 1 2	2	4 (3) 3 2 (3) 3	2	five possible endings
VIII	5 6 1	1	2 (1) 1	1	Three endings
Peregrinus	6 7̶	6	5 7̶ 6 5 (4) 4	5	2 4 (4) 3 2

*Tones 2, 3, 5, and 7 used a flex of a minor 3d since their reciting notes are either on "c" or "f," which would necessarily mean that a departure of a 2d would always be a minor interval on the leading tone. To avoid this, the minor 3d is used instead.

which, in Gregorian notation, is a white note; and figures with a dash above them indicate the upper octave of the scale—thus 1 actually stands for 8; 2 for 9, etc.

In addition there is an irregular psalm tone called the *tonus peregrinus* (LU, p. 117). It cannot be related to any specific mode since it has two Tenors. The first part of the formula has *la* (a) as its Tenor and the second has *sol* (g) as its Tenor. In Roman usage this tone is used only for Psalm 113 (*In exitu Israel*) which is the fifth or last of the Psalms for Sunday Vespers.

Ex. 3

Tonus Peregrinus

Strangely enough, in German Lutheran tradition, the *tonus peregrinus* has been used to chant the *Magnificat*. Its intonation has been slightly altered to a minor third instead of the minor second seen in the above example. (cf. Cantata No. 10, "Meine Seel' erhebt den Herrn" or the Schuebler Chorales by J. S. Bach). MAB

Readings: In addition to the bibliography given under chant, Gregorian, the following will be useful to the reader: Pierik, Marie, *The Psalter in the Temple and the Church* (Washington, D. C., 1957); Lindemann, Herbert and Newman Powell, *The Sunday Psalter* (St. Louis, 1961); Christensen, Albert and Harold Schuneman, *Proper of the Service* (New York, 1947).

See also: canonical hours; canticle; chant, Anglican; chant, Gregorian; church modes; church music history, medieval; *HCM*, III, IV

Renaissance instruments

Before 1400, instrumentalists generally accompanied singing; after that time they gradually became more independent and took over all kinds of vocal forms in addition to their own dance music. As late as the 17th century, printed collections of music bore the indication, "to be sung or played." Styles characteristic of certain instruments also began to be developed, and composers created exclusive instrumental forms of composition.

Instruments between 1400 and 1600 were made in families or *consorts* and were often played in these homogeneous groups. As the number of voice

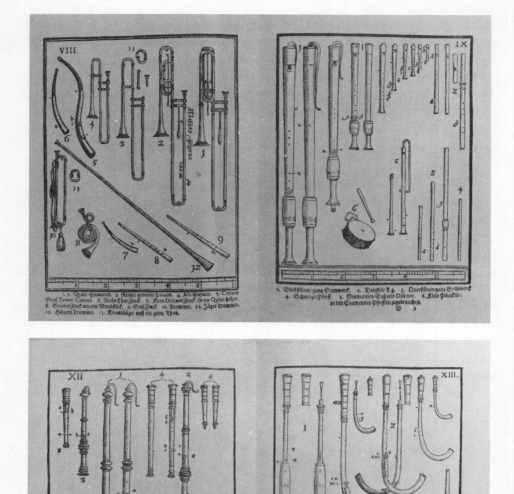

Typical Renaissance instruments as depicted in Michael Praetorius' *Theatrum instrumentorum* of 1620.

parts increased in 16th-century compositions, so did the number of instrument sizes within a family.

Stringed Instruments

lute. One of the most popular instruments of this period, the lute was derived from the Arabian *al'ud.* It was pear-shaped with an elongated neck at the end of which was a pegbox placed at a right angle. By the year 1500 the lute had six strings tuned G, C, F, A, D, and g. The neck was fretted at half-step distances. The ribs of the sound box were usually made of sycamore; sometimes of ebony, rosewood, cypress, sandalwood, or ivory. During the 16th century many transcriptions of dance music or of songs appeared in lute tablature.

vihuela. This Spanish lute had a flat back and was generally plucked with the fingers from the 16th century on. It had five double strings and one single string just like the lute and was also tuned similarly.

guitar. In the second half of the 16th century the guitar became very popular in Spain. The Spanish guitar had five strings while the continental guitar had four strings. Unlike the lute, its sound box had a flat chest.

cittern. This short-lived stringed instrument was popular with the upper middle classes in the 16th century. It had a flat back, a fairly elongated neck, and metallic double strings.

harp. The continental harp remained diatonic during the renaissance, but it received a greater number of strings. This caused the frame to be strengthened, and so the harp increased in size and weight.

viola da gamba. The large bowed medieval fiddle developed into the viol during the 15th century. The tenor viol was the standard member of the viol family. The tuning of the six strings was identical with the lute, so any lutenist could learn to play the viol without much difficulty. The sound box, generally with a flat back, often terminated in a point at the top. The C-shaped sound holes were placed symmetrically on each side of the bridge. The neck had frets like the lute and ended in a pegbox which bent backwards. This same structure served all the viols of the viola da gamba family from the smallest (pardessus de viole, about 2' long) to the double bass viol (7' long).

viola da braccio. This instrument developed from the small medieval fiddle. Its belly and back were slightly humped and edged with inlaid threads. The upper part of the sound box was rounded. It was not fretted but had a bent-back pegbox like the lute. It had four strings and the sound holes were in the shape of two C's, one superposed and reversed (♉). The viola da braccio family included the four-stringed instruments that extended from the violin down to the cello.

lira da braccio. Another bowed stringed instrument, the lira da braccio was popular in Italy from the 14th to the 16th centuries. It had a straight pegbox and five strings, the two longest of which were placed off the neck and served as drones. The tuning was in fifths.

Wind Instruments

recorder. During this period the recorder was made in various sizes. Praetorius, in the early 17th century, mentions nine sizes; the smallest was about 8″ long and the great bass was 6′ 6″ long.

flageolet. Popular with all classes of society, this instrument was invented in Paris in 1581. It had six holes, four in front and two in back. It soon was called the flauto piccolo and was the highest instrument of the orchestra.

transverse flute. This instrument was represented by a family of four differently pitched flutes. It continued to have a cylindrical bore.

shawm. The double reeds were the principal reed instruments and developed from the medieval shawm. The shawm was the most popular of the higher-pitched double reeds. It had a narrow and slightly conical bore, and its double reed remained uncovered. There were seven holes in the shawm, the last one of which was fitted with an open key.

pommer. The pommer was a lower-pitched double reed. It also had a narrow and slightly conical bore with an open double reed. Like the shawm, it had seven holes with an open key fitted to the last hole. Since the pommer was quite long, it had a crook like the bass recorder, and the double reed was fixed to the end of it. There were seven sizes of pommers.

curtal (Ger.: *Kortholt*). This was another double reed with its reed enclosed in a cap. The bore was cylindrical, and it was bent back in the shape of a "U" at its lower end and terminated in a flared bell.

hautbois. At the end of the 15th century, hautbois and shawm were sometimes used to designate any double reed instrument, whatever size or shape. During the 17th century, the name hautbois gradually replaced shawm.

bassoon (Ger.: *Fagott*; Fr.: *doucaine*; Eng.: *dulzian*; Sp.: *bajon*). This instrument developed from the pommer in the 16th century. It was constructed of two adjacent tubes coupled at the bottom to form a single tube of double length. The bassoon also appeared in different sizes.

sordone. Among double-reed instruments with a cylindrical bore was the sordone, made in five different sizes. It was low in pitch and bored in a single piece of wood with a hole in the side which served as a bell.

racket. This instrument consisted of a short, squat, ivory cylinder, in which were bored parallel channels joined to make one continuous tube. A crook was attached to the top of the first channel and contained the double reed. The crook and part of the reed were covered in an ivory protective shield. Around the body of the instrument were 12 holes connected with one or another of the channels at different levels. It produced a sweet but weak sound.

crumhorn. Enjoying great importance during this period, the crumhorn was made of a wooden tube, fairly thin and bent downwards. The double reed was enclosed in a cap, preventing contact with the player's lips. The crumhorn was also made in various sizes. The complete family was known in France already in the 15th century. In 1459 the name appeared in a document to designate an organ voice.

cornett (Ger.: *Zink*). The cornett obtained widespread use during the 16th and 17th centuries. It was made of an animal horn originally, later of ivory or wood. The highest-pitched of the cornett family had a straight tube, while the others had a curved form. Its timbre blended well with the human voice, and so it was used to double or replace singers.

trumpet. The 16th century trumpet was very much like the modern instrument. It had a narrower bell and deeper mouthpiece. It had a soft sound and could participate well in chamber music. Five sizes were designated as Clarino, Quinto, Alto, Vulgaro, and Basso. A more developed technique was required to play the high Clarini, and so players of these instruments formed a guild of true virtuosi.

sackbut (It.: *trombone;* Ger.: *Posaune*). The name sackbut was used in the 15th and 16th centuries to denote a bass trumpet. The sackbut had two straight tubes, parallel and joined to one another by a third tube, which was bent double and could slide along the first two. Sackbuts were used in festive mass celebration in the 16th century and made their way into the opera orchestras in the 17th century.

Percussion Instruments

timpanum. The timpanum or kettledrum was very much like the modern kettledrum, except that it lacked the keys around its circumference to vary the tension of the skin. The instrument was generally mounted in counterbalanced pairs, one on each side of a horse, upon which the player rode. Kettledrums, played on horseback, became one of the symbols of power, and in the 17th century in northern Europe, no one under the rank of baron was allowed to own them.

xylophone. This was another name for the medieval échelette. It was well known for its dry and sharp sounds and often appears in paintings on the "dances of death" theme.

bells. Manually operated chime bells survived into the 15th century. After bells were installed in church towers and belfries, the use of a cylinder replaced the manual operation. In the 16th century, chime bells were given a keyboard, thus becoming the carillon. After this time, clock towers and belfries included more and more bells, especially in Flanders.

Keyboard Instruments

harpsichord. This instrument continued to enrich its tonal possibilities during the Renaissance. Combinations of stops (4', 8', 16') became more numerous. Since it did not have a very extensive keyboard, its lower octave was reduced, retaining only diatonic notes, except for B♭, allowing the instrument to reach the lowest note possible (the "short octave").

The harpsichord had a wing-shaped soundboard, and its strings ran at right angles to the length of the keyboard. The spinet also had a wing-shaped soundboard placed sideways with the strings parallel to the length of the keyboard. On the other hand, the virginal was contained in a rectangular case with its strings placed in a slanting position in relation to the keyboard.

clavichord. The only keyboard instrument with struck strings was the clavichord. Until the 18th century, the clavichord had more keys than strings. This "fretted" mechanism made it impossible to play two sounds belonging to the same string at the same time. One of its unique characteristics, however, was its ability to produce a vibrato tone. When the metal tangent struck the key, it remained in contact with it as long as the player's finger did not leave the key. By applying a gentle, rapid repeated pressure to the key, a quivering sound was produced (Ger.: *Bebung*).

organ. Some important modifications and additions were made to the organ during the Renaissance. The pedal board was invented in 1306. A second manual keyboard appeared in 1386. Many solo stops were added; such as oboe, flute, crumhorn, and trumpet. In general, the overall number of pipes continually increased. In 1429 the full organ at Amiens had 2,000 pipes. In the latter part of the 15th century, German and Flemish organ makers were producing stopped pipes, pipes of inverted conical bore, and reed pipes. In 1491 the tremolo stop appeared at Hagenau. Compositions specifically designated for the organ began to appear after 1450.

The regal organ appeared for the first time in 1519. It comprised a single rank of beating reed pipes. The air was blown through a pair of bellows operated by an assistant. It was used wherever a full church organ could not be afforded.

In 1550 a regal organ of a small size was invented whose keyboard and reed pipes could be taken apart and fitted into a large hollowed-out imitation "Bible." It was thus called a Bible regal. ERi

Readings: Bragard, Roger and Ferdinand J. De Hen, *Musical Instruments in Art and History* (New York, 1968); Harrison, Frank and Joan Rimmer, *European Musical Instruments* (London 1964); Praetorius, Michael, *Theatrum Instrumentorum,* supplement to *Syntagma musicum*, Band II, reprint of 1620 edition (Kassel, 1958); Sachs, Curt, *The History of Musical Instruments* (New York, 1940).

See also: baroque instruments; church music history, Renaissance—the Latin tradition; church music history, Renaissance—the Reformation tradition; medieval instruments; organ, history

Roman school

A group of composers, active in Rome during the last half of the 16th century and first half of the 17th century, who wrote church music rooted in the style of 16th-century Flemish polyphony, in contrast to the more adventurous style of the composers of Venetian polychoral music, monody, and the madrigal. The leading figure of the Roman School was Giovanni Pierluigi da Palestrina (c. 1525—94).

The Council of Trent met intermittently from 1545 to 1563, and was but one part of the larger movement known as the Counter Reformation, which sought to purify, strengthen, and revitalize the entire church in the face of threatening forces from within and without its domain. Some of the most significant legislation arising from the council concerned the organization and practice of the liturgy. The nature of music appropriate for worship was discussed at length, and the resulting brief observations exercised a profound influence on Roman Catholic church music during the following four centuries. Music with specifically secular associations was considered "lascivious and impure"; a simple style of composition was favored, for the sacred texts were not to be obscured by confusing polyphony.

The musical style favored by the council was in many respects already being practiced by the Flemish composers Nicolas Gombert (c.1500—c. 1556), a pupil of Josquin Desprez (c. 1440—1521), Jacob Clement (c. 1510—c. 1556), and Jacob Arcadelt (c. 1505—68). During the course of its sessions the Council examined a variety of polyphonic works composed in the reformed idiom (including Masses by Palestrina and Orlando di Lasso (1532—94), but apparently was particularly impressed by the polyphonic *Preces speciales* (Special Prayers) of Jacobus de Kerle (c. 1531—91), which were frequently performed for the council.

One of the earliest Italian composers to adopt the northern contrapuntal practice was Constanzo Festa (c. 1490—1545). Others were Gasparo Alberti (c. 1480—1560) and Giovanni Animuccia (c. 1500—71). The Roman composer who most successfully combined adherence to the new decree with artistic imagination, consummate musical skill, and deep spiritual devotion was Palestrina. His compositions, nearly all sacred works, have been studied and analyzed with great care by generations of students: his style of writing has been consciously imitated by hosts of composers during and following his lifetime, not only because of its virtual canonization by the church as the ideal style of sacred music, but also because of its high intrinsic merit.

The Palestrina style is variously called *stile grave* (severe style), *stile antico* (old style), *stile a cappella* (choir style), and *stile osservato* or *legato* ("strict," "bound," or "smooth" style) with reference to particular aspects of the writing. While each appellation is valid, the first three terms require clarification. The music of Palestrina appears in print to be somewhat more severe or restrained than it really was. Contemporary evidence has established the prevalence in performance of improvised ornamentation, particularly diminution (breaking up larger intervals into smaller notes), in much of the choral polyphony of the Roman school, including that of Palestrina. Palestrina's composition was not "out of date" in its age. Rather, it was highly praised and defended by his contemporaries for its perfection. It was often referred to as the "first practice" of those contemporaries interested in the new monody and concerted music. Most composers of the age considered skill in writing Flemish counterpoint a normal part of their craft. For example, the Venetian composers Adrian Willaert (c. 1490—1562), Gioseffo Zarlino (1517—90), and Giovanni

Gabrieli (c. 1555—1612), all wrote in the so-called *stile antico*. Even the progressive Claudio Monteverdi (1567—1643) wrote some liturgical pieces in the Roman style. The term *a cappella* may be misleading as descriptive of Palestrina's style, for it identifies as normal a performance practice actually distinguished by its rarity. It was common for choral music of the Palestrina-style to be performed with instruments doubling the voice parts.

It is in Palestrina's Masses that his coolly objective style is most fully articulated. These works, usually written for four voices, present the liturgical texts clearly, adhering faithfully to the natural Latin accents. Dramatic points are delicately highlighted without resorting to exaggerated madrigalisms. The works breathe the spirit of Gregorian chant; even when a Gregorian *cantus firmus* does not form the basis of a Mass (an occurrence found in only 23 of 102 Masses), individual voices proceed with the smooth linear motion of the chant. The predominant contrapuntal texture is occasionally contrasted with areas written in chordlike style. The harmonies formed by the combined voices are drawn from the nonchromatic vocabulary now called triads and first-inversion chords. Dissonant tones are carefully prepared and controlled. Each voice moves in an independent rhythmic pattern, which, when combined with the rhythms of other voices, creates a highly sophisticated polyrhythmic texture.

Palestrina, who spent his entire life in Rome, serving at various times in each of the major musical churches of the city (St. Peter, St. Mary the Greater, and St. John Lateran), exerted considerable influence over his pupils, colleagues, and successors.

After Palestrina, the leading Roman composers are Ruggiero Giovannelli (c. 1560—1625), Giovanni Maria Nanino (c. 1545—1607), Annibale Stabile (c. 1535—95), Annibale Zoilo (c. 1537—92), Giovanni Dragoni (c. 1540—98), Felice Anerio (1560—1614), Francesco Soriano (1549—1620), Giovanni F. Anerio (c. 1567—1630), Gregorio Allegri (1582—1652), and Francesco Foggia (c. 1604—88).

Spanish musicians contributed significantly to composition in the Roman style, even though not all were residents of the Eternal City. Tomás Luis de Victoria (c. 1535/48—1611), who spent most of his productive life in Rome, was probably the most gifted composer of the Roman School next to Palestrina. All of his compositions were written for the church; they demonstrate, in addition to technical mastery, the mystical intensity and devotion often associated with Spanish religious music. Other

Spanish composers active in Rome were Cristóbal de Morales (c. 1500—53), Bartolomé Escobedo (c. 1515—63), Francisco Guerrero (c. 1527—99), and Juan Pujol (1573—1626).

In spite of the preeminence of Palestrina, the Roman School was not unaffected by the characteristic grandeur and spectacle of the burgeoning baroque period anticipated in the works of Giovanni Gabrieli and other composers of the Venetian School. After Palestrina's death a growing number of composers tried to combine the master's serene, restrained counterpoint with the sonorous and impressive Venetian style. The result was the creation of pompous works for several choirs of voices and instruments. The most prominent figure in this movement, called the "colossal baroque," was Orazio Benevoli (1605—72), a director of music at St. Peter's after 1646 and composer of a famous Mass for several choirs of voices and instruments—a total of 53 parts—for the dedication of the Salzburg Cathedral. Other composers in this extravagant style were Pablo Agostini (1593—1629), Antonio M. Abbatini (c. 1595—1680), Virgilio Mazzocchi (1597—1646), and Domenico Mazzocchi (1592—1665).

The durability of the Palestrina style through the 18th century is attested to by the *Gradus ad Parnassum* (1725) of Johann J. Fux (1660—1741), an immensely popular treatise supposedly based on Palestrina's style. In spite of its weaknesses, not the least of which is its disparity with Palestrina's actual practice, it is a remarkably effective pedagogical tool for the teaching of counterpoint and served as a guide for composers wishing to write in an approved "sacred" style.

The influence of the Roman School continued in the church long after the passing of its leading composers; the name of Palestrina was often evoked as a symbol of propriety and his style regarded as the proper ecclesiastical mode of composition. It was often reserved for use in the penitential Advent and Lenten seasons (hence the designation of some *a cappella* Masses as *Missae quadragesimales* (Masses of the Forty Days). Even where the Palestrina contrapuntal style was not faithfully perpetuated, elements of it were incorporated into other styles of composition as signs of "churchliness."

In the 19th century a formal movement to raise musical standards in the church and to revive the Palestrina style of composition took shape in the organization of the Caecilian Society in Germany in 1868 by Franz Xaver Witt (1834—88). The motu proprio *Tra le sollecitudine* (1903) of Pope Pius X decreed the music of Palestrina to be a model of church music composition. CM

Readings: Abraham, Gerald, ed., *The Age of Humanism (1540—1630)*, vol. IV of *New Oxford History of Music*, ed. J. A. Westrup *et al.* (London, 1968); Apel, Willi, ed., *Harvard Dictionary of Music*, 2d ed. rev. and enl. (Cambridge, Mass., 1969); Fellerer, Karl Gustav, *The History of Catholic Church Music*, tr. Francis A. Brunner (Baltimore, 1961); Grout, Donald J., *A History of Western Music*, rev. ed. (New York, 1973); Jeppesen, Knud, *The Style of Palestrina and the Dissonance* (London, 1927); Reese, Gustave, *Music in the Renaissance*, 2d ed. (New York, 1959).

See also: Caecilian movement; catholic pronouncements and decrees on church music; church music history, Renaissance—the Latin tradition; polychoral style; Venetian school

sequence

A form of Gregorian chant sung in the Roman rite after the gradual and Alleluia and before the Gospel lesson. Sequences were first written beginning about the 9th century and flourished from the 11th century to the reform of the mass at the Council of Trent in the 16th century, by which time sequences had been appointed for almost every day in the church year and for all the saints' days. At the Council of Trent the Roman Catholic church decreed that sequences could no longer be used. Four exceptions were allowed: *Victimae paschali* for Easter, *Veni, Sancte Spiritus* for Pentecost, *Lauda Sion Salvatorem* for the Feast of Corpus Christi, and *Dies irae* at masses for the dead. In 1727 a fifth sequence was also allowed, the *Stabat mater* for the Feast of the Seven Sorrows of the Blessed Virgin Mary. (These sequences may be found in *The Hymnal 1940*, Nos. 97, 109, 193—194, 468, and 76. The Latin texts and melodies are found in *Liber Usualis.*)

The predominant formal feature of the sequence is the repetition of musical phrases, resulting in a succession of paired lines of varying length and accentual structure. The early structure, which began and concluded with a single line may be diagrammed as follows: a–bb–cc–dd . . .x. Later developments included more regular versification and the occasional use of actual rhyme. The pattern of repetition became the standard form during the "middle period" of sequence composition during the 11th century. In the "later period" sequences became so highly formal in structure that they approximated the strophic forms of hymns. Adam of St. Victor (d. 1192), a Parisian monk, is the most famous writer of these later sequences.

His works are almost always in strict double versicles (aa-bb-cc-dd-ee-ff-gg etc.); the verses are of nearly equal length in recurring strophic structures (I: 8-8-7; II: 8-8-7).

The history of the sequence begins during the 9th-century Carolingian attempt to enforce a uniform liturgical practice on the Frankish empire. The arts, particularly those associated with the practice of worship, were also encouraged, with a resulting high level of virtuosity among the singers used in the mass. These singers apparently began to embroider the rigidly prescribed material of the official rite by singing long, textless melodies ("jubilations," Latin: *jubilus*) added to the end of the Alleluia on the concluding syllable "-ia." Amalar of Metz in the early 9th century speaks of rich additions of verses and sequences *(cum omni supplemento et excellentia versuum et sequentiarum).*

The first major figure (though certainly not the inventor) associated with the sequence is Notker the Stammerer *(Balbulus),* a monk of St. Gall in Switzerland. Late in the 9th century a monk fled to St. Gall before the Norman destruction of Jumiéges carrying a book with texts provided for the "most long melodies" of the jubilations *(longissimae melodiae),* which Notker found too long for easy memorization. Notker liked the idea of the texts but decided he could do better. As a result he wrote what is considered the first collection of texts for sequences, sometimes referred to as "proses" (from: *sequentia cum prosa*) or "sequence" (designating either the melody or the combination of melody and text). Thereafter, it was a

Comparison of Melodies
Based on the Easter Sequence

Sequence: *Victimae paschali (Liber Usualis,* p. 780)

Christ ist erstanden (The Lutheran Hymnal, No. 187)

Christ lag in Todesbanden (The Lutheran Hymnal, No. 195)

328

relatively simple thing to compose entirely new works, text and music, for insertion into the liturgy after the traditional Alleluias.

A classic example of an 11th-century sequence by Wipo of Burgundy is the *Victimae paschali,* which follows the structure a-bb-cc-d or, possibly a-bb-cd-cd-e. It will be noted that each verse incorporates internal assonance, as *paschali/Christiani, oves/peccatores, Maria/via,* etc. The only exception is the third verse.

The history of the sequences is particularly instructive to the modern church in that many sequence texts and melodies eventually became part of the church's hymnody. *Victimae paschali,* for example, is the source for the German chorales *Christ ist erstanden* and *Christ lag in Todesbanden,* as a comparison of the tunes will readily show. VG

Readings: Apel, W., "Sequence," *Harvard Dictionary of Music* (Cambridge, 1970); Apel, W., *Gregorian Chant* (Bloomington, 1966); Douglas, W., *Church Music in History and Practice* (New York, 1962).

See also: church music history, medieval; mass; trope; *HCM,* IV

Service

In Anglican churches, the portions of the liturgy that are sung by the choir, when composed in cyclical form, are collectively called a "Service."

Usually written in one key, a Service contains all or nearly all the invariable parts of Morning Prayer, The Communion, and Evening Prayer. In common practice it was chiefly the various canticles that received the greatest attention.

These texts are, in the Morning Service: the *Venite* (Ps. 95), the *Te Deum* or the *Benedictus es Domine* (from the apocryphal Song of the Three Children) or the *Benedicite* (a continuation of the above) and the *Benedictus* (Luke 1:68-79); in the Communion Service: the Decalog (Responses to the Ten Commandments) or the *Kyrie,* the *Credo* (Nicene Creed), the *Sanctus, the Benedictus qui venit,* (Matt. 21:9b) the *Agnus Dei,* and the *Gloria in excelsis;* in the Evening Service: the *Magnificat* (Luke 1:46-55 or *Cantate Domino* (Ps. 98) or *Bonum est confiteri* (Ps. 92), and the *Nunc dimittis* (Luke 2:29-32) or the *Deus misereatur* (Ps. 67) or *Benedic, anima mea* (Ps. 103:1-4, 20-22).

The *Venite* was not treated as a choral canticle after the Elizabethan era, and the Communion Service was usually limited to the Decalog or *Kyrie* and the *Credo.* The use of the new Book of Common Prayer after 1549 stimulated composers to set the *Te Deum* and the New Testament canticles listed above were used in their places. In the time of Charles I under had been set polyphonically. With the rise of Puritanism, the *Te Deum* and the New Testament canticles fell into disfavor and the alternate Psalms listed above were used in their places. In the time of Charles I under Archbishop Laud's influence, the *Sanctus* and *Gloria in excelsis* began to be set musically, a practice which became widespread in Queen Anne's reign in the 18th century. The *Benedictus qui venit* and *Agnus Dei* were added in the 19th century under the influence of the Oxford Movement.

An early model Service was the Dorian or Short Service, so called because of its direct, homophonic style, of Thomas Tallis (c. 1505—85). The Great Service—the term refers to a richer contrapuntal style—by William Byrd (1543—1623) is perhaps the outstanding choral work of the period in all Europe. Other composers of this period whose Services have remained in cathedral repertories are Thomas Morley (1557—1602), Thomas Tomkins (1572—1656), Thomas Weelkes (c. 1575—1623), and Orlando Gibbons (1583—1625). These men began by writing for full double choirs (of men and boys) which sang antiphonally and unaccompanied. Byrd began tentatively to set occasional verses for solo voices with organ accompaniment. This new style was developed into the Verse Service by his successors.

The mid-17th century Commonwealth in England saw a complete disruption of all cathedral choirs and service music. It took nearly another generation after the Restoration to rebuild cathedral choirs and service music to the former glory. The one outstanding new work was by Henry Purcell (c. 1659—95), the Service in B$\flat$, which has a fine, early setting of the *Benedicite*. In the 18th century, cathedral music was poorly supported and its new compositions uninspired. A few of the better Services are those of William Croft (1678—1727) in A, William Boyce (1710—79) in C, and John Clarke-Whitfield (1770—1836) in E.

In the 19th century the Oxford Movement, which led to a great revival of the use of plainsong and the sung, or fully choral, service, indirectly revived interest in cathedral music and helped restore many of the derelict choirs. This stirred fresh interest in the writing of Services on the part of Victorian composers. Among the best are John Goss (1800—80) in E, Samuel Sebastian Wesley (1810—76) in E, Thomas Attwood Walmisley (1814—56) in D minor, and Charles Villiers Stanford (1852—1924) in B$\flat$.

The Service has largely been a feature of the music in English cathedrals and collegiate churches where professional choirs of 20 to 50 men and boys have been maintained in connection with the cycle of daily worship. The 20th century has seen this cut back to the full cycle only on Sundays, maintaining daily Evensong (Evening Prayer). Native works that have found a permanent place in the repertory since 1900 are: Thomas Tertius Noble's (1867—1953) student Evening Service in B minor and a later Communion Service in the same key, Ralph Vaughan Williams' (1872—1958) in D minor, Herbert Howells' (b. 1892) St. Paul's Service, Michael Tippett's (b. 1905) Evening Service "Collegium Sancti Johannis Cantabrigiense," and Kenneth Leighton's (b. 1929) Missa brevis, op. 50.

In America the use of Services on Sundays and at Evensong has been a feature of the music in only a few cathedrals and larger parish churches. Hence no full services have been composed here, but there are a number of good, partial ones. Outstanding among these are the Horatio Parker (1863—1919) Evening Service in E, the David McK. Williams (b. 1887) unison Evening Service in A minor, Harold Friedell's (d. 1958) Evening Service in F, Leo Sowerby's (1895—1968) Communion Service in G and Evening Service in D, and Ronald Arnatt's (b. 1930) "Communion Service for the people" set for choir with unison congregation, brass instruments, and organ.

A development of the second quarter of the 20th century was the introduction of Services for unison voices. These have been particularly useful for nonprofessional parish choirs. A number of fine Morning, Communion, and Evening unison Services have been composed on both sides of the Atlantic. LE

Readings: Fellows, E. H., *English Cathedral Music*, rev. ed. by J. A. Westrup (London, 1969); Long, K. R., *The Music of the English Church* (New York, 1971); Shaw, W., "Church Music in England from the Reformation to the Present Day," *Protestant Church Music* (New York, 1974).

See also: canticle; church music history, baroque; *HCM,* I

tablature

The term tablature (from the German *Tabulatur*) is applied to the notation of early keyboard and instrumental music, in which pitches are indicated by letters or figures rather than by notes on a staff. Such symbols were used primarily in the notation of lute and keyboard music written during the 15th, 16th, and 17th centuries. There are three principal methods of lute tablature—Italian, French, and German. Of the two main types of keyboard tablature—Spanish and German—only the latter will be taken up here. For a discussion of those systems not treated here see the suggestions for further reading.

Old German Keyboard Tablature

Early German keyboard music used the so-called old German tablature—a semi-tablature with the uppermost voice notated on a staff and the lower voices written beneath it in letters. Some of the important collections in the old German tablature include:

"Old German" tablature with partial transcription. Basel, Universitaetsbibliothek Ms. F. IX. 22.

"Old German" partial transcription

Buxheimer Orgelbuch, c. 1460; Arnolt Schlick, *Tabulaturen etlicher Lobgesang und Lauten*, 1512; Basel, Universitaetsbibliothek Ms. F.IX.22 (Hans Kotter), 1513—32; Basel, Universitaetsbibliothek Ms. F.IX.58 (Hans Kotter), c. 1525; Johannes Buchner, *Fundamentum*, c. 1525; Berlin, Deutsche Staatsbibliothek Ms. 40026 (Leonhard Kleber), 1522—24; St. Gall, Stiftsbibliothek Ms. 530 (Fridolin Sicher), c. 1520; Cracow, Academy of Sciences Ms. 1716 (Jan de Lublin), 1537—48; and the Cracow Tablature, 1548.

To distinguish the various registers of the lettered parts, the intabulators use a large letter for the great octave, a small letter for the small octave, and dashes over small notes for the upper octaves. Changes of register occur on each *b-natural*.

Chromatic alterations include the pitches *c-sharp, d-sharp*, (transcribed as *e-flat*), *f-sharp, g-sharp*, and *b-flat*. The tone *b-flat* is indicated by the letter *b; b-natural* by the letter *h*. On the staff chromatic inflections of the pitches *c, d, f, g*, and *h* are indicated by a diagonal slash in a line below the note.

Rhythmic values are indicated above the notes or letters and are grouped into units equal to the semibreve. Either a small space or a vertical line serves to separate units of tactus.

New German Keyboard Tablature

The so-called new German keyboard tablature was introduced in 1571 by Elias Nicholaus Ammerbach (c. 1530—97). In this type of tablature all of the parts are represented by letters. Some of the important extant collections in new German tablature include:

Elias Nicholaus Ammerbach, *Orgel oder Instrument Tabulatur*, 1571; Elias Nicholaus Ammerbach, *Ein new kuenstlich Tabulaturbuch*, 1575; Elias Nicholaus Ammerbach, *Orgel oder Instrument Tabulatur*, 1583; Bernhard Schmid, the elder, *Zwey Buechner Einer Neuen Kuenstlichen Tabulatur auff Orgel und Instrument*, 1577; Johann Ruehling, *Tabulaturbuch auff Orgeln und Instrument*, 1583; Jacob Paix, *Ein Schoen Nuetz und Gebreuchlich Orgel Tabulaturbuch,* 1583; Jacob Paix, *Thesaurus Motetarum*, 1589; Basel, Universitaetsbibliothek Ms. F.IX.44 (Ruehling), 1583; Berlin, Deutsche Staatsbibliothek Ms. 40034 (Christoph Loeffelholtz), 1585; Dresden, Saechsische Landesbibliothek Ms. F.307m (*Tabulatur Buch Auff dem Instrument Christianus Hertzogk zu Sachsen*), c. 1580; Bernhard Schmid, the younger, *Tabulaturbuch von Allerhand ausserlesenen*, 1607; and Johann Woltz *Nova musices organicae tabulatura*, 1617.

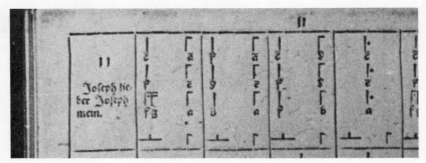

"New German" tablature with partial transcription. Munich, Bayerische Staatsbibliothek, Elias Nicholaus Ammerbach, *Orgel oder Instrument Tabulatur,* 1583, No. 11.

"New German" partial transcription

In the new German keyboard tablature the various octaves are distinguished in much the same fashion, as in the old tablature and the symbols for chromatic alteration are retained. Two important differences, however, reflect the expansion of the range of the keyboard and the redefinition of rhythmic values. HM

Readings: Apel, Willi, "Tablature," *Harvard Dictionary of Music,* 2d ed. (Cambridge, 1969); Apel, Willi, *The Notation of Polyphonic Music 900—1600,* 5th ed. (Cambridge, 1961); Blom, Eric, ed., "Tablature," *Grove's Dictionary of Music and Musicians,* 5th ed. (London, 1954).

See also: notation

theology of church music, early church fathers

Early Christian music was closely associated with the liturgy, and like the liturgy itself, was strongly influenced by Jewish synagog worship. St. Paul reflected this influence when he encouraged Christians to "sing psalms and hymns and spiritual songs to the Lord" (Col. 3:16, Eph. 5:19).

For centuries Jewish worship was centered on the chanting of the psalms, which were ordinarily sung by the cantor alternating with a choir or congregation. Services were held at fixed times of the day or night, and Christians continued the practice. New Testament songs, such as that of Mary, Simeon, Zechariah, were added to the Old Testament canticles, such as the song of Moses (Ex. 15:1-9) in early Christian hymnody. Although hymn singing was accepted as part of the Jewish heritage, most early churchmen condemned the use of any texts not taken directly from the Bible. Outside the New Testament there is evidence in Pliny's letter to Trajan (c. 112 A.D.) that Christians used hymns in worship, but the earliest example of a Christian hymn fragment with music comes from Egypt late in the 3d century (the so-called Oxyrhnchus hymn). Spiritual songs were the Alleluias and other exultant songs of praise which also came from the synagog. From the very beginning of Christian worship liturgical chant was an integral part of the service.

Despite the growing popularity of music in the liturgy, many churchmen viewed this trend with considerable reserve. They were especially opposed to the use of musical instruments to support the singing. Clement of Alexandria, who lived in the latter 2d and early 3d centuries, understood the Biblical references to instruments as referring to spiritual realities: the harp was Christ, the pipe was the Spirit, and a new song meant faith. Basil of Caesarea (c. 330—379) believed that music had an educational value, "that through the softness of the sound we might unawares receive what is useful in the words," but he opposed the use of the cithera or lyre. John Chrysostom (c. 347—407) was positive in his attitude toward music, citing Paul's song in prison as an example (Acts 16:25). The use of sacred songs, he said, lends itself to the worship of God by all sorts of people under many conditions: travelers, sailors, housewives, merchants, old and young. "But you have no need for the cithera, or for stretched strings, or for the plectrum, or for any instruments." Jerome (c. 348—c. 420) was not as positive as Chrysostom. Commenting on Eph. 5:19 he wrote, "Sing to God not with the voice but with the heart, and seek to please Him with your knowledge of Scripture rather than the noise of song." But Jerome also speaks of the office of a singer, indicating that by 400 A.D. there was a special person or group within the church whose task it was to lead in song. Athanasius (c. 296—373) is cited by Augustine as recommending that a chant should resemble speech as much as possible, "with little wavering of the voice." Churchmen were unanimous in their caution against the kind of tunes that would excite passions.

During the second half of the 4th century significant liturgical and musical advances had been made in Rome and Milan. Ambrose (340—397), bishop of Milan, established the singing of hymns and antiphonal psalmody as part of the Milanese liturgy. He also composed several hymns to popularize the orthodox doctrine of the Trinity such as "O Splendor of God's Glory Bright," and "O Trinity, Most Blessed Light." The Ambrosian liturgy was the first of four great Western liturgies which had significant influence on church music (others are the Mozarabic, Gallican, and Roman). The inclusion of Ambrose' hymns in the Benedictine Rule (526 A.D.) was the first time hymns officially became a part of prescribed liturgical practice.

Augustine (354—430), a disciple of Ambrose, took delight in congregational singing. "What better thing can the people do than sing? I know of nothing better than that." He encouraged his monks to sing while at work, but he also cautioned against music that made an excessive appeal to the emotions through tunes that called attention to themselves instead of to the text. Augustine was the first Christian to compose a treatise on music (*De musica*), but, strangely, the work does not discuss music in Christian life or worship.

Music became a fixed part of the Roman liturgy during the 4th century, where boys trained in special schools alternated in the chant with men and women. The establishment of the *schola cantorum* (school for singers) in the 5th century assured a vigorous musical life in the Roman church and the West. The cultivation and composition of plainsong chant was a primary concern of all Roman bishops since 400 A.D., but it was under Gregory I (c. 540—604) that liturgical chant took its definite and typical form which has become known as Gregorian.

The change in attitude of churchmen toward music, from suspicion to acceptance, was due in part to the conversion of the empire after Constantine (c. 274—337). In place of the catacombs and house churches there were now large basilicas and elaborate ceremonial. The chanted liturgy was more audible in these massive structures than the spoken word. When Christians were in the minority, music and the use of instruments were viewed as part of pagan culture, but when the empire became Christian the church felt more comfortable and less threatened by adapting to its own use what had earlier been suspect.

In the 6th century two prominent churchmen wrote positive treatises on the use of music. Boethius (c. 475—524) wrote *De institutione musica*, in which he transmitted the knowledge of ancient Greek music to the Middle Ages, and Cassiodorus (c. 475—c. 570) developed a philosophy of music in his *Institutes*, (Ch. 5), in which he said, "Music is closely bound up with religion itself. It lifts our sense to celestial things." But even these later fathers retained a certain ambivalence toward music, noting that it could both enhance or detract from the devout life. CV

Readings: McKinney, H. D. and W. R. Anderson, "Roman and Early Christian Music," *Music in History* (New York, 1940); Strunk, O., "The Early Christian View of Music," *Source Readings in Music History* (New York, 1950); Wellesz, E., "Early Christian Music," *Early Medieval Music up to 1300,* in *The New Oxford History of Music* (Oxford, 1954).

See also; canticle; church music history, Jewish; church music history, medieval; hymnody, Old Testament; hymnody, New Testament; hymnody, Greek; hymnody, Latin; medieval instruments

theology of church music, Reformers

Theology and music interacted rather strongly in the Reformation period because the rejection of Roman Catholic practices and the reform of the liturgy made necessary a new rationale for the use of music. The principal exponents of the reformers' positions are Martin Luther, John Calvin, and Ulrich Zwingli. Their varied viewpoints cluster around a common concern for worship but radiate along very different lines to produce widely separated results. At issue seems to be the consistency with which a theological position can be maintained in spite of pragmatic fears for the misuse of music.

Martin Luther

Martin Luther (1483—1546) is a clear example of theological consistency in understanding music. Luther was a singer, lutenist, and composer of some skill, a fact that may have aided in his development of a high regard for music. In his earlier, monastic period Luther recognized the power of music to move the emotions and consequently downgraded secular, worldly songs for their pernicious moral effects. His views were expressed with considerably different emphasis later in life, however, after he had come to grips with the full meaning of the Gospel, the power of God's Word, and joyful freedom—parts of the new life of God's people.

In 1530 Luther outlined a treatise on music, which he never finished.

The key sentence in that document, taken from Augustine, unlocks Luther's ideas about music: "For music is a gift and largess of God, not a gift of men." Luther saw music as part of God's creation, for there is a type of music in all things, from the sound of the wind to the song of the birds. That is natural music (*musica naturalis*). When man properly develops this gift of music into art (*musica artificialis*), he can fully adore the wisdom of God in creating it. Music, then, is God's creature with an existence all its own and with the power to praise God. This is radically different than saying music is a product of human art or an expression of human feelings.

The power of music, used for good purpose, could produce the same effects as the Word of the Gospel. Luther therefore honored music next to theology for its ability to witness to the joy of the redemption, claiming that "experience proves that, next to the Word of God, only music deserves being extolled as the mistress and governess of the feelings of the human heart. . . . For this reason the fathers and prophets desired not in vain that nothing be more intimately linked up with the Word of God than music." Music chased the devil from men's hearts, revealed the full wisdom of God, and proclaimed the Gospel. The last feature was especially characteristic. Music was a proclamation of God's Word. To "sing and say" the Gospel was a single concept, resulting from the inevitable eruption of joyful song in the heart of the Christian. "If any would not sing and talk of what Christ has wrought for us, he shows thereby that he does not really believe and that he belongs not into the New Testament, which is an era of joy, but into the Old, which produces not the spirit of joy, but of unhappiness and discontent."

Luther's reliance on the Gospel was consistent, even in his attitudes toward music, and brought him later to a more sweeping approval of all music than is found in his youthful writings. He insisted that children and young people must be thoroughly trained in music. Luther zealously promoted the singing of hymns by the congregation and the making of music in the home. Churchmen must be well trained in music. "A teacher must be able to sing; otherwise I will not as much as look at him. Also, we should not ordain young men into the ministry unless they have become well acquainted with music in the schools."

The music Luther was talking about in this way included not only the best in the tradition of folk song. Far more was Luther enchanted by God's gift of music in the very sophisticated art forms of the great composers of his time, such as Josquin Desprez and Ludwig Senfl—both Catholics. This music was to be taught to churchmen and to youth. Even music based on objectionable texts was to be revised and sung by Christians in a wholesome manner, so that Satan would not have all the good tunes.

Luther believed the Gospel allowed Christians the freedom to use all music without fear of sin. Such attitudes made possible the cultivation of the highest art, also in worship, without fear of worldliness or sin.

John Calvin

John Calvin (1509—64), the Reformed leader from Geneva, would have agreed with Luther that music is a gift of God and that its proper work is to praise God. It is capable of this work because of its power to fire the heart of the believer in the act of adoring God. Moreover, music can provide the proper "affect," without which a right understanding of the Word is impossible. Calvin could not, however, shake off a fear of the power of music. He believed that experience showed the proper use of music according to its creaturely function to be very rare. The Christian should, therefore, avoid the dangerous power of music as much as possible. These dangerous powers were due both to the explicit evil of coarse, ungodly texts and to the subtle dangers of aesthetic pleasure.

Where Luther was exhilarated by the pleasures of music, Calvin saw such pleasure as a distraction from the Word of God. The Word, in fact, was so predominant in Calvin's theology that it tended to exclude other considerations. Where Luther joined music to the Word because of their similar effects, Calvin limited this union to the single function of making the Word more understandable. Music was a "funnel," directing the Word into the heart of the believer. For this reason Calvin rejected all instrumental music and all polyphony. These idioms obscured the pure statement of the Scriptural text.

The practical result of this position has been called a kind of musical Puritanism. Calvin rejected the use of all instruments and the choir in worship in favor of congregational song which was to be as simple as possible. The congregation was to sing in unison, unaccompanied, both in the vernacular rhymed Psalm texts and some New Testament canticles. Other texts had no Biblical precedent and were excluded. The music of these settings was to have a certain gravity (*poids*) and solemnity (*majesté*), the characteristics basic to any church style.

Although Calvin's severe regulations were relaxed somewhat shortly after his death, his influence was enormous. The Reformed churches throughout Europe developed a magnificent practice of congregational song, however limited it was in the strict use of Psalms. Above all, it is Calvin who laid the foundations for the separation of sacred and secular music in terms of style, with the resulting isolation of church music from music in general and the secularization of aesthetic values in later centuries.

Ulrich Zwingli

Ulrich Zwingli (1484—1531), the third great reformer to have defined a music practice, is perhaps the most puzzling. Zwingli was a cultivated person who had some skill in music and expressed high regard for the art—but only in private house gatherings. He rejected all forms of music in worship, a fact that must be seen in close relationship to his concept of worship. Worship, for Zwingli, took place in a spiritualistic (i.e., abstracted) singing in the heart, as opposed to literal singing with the mouth. It was the moment of silence before God that constituted the real, undisturbed dialog with the Almighty to which all Christians aspired. Song only disturbed this dialog because of the sensual distraction of the music and because it drew one's thoughts into the whole of the congregation. Zwingli, therefore, located the action of the worship in the heart of the individual, not in the community of believers.

It is important to appreciate the wholeness of Luther's theological position in comparison with the Reformed views. His view of Christian joy and freedom permeated all aspects of music and all of life. Calvin, on the other hand, separates radically a sacred and a secular style, with the resulting failure of "sacred" music to demonstrate its relevance to the rest of life. Zwingli, even more radically, restricts music to strictly extraliturgical situations, refusing to allow one of the creatures of God to perform the function of a worshiping creature. VG

Readings: Blankenburg, W., "Church Music in Reformed Europe," *Protestant Church Music* (New York, 1974); Buszin, W., "Luther on Music," Pamphlet Series, No. 3 (1958); Kurzschenkel, W., *Die Theologische Bestimmung der Musik* (Trier, 1971); Routley, E., *The Church and Music* (London, 1950).

See also: chorale; church music history, Renaissance—the Latin tradition; church music history, Renaissance—the Reformation tradition

theology of church music, Pietism and rationalism

What Martin Luther had revitalized for Reformation musicians was the very important and fundamental understanding that music is a gracious gift of God. Because of current assumptions regarding God's creation, music, and words, such an acknowledgement was already behind most of 15th- and early 16th-century music. Luther, however, gave the hundreds of musicians sympathetic to his cause new impetus for prizing their art in terms of its high task of unfolding God's word.

Luther's insights were perpetuated well into the period of Lutheran orthodoxy through the writings of Johann Dannhauer (1603—66), Balthasar Meisner (1587—1626), and Hector Methobius, for instance, but a new emphasis developed alongside, generated in part by Dietrich Lobechius and Balthasar Mentzer (1614—79) who singled out those qualities in music that edified the worshiping Christian. Compared with Johann Sebastian Bach's classic definition of purpose ("to the glory of God and the recreation of my neighbor"), this remodeled view of music's purpose appears to be heavily one-sided. Yet it is faithful to the teachings of August H. Francke (1663—1727), (one of the central figures in the early pietistic movement). He maintained that the goal of worship—and hence worship music—is the upbuilding of the worshiper. In one way or another this anthropocentric goal was behind nearly the entire church musical enterprise connected with pietism and rationalism. The implications are reflected in the following viewpoints.

For more than a century after the Reformation most composers who wrote for the church understood their craft as a tool for begetting and generating a lively word in the midst of the congregation. Practically, that translated into showing one's ingenuity in treating fixed texts that were integral to the yearly span of liturgical life. For such exegetical work they used agreed-upon musical conventions that together formed the musical rhetoric of the day. However, with a change in focus came a change in methodology. In order to edify the worshiper, composers exercised a new freedom to choose only texts that would accomplish this purpose, and to bypass conventions in order to find the musical means that moved the hearer. It is no accident that the doctrine of affects (the theory that certain musical sounds cause predictable responses) reached popularity at a time when musicians were trying to arouse specific sentiments.

Music was made to fit the purpose of worship. For the pietists the integral relationships of music and worship were summarized as early as 1659 in the *Geistliche Seelenmusik* of Heinrich Mueller (1631—75). Mueller considered music to be a part of the soul's devotional exercise; the entire scheme included at least four steps: Act of Penitence, Act of Devotion, a Song of the Soul (meaning a soloistic hymn based on themes of love and the nearness of Jesus), and the Mystical Vision of God. According to its intended purpose, the song, hymn, or aria was supposed to equip as well as express the activated faith. The same view was shared by Pope Benedict XIV (1675—1758) years later in his encyclical *Annus qui* (1749): he urged church music as useful for "arousing the sentiments of the faithful so that they may be the more joyfully excited to piety and devotion."

The pietists were not alone in their designs. Early proponents of the enlightenment such as Jean Rousseau (1712—78) and the other encyclopedists, together with the adherents of the German version of the Rococo *(Empfindsamkeit)*, stressed the absolute independence of music (art for art's sake) and propagandized for its potential to make men better. Friedrich Schleiermacher (1768—1834), as a child of both the Enlightenment and Pietism, pointed out yet another facet: worship (music) designed to edify must be for every man, and therefore simple and radically popular. This, in turn, spawned a wave of amateurism, particularly among the pietists, who upheld the faith of the common man against the onslaught of the beast of rationalism. Contrapuntal music was no longer considered useful. The perfect slur of the critic during the last half of the 18th century was to call a piece of church music "learned." Simplicity (frequently naiveté) was elevated to ideal. Echoing rationalistic concerns, Benedict XIV said that "the very first concern must be to insure that the words can be clearly heard without any difficulty," meaning no elaborate musical distractions.

By establishing edification as music's chief goal, Pietists and rationalists alike opened the door to extraecclesiastical musical goods. Edification was thought to be available also outside of the church. Having expanded the market—while the liturgy was crumbling from lack of maintenance—the church's worship leaders set out to import opera arias and other nonreligious music for public worship. For the rationalists, at least, this embracing of the theater was done "to beautify worship," for that meant the good feeling of having been uplifted and edified.

Just how much of this beauty they wanted was determined by the worshipers. Musical edification they could take or leave; as it was, church music was occasionally performed after the service—all to demonstrate its theological essence as adiaphoron. For Luther music followed the Gospel automatically if not necessarily. Not any more. Forced to the question by the Zwinglians who wanted to know if music was really commanded by God, the orthodox Lutheran theologians such as Johann Gerhard (1582—1637) (*Loci theologici*) held to its nature as an adiaphoron. In the 17th century, Mengering (1596—1647) argued that "music does not justify itself if it does not meet with receptivity in the hearers, or if it is practiced for its own sake" (quoted by Friedrich Kalb, p. 148).

While some welcomed opera to worship, others—particularly the pietists—began to set restrictions. They were suspicious of worldly things, e.g., instrumental church music. Theophil Grossgebauer (1627—61) (*Waechterstimme*. 1667) complained of the musicians, many "unspiritual," who would give forth meaningless noises. Since the nonvocal could not edify, Grossgebauer played down its usefulness, a sharp contrast to the Romantics of a little more than a century later. This reduction of musical expression among Protestants and Catholics alike resulted in stylistic favoritism, as illustrated by the fostering of the Palestrina style (*stile antico*) among Roman Catholics at a time when the baroque style (*stile moderno*) was at its height and fully tested for church musical purposes.

When the goals of the rationalists were mixed with a theology of edification, the theology of church music was further affected. In 1724, Johann C. Gottsched announced that the source of evil is to be found in man's weak mind and that a remedy was to press on as best as possible to enlightened thought. This heralding of the Enlightenment or rationalism had been anticipated already in 1733 when Johann Stryk advised in his *De jure Sabbathi* that all the misunderstandings (due to textual and musical complexities) which resulted from the usual hearing of most church music were sure to lead to superstition, and that therefore most church music should be banned from worship. More positively, Friedrich Klopstock (1724—1803) in 1758 directed the search for ideal church music to the simple, to epitomize adoration and devotion. For the rationalist, however, adoration meant being filled with useful knowledge of God. To achieve that, he summoned the edifying help of the hymn and hymnlike church music. Why the hymn model? It was simplest; through its slow and quiet execution, the worshiper, undistracted, would have the opportunity to absorb all that was useful. To insure the results, texts had to be constructed with utmost care, and purged (*verbessert*), if necessary.

Throughout the period (c. 1670—1817), the prevailing evaluation of music from the theologians was its usefulness for building up the worshiper. Pietists and rationalists offered their own interpretations of this understanding. Just how prevalent this notion was among the faithful folk is a question necessarily informed also by the music that was written and performed at the time. MB

Readings: Blume, Friedrich, *Protestant Church Music* (New York, 1974); Graff, Paul *Geschichte der Aufloesung der alten gottesdienstlichen Formen in der evangelischen Kirche Deutschlands,* 2 vols. (Goettingen, 1939); Kalb, Friedrich, *Theology of Worship in 17th-Century Lutheranism* (St. Louis, 1965); Wienandt, Elwyn A., *Opinions on Church Music* (Waco, Texas, 1974).

See also: church music history, classic and romantic; theology of church music, Reformers

theology of church music, 19th century

The reserved and coldly superficial worship advocated by the "enlightened" apparently proved to be too sterile for many 19th-century folk, since they often and vigorously resisted attempts at introducing rationalist-inspired hymnals. They were given intellectual support. Early in the century Johann Herder (1744—1803) mounted a critique against the heartless worship of his time. Yet the effects of rationalism and Pietism were felt through a good part of the 19th century. Wilhelm Schroeter (1809) perpetuated the current understandings of church music when he pointed out its capacity for nurturing religiosity. Edification remained the key understanding, and hymnals containing new and purged hymns that urged pious virtues and moral uprightness continued to be published well into the latter part of the century.

Meanwhile, esoteric distinctions between religious music and church music had not yet filtered down to the masses. When the 300th anniversary of the Reformation was celebrated, portions of Haydn's *Creation* were sung with new texts: chaos, for instance, was pictured as the Middle Ages, and the appearance of light was likened to the star from Eisleben (Martin Luther). A new surge of Pietism about 1820 helped to keep alive the tradition of "Jesus songs" and other music designed to stir up faith. Formal theological evaluations of these practices were at a minimum, though Friedrich Schleiermacher (1768—1834) provided some insight by insisting that the purpose of worship—and by extension religious music—is edification. Yet in the context of the entire century and its diverse activities in church music, his view of worship can hardly be claimed as an epitomy of theological notions regarding music. Something closer to that results from understanding the 19th century as the outcome of a gradual transformation of musical experience: preoccupation with the music of heaven (*musica coelestis*—a Reformation concept) had been turned to preoccupation with the heavenly in music (the romantic's credo).

The artists and musicians developed their own theology. It was never well systematized, nor understood as deliberately a-Christian, but it was widely-embraced, long-lasting, and influential among many church people. At the center was the optimistic belief that the divine could be made accessible in music through the efforts of the priestlike composer. Incarnations of this sort were not necessarily immediately or universally apprehensible, but they were declared possible and became one of the chief objectives of musical involvement. Hector Berlioz (1803—69) fearlessly set out to incarnate the last judgment, and of his *Te Deum* he proudly said that it was "colossal, Babylonian, and Ninevite."

The accepted theology altered musical technique. Because the romantic composer imagined himself in the presence of the divine, according to Wilfrid Mellers, he showed his preference for the unending, asymmetrical, spiritual, additive rhythms over against the structured, balanced, corporal, divisive rhythms of previous years. It is why he was fond of the closed, definitive, all-inclusive, cyclic sonata form as opposed to open-ended forms, such as the fugue, that had been used to reveal—but always incompletely.

Musical incarnations could happen anywhere, it was thought. Franz Liszt (1811—86) in his 1834 essay on church music called for a new artistic religious music free from the "holy of holies." This desire for a new home was reinforced by a growing value placed on instrumental music, for it was increasingly looked to for incarnational experiences rather than traditionally honored vocal music.

With the joy of having found a new means of grace the flocks looked with admiration to their new spiritual mentor—the composer gifted with charismatic genius. The elevation of genius was far from the 16th-century appraisal of music as gift of God, and provided the recipient with the frightening temptation to withhold it or to dispense it at great price. Composers and virtuosi jealousy guarded their aristocratic, hierarchical recognition, and so brought into being a class of second-level church composers who produced *kitsch*, as it was later called—music made to exude aural religiosity. It led to pedestrian attempts at creating transcendent effects; e.g., a pastor from Duisburg in 1808 arranged to place his choir and organ behind a screen, so that the music would appear to come from the "beyond."

The effects of music were highly estimated. Richard Wagner (1813—83), who believed music to be the logical progression beyond conceptual thought, encouraged the notion that his operas would bring a kind of redemption and regeneration—a promise more systematically propagandized by Arthur Schopenhauer (1788—1860). Church music must be brought to the people, Liszt said, in order to comfort and empower them, to help them discover the heavenly in music.

While some composers and musicians sought ways of achieving greater public notice, others explored the communalizing capacities of music. Liszt envisioned a utopian age when all people would sing and write songs in praise of God and for men as a grand musical accompaniment to a socialistic society. His visions were realized at least on a small scale. The ever-popular oratorio societies and music-promoting clubs served to accommodate the communal musical experience of the divine so as to become "brotherhoods bound together by enchanting miracles," as Liszt had said.

It is difficult to determine just how much impact these views had on the practice of church music. For many the art-for-art's-sake credo had replaced theological foundations as the primary motivation. Edification remained the single most accepted purpose for worship music, though numerous exceptions to that could be cited (e.g., Johann Herder [1744—1803] and Anton Bruckner [1824—96]). The new sense of community discovered in the music societies was likely envied by church musicians busy devising ways of achieving fuller participation in hymn singing. Meanwhile, the people were encouraged to seek out the heavenly in music, and music in turn was designed to fulfill these needs. The religious function attributed to all music created a dilemma for talented and dedicated church composers such as Felix Mendelssohn; artists of his caliber were never sure whether their efforts should be expanded within or without the church. Finally, the merging of generally religious music and church music led some to consider fresh canons of church music, if only to help sort out the mass of material that was being published.

The 19th century was never without its critics. At the beginning of the century, Johann Herder (1744—1803), enthralled with the song of the folk and with Hebrew poetry, upheld the ideal of vocal church music and pointed to the music of Palestrina as the prime example. E. T. A. Hoffmann (1776—1822) joined in the search for "true" church music also elevating Palestrina. The attraction to 16th-century polyphony was experienced also by Felix Mendelssohn (1809—49) and Beethoven (1770—1827). Many participated in this search for "true" church music through the backward-looking Caecilian movement, an effort to unearth, study, perform, and foster Renaissance vocal music. It had Roman Catholic as well as Protestant versions, the latter helped by the ninety-five anniversary theses posted by Claus Harms (1778—1855) in 1817.

For the theology of music this growing fascination with old choral music meant three things. First, there emerged a pervasive belief that the old was holy or holier—a belief consonant with the basic tenets of Romanticism—but which at the same period provided a challenge to the evolutionary theory of progress so current among late-romantic music historians. Theologically, the value one attached to the old was determined to a large extent by his view of divine action in all of history. Second, as a corollary of the first, a concern for the holy old eventuated in a concern which elevated musical style to an important place with a subsequent tendency toward compositional imitation of "approved" styles, all of which raised questions as to just what music was sacred for worship. Third, the concern for a distinction between the sacred and the secular led to restrictions such as those submitted by Ludwig Schoeberlein (1813—81) in 1859 *(Ueber den liturgischen Ausbau)* regarding the suppression of instrumental music in worship.

Whether or not the Caecilian sympathizers ever found incarnations of the divine in the music of the 16th century is not verifiable. That increasing numbers joined the search suggests that many were not completely satisfied with the 19th-century version of the divine, a dissatisfaction expressed in an entirely different way by later romantics such as Richard Strauss (1864—1949) and the young Arnold Schoenberg (1874—1951) when they questioned the very foundations of romantic music.

In one way or another the edification theology from the Enlightenment, the incarnational theology of romanticism, and the notions of "true" church music have persisted into the 20th century. The Caecilian movement in its broadest sense, however, was most fecund with promise. When combined with a revival in Biblical studies, with parallel historical studies, and with access to an ever-increasing store of musical material, it provided the impetus and resources to uncover Reformation theologies of music ready to be tailored for the needs of a new century. MB

Readings: Bangert, Mark, "Franz Liszt's Essay on Church Music (1834) in the Light of Felicite Lamennais' Religious and Political Thought," *Church Music,* 73·2, pp. 17—25; Blume, Friedrich, *Protestant Church Music* (New York, 1974); Hutchings, Arthur, *Church Music in the Nineteenth Century* (New York, 1967); Mellers, Wilfrid, *Caliban Reborn* (New York, 1967); Wienandt, Elwyn, *Opinions on Church Music* (Waco, Tex., 1974).

See also: Caecilian movement; theology of church music, Pietism and rationalism

theology of church music, 20th century

Although very little systematic work on the theology of music has appeared in this century, some major emphases have surfaced. The point of departure for theological consideration is a general perception of the 19th century's Romanticism as a period of decline in church music. To complicate this situation, theology has had to come to grips with the concept of "art" in music, an aspect of recent music history which our century has been unable to transcend. Anthropocentric Romantic art, either as the expression of an individual artist's vision or as an end in itself *(l'art pour l'art),* seems incompatible with theology's emphasis on the congregation as the locus for church music practice and on the primacy of the Word of God in the liturgy.

It is not unfair to say that the challenges thus posed to the church have not received thorough theological treatment in the English-speaking world. Writers such as Archibald Davison (1883—1961) accepted a technical distinction between sacred and secular music on the assumption that a sacred style could be defined by reference to the past great ages of church music. Church music was denied any autonomous artistic claims. It was to deal with the feelings and emotions of the worshiper in a liturgically appropriate manner. It was assumed that only music as great as that of Bach, Gregorian chant, or the "golden period" of polyphony would meet this need. Such views, which have been paralleled in England, do not take into account the phenomenon of music in general, remaining content to devise a rationale for an existing practice. Theological considerations focus only on feelings about music or the meanings people attach to music.

Roman Catholic thought on the matter must be considered in two phases: the period after the 1903 motu proprio of Piux X and the period since the Second Vatican Council (1962—65). Both phases are united in viewing music as a component within the liturgy. The earlier music practice, defined so pointedly in the motu proprio, required church music to conform itself to the aesthetic and stylistic standard of Gregorian chant or the polyphony of the Palestrina model. Theologically this was justified in Catholic writing by a belief that the arts exist to direct attention to the infinite beauty of God. Art praises God in his infinite perfection and, by fashioning beauty, demonstrates the relationship of the creature to the creator. Creation yearns for its source and tries to imitate it. An experience of art which is truly constituted to fulfill this function provides a way of intuiting the transcendent in spite of the boundaries of our existence in the world. Art offers visible symbols of the invisible realm— just as the liturgy offers an ineffable vision otherwise beyond our limitations.

It is too early to begin to describe any sort of systematic thought following Vatican II. Enormous changes are taking place nonetheless. The "newer" Roman Catholic music grows out of a deeper awareness of the role of the congregation in worship, as expressed in the *Constitution on the Sacred Liturgy* (1963), which contains the council's thought in this matter. For that reason, the older stylistic absolutes have been discarded in practice, if not always in theory. This development has touched off a bitter dispute between the tradition-oriented professional church musicians and the more reform-minded liturgists who take the *Constitution's* exhortation to use responsibly the music of all peoples to mean that the most popular styles are liturgically appropriate. Music in this sense is likewise subordinated to the liturgy, but the conception of the liturgy is changed. Its purpose is the celebration of the life of Christ's people now and the presence of Christ in this world rather than the striving for transcendent experiences by which one approaches the contemplation of the divine.

The most thorough theological discussions of music have occurred among German theologians. A considerable amount of reflection about the nature of music took place in the church music renewal movement of the German Lutheran church, which began in the 1920s. As might be expected, theological considerations took their point of departure from opinions of Martin Luther. Strongly antiromantic views led to a renewed appreciation for objective values in music, for polyphony rather than Romantic harmony, and for the "purer" styles of baroque and Renaissance music. Luther's theology and these older styles were congruent. Church musicians, moreover, went on to write a "new" church music reflecting the values of those older styles. That development is a separate history. It does, however, provide a springboard for systematic theological thought on music.

Some major lessons have surfaced in this small but important body of literature. The nature of music has been defined within the tension between freedom and order. Theologians like Edmund Schlink, Karl Barth, René Wallau, and Winfried Zeller have been strongly influenced by Johan Huizinga's *Homo ludens*, a theory of the play element in culture. Schlink particularly deals with the ability of man to "play" in freedom although required to observe the order of law. Plato, Luther, and the medieval tradition observed both the order imposed by the musician on sound (harmony, conformity to rule, form) and the freedom to transcend music's concrete forms in lofty expressiveness. The Christian recognized the requirement of God's law as it confronts the world fallen into disorder. Music can reflect the order implanted by God in creation and thus provide man with a taste of freedom from the very different confines of law in a fallen world. That taste of freedom is the companion of the joy the redeemed person feels in Christ. In Christ man is free to play without threat of death, to play nonrationally without regard to external necessity, to play in the full enjoyment of the creation for its own sake. All that is a foretaste of the free play to take place in heaven before the throne of God. The technical mastery of a Bach (so Soehngen) or a Mozart (so Karl Barth) is evidence of this transcendent freedom to play. The nature of church music is defined wherever music can be seen to collaborate with the Word of God. Where the Word is allowed to determine the significance of the musical event, the believer perceives both the limitations of the music played within the order of this world and the freedom in the new order revealed in Christ. There is, therefore, no limit to the stylistic possibilities for church music, but the realities of the congregation's ability to perceive the relationship between the Word and music impose limits on the repertoire. At the same time, the congregation has the responsibility to bring all creation—and its music—within its vision of the new life in Christ.

Other schemes for a theology of music have been proposed to deal with these same problems. Oskar Soehngen, the leading theological spokesman for the church music renewal movement, begins with a commitment to

Luther's thought and moves on to a Trinitarian understanding of music. Music's true nature can be located in the fact that it is a creature of God. In the new creation won by Christ's work mankind is able to sing "the new song" of joy because of his freedom from the curse of the Law. Finally, music in the time before Christ's return is a tool of the Holy Spirit. Only the Spirit can give music (both instrumental and vocal!) its highest office, namely the proclamation of the Word of God. Only those filled with the Spirit of God can perceive that Word of promise under the form of music.

There is no satisfactory review of the theology of music or church music in the English language. The reader is referred to the following works for a cursory discussion of some of the problems in this field. The German works of Soehngen and Kurzschenkel, however, are to be recommended as the best materials appearing to date. VG

Readings: Kurzschenkel, W., *Die theologische Bestimmung der Musik* (Trier, 1971); Pike, A., *A Theology of Music* (Toledo, 1953); Routley, E., *Church Music and Theology* (Philadelphia, 1959); Soehngen, O., *Theologie der Musik* (Kassel, 1967); Wilkey, J. W., "Prolegomena to a Theology of Music," *Review and Expositor* (1972).

See also: Catholic pronouncements and decrees on church music

thoroughbass

A unique technique of the baroque and early classic periods in which harmonies are improvised over a continuous bass line. The chief intervals and chords to be played are often, but not always, designated by figures. The function of the thoroughbass, or *continuo*, is to provide a relatively uninterrupted harmonic background for a composition. Whereas Renaissance counterpoint was conceived as a conjunction of intervals (*concentus*) produced by a combination of voices, 17th- and 18th-century composition is based on a harmonic polarity between the bass and soprano in which harmonies are generated from the bass—thus the *raison d'etre* for a *basso continuo*, or continuous bass. Normally, the *continuo* is comprised of a keyboard instrument plus a low reenforcing wind or stringed instrument.

Thoroughbass (*basse chiffrée, Generalbass, basso continuo*) began as a practical matter. Organists of the late Renaissance often had to accompany the choirs and supply missing voice parts when necessary. Since there were no scores, they wrote out a continuous bass line that consisted of the lowest sounding part (*basso sequente*) of a composition and added the harmonies above it. This improvisatory practice was first described in detail by Agostino Agazzari in *Del sonore sopro il basso* (1607) and continued to be developed and refined until the last decade of the 18th century. For example, Haydn's early quartets and symphonies include a *continuo* part as do Mozart's church sonatas. The last major treatise is D. G. Tuerk's *Kurze Anweisung zum Generalbassspielen* (1791).

The realization or working out of a *continuo* parts depends on the style of the composition, the place of performance, the instruments or voices employed, and the size of the ensemble. For example, an early baroque solo performed in a small room might require only a lute, chitarrone, or harpsichord for the *continuo*. In most later chamber music, harpsichord plus cello or viola da gamba are most common. In large ensembles of the 18th century, such as concertos, it was standard practice to use two harpsichords, melodic bass instruments, and one or more lutes.

The following points may be taken as a general guide to realizing a thoroughbass:

1. All intervals are reckoned from the bass. The intervals of the third, fifth, and octave are generally assumed. The signs ♯, ♮ or ♭, when standing alone, refer to the third. Chromatic alterations are indicated before or after a figure, such as ♯6 or ♭7. They may also be indicated by slashes and plus signs, such as ♯6=6̷, ♯5=5̷, and ♯4=4+. During the early baroque, the figures often indicated the actual distance from the bass (Ex. 1). Although this practice died out by the middle of the century, successive numbers over or under one bass note continued to indicate not only intervals, but also

Ex. 1

from *Le Nuove Musiche,* Giulio Caccini (c. 1546–1618)

Ex. 2

voice leading. Normally, only the essential figures are given; others must be assumed (Ex. 2)

2. The harmonies are generally conceived in three or four parts, in which the left hand plays the bass note and the right hand the others. An organist should avoid using the pedal unless the forces he is accompanying are unusually large. If three- or four-part texture is not adequate for a large work, a full-voiced accompaniment should be invented.

3. Harmonies should not be added to nonharmonic tones in the bass. If the bass moves quickly, few chords need to be added.

4. Some kind of countermelody in the realization is permissible when accompanying a soloist. Doublings should be avoided, and rules of voice-leading, such as preparation of dissonances, must be observed (see Ex. 2). The accompaniment should sound complete in itself, and reflect accurately the rhythm of the piece.

5. Ornamentation should be an inherent part of a good *continuo*, particularly the addition of appoggiaturas, internal and final cadence trills, and arpeggiations, both free and measured.

6. Because recitatives are in free rhythm, the *continuo* should not indulge in undue melodic elaborations, but should give the singer a firmly rhythmic impetus into each subsequent phrase.

Although the very nature of thoroughbass is improvisatory, and there is no single solution for a piece, one might find it instructive to study two realizations by J. S. Bach. One is a realization of an Albinoni sonata by H. N. Gerber and corrected by Bach. This may be found in Philipp Spitta's classic work, *Johann Sebastian Bach*. The other is the beginning of Bach's realization of his own unfigured *continuo* part to the bass aria in Cantata No. 3, "Ach Gott, wie manches Herzeleid" (Ex. 3). NJ

Ex. 3

Unfigured realization by J.S.Bach (Bass aria, Cantata No. 3, "Ach Gott, wie manches
Herzeleid")

(sic)

Bass

Emp-find ich

Readings: Arnold, F. T., *The Art of Accompaniment from a Thoroughbass,* reprint, 2 vols.
(New York, 1965); Donington, R., *A Performer's Guide to Baroque Music (London, 1973);*
Donington, R., The Interpretation of Early Music (New York, 1963); Keller, H., *Thoroughbass*
Method, tr. and ed. by Carl Parrish (New York, 1965).

See also: church music history, baroque; performance practice

trope

The trope is a *genus* of chant that flowered from the 9th through the
12th centuries. Essentially an accretion to the Roman liturgy, the trope is
both a literary and musical phenomenon. Textually the trope is an addition
to the official liturgical text, the equivalent of the gloss in literature and
logic. Like the gloss the trope usually expands, clarifies, or interpolates the
liturgical text. The music to which the trope was sung was either
borrowed from existing chant or newly composed in the style of Gregorian
chant.

Of the proper of the mass the introit, gradual, Alleluia, tract, and
offertory were often subjected to troping. The sequence or prose, an added

chant that follows the Alleluia, is a particularly important type of trope. Of the ordinary of the mass the Kyrie was the most common item to be troped. Even today masses are labeled in the chant books after trope texts that once were added to the Kyries. Thus, the *Missa Cunctipotens Genitor* at one time included a Kyrie troped with the text *Cunctipotens Genitor.* Likewise with other masses such as those labeled *Lux et origo, De angelis, Orbis factor, Cum jubilo,* or such Kyries as the *Kyrie Deus sempiterne, Kyrie Rex Genitor, Kyrie magnae Deus potentiae,* and so on.

The Kyrie trope *Kyrie fons bonitatis* can serve as an example of the phenomenon of troping. Although the chant melody of *Kyrie fons bonitatis* dates from the 9th century, the troped text first appeared in the 11th century. The full Latin text follows. Troped material is given in brackets.

Kyrie [fons bonitatis, Pater ingenite, a quo bona cuncta procedunt] *eleison.*

Kyrie [qui pati Natum mundi pro crimine, ipsum ut salvaret misisti] *eleison.*

Kyrie [qui septiformis dans dona Pneumatis, a quo caelum, terra replentur] *eleison.*

Christe [unice Dei Patris Genite, quem de Virgine nasciturum mundo mirifice sancti praedixerunt prophetae] *eleison.*

Christe [hagie, caeli compos regiae, melos gloriae cui semper adstans pro numine Angelorum decantat apex] *eleison.*

Christe [caelitus adsis nostris precibus, pronis mentibus quem in terris devote colimus, ad te pie Jesu clamantes] *eleison.*

Kyrie [Spiritus alme, cohaerens Patri Natoque, unius usiae consistendo, flans ab utroque] *eleison.*

Kyrie [qui baptizato in Jordanis unda Christo, effulgens specie columbina apparuisti] *eleison.*

Kyrie [ignis divine, pectora nostra succende, ut digne pariter proclamare possimus semper] *eleison.*

As is true with much of Reformation hymnody, the ancient *Kyrie fons bonitatis* was adapted for use in the Lutheran liturgy by the 16th-century Reformers. The Lutheran chorale, *Kyrie, Gott Vater in Ewigkeit* closely paraphrases *Kyrie fons bonitatis.* The evangelical text follows the Trinitarian plan of its Gregorian predecessor even though the petitions are reduced from nine to three. An English translation of the evangelical Kyrie trope follows, the troped material enclosed in brackets.

Kyrie [God Father in heav'n above, Great art Thou in grace and love, Of all things the Maker and Preserver] *eleison, eleison.*

Kyrie [O Christ, our King, Salvation for sinners Thou didst bring. O Lord Jesus, God's own Son, Our Mediator at the heav'nly throne, Hear our cry and grant our supplication] *eleison, eleison.*

Kyrie [O God the Holy Ghost, Guard our faith, the gift we need the most; Do Thou our last hour bless; Let us leave this sinful world with gladness] *eleison, eleison.*

See the comparison of the initial phrases of the *Kyrie fons bonitatis* to the first section of *Kyrie God Father in heav'n above. HM*

Readings: Apel, Willi, *Gregorian Chant* (Bloomington, 1958); Handschin, Jacques,

"Trope, Sequence, and Conductus," *New Oxford History of Music*, II (London, 1954), 128—174; Palmer, Larry, "Organ Compositions Based on Kyrie Fons Bonitatis," *The Musical Heritage of the Church*, VI (1963), 92—104.

See also: chant, Gregorian; church music history, medieval; mass; sequence

Venetian school

A term identifying the composers, directors, organists, singers, and instrumentalists of Flemish and Italian origin who were associated with Venice and St. Mark's Cathedral in the 16th and early 17th centuries. The chief identifying musical characteristics of the Venetian School were an impressive polychoral technique and independent instrumental composition. The leading figures were Adrian Willaert (c. 1490—1562), Andrea Gabrieli (c. 1520—86), and Giovanni Gabrieli (c. 1555—1612).

In the 16th century Venice was indeed the Queen of the Adriatic (if not of the Mediterranean), and St. Mark's was her crown. The city had prospered for centuries through her position as chief commercial link between East and West. The ruling doges of the well-organized Venetian state provided an atmosphere in which the visual and musical arts were encouraged to dazzle the eye and impress the ear with an exotic mixture of Occidental strength and Oriental mystery. The wealthy city provided ample opportunities for the creation and performance of a variety of secular and sacred music. Byzantine-touched St. Mark's Cathedral and its companion Piazza gave to the musician magnificently resonant settings for display of sonorities. The plaza was the forestage for the elaborate state processions; the Cathedral, governed by the doges, became the central site of state-church ritual. The building itself, formed in the shape of an immense Greek cross, was richly receptive to musical performance, but as a special attraction the ample twin choir galleries above and to either side of the high altar were both furnished with independent organs about 1490. While many large churches of the day possessed two or more organs, it was first at St. Mark's that musicians capitalized on the dual possibilities of architectural advantage and ceremonial need for colorful and sonorous accompaniment to develop the brilliant polychoral style.

The Flemish master Adrian Willaert became St. Mark's choirmaster in 1527, and as performer, composer, and teacher during the next 35 years brought unprecedented musical prominence to the city. His masses and motets display a complete command of Flemish contrapuntal technique, including flawless skill in text declamation, tonal color, and modulation. One of his most noteworthy accomplishments was the distinction and prominence he gave to writing for divided choirs (*cori spezzati*) in his *Salmi spezzati* (1550), in which two four-voice choirs sing alternately, joining for eight-voice performance of selected phrases. Willaert thus built upon the technique of earlier Northern composers who commonly divided choir voices for "paired-imitation" or other types of alternation within one choir. Antiphonal effects between two four-voice choirs had also been achieved by other Italian composers at least as early as the middle of the 15th century.

Willaert was succeeded as choirmaster by two pupils: Cipriano de Rore (1516—65) and Gioseffo Zarlino (1517—90). Rore, a brilliant composer, continued the transmission of the Flemish technique during his brief tenure (1563—64), although his chief accomplishments were to lie in the field of the madrigal. Zarlino, who served as choirmaster from 1565 to 1590, achieved prominence through publication of theoretical treatises that clearly identified the priority of the modern major and minor modes, thereby contributing to the increasing emphasis upon tonal writing in Venice.

Andrea Gabrieli, appointed second organist in 1564 and first organist in 1585, did not abandon Flemish counterpoint, but turned increasingly to a more homophonic style in antiphonal choral writing in compositions for one choir and in works for two or more choirs. As early as 1565 he indicated instrumental participation in performance of his sacred choral works, thus reflecting common 16th-century performance practice as well as capitalizing upon the instrumental and acoustic resources of St. Mark's.

Andrea's nephew and pupil, Giovanni Gabrieli, who served primarily as second organist from 1584 to 1612, brought Venetian polychoral composition to its highest level of splendor and magnificence. He created striking harmonic effects while contrasting vocal and instrumental timbres in antiphonal exchange, thereby expanding the resources of church music. In the *Sacrae symphoniae I* (1597) and *II* (1615) he specified instruments (by name) for participation with choral forces in *sinfonie*, and interspersed these between movements of larger compositions. Such works as *In ecclesiis* and *Surrexit Christus* call for a great variety of solo and ensemble instruments (*cornetti*, trombones, *violini*, and organs), which perform with the vocal soloists and choirs. The *Canzoni 'da sonar* (1597) provide no less than six types of alternation of musical resources: motion of voices, meter, dynamics, size of groups, texture, and theme.

Performance of the polychoral works must have created an overwhelming impression upon the listener, who was surrounded by choirs of voices and instruments. The first choir sang from the gallery of the first organ; the second choir or *cappella* (possibly doubled by the second organ), the third, "high," choir, the fourth, "low," choir, and numerous supporting and independent instrumentalists were situated at various points in the basilica, some possibly on specially constructed platforms.

Other Venetian composers of sacred choral music include Jacques Buus (c. 1500—c. 1564), Annibale Padovano (c. 1527—75), Baldassare Donato (c. 1530—1603), Claudio Merulo (1533—1604), Gioseffe Guami (c. 1540—c. 1611), Giovanni Croce (c. 1557—1609), and Giovanni Bassano (fl. 1595), probably the first to write motets with an organ bass.

The Venetian polychoral style had broad and deep influence throughout Europe. The impressive effects achieved by the Venetian polychoral writers were eagerly adapted by the Roman School composers, but without great success. The Romans, schooled in Palestrina's counterpoint, multiplied choirs and added instruments—up to 53 parts—but achieved mostly massive, not brilliant effects. Domenico and Virgilio Mazzocchi (1592—1665, 1597—1646), Paolo Agostini (1593—1629), and Antonia M. Abbatini (c. 1595—1677) are representative composers, along with the leading figure, Orazio Benevoli (1605—72).

Hans Leo Hassler (1564—1612), who studied with Andrea Gabrieli in 1584, first carried the Venetian style to Germany, where it was continued by Hieronymous Praetorius (1560—1629), Michael Praetorius (1571—1621), who specialized in application of the polychoral style to the chorale, Samuel Scheidt (1587—1654), Johann H. Schein (1586—1630), and Heinrich Schuetz (1585—1672), a student of Giovanni Gabrieli from 1609 to 1612. Composers in other lands were also influenced: in Bohemia, Jacobus Gallus (Handl, 1550—91), in Spain, Juan Bautista Comes (1568—1643), in Holland, Jan P. Sweelinck (1562—1621), and in Poland, Mikołaj Zieleński (fl. 1611).

It is not by accident that many of the Venetian composers were organists, for the cultural and acoustic aspects of the practice of church music at St. Mark's encouraged composition of independent music for organ, and for organ with choirs and instrumental ensembles. A Venetian decree of 1546 indicates the esteem in which organ music was held: "No canons or priests should interrupt performing organists, but should remain quiet and patiently await the end of a piece." Compositions took a variety of forms and names among which *ricercar, toccata, intonazione*, and Magnificat are prominent. The chief composers of organ music were Jacques Buus, Annibale Padovano, said to be the first to develop the antiphonal possibilities of the two organs, Vincenzo Bell'haver (c. 1530—87), Claudio Merulo, Giuseffe Guami, Girolamo Diruta (b. 1561), and Andrea and Giovanni Gabrieli.

Although composition of madrigals took place in most Italian cities during the 16th century, Venice provided a particularly congenial setting for their creation. Subsequent to Adrian Willaert's pioneering innovations, nearly all musicians associated with St. Mark's wrote madrigals: Cipriano de Rore, Andrea Gabrieli, Annibale Padovano, Constanzo Porta (c. 1529—1601), Vincenzo Bell'haver, Baldassare Donato, Claudio Merulo, Gioseffe Guami, Giovanni Gabrielli, and Giovanni Croce.

Instrumental ensemble compositions were also popular in Venice as composers sought to extend the advances achieved in polychoral and solo organ music to the instrumental ensemble idiom. The forms utilized were the *canzona*, sonata, *ricercar*, fantasia, and *sinfonia*. The early composers of ensemble pieces were Adrian Willaert, Jacques Buus, Cipriano de Rore, Andrea Gabrieli, Annibale Padovano, Gioseffe Guimi, Giovanni Croce, and Giovanni Bassano. Independent instrumental music gained particular prominence as Giovanni Gabrieli extended the principles of polychoral writing to instruments. The remarkable *Sonata pian e forte* is the earliest known ensemble piece to call for dynamic contrasts; it also calls for precise instrumentation. The orchestration of one *canzona* calls for alternate large and small forces, which suggests the later baroque concerto grosso. Instrumental groups of different timbre, pitch, and size are set against each other in order to heighten contrasts.

The vigorous musical life of Venice was complemented by its position as the most active music publishing center in Italy. In the years spanned by the lives of the Venetian School musicians, nearly 30 individual firms engaged in the publication of music.

With the death of Giovanni Gabrieli in 1612 and the assumption of musical leadership at Venice in 1613 by the renowned Claudio Monteverdi (1567—1643), the music associated with the city became increasingly representative of the baroque concerted style, and, although sacred music was not neglected, its form and thrust changed, and secular music assumed an increasingly prominent position, leading to the ultimate domination of the musical life of the city by opera production. CM

Readings: Abraham, Gerald, ed., *The Age of Humanism (1540—1630),* vol. IV of *New Oxford History of Music,* ed. J. A. Westrup *et al.* (London, 1968); Apel, Willi, ed. *Harvard Dictionary of Music.* 2d ed. rev. and enl. (Cambridge, Mass., 1969); Arnold, Denis, *Giovanni Gabrieli* (London, 1974); Reese, Gustave, *Music in the Renaissance,* 2d ed. (New York, 1959); Woerner, Karl, *History of Music,* 5th ed., tr. and supplemented by Willis Wager (New York, 1973).

See also: chorale, vocal settings; concertato style; polychoral style

voluntary

The term voluntary generally denotes a free organ composition performed in the Anglican service. The content, style, and function of the voluntary have varied from one historical period to the next, and an exact definition of the term is problematic. A brief overview of its development through the 19th century is perhaps the most helpful approach to an understanding of the term.

The earliest voluntaries appear in the 16th-century English manuscripts (e.g., *Mulliner Book* and *My Ladye Nevells Booke*). They are free imitative pieces more akin to the ricercar rather than to works based upon a cantus firmus. Thomas Morley (1557—1603) in his *A Plaine and Easie Introduction to Practicall Musicke* (1597) observes that "to make two parts upon a plaine song is more hard than to make three parts into a voluntarie." This observation probably applies to the improvisation of voluntaries as well as the composition of such works.

In the late 17th and early 18th centuries two distinct types of voluntary may be distinguished. In addition to the "single voluntary" (for one-manual organs) the "double voluntary" (for two-manual organs) came into being. The upper manual ("Double," "Bass," "Great") was the louder one and was used to feature solo passages. The lower manual ("Single," "Tenor," "Little," "Chair") was softer and possessed fewer stops. If a third manual ("Echo") were included, like the "double" it was used for solo passages. Examples of the single and double voluntary were the "diapason voluntary," usually a slow movement of relatively short duration, and the "cornet voluntary," a fast virtuosic piece with solo and often echo sections.

Some of the important composers of voluntaries in the late 17th and early 18th centuries include: John Barrett (c. 1674—c. 1735), John Blow (1649—1708), William Croft (1678—1727), Maurice Greene (1695—1755), George Frideric Handel (1685—1759), Matthew Locke (1630—77), Henry Purcell (1659—95), Thomas Roseingrave (1690—1766), Charles John Stanley (1713—86), and John Travers (c. 1703—58).

The most significant composer of voluntaries in the late 18th and early 19th centuries was Samuel Wesley (1766—1837). Others include: Thomas Adams (1785—1858), John Bennett (c. 1735—84), William Boyce (1710—79), Thomas Dupuis (1733—96), William Russell (1777—1813), and William Walond (1725—70).

In the late 18th-century Anglican service at least three voluntaries were commonly played—at the beginning and end of the service and after the first lesson. Voluntaries might also be improvised or played before the first lesson or between the end of Morning Prayer and the beginning of the Communion Service. In the 19th century voluntaries began to be called preludes, postludes, and offertories. These latter usages are the ones which are most often encountered in Protestant services today. Whereas the voluntary originally served a serious liturgical purpose, the late 19th-century voluntary often degenerated into a mere transcription of an anthem, oratorio, or instrumental work.

The disintegration of the voluntary form in the 19th century is illustrated by the fact that Felix Mendelssohn (1809—47) was called upon to write "three voluntaries" but requested that his work be called "Three Sonatas for the Organ." In writing to the publisher Mendelssohn wrote:

> I have been busy about the organ pieces which you wanted me to write for you, and they are nearly finished. I should like you to call them "Three Sonatas for the Organ" instead of "voluntaries." Tell me if you like this title as well; if not, I think the name of "voluntaries" will suit the pieces also, the more so as I do not know what it means precisely. HM

Readings: Blom, Eric, ed., "Voluntary," *Grove's Dictionary of Music and Musicians,* 5th ed. (London, 1954); Routh, Francis, *Early English Organ Music from the Middle Ages to 1837* (New York, 1973); Scholes, Percy, "Voluntary," *The Oxford Companion to Music,* 10th ed. (London, 1970).

See also: organ, literature; *HCM,* V

Notes on the Contributors

Mark Bangert teaches at Christ Seminary—Seminex, St. Louis, Mo., is a member of the Liturgical Texts Committee of the Inter-Lutheran Commission on Worship, and a contributing editor to *Church Music*.

M. Alfred Bichsel, former head of the department of church music at the Eastman School of Music of the University of Rochester, Rochester, N. Y., is a member of the editorial board of *Church Music*.

Paul Bunjes teaches at Concordia Teachers College, River Forest, Ill., is the author of *The Praetorius Organ, The Formulary Tones Annotated*, and the *Service Propers Noted*, and editor of the critical edition of Georg Rhau's *Postremum vespertini officii opus . . . Magnificat octo . . . tonorum*, a widely recognized authority on organ construction and design, and a member of the editorial staff of *Church Music*.

Gerhard Cartford is on assignment in Columbia, South America, as a resource person in worship and church music with the Division of World Missions and Inter-Church Cooperation of the American Lutheran Church. He is a member of the Liturgical Music Committee of the Inter-Lutheran Commission on Worship.

Louise Cuyler is a widely recognized authority on Renaissance music and a former member of the faculty of the University of Michigan, Ann Arbor, Mich.

Theodore DeLaney, former Executive Secretary of the Commission on Worship of The Lutheran Church—Missouri Synod, is a member of the editorial board of *Church Music* and pastor of the dual parish of St. Paul, Red Bluff, and Mt. Olive, Corning, Calif.

Leonard Ellinwood is the author of *The History of American Church Music*, editor of *The Works of Francesco Landini*, chief author of *The Hymnal 1940 Companion*, and a contributing editor to *Church Music*.

Victor Gebauer teaches at Concordia College, St. Paul, Minn., and is editor of *Response* and a contributing editor to *Church Music*.

Ralph Gehrke teaches at Pacific Lutheran University, Tacoma, Wash., and is the author of a Biblical *Commentary on 1 and 2 Samuel* and *Planning the Service,* coauthor of *Our Way of Worship*, and a contributing editor to *Church Music*.

Thomas Gieschen teaches at Concordia Teachers College, River Forest, Ill., has edited various choral and organ collections, and is a contributing editor to *Church Music*.

Herbert Gotsch teaches at Concordia Teachers College, River Forest, Ill., and is a member of the editorial staff of *Church Music*.

Richard Hillert teaches at Concordia Teachers College, River Forest, Ill., is widely recognized as a composer, and is a member of the Liturgical Music Committee of the Inter-Lutheran Commission on Worship and assistant editor of *Church Music.*

Wesley W. Isenberg teaches at Concordia Teachers College, River Forest, Ill., and is a member of the international team of scholars editing and translating the Coptic Gnostic codices from Nag Hammadi.

Natalie Jenne teaches at Concordia Teachers College, River Forest, Ill., and is widely known as a harpsichord recitalist and authority on performance practice.

Donald Johns teaches at the University of California—Riverside, Riverside, Calif., and is a contributing editor to *Church Music.*

Edward Klammer is the editor of many church music publications, has long been associated with the music department of Concordia Publishing House, is a member of the Hymn Music Committee of the Inter-Lutheran Commission on Worship, and is a member of the editorial staff of *Church Music.*

Gerhard Krapf teaches at the University of Edmonton, Edmonton, Alberta, Canada, has a wide reputation as a composer and organ recitalist, and is the author of *Liturgical Organ Playing* and *Organ Improvisation* and the translator of *The Organ Handbook.*

Harlan McConnell, formerly a member of the faculty at Concordia Teachers College, River Forest, Ill., is a frequent contributor to *Church Music* and teaches privately in Denver, Colo.

Carlos Messerli teaches at Concordia Teachers College, Seward, Nebr., and is a member of the Liturgical Music Committee of the Inter-Lutheran Commission on Worship.

Ewald Nolte teaches at Salem College, Winston-Salem, N. C., and was formerly the director of the Moravian Music Foundation.

Herbert Nuechterlein, former member of the faculty at Concordia Senior College, Ft., Wayne, Ind., is a contributing editor to *Church Music.*

Elmer Pfeil is associated with the Office for Divine Worship of the Archdiocese of Milwaukee and is a member of the faculty at St. Francis Seminary, Milwaukee, Wis.

Frederick Precht, former member of the faculty at Concordia Theological Seminary, Springfield, Ill., is a member of the editorial board of *Church Music.*

Evangeline Rimbach teaches at Concordia Teachers College, River Forest, Ill., and is a contributing editor to *Church Music.*

Erik Routley teaches at Westminster Choir College, Princeton, N. J., is the author of many books, including *The Music of Christian Hymnody, The English Carol,* and *Words, Music, and the Church,* and is a contributing editor to *Church Music.*

Carl Schalk teaches at Concordia Teachers College, River Forest, Ill., has edited many church music publications, and is a member of the Hymn Music Committee of the Inter-Lutheran Commission on Worship and the editor of *Church Music.*

Carl Volz teaches at Luther Seminary, St. Paul, Minn., and is the author of *The Church of the Middle Ages.*

Elwyn Wienandt teaches at Baylor University, Waco, Tex., and is the author of *Choral Music in the Church,* coauthor of *The Anthem in England and America,* editor of *Opinions on Church Music,* and compiler of a three-volume *Bicentennial Collection of American Music.*

Edward Wolf teaches at West Liberty State College, West Liberty, W. Va.

Carlton R. Young teaches at Scarritt College for Christian Workers, Nashville, Tenn., is the editor of the Methodist *Book of Hymns,* coauthor of the *Companion to the Hymnal,* composer and editor of many choral publications, and a contributing editor to *Church Music.*